Sufism and the Scriptures

Sufism and the Scriptures

Metaphysics and Sacred History in the Thought of ʿAbd al-Karīm al-Jīlī

Fitzroy Morrissey

I.B. TAURIS
LONDON • NEW YORK • OXFORD • NEW DELHI • SYDNEY

I.B. TAURIS
Bloomsbury Publishing Plc
50 Bedford Square, London, WC1B 3DP, UK
1385 Broadway, New York, NY 10018, USA
29 Earlsfort Terrace, Dublin 2, Ireland

First published in Great Britain 2021
This paperback edition published in 2022

A catalogue record for this book is available from the British Library.

A catalog record for this book is available from the Library of Congress.

ISBN: HB: 978-0-7556-1831-6
PB: 978-0-7556-3686-0
ePDF: 978-0-7556-1833-0
eBook: 978-0-7556-1832-3

Typeset by Deanta Global Publishing Services, Chennai, India

Contents

Acknowledgements vi

Introduction 1
1 Al-Jīlī and *al-Insān al-kāmil* 5
2 Muslim views of sacred history 19
3 The Qur'an 33
4 The Torah 59
5 The Psalms 103
6 The Gospel 135
Conclusion 167

Notes 175
Bibliography 221
Index 239

Acknowledgements

This book is an expanded and revised version of my DPhil thesis at the University of Oxford. Both in writing that thesis, and in converting it into this monograph, I have been heavily indebted to the guidance and support of my supervisor, Ron Nettler. Ron and I began reading al-Jīlī's *al-Insān al-kāmil* in 2015, while I was an MPhil student in Islamic Studies and History, and the present book is the result of five years of reflection on that text, under Ron's expert supervision.

Alongside Ron, there are several people and institutions without whose support this book would never have been written. For my DPhil, I was fortunate enough to benefit from a doctoral scholarship from the Clarendon Fund. The Oriental Institute at Oxford has provided me with an immensely stimulating academic home over the last decade. The Warden and Fellows of All Souls College, in unexpectedly electing me to an Examination Fellowship in 2017, provided me with the perfect environment in which to complete the thesis and turn it into this book. The support provided by the staff at the Oriental Institute Library was always second to none. My DPhil examiners, Nicolai Sinai and Toby Mayer, made several very helpful suggestions that have enabled the conversion of the thesis into a monograph. At I.B. Tauris, I have been very lucky to have Sophie Rudland as my editor. I am also very grateful to Mohamed Ben-Madani of *The Maghreb Review* for his kind permission to reproduce edited extracts from my article in that journal, "Abd al-Karīm al-Jīlī's Sufi View of Other Religions', copyright @ *The Maghreb Review*, volume 43, No. 2, 2018, pp.175–97, and to the Provost and Fellows of Eton College for permission to use an image from the Eton College Collections for the cover of the book.

I would have never even begun the research on this book without the support of my parents, who have always encouraged me to follow my talents and interests, wherever they may take me. Finally, my wife, Dyedra, was crucial to the project's inception, continuation and conclusion. She always helped me see the value of my work, and, through her loving companionship, kept me going through the years of writing and research.

Introduction

'Abd al-Karīm al-Jīlī's (d. 811/1408) *al-Insān al-kāmil fī maʿrifat al-awākhir wa-al-awāʾil* (*The Perfect Human in the Knowledge of the Last and First Things*) is one of the most important and influential works of Sufi metaphysics in the tradition of Ibn 'Arabī (d. 638/1240).[1] The latter was perhaps the most widely discussed Sufi thinker of any age, and al-Jīlī, who lived two centuries after the famous Andalusian Sufi thinker, is generally acknowledged to have been one of his most independent and thoughtful followers, and *al-Insān al-kāmil* his most important and widely read work. As its title indicates, al-Jīlī's book is principally concerned with the key Ibn 'Arabian idea of the 'Perfect Human' (*al-insān al-kāmil*), and within it al-Jīlī develops this idea in an original and highly influential way.[2] Yet it would be a mistake to imagine that the book is solely concerned with the Perfect Human, and that al-Jīlī's contribution to the history of ideas was limited to his elaboration of that idea. In fact, *al-Insān al-kāmil* is a comprehensive compendium of Ibn 'Arabian Sufi metaphysics – 'a remarkably clear, concentrated and profound expression of Sufi doctrine'[3] – which would come to be widely used by Sufi orders across the Islamic world as one of the key 'mediating works' in that intellectual tradition, introducing Sufi students to the Ibn 'Arabian Sufi world view in a relatively comprehensible and systematic fashion.[4]

Among the topics treated as some length in *al-Insān al-kāmil* is the issue of the different scriptures, prophets and religions, or what might be called 'sacred history', a key issue in Islamic thought. This issue is discussed most fully in chapters thirty-four to thirty-eight of the text, which are devoted to the scriptures universally recognized in Islam: the Qur'an (*al-Qurʾān*) (also called here the Furqan [*al-Furqān*]), the Torah (*al-Tawrāh*), the Psalms (*al-Zabūr*), and the Gospel (*al-Injīl*). Yet despite their importance within al-Jīlī's work, these chapters – and therefore al-Jīlī's treatment of the issue of sacred history – remain little known or discussed, both in academic scholarship on Ibn 'Arabian Sufi thought and in more general writing on Sufism and Islam.[5] They were not included in Titus Burckhardt's partial 1952 translation of *al-Insān al-kāmil* into French, *De l'homme universel*,[6] nor in the translated extracts from al-Jīlī's book presented by Margaret Smith in her anthology of Sufi literature,[7] nor in the French translation of a chapter of *al-Insān al-kāmil* included by the scholar of Shīʿi and Sufi thought Henry Corbin in his *Terre céleste et corps de résurrection, de l'Iran mazdéen à l'Iran shīʿite* (1960).[8] Nor do they make an appearance in Muhammad Iqbal's presentation of al-Jīlī's thought, based on his reading of *al-Insān al-kāmil*, in his major work *The Development of Metaphysics in Persia* (1908).[9] The best introduction to the chapters on the scriptures, in fact, remains the few pages devoted to them by the great Cambridge orientalist R. A. Nicholson in his seminal *Studies in Islamic Mysticism* (1921), which was first published a century ago.[10]

This gap in the scholarship is a source of regret, not only because of the intrinsic interest of al-Jīlī's treatment of the scriptures, the insight that these chapters give into his wider Ibn ʿArabian Sufi metaphysics, and al-Jīlī's general significance within the history of Sufi thought,[11] but also because they raise issues that are of relevance both to the history of Sufism and Ibn ʿArabian Sufi metaphysics, and, as already indicated, to important topics in the study of Islam and Islamic thought: specifically, Islamic ideas about scripture, prophethood and sacred history, and how Muslims have historically thought about the relationship between Islam and other religions at a more abstract, theoretical level (as opposed to at the level of day-to-day lived experience). Connected to that last point, these chapters are also of relevance to an important issue in the study of Ibn ʿArabian Sufi thought, namely, the question of the stance that Ibn ʿArabian Sufis – al-Jīlī included – have taken towards other religions. As we shall see, a notable feature of much modern writing on Ibn ʿArabian Sufism – and Sufism more generally – is the emphasis on the more inclusivist or pluralist stance taken by thinkers in the intellectual tradition towards non-Muslims and their religions.[12] The chapters of *al-Insān al-kāmil* on the scriptures shed some light on the validity of this idea, particularly insofar as it has been applied to the thought of al-Jīlī and the Ibn ʿArabian Sufis, and, so I argue, suggest that it ought to be somewhat modified.

In light of the significance of these chapters, therefore, and in the absence of focused scholarly studies on them, the present book undertakes to present and analyse this key section of al-Jīlī's major work.[13] I undertake a close reading of the chapters on the scriptures, an approach designed to enable us to follow the internal logic of al-Jīlī's ideas, and so to avoid, as far as possible, reading into the texts any preconceptions of what his views were or ought to have been, or imposing our own questions or an artificial coherence onto the text.[14] In following this close reading approach, I pay particular attention to the key terms that he uses, the concepts that those terms denote, the particular conceptions that al-Jīlī has of those concepts and the way in which he arranges them into particular patterns or groups of terms that together make up a coherent text. In this way, I attempt to identify the key terms and groups of terms that form the building blocks of his conception of both the individual scriptures, and of sacred history as a whole, and so to elucidate the key features of that conception, all the while keeping sight of the flow of his reasoning. Although this method can, I think, be usefully applied to the interpretation of all texts and systems of thought,[15] it is particularly applicable to the writing and thought of al-Jīlī, since, in addition to his immersion in the Arabic vocabulary of the Qur'an, Sufism, *kalām* and *falsafah*, he primarily expresses his ideas using the distinctive technical vocabulary – what Suʿād al-Ḥakīm has called the 'new language' (*lughah jadīdah*) – of Ibn ʿArabī and his interpreters.[16] Furthermore, I supplement this close reading approach with a history of ideas perspective, reading al-Jīlī's text against the background of Sufi and other widely held Islamic conceptions of sacred history, particularly what I call 'the Qur'an-centred view of sacred history'. This is intended to allow us both to consider the originality of al-Jīlī's ideas about the scriptures, prophets and religions and to enter into broader debates regarding Ibn ʿArabian Sufi views on sacred history and other religions and their supposedly pluralistic nature.

Based on my reading of the chapters on the scriptures, I shall argue that, while al-Jīlī's view of the scriptures is to a large extent conditioned by his key Sufi metaphysical ideas (particularly what I describe as the ideas of 'universal theophany', the 'levels of existence', and 'the Perfect Human'), nevertheless his view of sacred history is consistent with the Qur'an-centred view. We shall see that his view of the pre-Qur'anic scriptures – the Torah, Psalms and Gospel – and the pre- or non-Islamic communities to which they were revealed – the Jews and Christians – is marked by a certain ambivalence, and that, consistent with the Qur'an-centred view, he maintains the superiority of the Qur'an, Muhammad and Islam over the other scriptures, prophets and religions. This being the case, the findings of the present book challenge and complicate prevailing views regarding the pluralistic quality of Ibn 'Arabian Sufi views on other religions, and supplement and support the argument recently made in relation to Ibn 'Arabī by Gregory Lipton in his *Rethinking Ibn 'Arabi* (2018).[17] In this way, the present book should, I hope, be of interest and use not only to scholars and students of Sufism and the Ibn 'Arabian Sufi tradition but also to those interested in the history of Muslim-Jewish and Muslim-Christian relations and Islamic views of the religious 'other'.

1

Al-Jīlī and *al-Insān al-kāmil*

Al-Jīlī's life and works

We know little about al-Jīlī's life with any great certainty. Such is the paucity of surviving information on his life, in fact, that Claude Addas, the leading modern biographer of Ibn 'Arabī, has gone so far as to ask, albeit rhetorically, whether al-Jīlī really existed.[1] Thanks to the work done by Riyadh Atlagh, however, we do now have the basic outlines of his biography.[2] Al-Jīlī was born in Calicut on the Malabar Coast of India in 767/1365. As a boy he travelled with his father to Aden in Yemen, following a route well traversed by traders and scholars then and in later periods. From Aden he went to Zabid on Yemen's western coastal plain, which he subsequently made his home. In Zabid he joined the Sufi community led by the famous *shaykh* Ismā'īl al-Jabartī (d. 806/1403) of the Ahdalī branch of the Qādiriyyah *ṭarīqah*. Al-Jabartī was close to the Rasulid sultans of southern Yemen, al-Ashraf Ismā'īl (r. 778–803/1376–1400) and al-Nāṣir Aḥmad (r. 803–27/1400–24), whom he counted among his disciples, affording the Sufi community political patronage and protection from its critics among the anti-Sufi *fuqahā'*. Al-Jabartī's Sufi circle was known for making *samā'* (Sufi mystical concerts) central to its ritual practice and for its adherence to the ideas of Ibn 'Arabī and his followers. Al-Jabartī taught his disciples Ibn 'Arabī's two major works, *Fuṣūṣ al-ḥikam* – along with its famous commentaries by al-Jandī (d. c. 700/1300), al-Qāshānī (d. 730/1329) and al-Qayṣarī (d. 751/1350/1) – and *al-Futūḥāt al-Makkiyyah*.[3] It is therefore likely that al-Jīlī was first exposed to Ibn 'Arabian Sufi thought in a deep and sustained manner in the course of his instruction by al-Jabartī. While Zabid became his home, al-Jīlī also travelled widely, visiting Mecca and Medina, India, Iran, Damascus, Gaza, Cairo and Sanaa over the course of his life. It seems that he died and was buried in Zabid in 811/1408.[4]

Though we know relatively little about the details of al-Jīlī's life, we are able to build up a fairly comprehensive picture of his thought based on the several writings of his that have come down to us. He wrote approximately twenty works (including two made up of several shorter treatises), of which eleven are extant.[5] All of the surviving works deal with Ibn 'Arabian Sufi metaphysical topics. Indeed, at least one of them is a direct commentary (*sharḥ*) on a work of Ibn 'Arabī's: *Sharḥ mushkilāt al-Futūḥāt al-Makkiyyah*, a partial commentary on the summative penultimate chapter (chapter 559) of the *Futūḥāt*, written at some point between 805/1402/3 (which al-Jīlī mentions in the *Sharḥ* as the year of a particularly significant dream he had in Sanaa) and his death.[6] Besides this commentary, his most important works are, in chronological order: *al-Kahf wa-al-raqīm fī sharḥ bism Allāh al-raḥmān al-raḥīm*, his first work, a short treatise on the hidden meaning of the letters of the *basmala*;[7] *al-Nādirāt al-'ayniyyah*, a mystical poem of 536 verses, on which the famous later Ibn 'Arabian Sufi of Damascus 'Abd al-Ghanī al-Nābulusī (d. 1143/1731) wrote a commentary;[8] *al-Insān al-kāmil*, his magnum opus, which, though principally focused on the idea of the Perfect Human, is in fact a compendium of his Sufi metaphysics as a whole;[9] *al-Manāẓir al-ilāhiyyah*, a book setting out 101 stages of the mystical path;[10] *Ghunyat arbāb al-samā' fī kashf al-qinā' 'an wujūh al-istimā'*, a treatise on symbolism and rhetoric in poetry from al-Jīlī's Sufi perspective;[11] *al-Kamālāt al-ilāhiyyah fī al-ṣifāt al-Muḥammadiyyah*, in which he explains how the Prophet Muhammad is a locus of manifestation for the traditional ninety-nine most beautiful names of God;[12] *Qāb al-qawsayn fī multaqá al-nāmūsayn*, a treatise on how to 'attach oneself' (*al-ta'alluq*) mystically to the Prophet;[13] and *Marātib al-wujūd*, a concise exposition of the forty levels of existence written towards the end of his life.[14] All of these works provide useful insights into some of al-Jīlī's key ideas, such as his notion of the levels of existence or his conception of the Prophet Muhammad as the Perfect Human. Nevertheless, it is *al-Insān al-kāmil*, the work on which his fame in later Islamic thought depends, which provides the most comprehensive overview of al-Jīlī's thought, and it is on this work, therefore, that the present book shall concentrate.

Al-Insān al-kāmil

(a) Structure and contents

As already noted, while it is ostensibly devoted to the idea of the Perfect Human, *al-Insān al-kāmil* in fact ranges over almost every topic that al-Jīlī deemed important from his Ibn 'Arabian Sufi metaphysical perspective. Each of its sixty-three chapters is devoted to a specific key term and concept, the majority of which are rooted in the Qur'an or were important subjects within Islamic theology (*kalām*) and/or Ibn 'Arabian Sufi metaphysics. The book is divided into two parts,[15] the first of which deals with the divine essence (*al-dhāt*), names (*al-asmā'*) and attributes (*al-ṣifāt*), and the second of which is mainly devoted to key Qur'anic concepts such as the Preserved Tablet (*al-lawḥ al-maḥfūẓ*) and the Holy Spirit (*rūḥ al-quds*), though the dividing line between the two parts is not a completely sharp one. The chapters on the scriptures are located towards the end of the first part of the book. This is because, as we shall see, the scriptures are associated in al-Jīlī's thought with the divine essence, names and attributes, yet are also Qur'anic themes. In this sense, they can be viewed as a bridge connecting the two parts of the book, and therefore as central to the work as a whole – providing further justification for our decision to focus upon them in the present book.

As can be seen, the contents of *al-Insān al-kāmil* are heavily coloured by Qur'anic imagery and vocabulary; indeed, we can go so far as to say that the book is a kind of lexicon of Qur'anic terminology, with the Qur'anic key terms defined according to al-Jīlī's Sufi metaphysical ideas. Thus, he begins each chapter with an explanation of

Table 1 The chapter headings of *al-Insān al-kāmil*

Part One:

1. The Essence (*al-dhāt*)
2. The Name (*al-ism*)
3. The Attribute (*al-ṣifah*)
4. Divinity (*al-ulūhiyyah*)
5. Unqualified Oneness (*al-aḥadiyyah*)
6. Qualified Oneness (*al-wāḥidiyyah*)
7. All-Mercifulness (*al-raḥmāniyyah*)
8. Lordship (*al-rubūbiyyah*)
9. The Cloud (*al-ʿamāʾ*)
10. Divine Incomparability (*al-tanzīh*)
11. Divine Comparability (*al-tashbīh*)
12. The Manifestation of the Divine Acts (*tajallī al-afʿāl*)
13. The Manifestation of the Divine Names (*tajallī al-asmāʾ*)
14. The Manifestation of the Divine Attributes (*tajallī al-ṣifāt*)
15. The Manifestation of the Essence (*tajallī al-dhāt*)
16. Divine Life (*al-ḥayāt*)
17. Divine Knowledge (*al-ʿilm*)
18. Divine Will (*al-irādah*)
19. Divine Power (*al-qudrah*)
20. Divine Speech (*al-kalām*)
21. Divine Hearing (*al-samʿ*)
22. Divine Vision (*al-baṣar*)
23. Divine Beauty (*al-jamāl*)
24. Divine Majesty (*al-jalāl*)
25. Divine Perfection (*al-kamāl*)
26. Ipseity / He-ness (*al-huwiyyah*)
27. Egoicity / I-ness (*al-aniyyah*)
28. Sempiternity (*al-azal*)
29. Everlastingness (*al-abad*)
30. Pre-eternity (*al-qidm*)
31. The Days of God (*ayyām Allāh*)
32. The Ringing of the Bell (*ṣalṣalat al-jaras*)
33. The Mother of the Book (*umm al-kitāb*)
34. The Qurʾan (*al-Qurʾān*)
35. The Furqan (*al-Furqān*)
36. The Torah (*al-Tawrāh*)
37. The Psalms (*al-Zabūr*)
38. The Gospel (*al-Injīl*)
39. The Descent of the Real (*nuzūl al-ḥaqq*)
40. The Opening of the Book (*fātiḥat al-kitāb*)
41. Mount Sinai (*al-ṭūr*)

Part Two:

42. The Highest Cushions (*al-rafraf al-aʿlá*)
43. The Bed and the Crown (*al-sarīr wa-al-tāj*)
44. The Two Feet and the Two Sandals (*al-qadamayn wa-al-naʿlayn*)
45. The Throne (*al-ʿarsh*)
46. The Footstool (*al-kursī*)
47. The Highest Pen (*al-qalam al-aʿlá*)
48. The Preserved Tablet (*al-lawḥ al-maḥfūẓ*)

(*Continued*)

Table 1 (Continued)

49. The Lote-Tree of the Furthest Bounds (*sidrat al-muntahá*)
50. The Holy Spirit (*rūḥ al-quds*)
51. The Angel called 'The Spirit' (*al-malak al-musammá bi-al-rūḥ*)
52. The Heart (*al-qalb*)
53. The First Intellect (*al-'aql al-awwal*)
54. The Conjectural Faculty (*al-wahm*)
55. Aspiration (*al-himmah*)
56. Thought (*al-fikr*)
57. Imagination (*al-khayāl*)
58. The Muhammadan Form (*al-ṣūrah al-Muḥammadiyyah*)
59. The Soul (*al-nafs*)
60. The Perfect Human (*al-insān al-kāmil*)
61. The Signs of the Hour (*ashrāṭ al-sā'ah*)
62. The Seven Heavens (*al-sab' al-samawāt*)
63. All of the Religions and Forms of Worship (*sā'ir al-adyān wa-al-'ibādāt*)

the meaning of the particular term under discussion, as in a lexicon. Both this Qur'an-centredness and focus on key concepts and terminology will become apparent when we come to look at the chapters on the scriptures.

(b) The Sufi metaphysics of *al-Insān al-kāmil*

Ibn 'Arabian Sufi metaphysics:

Al-Jīlī's *al-Insān al-kāmil* reveals his almost total commitment to the underlying Sufi metaphysical world view of Ibn 'Arabī and his interpreters. The major contribution of this intellectual tradition to the history of ideas, and the central idea within its metaphysical system, is what I have termed 'the idea of universal theophany'. This is the idea that the entire phenomenal world is, as Syed Muhammad Naguib al-Attas has rather poetically phrased it, the 'theatre of [God's] manifestation'.[16] This is to say that the existence or being (*wujūd*) of the things which we see all around us is not an independent or separate kind of existence, but rather a 'limited' (*muqayyad*) reflection of the existence of God, whose 'unlimited' (*muṭlaq*) existence is in fact the one and only 'real' existence. For the Ibn 'Arabians, therefore, the first half of the *shahādah*, 'There is no god but God', the fundamental tenet of Islamic monotheistic faith, means nothing less than that 'there is no *existence* but God's',[17] or as al-Jīlī puts it, 'The Real is everything (*al-ḥaqq huwa al-kull*)'.[18] This idea of universal theophany features (whether explicitly or implicitly) on almost every page of the writings of Ibn 'Arabī and his followers, including al-Jīlī's *al-Insān al-kāmil*, where it is figured by the often recurring key terms *tajallī* ('unveiling', 'manifestation', 'self-disclosure') and *ẓuhūr* ('appearance', 'manifestation') and their *ism makān* forms *majlá* and *maẓhar* ('locus of manifestation', the literal version of al-Atas' more poetic rendering).[19] As Izutsu puts it, '*tajallī* is the pivotal point of Ibn 'Arabī's thought. Indeed, the concept of *tajallī* is the very basis of his world-view';[20] hence, Ibn Khaldūn (d. 808/1406) calls the Ibn 'Arabian Sufis 'the partisans of [divine] manifestation, loci of appearances, and presences' (*aṣḥāb al-tajallī wa-al-maẓāhir wa-al-ḥaḍarāt*).[21]

Though, for Ibn 'Arabī and his followers, therefore, it is true to say that only God really exists, what 'appears' or 'becomes manifest' in the phenomenal world is not God's essence (*al-dhāt*) itself. Rather, it is specifically through His *names and attributes* (*al-asmā' wa-al-ṣifāt*) that God reveals Himself within the world;[22] hence, in another work, Ibn Khaldūn also refers to the Ibn 'Arabians as 'the partisans of manifestation, loci of manifestation, *divine names*, and presences' (*aṣḥāb al-tajallī wa-al-maẓāhir wa-al-asmā' wa-al-ḥaḍarāt*)'.[23] It is the divine names and attributes, then, that serve as 'connections' (*nisab*) between God and His creation.[24] This is significant, insofar as these divine names and attributes reveal different aspects of God, and reflect the divine reality to different degrees of completeness. As al-Jīlī puts it in his *Sharḥ mushkilāt al-Futūḥāt*, 'It is clear that His names and attributes have a [hierarchical] order (*tartīban*) that applies to every attribute.'[25] We can refer to this notion as 'the idea of the levels of existence', *marātib al-wujūd* ('the levels of existence') being a term often employed by Ibn 'Arabī and his followers, including al-Jīlī himself, who, as we have already seen, authored a work of that title.[26] (A near synonym for that term is 'presences' [*ḥaḍarāt*], hence the inclusion of that term in Ibn Khaldūn's name for the Ibn 'Arabians.[27]) The significance of the idea of the levels of existence lies in the fact that, if the different existents (*mawjūdāt*) within the phenomenal world constitute 'loci of manifestation' (*maẓāhir*) of the different names and attributes, and if these names and attributes reflect the divine to different degrees of completeness, then it follows that phenomenal existents will also reflect the divine existence in different ways and to different degrees of completeness, in accordance with the particular divine names that they manifest.[28] While the key Ibn 'Arabian idea of universal theophany signals the *unity* (*waḥdah*) of God and creation, therefore, the idea of the levels of existence points towards the *diversity* or *multiplicity* (*kathrah*) within both the Godhead and the phenomenal world; hence, the Ibn 'Arabian Sufis sometimes speak of 'unity within multiplicity' and 'multiplicity within unity': 'The Shaykh [Ibn 'Arabī] witnessed the oneness (*wāḥidiyyah*) of God', writes al-Jīlī in his commentary on the *Futūḥāt*, 'in the multiplicity (*kathrah*) of existents.'[29] If we are to understand the Sufi metaphysics of al-Jīlī, it is important that we acknowledge the existence of both of these perspectives – that is, of unity *and* multiplicity – in the Ibn 'Arabian world view. This holds especially true for his views on the scriptures and sacred history, for, as we shall see, al-Jīlī professes a belief both in the underlying unity of revelation and religion, as forms of divine manifestation, and, at the same time, in their diversity, and the superiority of some of the scriptures, prophets and religions over others.

Universal theophany and the levels of existence in al-Insān al-kāmil:

Perhaps the clearest window into al-Jīlī's adoption and elaboration of the key Ibn 'Arabian ideas of universal theophany and the levels of existence, and, therefore, into the ideas that underlie his whole Sufi metaphysics, is provided by the opening chapters of *al-Insān al-kāmil*. In those chapters, al-Jīlī takes the reader on a journey through the highest levels of existence, beginning with the most exalted level – the divine essence in its simplest, most imperceptible form – and continuing down through the levels associated with the different divine names and attributes. For the purposes of the present book, it is these highest levels of existence that are of most relevance to us, for, as we shall see, al-Jīlī views the scriptures as 'expressions' (*'ibārāt*) of these levels of existence and the divine names and attributes associated with them. In what follows, therefore, I summarize the Sufi metaphysics of *al-Insān al-kāmil* based on a close reading of these opening chapters, paying close attention to the key terms and concepts within his treatment of the highest levels of existence.[30]

Existence, as al-Jīlī sees it, originates in the divine essence (*al-dhāt*). The essence of God, he tells us, is a 'pure existent' (*mawjūd maḥḍ*). This means that its existence is real, necessary and absolute – unlike the existence of created things, which is 'attached to non-existence' (*mulḥaq bi-al-ʿadam*). It is 'imperceptible' (*lā tudrak*), for it has no essence (*dhāt*), name (*ism*), shadow (*ẓill*), trace (*rasm*), spirit (*rūḥ*), description (*waṣf*), qualification (*naʿt*) or mark (*wasm*). For this reason, no expression (*ʿibārah*) or allusion (*ishārah*) can capture it,[31] and it is called, among other names, 'the Cloud' (*al-ʿamā*'),[32] 'the Self of the Self of God' (*nafs nafs Allāh*) and 'the Reality of Realities' (*ḥaqīqat al-ḥaqā'iq*).[33] At the same time, however, everything is latent within it, for the 'entities' (*aʿyān*) or prototypical forms of all the names and attributes depend on it. Al-Jīlī therefore tells us that from another perspective the essence has two accidents (*ʿaraḍān*) – sempiternity (*al-azal*) and everlastingness (*al-abad*);[34] two descriptions (*waṣfān*) – the Real (*al-ḥaqq*) and creation (*al-khalq*); two qualifications – pre-eternity (*al-qidm*) and origination (*al-ḥudūth*);[35] two names (*ismān*) – Lord (*al-rabb*) and servant (*al-ʿabd*); two faces (*wajhān*) – the apparent (*al-ẓāhir*) or the lower world (*al-dunyā*) and the hidden (*al-bāṭin*) or the other world (*al-ukhrá*); two governing principles (*ḥukmān*) – necessity (*al-wujūb*) and contingency (*al-imkān*) and so on and so forth.[36] Based on this, it can be said that the essence is utterly simple, unqualified and unknown/unknowable in itself, yet complex, qualified and known/knowable in its manifestations, which exist within the simple essence in a state of latency. The essence, in other words, contains both God and creation within itself.[37]

The second level of existence in al-Jīlī's scheme, at least as presented in *al-Insān al-kāmil*,[38] is that of 'divinity' (*al-ulūhiyyah*), the level associated with the greatest divine name, *Allāh*. The name *Allāh*, according to al-Jīlī, can only be applied to the essence of 'the One whose existence is necessary (*dhāt wājib al-wujūd*)', the most common 'philosophical' name for God in post-Avicennan Islamic thought.[39] At the same time, all of the names and attributes, and therefore all divine manifestations (*tajalliyyāt*), are beneath the name *Allāh* and contained within it.[40] The level of divinity (*al-ulūhiyyah*), therefore, encompasses all of the realities of existence (*jamīʿ ḥaqā'iq al-wujūd*) and 'preserves' (*ḥifẓ*) them at their respective levels. Divinity thus encompasses both the Real and creation (*al-ḥaqq wa-al-khalq*) – that is, all the 'divine levels' (*al-marātib al-ilāhiyyah*) and 'levels within the universe' (*al-marātib al-kawniyyah*) – and gives every level of existence its reality. For this reason, it can be regarded as 'the highest of the loci of appearance of the essence' (*aʿlá maẓāhir al-dhāt*) and the best (*afḍal*) of the manifestations of the essence to itself and to others.[41]

The third level of existence, according to *al-Insān al-kāmil*, is the level of 'unqualified oneness' (*al-aḥadiyyah*), a term seemingly derived by the Ibn ʿArabian Sufis from the famous opening verse of *Sūrat al-Ikhlāṣ*, '*qul huwa Allāhu aḥad*' ('Say, "He is God, the One."').[42] This level is 'the locus of manifestation of the essence' (*majlá al-dhāt*). It is, in al-Jīlī's words, 'the first of the descents of the essence (*awwal tanazzulāt al-dhāt*) from the darkness of the Cloud (*min ẓulmat al-ʿamā*') into the light of the loci of manifestation (*ilá nūr al-majālī*),' and 'the highest of the loci of manifestation', since every other level (except the level of the simple essence itself) is more qualified and particular than it. Though it constitutes the beginning of the simple essence's descent into phenomenality, therefore, nevertheless 'neither the names, nor the attributes, nor any of its effects have any appearance within it'. Rather, it is a name for the 'simplicity of the essence' (*ṣarāfat al-dhāt* / *maḥḍ al-dhāt al-ṣarf*) that has been 'purified' (*mujarradah, munazzahah*) of all attributes, names, allusions, connections and perspectives. In other words, it signifies the divine essence in its state of incomparability (*al-tanzīh*) and hiddenness (*al-buṭūn*). It is never possessed by created beings, but is instead specific to God.[43]

While *al-aḥadiyyah* is the level of the divine essence in its undifferentiated state, the fourth level, 'qualified oneness' (*al-wāḥidiyyah*), is the level at which the divine essence takes on the names and attributes. Al-Jīlī therefore also calls it the 'differentiation' (*furqān*) of the essence, for it is at this level that multiplicity begins to appear. Nevertheless, at this level all of the names and attributes are united, such that 'the Avenger is the same as the Bounteous (*al-muntaqim 'ayn al-mun'im*)' and so forth. This unity of the attributes, al-Jīlī explains, is because the essence is in all of them, and they are all in the essence. For this reason, at the level of *al-wāḥidiyyah*, the one and the many are united: it is 'the locus of the synthesis of the difference in the attributes' (*majma' farq ṣifātī*); 'everything within it is one and multiple' (*al-kull fī-hā wāḥid mutakaththir*); it is 'an expression of the reality of multiplicity in unity, without being scattered' (*'ibārah 'an ḥaqīqat kathrah fī waḥdah min ghayr mā ashtātī*). It is below the levels of divinity and unqualified oneness, because it represents the divine in a more qualified state than at those levels, yet it is above all of the other levels, because of its synthetic and unitive nature.[44] Moreover, in its hidden, invisible (*bāṭin, ghayb*) aspect it is called ipseity or 'He-ness' (*al-huwiyyah*),[45] and in its apparent, visible (*ẓāhir, shahādah*) aspect it is called 'I-ness' (*al-aniyyah*).[46]

The fifth level of existence, according to al-Jīlī's scheme in *al-Insān al-kāmil*, is the level of 'all-mercifulness' (*al-raḥmāniyyah*). For al-Jīlī as for Ibn 'Arabī,[47] divine mercy (*al-raḥmah*) is the source (*aṣl*) of all existence, that is, the cause of God's existentiation (*ījād*) of the realities latent within Himself, and therefore of the creation of all things – a notion that might be called 'the idea of universal mercy'. 'The first mercy (*awwal raḥmah*) by which God had mercy upon existents', says al-Jīlī, 'was His giving of existence (*wajada*) to the world from Himself.' It is on account of this existentiating, universal mercy that the Sufis speak of the 'pervasiveness' (*sarayān*) of the divine existence in creation. For this reason, the level of all-mercifulness is defined as the level of 'making the realities of the names and attributes appear' (*al-ẓuhūr bi-ḥaqā'iq al-asmā' wa-al-ṣifāt*). In this sense, all-mercifulness is like divinity (*ulūhiyyah*), the second level, for they both serve to bring creation into existence. Indeed, all-mercifulness is a more specific (*akhaṣṣ*) form of divinity, the relationship between them, according to al-Jīlī, being like that of rock candy to sugar cane, because the level of divinity, as will be remembered, gives all levels (including that of all-mercifulness) their existence. Thus while the name *Allāh* encompasses all of the divine names, the name *al-raḥmān* stands between 'the names of the essence' (*asmā' al-dhāt*) – that is, those names that belong to God alone – and what he calls 'the names of the self' (*al-asmā' al-nafsiyyah*) – that is, those names like the Powerful (*al-qādir*), the Knowing (*al-ʿalīm*), the Hearing (*al-samīʿ*), which have 'their face turned towards created beings' (on which see further).[48]

The sixth level of existence is the level of 'lordship' (*al-rubūbiyyah*). This is the level associated with those divine names that require a counterpart in creation, and which are likewise themselves required by that counterpart. The Lord (*al-rabb*), in other words, requires an 'object of lordship' (*marbūb*), that is, a servant (*ʿabd*), in creation, in order to be Lord – an idea that is taken from Ibn ʿArabī.[49] The same applies to the names of the self (on which see further), for the Knower requires something to know (*al-ʿalīm yaqtaḍī al-maʿlūm*), the Powerful requires something to have power over (*al-qādir yaqtaḍī maqdūran ʿalayhi*) and so forth, as well as to other names like the King (*al-malik*) and the Sustainer (*al-qayyūm*).[50] In this way, at the level of lordship a 'connection' (*nisbah*, *ṣilah*) of mutual dependency between God and creation is established,[51] even if the divine retains its superiority over creation (the lord or king being superior to the servant or subject).[52]

Below the level of lordship comes the level associated with those divine attributes that al-Jīlī terms the 'attributes of the [divine] self' (*al-awṣāf/al-ṣifāt al-nafsiyyah*),[53] and which were more commonly known in *kalām* as 'the attributes of the essence'.[54] There are seven such attributes: life, knowledge, will, power, speech, hearing and sight.[55] Al-Jīlī devotes a separate chapter to each of them, the order with which he deals with them reflecting their order, it seems, in the hierarchy of existence:

- Life (*al-ḥayāh*): God, al-Jīlī tells us, possesses 'complete life' (*al-ḥayāh al-tāmmah*), which he defines as 'the existence of a thing through itself', in contrast to the 'additional life' (*ḥayāh iḍāfiyyah*) that belongs to creation, which he defines as 'the existence of a thing through something else'. God's life appears in creation as a 'single and complete' (*wāḥid tāmmah*) life, but created beings differ in their manifestation of it: at the top of the hierarchy, the Perfect Human (*al-insān al-kāmil*) manifests the divine life in a complete way, followed by the highest angels, then ordinary human beings, angels and jinn, then other animals, and finally plants and minerals.[56]
- Knowledge (*al-ʿilm*): God's knowledge is the nearest attribute to His life. As al-Jīlī sees it, God's knowledge of Himself and of His creation is one and the same. In this regard, he criticizes Ibn ʿArabī for suggesting that the objects of God's knowledge (*al-maʿlūmāt*) give Him knowledge from themselves.[57] Rather, says al-Jīlī, God knows the objects of knowledge via 'a form of knowledge that originates in him' (*bi-ʿilm aṣlī minhu*).[58]
- Will (*al-irādah*): Al-Jīlī sees the divine will as a manifestation of the divine knowledge, for God's act of willing constitutes 'the designation of the objects of His knowledge with existence'. There is no cause or reason for God to will the creation of existents; rather, the will to create is 'simply a free choice of God's' (*maḥḍ ikhtiyār ilāhī*). In this regard al-Jīlī again criticizes Ibn ʿArabī, this time for supposedly saying that God cannot be called 'one who acts through free choice' (*mukhtār*), because He acted in accordance with what the world demanded – that is, because He responded to the 'desire' of the essences of possible beings, which were latent within His knowledge, to be given phenomenal existence.[59]

- Power (*al-qudrah*): God's power consists in His ability to give existence to that which does not exist (*ījād al-ma'dūm*), that is, to bring things from a state of hiddenness (*al-buṭūn*) to one of appearance (*al-ẓuhūr*). Once again, in defining *al-qudrah* in this way, al-Jīlī explicitly sets himself against Ibn 'Arabī. For Ibn 'Arabī, al-Jīlī tells us, God's power consists in His ability to bring things from 'intellectual existence' (*wujūd 'ilmī*) – that is, existence in His knowledge – into 'visual existence' (*wujūd 'aynī*) – that is, existence in the phenomenal world.[60] As al-Jīlī sees it, by contrast, God brought things first from non-existence (*al-'adam*) into His knowledge (*al-'ilm*), and then from His knowledge into the visible realm (*al-'ayn*). God's power to bring the non-existent into existence in this way establishes His lordship (*al-rubūbiyyah*) and indicates that God has primary existence (*al-wujūd al-awwal*), while phenomenal existents, being in need of Him, have secondary existence (*al-wujūd al-thānī*).[61]
- Speech (*al-kalām*): God's speech primarily represents His phenomenal existence (*al-wujūd al-bāriz*), for it is the act of giving phenomenal existence to the 'letters' (*aḥruf*) – that is, the latent essences of possible things (*a'yān al-mumkināt*) – that exist undifferentiated in His knowledge. This conception of the divine speech as a creative – or rather, existentiating – act is grounded in the recurring Qur'anic motif that when God desires a thing to come into existence, He simply says to it 'Be!' and it is (*kun fa-yakūn*) (see e.g. Q 2.117, 3.47, 3.59).[62] Al-Jīlī also understands the divine speech in two other senses. In the first sense, it corresponds to the divine command (*amr*) to worship Him, a form of speech that comes from the level of divinity (*al-ulūhiyyah*), and to which all existents respond with worship (*al-'ibādah*) and obedience (*al-ṭā'ah*) – the basis of what I call 'the idea of universal monotheism' (on which see below). The second, narrower kind of divine speech is that which is contained in the scriptures (*al-kutub*) sent down by God to His prophets or in the direct conversations (*al-mukālamāt*) that He has with them. The commandments (*al-awāmir*) contained in this form of speech, which come from the lower level of lordship (*al-rubūbiyyah*) and are in human language (*bi-lughat al-ins*), are met with both obedience and disobedience (*al-ma'ṣiyah*).[63] The free choice (*al-ikhtiyār*) of individuals to respond positively or negatively to this form of speech thus allows for the justice of the divine punishment (*al-jazā'*) and reward (*al-thawāb*) to be preserved.[64]
- Hearing (*al-sam'*): God's hearing is also a manifestation of His knowledge: it denotes, in al-Jīlī's phrase, 'the Real's knowledge of things, through their speech (*kalām*), without a mirror'. This 'speech' of existents can either be actual speech (*talaffuẓ*, *manṭiq*) or a spiritual state (*ḥāl*): God 'hears' both, just as He hears His own speech. In addition, there is also a second type of hearing, which al-Jīlī calls 'the second hearing/listening' (*al-sam'/al-istimā' al-thānī*). This denotes the 'teaching of the Qur'an' (*ta'līm al-Qur'ān*) to those unique individuals who are singled out to receive the manifestation of the divine essence, and whom al-Jīlī variously calls 'the people of the essence' (*al-dhātiyyūn*), 'the Unique Ones who attain realization' (*al-afrād al-muḥaqqiqūn*), and, based upon a *ḥadīth qudsī* that he quotes, 'the people of the Qur'an' (*ahl al-Qur'ān*), 'the people of God' (*ahl Allāh*) and 'God's elect' (*khāṣṣat Allāh*). These terms all denote the Perfect Humans.

The second type of hearing, then, is that which God loans (*a'āra*) to His perfect servants, who are thus able to 'hear' – that is, to know – the true meaning of the Qur'an. The archetype of such Perfect Humans is Muhammad; hence, those who attain this status are called 'Muhammadan people of the essence' (*al-dhātiyyīn al-Muḥammadiyyīn*), and their station is 'the station of the Beloved' (*maqām al-ḥabīb*) – *ḥabīb Allāh* being a traditional title for Muhammad. Below this level of Perfect Humans, meanwhile, is the level of those who receive the manifestation not of the essence itself, but only that of the attributes of the divine self. These individuals are taught not the Qur'an – which, as we shall see, al-Jīlī considers a manifestation of the essence – but rather the Furqan – which is an expression of the qualified oneness of God, or the essence qualified by names and attributes. The model for such individuals is Moses; hence, they are called 'the Mosaic people of the self' (*al-nafsiyyūn al-mūsawiyyūn*),[65] and their station is 'the station of the One Spoken To' (*maqām al-kalīm*), *kalīm Allāh* being the traditional title of Moses.[66]

- Sight (*al-baṣar*): God's sight denotes 'His witnessing of the objects of [His] knowledge' (*shuhūdihi li-al-ma'lūmāt*). Like several of the other attributes of the divine self, then, God's sight is also a form of His knowledge: 'The locus of His knowledge is the locus of His eye (*maḥall 'ilmihi maḥall 'aynihi*). Thus, though His knowledge and sight are two attributes (*ṣifatān*), nevertheless they are one thing (*shay' wāḥid*).' Just as nothing is outside of God's knowledge, so too is nothing veiled from His sight, though He only gazes upon things if He wills; hence, God's gaze (*naẓar*) is considered an act of divine mercy (*raḥmah ilāhiyyah*).[67]

The eighth level of existence, in al-Jīlī's scheme, is that of the divine 'beauty' (*al-jamāl*) and the names and attributes associated with it. God's beauty, says al-Jīlī in this regard, denotes God's 'most exalted names and most beautiful attributes' (*awṣāfihi al-'uliyā wa-asmā'ihi al-ḥusná*). More particularly, the divine beauty points towards the divine attributes of mercy (*al-raḥmah*), knowledge (*al-'ilm*), kindness (*al-luṭf*), grace (*al-ni'mah*), generosity (*al-jūd*), sustaining (*al-razzāqiyyah*), creating (*al-khallāqiyyah*), granting benefits (*al-naf'*) and so forth. There are also some names, al-Jīlī informs us, such as *Allāh*, *al-rabb* and *al-raḥmān*, which are names of beauty from one perspective, and names of majesty (*al-jalāl*) (on which see further) from another perspective; hence, they are called 'shared' (*mushtarakah*) names or attributes. Moreover, there are two types of divine beauty: (i) that which pertains to God's inner meaning (*ma'nawī*), that is, to the inner meanings of the most beautiful names and most exalted attributes, the witnessing of which is particular to God alone; and (ii) that which pertains to His outer form (*ṣūrī*), which is the beauty seen in the phenomenal world (*al-'ālam*) and the creatures (*al-makhlūqāt*) within it. On account of this latter type of beauty, it can be said that the divine beauty or goodness (*al-ḥusn*) is present in the original nature (*aṣālah*) of all existents, while ugliness (*al-qubḥ*) is only a matter of perspective, which is to say that it is non-essential. All things that are qualified by existence, of whatever type, therefore, are forms or loci of manifestation of the divine beauty.[68]

Like God's beauty, God's majesty (*al-jalāl*), the ninth level of existence, denotes another category of His names and attributes. In this case, it denotes attributes such as grandeur (*al-'uẓmah*), greatness (*al-kibriyā'*), eminence (*al-majd*), praise (*al-thanā'*) and so forth. There are thus four categories (*aqsām*) of divine names/attributes: (i) the attributes of beauty; (ii) the attributes of majesty; (iii) the attributes shared between beauty and majesty, which are also called the attributes of perfection (*ṣifāt al-kamāl*); and (iv) the essential attributes (*ṣifāt dhātiyyah*), which are those that qualify the divine essence alone.[69] All existents, as we have seen, are loci of manifestation of (an aspect of) God's beauty, because, in accordance with the idea of 'universal mercy', they attain existence by receiving God's mercy – which is an attribute of beauty. While God's majesty is also manifest in creation, it does not embrace all existents in the same universal way that God's beauty does. This, says al-Jīlī, is the mystery of the hadith beloved by Ibn 'Arabī and his followers, and which is a key scriptural source for the Ibn 'Arabian idea of universal mercy:[70] 'My mercy precedes My wrath.'[71]

This detailed exposition of al-Jīlī's conception of the levels of existence helps us to understand his conception of the relationship between God and creation, and his view of reality more generally. Simply put, as al-Jīlī sees it, existence originates in the divine essence. This essence is utterly one, simple and unknowable. However, as al-Jīlī notes in the introduction to *al-Insān al-kāmil*, God is not just His essence; rather, He possesses an essence, names and attributes.[72] This being the case, as those names and attributes become manifest, so too does the unity of God emerge into multiplicity. This process begins with the level of *al-aḥadiyyah*, at which the names and attributes, while not outwardly apparent, are latent within the divine essence, and continues through the levels of *al-wāḥidiyyah*, *al-ulūhiyyah*, *al-raḥmāniyyah* and so forth, at which the divine is increasingly qualified by names and attributes, and increasingly manifest. It is through the progressive manifestation of the different names and attributes at the different levels, therefore, that God's simple, unqualified existence becomes the complex, qualified existence of creation. Moreover, these divine names and attributes that become manifest in the world also fall under different categories, some being attributes of 'beauty', and others of 'majesty'. The requirement that these different kinds of attributes possess counterparts in creation – for example, the sinner who is worthy of God's 'majestic' vengeance, and the penitent who is worthy of His 'beautiful' forgiveness – further adds to the diversity of the created realm.

With respect to al-Jīlī's treatment of the scriptures and his view of sacred history, what is most important to take from all of this is that, as already indicated, while creation as a whole is a locus of divine manifestation, nevertheless there is a *hierarchy* of divine manifestation within creation, which mirrors the hierarchy of names and attributes within the Godhead. Some created beings, therefore, are more complete manifestations of God's essence, names and attributes than others, and/or complement the higher or more 'beautiful' divine attributes. This, as we shall see, also applies to the scriptures, their prophets and their religious communities; indeed, there is already a hint of this in the hierarchical distinction that al-Jīlī draws, in his discussion of God's 'hearing', between the Qur'an and Furqan, and between 'the Muhammadan people of the essence' and 'the Mosaic people of the self'.

This leads us on to the final key idea underlying the whole of *al-Insān al-kāmil*, namely, al-Jīlī's idea of the Perfect Human, which, as the title indicates, is the central idea of the book.[73] The term *al-insān al-kāmil* and the related concept are found in the works of Ibn 'Arabī and his interpreters, for whom the Perfect Human is above all a 'synthetic being' (*kawn jāmi'*) who unites the created and the divine.[74] Al-Jīlī adopted and developed this idea.[75] For him, humanity is the fortieth and final level of existence. Man therefore synthesizes all of the other levels and is the most complete locus of divine manifestation: as we saw previously, in the context of al-Jīlī's discussion of God's attribute of 'life', the Perfect Human is the individual who manifests the divine life in the most complete and perfect way. In this sense, the human being is both a microcosm of the cosmos and a 'copy' (*nuskhah*) of the divine names and attributes that are manifest in the phenomenal world.[76] Not all humans, however, actually realize their potentially all-comprehensive nature. Those who do so are the Perfect Humans.[77] One of al-Jīlī's most important innovations in this regard is his clear and absolute insistence that the only individual who has fully achieved this, and who therefore deserves to be called the Perfect Human, is the Prophet Muhammad: 'Wherever the term "Perfect Human" in an unqualified sense occurs in my writings,' he writes, 'I only mean by it Muhammad.'[78] That said, al-Jīlī does also leave open the possibility of other individuals having become or becoming Perfect Humans, or what he calls 'Perfect Ones' (*kummal*), through his adoption of the Ibn 'Arabian concept of the Muhammadan Reality (*al-ḥaqīqah al-muḥammadiyyah*). According to al-Jīlī, this Muhammadan Reality appears in the forms or 'garments' (*malābis*) of other prophets and saints or 'Friends of God' (*awliyā'*), thereby transferring Muhammad's perfection onto them.[79] As he puts it in his commentary on the *Futūḥāt*, 'The perfect meanings (*al-ma'ānī al-kamāliyyah*) existent in the Muhammadan Reality become illuminated (*ushriqat*) in our [the Perfect Humans'] essences.'[80] Nevertheless, there remains a hierarchy of perfection – both in *al-Insān al-kāmil* and elsewhere in his writings, al-Jīlī indicates that there are different 'stations' (*maqāmāt*) or 'isthmuses' (*barāzikh*) of perfection[81] – and, within this hierarchy, Muhammad is indisputably the 'most perfect' (*akmal*) of the Perfect Humans.[82] Al-Jīlī's other important innovation, meanwhile, is to go further than Ibn 'Arabī and his interpreters in blurring the distinction between God and Muhammad, the Perfect Human, a point that we shall touch upon when we come to look at his conception of the Qur'an in Chapter 3. This highly exalted conception of Muhammad, as the one and only true Perfect Human, and even a quasi-divine figure, is of clear relevance to al-Jīlī's view of sacred history.

Indeed, as we shall see presently, each of the key Sufi metaphysical ideas that have just been set out plays a crucial role within al-Jīlī's Sufi metaphysical treatment of the scriptures in chapters thirty-four to thirty-eight; in fact, it can be said that they determine his view of sacred history. First, in keeping with the idea of universal theophany, he views God's revelation of the Qur'an, Torah, Psalms and Gospel to His prophets not merely as God's 'sending down' (*inzāl*) of the different scriptures, but more fundamentally as an expression of different forms of divine 'manifestation' or self-disclosure (*tajalliyyāt*). Second, and connected to his notion of the levels of existence, al-Jīlī holds that the divine 'manifestations' represented by the different scriptures are of different degrees of completeness, depending on the kind of divine names and attributes that the scriptures represent. The scriptures, in other words, correspond to different levels within the hierarchy of existence. This means that there is a hierarchy of scriptures, just as there is a hierarchy within the levels of existence. We shall see that this hierarchy of scriptures is in keeping with what I call 'the Qur'an-centred view of sacred history', according to which the Qur'an stands at the top of the hierarchy of scriptures. Third, we shall see that al-Jīlī views the prophets, who are the recipients of these scriptures or divine manifestations, as Perfect Humans, that there is also a hierarchy among these prophets, and that, in accordance with the Qur'an-centred view, Muhammad stands at the top of this hierarchy of prophets, and his community (the Muslims) at the top of the hierarchy of religious communities. In this, we can begin to see both that al-Jīlī's view of sacred history is fundamentally a Sufi metaphysical one, and that this Sufi metaphysical view of sacred history does not conflict with the more conventional Islamic view of sacred history. This, in brief, is the argument put forward in this book.

2

Muslim views of sacred history

The Qur'an-centred view of sacred history

While al-Jīlī's Sufi metaphysics determines his view of the scriptures and renders his view of sacred history distinctive (at least from non-Ibn 'Arabian views of sacred history), this does not mean, as already suggested, that his views violate the Qur'an-centred view of sacred history. In order to establish this point, it is first necessary that we have some idea of the key elements of that Qur'an-centred view. This raises first the issue of terminology: What does it mean to talk about the 'Qur'an-centred view of sacred history'?

Sacred history can be generally understood as an 'account of God working through His human agents to accomplish His will',[1] where those 'human agents' are prophets, in particular. Understood in this way, it can be said that history in the Qur'an *is* sacred history: as Kenneth Cragg notes, the 'time-perspectives' of the Qur'an are 'backwards to the prophets and their generations, and forwards to the judgment-end'.[2] Secular history, by contrast, receives little attention in the Islamic scripture.

What I am calling 'the Qur'an-centred view of sacred history', however, is not confined merely to what the Qur'an itself says about the prophets and their scriptures and communities; rather, the term refers to the common framework in which most Muslims prior to modernity (and in many cases, up to the present day) thought about the prophetic past.[3] As such it includes ideas about sacred history found in various genres of post-Qur'anic Islamic literature, such as hadith, Qur'anic exegesis (*tafsīr*), doxography, religious polemic, tales of the prophets literature (*qiṣaṣ al-anbiyā'*) and historical chronicles (*tārīkh*), as well as the Qur'an itself. Nevertheless, this view of sacred history is 'Qur'an-centred' in two respects. First, though supplemented by the sources just mentioned, it is primarily rooted in what the Qur'an itself says about sacred history. Second, this view of sacred history, as we shall see presently, makes the revelation of the Qur'an to Muhammad *the* central event in history, in the sense that all that went before this event is believed to lead up to it, and all that will come after must look back to it.

The central theme running through the Qur'an-centred view of sacred history is the need for mankind to acknowledge, believe in, submit to and worship the one God (*Allāh*) who created the heavens and the earth – obligations figured by the key Arabic terms *tawḥīd*, *īmān*, *islām* and *'ibādah*.[4] Those who perform these obligations will be admitted to paradise, and those who do not will be condemned to hell (see e.g.

Q 4.122-123; 6.48; 11.13; 30.15-16). This simple, straightforwardly monotheistic message, it is said, is the original religion of mankind (*dīn al-fiṭrah*).[5] Yet, since human beings are neglectful of – and often actively resistant to – this message (see e.g. Q 16.82-83), God has sent to them inspired individuals called prophets (*anbiyā'*, *nabiyyīn*) – from Abraham, the archetypal pre-Jewish and pre-Christian monotheist (*ḥanīf*) (Q 2.135, 3.67), up to Muhammad, 'the seal of the prophets' (*khātam al-nabiyyīn*) (Q 33.40) – in order to remind them of the true religion (*tadhkīr*) (e.g. Q 20.1), and to bring the good news of salvation to the believers (*tabshīr*) and warn the unbelievers of their impending doom (*tandhīr*) (see e.g. Q 6.19, 6.92, 7.1, 8.7, 33.45, 46.19). 'Every messenger We sent before you [i.e. Muhammad]', God is quoted as saying in the Qur'an (Q 21.25), 'We inspired [with the message]: There is no god but God. So worship Me (*fa-'budūni*).'

According to post-Qur'anic tradition, the prophets were of two kinds: 'messengers' (*rusul*, sing. *rasūl*), who were those prophets to whom God sent down (*anzala*) a 'book' (*kitāb*), that is, a scripture, which they were instructed to propagate (*tablīgh*) to their community, and ordinary prophets, who, though they worked miracles (*mu'jizāt*) and were divinely inspired, were not given their own scripture, instead being commanded to call people (*da'wah*) to follow the scripture of the messenger who had preceded them.[6] Although the Qur'an does not itself appear to make so rigid a distinction, it does perhaps contain the germ of the idea (see e.g. Q 57.25, which specifically connects God's *messengers* with the receiving of 'the book'). It tells us, moreover, that 'every community (*ummah*) was given a messenger', (Q 10.47) meaning that 'every people (*qawm*) has had someone calling them to believe in the oneness of God (*tawḥīd Allāh*) and to worship Him (*'ibādatihi*)'.[7]

The Qur'an makes special mention, however, of four messengers and their scriptures and communities: Moses (*Mūsá*),[8] who was given the Torah (*al-Tawrāh*),[9] which he was ordered to propagate to the Jews (*al-Yahūd*) or Children of Israel (*Banū Isrā'īl*);[10] David (*Dāwūd*),[11] who was given the Psalms (*al-Zabūr*),[12] which is also a scripture of the Children of Israel, though unlike the Torah is generally understood not to contain a new law;[13] Jesus (*'Īsá*),[14] who was given the Gospel (*al-Injīl*),[15] the scripture of the Christians (*al-Naṣārá*);[16] and Muhammad,[17] who was given the Qur'an (*al-Qur'ān*) itself,[18] the scripture of the Muslims (*al-Muslimūn*) or Believers (*al-mu'minūn*).

Each of these scriptures is believed to exist, in archetypal form, in a heavenly book called (using Qur'anic terms) 'The Mother of the Book' (*umm al-kitāb*) or 'The Preserved Tablet' (*al-lawḥ al-maḥfūẓ*),[19] meaning that in their original, divinely ordained forms, the Torah, Psalms, Gospel and Qur'an are thought to contain the same message of basic, primordial monotheism. A tradition attributed to the famous *ḥanīf* and contemporary of the Prophet Waraqah ibn Nawfal has it that, 'This [Qur'an] and that which Moses brought truly derive from a single lamp (*mishkāh wāḥidah*)'.[20] Each of the four scriptures, therefore, is a true, divinely revealed scripture: 'God – May He be exalted – truly (*ḥaqqan*) sent down the Torah to Moses', writes the Andalusian Ẓāhirī scholar Ibn Ḥazm (d. 456/1064), 'and He truly sent down the Psalms to David, and He truly sent down the Gospel to Jesus.'[21] Reflecting this idea, the Qur'an styles itself as a 'confirmation' (*muṣaddiq*) of the earlier scriptures (see e.g. Q 2.41, 2.97, 3.3), commanding its audience to 'believe in all the scriptures that God has sent down', (Q 42.16) and instructs them, when in doubt about the meaning of a Qur'anic passage, to consult those communities who had previously been given a scripture, that is, the Jews and Christians (see Q 10.94). The different messengers, similarly, are believed to have practised and taught the same religion: 'I am nothing new (*bid'an*) among the messengers', Muhammad is told to say (Q 46.9); 'Do not draw distinctions between the prophets of God', the Prophet instructs his followers in a hadith (see also Q 4.150-2, which warns against discriminating between messengers);[22] 'The religion of the prophets and messengers is a single religion (*dīn wāḥid*)', writes the famous Ḥanbalī jurist Ibn Taymiyyah (d. 728/1328).[23] And this means in turn that the earlier monotheistic communities, the Jews and Christians, are afforded the special status of 'People of Scripture' (*ahl al-kitāb*) (see e.g. Q 2.105, 2.109), and that they are recognized as religious communities who worship the same God as the Muslims (see Q 29.46), and follow the same line of prophets.[24]

This is the potentially more pluralist or inclusivist dimension of the Qur'an-centred view of sacred history; indeed, much like a modern religious pluralist,[25] the Qur'an even suggests that religious diversity is willed by God (see Q 5.48; 11.118). Yet this pluralism is heavily qualified by the sense that the Jewish and Christian scriptural communities have taken a seriously wrong turn. 'God rebuked (*dhamma*) the People of Scripture [who came] before us', writes the prominent later-medieval Qur'anic commentator and historian Ibn Kathīr (d. 774/1373), 'for turning away from the Book of God that had been given to them, and turning to the lower world and its affairs, and for being occupied with other than following the Book of God, as they had been commanded.'[26] In particular, the Qur'an and post-Qur'anic tradition charge the Jews and Christians with the 'corruption' (*taḥrīf*) or 'alteration' (*tabdīl*) of their scriptures (see e.g. Q 2.42, 2.79, 3.78, 4.46, 5.13-14, 5.15, 6.92 for the Qur'anic verses used as the basis of the charge).

In the post-Qur'anic tradition, the charge of *taḥrīf* was generally understood in one of two senses: corruption of the text itself (*taḥrīf al-naṣṣ*), that is, the charge that the Jews and Christians had changed, removed material from or added material to the original, divinely revealed versions of their scriptures; or corruption of the meaning of scripture (*taḥrīf al-ma'ná*), that is, the charge that the Jews and Christians had altered the meaning of their scriptures through misinterpretation of the text.[27] *Taḥrīf al-ma'ná* seems to have been the original, Qur'anic meaning of the charge,[28] and the concept is found in this sense in earlier Muslim polemical works,[29] as well as in the writings of major later figures like al-Shahrastānī (d. 548/1153), Fakhr al-Dīn al-Rāzī (d. 606/1210) and Ibn Khaldūn.[30] Yet the concept of *taḥrīf al-naṣṣ* is found in a well-known and canonical hadith report,[31] and as time went on this became 'the standard interpretation of *taḥrīf*',[32] featuring prominently (alongside the charge of *taḥrīf al-ma'ná*) in the Mu'tazilite theologian and judge 'Abd al-Jabbār's (d. 415/1025) critique of Christianity,[33] the famous doxographical work of Ibn Ḥazm[34] and the polemical works of Ibn Taymiyyah and his disciple Ibn Qayyim al-Jawziyyah (d. 751/1350),[35] to name only some of the best-known examples. The result of this *taḥrīf* (whether of the meaning or text of scripture), Muslims believed, was that the scriptures used by the Jews and Christians were *missing* vital material – most notably, predictions of the coming of Muhammad;[36] that they contained (or were understood to contain) *additional* false doctrines – such as, in the Christian case, the doctrines of the Incarnation (*ḥulūl, ittiḥād, tajassud*) and the Trinity (*tathlīth*)[37] – or false reports – such as the sinful conduct (*fawāḥish*) attributed to many of the prophets by the Hebrew Bible;[38] that the scriptures in the possession of the Jews and Christians contained numerous *contradictions* (*munāqaḍāt*) and chronological and geographical *inaccuracies*;[39] and that the Jews and Christians were beset by *disagreements* (*khilāfāt*) both between each other and among themselves.[40]

All in all, the distorting effect of *taḥrīf* means that the scriptures used and held sacred by the Jews and Christians are not the same as the 'Torah', 'Psalms' and 'Gospel' mentioned in the Qur'an. As the late-medieval Cairo-based Ḥanbalī theologian Najm al-Dīn al-Ṭūfī (d. 716/1316) put it, 'With regard to these four Gospels that are in the possession of the Christians, no part of them is identical to the Gospel revealed to Jesus son of Mary.'[41] According to the Qur'an-centred view, this is the context in which the revelation of the Qur'an to Muhammad needs to be understood. With the Jews and Christians beset by error and their scriptures in a state of corruption, Muhammad's mission was to call mankind back to the path of monotheism. Through Muhammad, Ibn Taymiyyah explains, God 'made manifest what was hidden among the People of Scripture; clarified the ways in which they had strayed from the right course (*minhaj al-ṣawāb*), realized what the Torah, Psalms and Gospel had promised, and revealed what falsehood (*bāṭil*) they contained due to corruption and alteration (*al-taḥrīf wa-al-tabdīl*).'[42] If they truly wished to follow the religions brought by their prophets, therefore, the Jews and Christians ought to follow Muhammad: 'This Qur'an relates to the Children of Israel most of what they disagree over', (Q 27.76) says the Qur'an. 'They could only adhere to [their scriptures]', writes al-Shahrastānī, 'by adhering to the Qur'an.'[43]

The Qur'an, then, not only 'confirms' the earlier scriptures, it also 'dominates' (*muhaymin*) and 'abrogates' or 'supersedes' (*naskh*) them.[44] 'The Qur'an', writes Ibn Taymiyyah,

> includes every good thing contained in the [earlier] scriptures, and many more things that are not found in the scriptures, and for this reason it confirms the existing Book and dominates it, and affirms that which is true within them, and falsifies what is corrupt in them, and abrogates (*yansakh*) what God has abrogated, and so affirms the true religion.[45]

As the uncreated speech of God (according to the Sunni view),[46] the Qur'an is perfect or complete (see e.g. Q 6.11) and flawless (see Q 18.1, 39:38), and 'the best of speech' (*aḥsan al-ḥadīth*) (Q 39.23). With its revelation, Muslim exegetes took Qur'an 5.3 to mean, religion had been perfected;[47] hence, according to Ibn Khaldūn, 'The religious law has forbidden the study of all revealed scriptures except the Qur'ân.'[48] In the Qur'an-centred view of sacred history, therefore, the Qur'an is undoubtedly the best of scriptures.

This being the case, the Qur'an-centred view also recognizes Muhammad as the greatest prophet. The Qur'an declares that God 'preferred some prophets to others', (Q 17.55) and Muhammad's title of 'Seal of the Prophets' (Q 33.40) was understood not only to mean that he was the last of the prophets but also that he was the best of them.[49] He was, as the Muʿtazilite exegete al-Zamakhsharī (d. 538/1144) puts it, 'the best of those to whom divine revelation was given (*khayr man ūḥiya ilayhi*)', [50] or as Ibn Kathīr has it, 'the lord of mankind (*sayyid al-nās*) at every station'.[51] The canonical hadith collections, similarly, contain sections featuring hadiths on the superiority of Muhammad over the other prophets: 'Were Moses alive he would have to follow me', runs one famous hadith report; 'I have been preferred over the other prophets for six things', begins another;[52] and when Jesus returns at the end of time, it is said, he will follow the law (*sharīʿah*) of Muhammad, 'praying towards his [i.e. Muhammad's] *qiblah*, as if he were a member of his community'.[53] While the earlier messengers were believed to have been sent to a particular community, Muhammad's message was thought to be *universal*: 'We have sent you to all men', (Q 34.28) says God to Muhammad in the Qur'an, and it was thought that Muhammad 'had taken on the message and propagated it to the people of the east and the west, to all races among the Children of Adam'.[54] And such was the reverence for Muhammad that, from al-Shāfiʿī (d. 204/820) onwards, the Prophet's customs (*sunnah*) and sayings (*aḥādīth*) were elevated in Sunni Islam to a quasi-scriptural status, almost equal to the Qur'an itself.[55]

In the Qur'an-centred view of sacred history, finally, the superiority of the Qur'an over the other scriptures and of Muhammad over the other prophets entail the superiority of the Islamic *ummah* over the other religious communities. 'You are the best community (*khayr ummah*) sent out to mankind', (Q 3.110) says the Qur'an, and this was taken by Muslim exegetes to be a declaration of Muslim superiority. 'This noble community', writes Ibn Kathīr, 'even if it is the last community to have been created, will nevertheless be the first community (*awwal al-umam*) on the Day of Resurrection', and this 'brocade of nobility' (*qaṣab al-sharaf*), he explains, is 'due to the nobility of its messenger'.[56] The Jewish and Christian communities, by contrast, are believed to have been made 'rotten' (*fāsid*) by *taḥrīf*;[57] they are, respectively, 'those who have earned [God's] wrath' (*al-maghḍūb ʿalayhim*) and 'those who are astray' (*al-ḍāllīn*) mentioned in the final verse of the Qur'an's opening *sūrah* (Q 1.7).[58]

This is the more exclusivist, or what might be called the 'supersessionist', dimension of the Qur'an-centred view of sacred history. The Qur'an, Muhammad and the Muslim community are presented as superior to the earlier scriptures, prophets and religious communities, their purpose being to supersede – that is, render superfluous – those earlier scriptures, prophets and religions. As we have seen, however, the attitude taken towards those earlier scriptures, prophets and religious communities is by no means unremittingly negative or exclusivist. In their original form, the earlier scriptures are viewed as a genuine revelation from God, while the earlier prophets are seen as genuine divine messengers whose example provides a model for Muhammad. And though the Jews and Christians have fallen into error, there are still righteous people among them, who can justifiably hope for salvation (see e.g. Q 2.62). In sum, then, the Qur'an-centred view of sacred history takes what might be called an equivocal or ambivalent attitude towards the earlier scriptures, prophets and religious communities.[59] Within this ambivalent framework, of course, Muslim thinkers could take a harsher, more exclusivist position or a softer, more inclusivist or pluralist stance, yet the overall framework, with its insistence on the superiority of the Qur'an, Muhammad and the Muslim community, remains the same.

Sufi views of sacred history

Sufis have always insisted that their ideas are rooted in the Qur'an and Sunna,[60] and, since Massignon,[61] most modern scholars have been inclined to agree.[62] This Qur'an-centredness applies, too, to how most Sufis have viewed sacred history, at least prior to modern times. In keeping with the Qur'an-centred view, the Sufis have tended to recognize a hierarchy of scriptures, prophets and religions, with the Qur'an, Muhammad and Islam occupying the highest rank. For example, with respect to the superiority of the Qur'an, the early Sufi Qur'an commentator Sahl Tustarī (d. 283/896) describes how the Qur'an 'is elevated (*rafīʿ*) over and masters (*mustawlin*) all of the other scriptures'.[63] The Andalusian Sufi, and influence on Ibn 'Arabī, Ibn Barrajān (d. 536/1141), who viewed all of the scriptures mentioned in the Qur'an as potentially valid sources of knowledge, nevertheless wrote in that same *tafsīr*, 'Whenever you desire to read the Torah, the Gospel, the Scrolls of Abraham, Moses, Noah, Salih, or any other prophet or messenger, then read the Qur'an [instead]. For it [i.e. the Qur'an] is God's straight path to which all previously sent [messengers] were guided.'[64] And Ibn 'Arabī himself, describing a vision of the four rivers of paradise in the *Futūḥāt*, compares the 'greatest river' (*al-nahr al-aʿẓam, al-nahr al-kabīr al-ʿaẓīm*) to the Qur'an, and the three tributaries as the Torah, Psalms and Gospel. And though he declares, in a more pluralist or inclusivist vein, that 'all [the scriptures] are true (*ḥaqq*), for they are the speech of God (*kalām Allāh*)',[65] he also instructs his readers, from a more exclusivist perspective, to follow the course of 'the river of the Qur'an', which he glosses as 'the river of Muhammad', 'for Muhammad was given all forms of [divine] speech (*jawāmiʿ al-kalim*), and was sent to all people, and through him were abrogated (*nusikhat*) all the tributary rulings (*furūʿ al-aḥkām*)'.[66] Indeed, like Ibn Barrajān,[67] Ibn 'Arabī believed in the corruption (*taḥrīf*) of the pre-Qur'anic scriptures: 'I saw the Torah', he wrote in chapter 367 of the *Futūḥāt*, 'and the specific knowledge God wrote in it by His own hand. But I was astonished at how, even though He wrote it by His own hand, God did not protect it from alteration (*tabdīl*) and corruption (*taḥrīf*) by the Jews, the companions of Moses, who corrupted it (*ḥarrafahā*).'[68] By contrast, he writes, 'no letter or word from the Qur'an [will] be changed'.[69]

In keeping with this strong sense of the superiority of the Qur'an over the other scriptures, the Sufis clearly believe in the superiority of Muhammad over the other prophets. Tustarī tells us that Muhammad, 'the Beloved' (*al-ḥabīb*), 'was elevated (*rufiʿa*) over the station of the Friend (*al-khalīl*) [i.e. Abraham] and of the One Spoken To (*al-kalīm*) [i.e. Moses], and over the stations of all the prophets brought near [to God] (*al-anbiyāʾ al-muqarrabīn*). . . . All the prophets and angels have proximity (*qurbah*) to God, but Muhammad is the nearest (*aqrab*) of them'.[70] Similarly, Abū al-Qāsim al-Qushayrī (d. 465/1072), author of the most famous manual of classical Sufism, writes in his Sufi *tafsīr*, commenting on Qur'an 17.55:

> [God] preferred (*faḍḍala*) some of the prophets over others in prophethood (*nubuwwah*) and degree (*darajah*) and in messengership (*risālah*), subtle realities (*laṭāʾif*) and particular qualities (*khaṣāʾiṣ*), and He made our Prophet – May God bless him and grant him peace – the best of them (*afḍalahum*), for they are like the

> stars, and he is among them like the full moon (*badr*), or they are like the moons, and he is among them like the sun, or they are like the sun, and he is the sun of suns (*shams al-shumūs*).[71]

As for Ibn ʿArabī and his followers, a 'recurrent theme' in the *Futūḥāt* is the idea that Muhammad is 'king and master of all the children of Adam'.[72] This includes the other prophets: 'All of the prophets in the world', Ibn ʿArabī writes, 'were Muhammad's deputies (*nuwwāb*), from Adam to the last of the messengers.'[73] As Michel Chodkiewicz has put it, for Ibn ʿArabī Muhammad 'is the sum of all the prophetic types and consequently integrates within himself the particular virtues of each'.[74] Likewise, linking the superiority of Muhammad to the superiority of the revelation that he received and of the community that he established, al-Qāshānī informs the readers of his widely read commentary on the *Fuṣūṣ* that 'his speech was the truest speech (*aqwam al-aqwāl*), even if the speech of all the prophets was true (*ḥaqq*), for he was the most perfect (*akmal*) of them and his community was the best of communities'.[75]

This comment of al-Qāshānī's indicates that, alongside the superiority of the Qur'an and the Prophet Muhammad, Sufi thinkers have typically insisted on the superiority of Islam and the Muslim community (*ummah*) over the other religions and religious communities; indeed, like other Muslim thinkers, they have tended to connect the superiority of the Muslim community to the superiority of their Prophet. As al-Qushayrī writes in his interpretation of the phrase *khayr al-umam* in Qur'an 3.110:

> Since Mustafa [i.e. Muhammad] was the noblest of the prophets (*ashraf al-anbiyā'*), his community was the best of communities (*khayr al-umam*); and since they were the best of communities, they were the noblest of communities (*ashraf al-umam*); and since they were the noblest of communities, they were the community that longed the most [for God] (*ashwaq al-umam*); and since they were the community that longed the most, He made their lifespan the shortest, and made them the last of peoples (*ākhir al-aqwām*), so that their life upon this earth would not be too long. Their being the best was not a result of their many prayers and acts of devotion, but of their enhanced acceptance (*iqbāl*) [of God] and His specification of them.[76]

Such a statement is a good example of how the Sufis have remained within the overall framework of the Qur'an-centred view of sacred history, while giving it a Sufi colouring – a tendency that is particularly discernible, as we shall see, in al-Jīlī's treatment of the scriptures.

This Sufi belief in the superiority of the Islamic religion and the Muslim community extends, moreover, to a general acceptance of the concept of *naskh*. According to Yousef Casewit, 'Ibn Barrajān was a firm believer in the dogma of "supersessionism" whereby Islam supersedes or abrogates Christianity, just as the latter is understood to have abrogated Judaism.'[77] Gregory Lipton has likewise recently shown that Ibn ʿArabī advocates 'a traditionally derived supersessionism based on the exclusive superiority of Islam and its abrogation of all previous religious dispensations'.[78] Ibn ʿArabī's statement, quoted earlier, on Muhammad's 'abrogation' of all the 'tributary rulings' supports this view, and further support is supplied by an often-quoted and much-debated passage from chapter 339 of the *Futūḥāt*, in which Ibn ʿArabī, echoing al-Qushayrī's commentary on Qur'an 17.55 quoted above, compares Islam's relationship with the pre-Islamic religions to that of the sun and the stars: the stars, he writes, 'were hidden' (*khufiyat*) by the sun, in the same way that the religious law (*sharīʿah*) brought by Muhammad 'abrogated' (*nasakhat*) all previous religious laws.[79] The Kubrawī Sufi, and contemporary of Ibn ʿArabī, Najm al-Dīn Rāzī (d. 654/1256), similarly devotes a whole chapter of his influential Sufi manual *Mirṣād al-ʿibād* to 'The Abrogation of Previous Religions' by the religion of Muhammad,[80] in the course of which he repeats the comparison of Islam and other religions to the sun and the stars.[81]

It seems clear, then, that the Sufis have generally accepted and reproduced the main features of the Qur'an-centred view of sacred history, even if they sometimes present that Qur'an-centred view in Sufi terms. There are, however, grounds for thinking that, at another, 'inner' (*bāṭin*) level, the Sufis have diverged from the Qur'an-centred view. For instance, the Ibn ʿArabian idea of 'universal theophany', when taken to its logical conclusion, can be taken to imply that, since all things are a locus of divine manifestation (*maẓhar*), whatever one worships, one is in fact worshipping a form of the one true God – what I refer to as 'the idea of universal monotheism'. In several places, indeed, Ibn ʿArabī and his followers appear to spell out this idea explicitly. 'The face of the Real is in everything that is worshipped (*fa-inna li-al-ḥaqq fī kull maʿbūd wajh*)', writes Ibn ʿArabī in the *Faṣṣ* on Noah, 'so in all that is worshipped, nothing is worshipped but God (*fa-mā ʿubida illā Allāh fī kull maʿbūd*).'[82] The same idea is repeated by al-Jandī in his commentary on the *Fuṣūṣ*: 'God is worshipped (*maʿbūd*)', he writes, 'in every place (*makān*), in all that has been worshipped and is worshipped, and prostration is rendered to Him (*masjūd lahu*) at every moment, and at every instant that prostration is rendered to something, from among all the things that can be imagined, conceived, thought of, or witnessed.'[83] By this standard, even idol-worshippers are worshipping the one true God; hence, in the chapter on Aaron in the *Fuṣūṣ*, Ibn ʿArabī explains that Moses knew that, in worshipping the calf, his people were in fact worshipping the real God,[84] for 'the perfect gnostic (*al-ʿārif al-mukammal*) is he who sees every object of worship (*kull maʿbūd*) as a locus of manifestation (*majlá*) of the Real.'[85] And though apparently unconventional, this Ibn ʿArabian idea of universal monotheism is also Qur'an-centred: Ibn ʿArabī supports his position by making reference to Qur'an 17.23 – 'Your Lord decreed that none be worshipped but Him' – which, in Ibn ʿArabī's interpretation, means that nothing *can* be worshipped other than God,[86] while elsewhere in his commentary al-Jandī refers to God's statement in Qur'an 5.48 – 'We have given each of you a law (*shirʿah*) and a way (*minhāj*)' – in support of the related idea that everyone and everything has a particular path to God.[87]

Statements such as these have led some modern scholars, such as Toshihiko Izutsu and others (as we shall see in the next section), to take the view that 'it is [Ibn ʿArabī's] unshakeable conviction that all religions are ultimately one because every religion worships the Absolute in a very particular and limited way'.[88] Yet it should be said that, even if everything is a manifestation of the divine in the Ibn ʿArabian view, this does not necessarily mean that Ibn ʿArabī and his followers think that everything manifests the divine to the same degree of completeness or perfection. Indeed, as we have seen, the notion of a hierarchy of manifestation is a corollary of the key Ibn ʿArabian idea of the 'levels of existence', which is central to al-Jīlī's thought. Connected to this notion of a hierarchy of divine manifestation is the crucial Ibn ʿArabian concept of 'preparedness' (*istiʿdād*) or 'receptivity' (*qābiliyyah*), according to which created beings are viewed as 'receptacles' (*qawābil*), which receive the divine manifestation in accordance with the degree of their preparedness for that manifestation. Because the preparednesses of created beings are different, it follows that created beings manifest the different divine names and attributes to different levels of perfection.[89]

This applies, too, to the scriptures, prophets, religious communities and their objects of worship. As Ibn ʿArabī puts it in his preface to the *Fuṣūṣ*, 'the sects and religions differ because of the differences between peoples (*ikhtalafat al-niḥal wa-al-milal li-ikhtilāf al-umam*)',[90] a statement that al-Jandī explains in the following way:

> The people of every era are distinguished (*yakhtaṣṣūn*) in their conditions, works, sciences, morals, customs, habits, and beliefs, these being matters that the people of no other age share with them. . . . The distinguishing features (*al-khuṣūṣiyyāt*) entail the particularization of the one divine religion (*taʿayyun al-dīn al-wāḥid al-ilāhī*) and the divine wisdom sent down to the perfect one of that age, in accordance with what is required by the preparednesses (*istiʿdādāt*) of his community, and their states, customs, sciences, and beliefs.[91]

It is on account of this belief in the differences between peoples, in their 'preparednessnes' and in other respects, that Ibn ʿArabī and his followers and fellow Sufis are able to insist, as in the statements quoted above, on the superiority of the Qur'an, Muhammad and Islam over the other scriptures, prophets and religions.[92] In fact, at the practical, that is socio-political and juridical, level, Sufis like Ibn ʿArabī declared this belief in the superiority of Islam in no uncertain terms, as in, for instance, Ibn ʿArabī's letter to the Seljuq Sultan of Rūm Kaykāʾūs (r. 607–16 / 1211–20) urging the strict application of the *dhimmī* laws.[93] While it may be true, therefore, that some of the Sufis' more 'esoteric' ideas have put them towards the softer, more inclusivist/pluralist end of the Islamic spectrum on the issue of religious diversity (including, as we shall see, on the issue of soteriology),[94] nevertheless their general commitment to the Qur'an-centred view of sacred history ought to be acknowledged. As we shall see, this holds true as much for al-Jīlī as it does for Ibn ʿArabī or any other Sufi.[95]

Modern assessments and interpretations

This being said, it is fair to say that most modern writers on Sufism have tended to place more emphasis on the Sufis' supposedly more inclusivist or pluralist approach to religious difference. This tendency goes back to some of the earliest orientalist scholarship on Sufism in the nineteenth century,[96] and can also be discerned in the writings of some of the leading twentieth-century scholars of Islamic Studies.[97] It is perhaps most pronounced, however, in the work of those scholars who straddle the boundary between the 'insider' and 'outsider' perspectives on Sufism – that is, who both engage in academic scholarship on Sufism *and* write on contemporary issues from a Sufi-minded perspective, a tendency that is particularly strong among scholars associated with the Perennialist or Traditionalist school, which advocates belief in 'the transcendent unity of religions'.[98] Significantly for the purposes of the present book, these scholars have drawn in particular on Ibn 'Arabian thinkers, from Ibn 'Arabī himself, through his major interpreters like al-Qāshānī and (notably for us) al-Jīlī, to the nineteenth-century Ibn 'Arabian thinker and politico-military leader 'Abd al-Qādir al-Jazā'irī (d. 1300/1883),[99] in order to demonstrate the supposedly more inclusivist or pluralist stance of the Sufis and its relevance for the contemporary world.[100]

For example, William Chittick, who has rightly been described as 'the major American expert on the legacy' of Ibn 'Arabī,[101] suggests in his book of collected essays *Imaginal Worlds: Ibn al-'Arabī and the Problem of Religious Diversity* (1994) that Ibn 'Arabī advances a radically relativist perspective on the issue of religious diversity that is akin to that of twentieth-century postmodernists, but which is at the same time rooted in an authentically Qur'anic position.[102] In support of this, Chittick argues that the aforementioned passage from the *Futūḥāt* in which Ibn 'Arabī compares Islam's relationship with the other religions to that of the sun with the stars in fact indicates Ibn 'Arabī's *rejection* of the doctrine of *naskh*, on the basis that the Sufi maintains that the earlier religions have not been rendered 'false' or 'null and void' (*bāṭil*) by the coming of Islam.[103] Significantly, in Chittick's view Ibn 'Arabī's supposedly relativist or inclusivist approach to religious difference is relevant for the contemporary 'student of religion': addressing the latter, Chittick advises 'taking up the Shaykh's [i.e. Ibn 'Arabī's] standpoint' by 'untying' the 'knots' that tie us to our particular, limited forms of religious belief.[104] This idea of the contemporary relevance and usefulness of Ibn 'Arabī's views on religious diversity and sacred history reflects a wider sense in Chittick's work that Ibn 'Arabī's ideas – for instance, on the divine origin of all things and the importance of the imagination – can help the secular, rationalist modern West recover a perspective that it has mistakenly abandoned.[105]

Even more explicit in his belief in the relevance of medieval Sufi ideas on religious diversity to the contemporary world is the Perennialist scholar Reza Shah-Kazemi. In his book *The Other in the Light of the One*, Shah-Kazemi aims to demonstrate, in the context of what he describes as 'the decline of spirituality and the rise of ideology in Islam as in other religions',[106] that the Qur'an 'contains the principles for elaborating . . . a "transcendently-ordained tolerance"',[107] that is, a vision of religious diversity as something that is divinely willed, and of the different revelations as 'expressions of one and the same religious essence'.[108] This Qur'anic 'universalism', as Shah-Kazemi calls it, can be more clearly discerned, he argues, when the Islamic scripture is read in the light of the Sufi exegetical tradition, and to this end he draws upon the commentaries of Ibn 'Arabian Qur'anic exegetes like al-Qāshānī and the Shī'ī Sufi Ḥaydar Āmulī (d. 787/1385), as well as what he calls 'informal commentaries' like Ibn 'Arabī's *Fuṣūṣ al-ḥikam*. From this Ibn 'Arabian perspective, Shah-Kazemi proposes that 'all revelations . . . can be seen as so many different facets of one principle: the self-disclosure [i.e. *tajallī*] of the divine Reality',[109] a view that, as we shall see, partly echoes the position taken by al-Jīlī in his treatment of the scriptures. For Shah-Kazemi, this inclusive view of the different revelations can form the basis for what he calls a 'metaphysics of dialogue', where 'the holiness of all religions' and their status as 'valid paths to salvation' are recognized, without the differences in their 'outward forms', nor, indeed, the ultimate superiority of Islam over the other religions, being overlooked or obscured.[110] In this way, Shah-Kazemi attempts to construct an authentically Islamic – that is Qur'anic and Sufi – universalism, as a potentially more attractive and therefore effective alternative to the more radical religious pluralism of John Hick and his followers.[111]

A similar argument has also been recently advanced by Vincent Cornell, a leading American scholar of medieval North African Sufism, in an essay titled 'Practical Sufism. An Akbarian Foundation for a Liberal Theology of Difference'[112] – the juxtaposition of 'liberal' and 'Akbarian' being a sure sign that we are dealing here with a modern interpretation of Ibn 'Arabian thought.[113] Cornell argues that, because 'Sufi thinkers were more inclined than their exoteric counterparts to view Islam from a wider perspective and deal meaningfully with religious difference', their perspective on other religions can form a solid basis for an authentically Islamic 'liberal theology of difference'. As his title suggests, Cornell deems Ibn 'Arabian ('Akbarian') Sufi thought particularly suitable for this purpose, and, significantly for the present book, takes al-Jīlī's treatment of other religions in the final chapter of *al-Insān al-kāmil* as a representative example of the religious pluralism of the Ibn 'Arabian tradition. Noting that, according to al-Jīlī, 'the existence of religious differences is God's will, and . . . all human beings, even unbelievers, practice religion as God intended them to do', Cornell concludes: 'Contemporary Muslims should carefully consider Jili's reasoning and the Qur'anic verses that support it.'[114]

Cornell's perspective on al-Jīlī dovetails closely with the work of another leading scholar of Ibn 'Arabian Sufism, Samer Akkach, who has devoted several studies to the prominent late-seventeenth-century Ibn 'Arabian Sufi thinker – and commentator on al-Jīlī – 'Abd al-Ghanī al-Nābulusī. In his Arabic introduction to the biography of al-Nābulusī written by Muhammad Kamāl al-Dīn al-Ghazzī (d. 1214/1799), Akkach refers to 'al-Nābulusī's assiduousness in adopting the ideas of Ibn 'Arabī in relation to religious tolerance (*al-tasāhul al-dīnī*) for the People of the Book, in spreading them within Damascene society, and in defending them against religious zealots (*al-mutashaddidīn*)'.[115] Significantly for us, elsewhere Akkach indicates that al-Nābulusī derived this rather modern sounding 'religious tolerance' not only from Ibn 'Arabī but from al-Jīlī as well. In a biography of al-Nābulusī written for a more general readership, Akkach discusses a debate between al-Nābulusī and the Medinan scholar (and Ibn 'Arabian Sufi) Aḥmad al-Qushāshī (d. 1071/1660/1) concerning al-Jīlī's views on the different religions, as presented in the aforementioned final chapter of *al-Insān al-kāmil*.[116] In the context of his discussion of this debate, Akkach refers to al-Qushāshī's objections to 'al-Jīlī's Sufi ecumenism that presents all major religions as legitimate forms of worship that are, in one form or another, grounded in divine unity'. In response to al-Qushāshī's criticisms, Akkach tells us, al-Nābulusī 'felt the need to defend Sufi ecumenism and re-enforce al-Jili's ideas', and so authored 'a treatise on the transcendent unity of religions that revealed his life-long struggle with the contrasting perspectives of the truth and the law'.[117] Just as his use of the terms 'religious tolerance' and 'religious zealots' in his introduction to al-Ghazzī's biography indicated that he was reading back modern concepts into the thought of Ibn 'Arabī and his later follower, so here Akkach's use of the Perennialist term 'the transcendent unity of religions' indicates that he is applying a modern, Perennialist perspective to his interpretation of al-Jīlī's and al-Nābulusī's thought. Indeed, a few pages on, he declares that al-Jīlī 'argued for the transcendent unity of religions, explaining that all religions are but different pathways to the same end, and that all people worship – by necessity and providence, not by choice – one and the same God'. This 'ecumenical perspective of the transcendent unity of religions', he explains, 'tends to undermine the core discriminatory and exclusivist elements that all religions have, by necessity, inherent in their belief systems in order to maintain the credibility of their exclusive promise for, and access to, salvation.'[118] It is clear from the context that, from his modern, apparently Perennialist standpoint, Akkach is sympathetic to this 'ecumenical perspective', which he associates with 'Sufis in general, and Ibn 'Arabi's school in particular'.[119]

Similar perspectives to those of Chittick, Shah-Kazemi, Cornell and Akkach can also be found in contemporary Arab–Islamic scholarship. For example, the Egyptian scholar Naṣr Ḥāmid Abū Zayd (d. 2010), who is best known for his controversial historical–critical hermeneutics of the Qur'an,[120] argues in his 2002 book *Hākadhā takallama Ibn 'Arabī* (*Thus Spake Ibn 'Arabī*) that the Sufi thought of Ibn 'Arabī contains the potential solution to many of the problems of our modern world, including the existence of a 'Clash of Civilizations' narrative, pushed, on the one hand, by Western intellectuals hostile to Islam, and, on the other hand, by those 'Salafi' Muslims who have in recent decades dominated what he calls the 'Islamic discourse' (*al-khiṭāb al-islāmī*).[121] Engaging with Ibn 'Arabī's thought on religious diversity, Abū Zayd attempts to explain away the more exclusivist aspects of Ibn 'Arabī's position (as seen, for instance, in his letter to Kaykā'ūs) as a result of the pressures of historical circumstance, particularly the 'weakness of Islam' in the face of Christian military victories in Spain and the Near East. While acknowledging the relevance of 'historical experience' (*al-tajribah al-tārīkhiyyah*) to Ibn 'Arabī's thought, therefore, Abū Zayd, like Akkach, proposes that, at the level of 'universal spiritual experience' (*al-tajribah al-rūḥiyyah al-kawniyyah*), Ibn 'Arabī in fact advocates a 'permissive' or 'tolerant' (*mutasāmiḥ*) approach to other religions, as in his famous lines on 'the religion of love' (which Abū Zayd quotes in the introduction to his book).[122] Abū Zayd seems to view this more 'tolerant' side of Ibn 'Arabī's thought on other religions as the basis for a contemporary Islamic religious pluralism and the answer to one of the aforementioned problems of the modern world.

To cite one final example, which is again particularly relevant for the present book, the noted Egyptian novelist, academic and public intellectual Youssef Ziedan (b. 1958) has proposed that Judaism, Christianity and Islam constitute three 'manifestations' (*tajalliyyāt*) of a single religion (*diyānah*).[123] Significantly for our purposes, this view seems to be rooted in the Ibn 'Arabian idea of 'universal monotheism', and in particular in its formulation by al-Jīlī, whose thought was the subject of Ziedan's master's thesis at the University of Alexandria, and whose poem *al-Nādirāt al-'ayniyyah* and commentary on chapter 559 of the *Futūḥāt* Ziedan has edited. Reflecting on his time as a postgraduate student at the University of Alexandria, Ziedan writes:

> I spent many years with 'Abd al-Karīm al-Jīlī filled with wonderment (*dahshah*), flying over the boundless horizons of the Sufis. I came to know the rockiness of his language, the delicateness of his symbols, and the charm of his ideas, and I understood then the famous Sufi saying, which the Sufi utters when his vision is expanded: 'My ocean has no shore!' And one of the strangest sources of wonderment to me, in al-Jīlī's Sufi philosophy, was his particular vision of religions (*diyānāt*), and his Sufi understanding of the essence of beliefs and the differences between people on account of them.[124]

Drawing in particular, like Cornell, on chapter sixty-three of *al-Insān al-kāmil*, Ziedan concludes that, in al-Jīlī's view, 'the fundamental essence (*jawharuhā al-aṣlī*) of the different religions is connected to God (*muta'alliq bi-Allāh*)', and that 'the essence of [Judaism and Christianity] is fundamentally correct (*fī al-aṣl ṣaḥīḥ*)'.[125] It seems that, for Ziedan, such a perspective holds the solution to the problem of religious violence, the topic of his major work of non-fiction, *al-Lāhūt al-'arabī wa-uṣūl al-'unf al-dīnī* (*Arab Theology and the Roots of Religious Violence*) (2009).[126]

I view all of these as well intentioned and in many respects valid modern interpretations and uses of Ibn 'Arabian views on religious diversity, and any student of Ibn 'Arabī or al-Jīlī will certainly learn much from reading them. Nevertheless, the present book differs from them in two principal ways. First, in pursuing a close reading and a history of ideas approach, and being written by an 'outsider' to the Ibn 'Arabian Sufi tradition, it attempts to understand and present al-Jīlī's thought on sacred history and religious difference *on its own terms*, rather than in terms of its potential usefulness or relevance for contemporary debates on how Muslims and others should relate to the religious 'other'. This is not to say that I reject the modern interpretation or use of Ibn 'Arabian thought as a necessarily invalid or unfruitful exercise; but only that such modern, 'insider' interpretations are something different to the history of ideas, and that the line between the two should not be blurred.[127]

Second, though it is true that all of the scholars mentioned – particularly Shah-Kazemi, who tries to maintain a Sufi-inspired Islamic 'particularism' within the overall framework of his Qur'anic universalism – recognize, to some extent, that Ibn 'Arabī, al-Jīlī and other medieval Sufi thinkers believed in the superiority of Islam over the other religions,[128] nevertheless, they all clearly place the emphasis on the pluralistic or inclusivist dimension of these Sufis' thought on other religions. Ultimately, in other words, the impression left on the readers of their works is that the Sufi thinkers discussed were religious pluralists, inclusivists or universalists (even if of a qualified sort), whose thought might therefore serve as the basis for a modern Islamic pluralism. By contrast, the close reading of al-Jīlī's treatment of the scriptures undertaken in the present book will show that although al-Jīlī sometimes *does* take a more inclusivist or pluralistic position on Judaism and Christianity, overall his Sufi metaphysical views on the scriptures, prophets and religions are fully in accordance with – and are in fact grounded upon – the Qur'an-centred view of sacred history. This is to say that, like Ibn 'Arabī and other medieval Sufis, al-Jīlī takes an ambivalent view of the pre-Qur'anic scriptures and religions, and advocates a hierarchy of scriptures, prophets and religions in which the Qur'an, Muhammad and Islam stand at the summit.

3

The Qur'an

We begin our reading of al-Jīlī's Sufi metaphysical conception of the scriptures with an analysis of chapter thirty-four of *al-Insān al-kāmil*, which is devoted to the Qur'an (*al-Qur'ān*), the scripture revealed to Muhammad – the event, as we have seen, which constitutes the apex of sacred history in the Qur'an-centred view. The Qur'an is the first scripture to which al-Jīlī devotes a specific chapter in *al-Insān al-kāmil.*[1] This is notable, because his treatment of the scriptures is otherwise chronological. Thus chapter thirty-six is dedicated to the Torah (*al-Tawrāh*), chapter thirty-seven to the Psalms (*al-Zabūr*) and chapter thirty-eight to the Gospel (*al-Injīl*). (Chapter thirty-five is devoted to the Furqan, another name for the Qur'an, and will be partly analysed later in this chapter.) Al-Jīlī decision to put the Qur'an first, I think, reflects his belief in the superiority of the Qur'an and Muhammad over the other scriptures and prophets. At a more metaphysical level, meanwhile, it reflects the idea that Muhammad, as the spiritual principle known as the Muhammadan Reality (*al-ḥaqīqah al-muḥammadiyyah*),[2] actually existed *before* all of the other prophets, an idea indicated in the famous hadith often quoted by Ibn 'Arabī and his followers: 'I was a prophet even while Adam was between water and clay.'[3] From this Sufi metaphysical perspective, then, the Qur'an – which, as we shall see, Muhammad is closely connected to – can be said to have existed before the creation of mankind and therefore to be chronologically prior to the other scriptures as well as superior to them.

These preliminary remarks reflect the nature of al-Jīlī's treatment of the Qur'an. As will become clear, he displays relatively little interest in more mundane matters that were traditionally of interest to Qur'anic exegetes, such as the particular historical circumstances of revelation (*asbāb al-nuzūl*), the grammar, syntax and vocabulary of Qur'anic Arabic, or which verses abrogate which (*al-nāsikh wa-al-mansūkh*), showing much greater concern for the *metaphysical* signification of the revelation of the Qur'an and Muhammad's role as messenger. In this way, he integrates the Qur'an into his overall Sufi metaphysics. At the same time, his treatment of the Qur'an also reveals a conception of sacred history, which, as we can already begin to see, chimes with the Qur'an-centred view. In what follows, I shall attempt to bring out these key elements of al-Jīlī's conception of the Qur'an by undertaking a close reading of key extracts from chapters thirty-four and thirty-five.

The metaphysical meaning of the Qur'an

> Know that the Qur'an is an expression of the essence (*al-dhāt*), in which all of the attributes disappear (*yaḍmaḥill*). For it [i.e. the essence] is the locus of manifestation (*al-majlá*) that is called 'unqualified oneness' (*al-aḥadiyyah*).[4]

Al-Jīlī begins the prose section of the chapter on the Qur'an with a clear statement of his Ibn 'Arabian, Sufi metaphysical view of the scripture. The Qur'an, he tells us here, corresponds to the simple divine essence (*al-dhāt al-maḥḍ/al-sādhaj*) in its state of not being qualified by names or attributes. Indeed, in the opening poem that immediately precedes this line, he calls the Qur'an 'a simple essence' (*dhāt maḥḍ*).[5] The Qur'an, in other words, is a part of God, and the essential part at that. While al-Jīlī does not use the term here, this implies that the Qur'an is uncreated, in keeping with the Sunni view.[6] Yet whereas Sunni doctrine holds that the Qur'an is identical with one of God's attributes – namely, God's speech (*kalām Allāh*) – al-Jīlī, from his Sufi metaphysical perspective, goes further and identifies it with the very essence of God. The implication of this identification is that, with the revelation of the Qur'an, God in fact revealed His essence within the created world. This, as we shall see, is what al-Jīlī seems to believe, in apparent contradiction of the conventional theological view, found also in Sufi thought, that the divine essence is unrevealed and unknowable.[7]

However, al-Jīlī also indicates here that, when he calls the Qur'an an expression of the essence, he does not mean the hidden, utterly unmanifest aspect of the essence, but rather the essence at the 'locus of manifestation' (*majlá*) of unqualified oneness (*al-aḥadiyyah*).[8] The term *majlá* here signifies a *martabah* (as in *marātib al-wujūd*), that is, one of al-Jīlī's forty levels of existence. Though, as we saw in Chapter 1, al-Jīlī presents *al-aḥadiyyah* in *al-Insān al-kāmil* as the third level of existence, it is in fact – as he indicates in the later work *Marātib al-wujūd* – the second level in terms of being unqualified and unlimited; indeed, it is the level of absolute existence (*al-wujūd al-muṭlaq*), that is, the all-encompassing, utterly unqualified and unlimited existence of the divine essence.[9] Above it is only the interior, totally hidden aspect of the essence, or what he calls, among other names, 'the absolute unseen' (*al-ghayb al-muṭlaq*) and 'the quiddity of the true nature of the essence' (*māhiyyat kunh al-dhāt*).[10] *Al-aḥadiyyah* is therefore both the level at which the essence, as al-Jīlī notes again here, remains unqualified by any names or attributes (which can therefore be said to 'disappear') and also the level at which the divine existence begins to turn towards phenomenality, what he calls 'the first of the descents of the essence (*awwal tanazzulāt al-dhāt*) from the darkness of the Cloud into the light of the loci of manifestation'.[11]

The Qur'an, as an expression of *al-aḥadiyyah*, therefore, does not represent the divine essence in its state of complete and utter hiddenness, but rather in its outward, if still unqualified, aspect. The hidden aspect of the essence, meanwhile, is represented not by the Qur'an, but, as he tells us in chapter thirty-three, by the Mother of the Book (*umm al-kitāb*).[12] This makes sense, if we remember that, in the Qur'an-centred view of sacred history, the Mother of the Book represents the unrevealed heavenly archetype of the Qur'an and other scriptures, while the Qur'an *is* of course revealed in the phenomenal world. Even though the Qur'an represents the unqualified, simple essence, then, it must necessarily represent the unqualified essence turned towards manifestation. Al-Jīlī's presentation of the Mother of the Book and the Qur'an as the first and second 'levels of existence' can therefore be considered a recasting of the Qur'an-centred view in Ibn 'Arabian Sufi metaphysical terms.

We might well ask about the rationale for this 'Sufi metaphysicalization' of scripture. While al-Jīlī's identification of the Qur'an with the absolute existence or unqualified oneness of the divine essence is certainly idiosyncratic, it has roots in the connection made by the Qur'an and the post-Qur'anic Islamic tradition between the revelation that is the Qur'an and the 'revelation' that is creation. The Qur'an itself suggests a parallel between scriptural revelation – or what the noted scholar of the Qur'an (and Ibn 'Arabian thought) Toshihiko Izutsu called God's 'linguistic' or 'verbal' communication to mankind – and the revelation in nature – 'non-linguistic' or 'non-verbal communication'[13] – by using the term *āyah* ('sign') to denote both forms of revelation. *Āyah*, in other words, denotes both a unit of scriptural revelation (see e.g. Q 2.106, 3.13, 10.1, 12.1, 13.1), that is a 'verse' of the Qur'an, and a 'sign' in the phenomenal world, among which are cited natural phenomena, man, animals and inanimate objects (see e.g. Q 11.64, 13.2-3, 41.53, 51.20-1). These different forms of *āyāt*, moreover, have the same function, namely to direct man to believe in and worship God, and the possible responses to them are therefore the same: either belief (*al-īmān*) and the declaration that they are true (*al-taṣdīq*) or unbelief (*al-kufr*) and the declaration that they are false (*al-takhdhīb*).[14] This, moreover, was something noted by medieval Qur'an exegetes, several of whom, as Fazlur Rahman puts it, pointed out the 'parallel (or even the identity) between the revelation of the Qur'ān and the creation of the universe'.[15]

One can therefore see a conceptual basis, rooted in the Qur'an and the wider Islamic tradition, for al-Jīlī's identification of the Qur'an with a particular level of existence. Indeed, prior to al-Jīlī, the identification between the Qur'an and phenomenal existence had already been developed by thinkers in the Ibn 'Arabian tradition.[16] Ibn 'Arabī himself speaks of the world as a 'written book' (*kitāb masṭūr*) or 'the great book' (*al-kitāb al-kabīr*),[17] and identifies existents (*mawjūdāt*) or their prototypical forms (*al-a'yān al-thābitah*) with the divine 'words' (*kalimāt*),[18] and individual realities (s. *ḥaqīqah mufradah*) with 'letters' (*ḥurūf*).[19] Ibn 'Arabī's leading disciple Ṣadr al-Dīn al-Qūnawī (d. 673/1274), similarly, writes in his Ibn 'Arabian commentary on the *Fātiḥah* of how 'the Real – Glory be to Him and may He be exalted – made the first macrocosm, with respect to its form, a book (*kitāban*) carrying the forms of the names of the Real and the forms of the relations of His knowledge'.[20] Much like al-Jīlī here, meanwhile, al-Qāshānī in his Ibn 'Arabian Sufi *tafsīr* identifies the revelation of the Qur'an with 'the manifestation of the unqualified single essence (*al-tajallī al-aḥadī al-dhātī*)'.[21] And, to cite a final example, the fourteenth-century Persian Sufi metaphysician 'Azīz Nasafī (seventh/thirteenth century), who fell under the influence of Ibn 'Arabian thought, 'compared Nature to the Quran in such a way that each genus in Nature corresponds to a *sūrah*, each species to a verse, and each particular being to a letter'.[22]

Echoing these earlier Ibn 'Arabian thinkers, in chapter thirty-three of *al-Insān al-kāmil* al-Jīlī develops a highly detailed set of correspondences between the 'linguistic' and 'non-linguistic' forms of revelation, proposing that, in addition to the Qur'an corresponding to absolute existence, the *sūrahs* of the Qur'an denote the 'essential forms' (*al-ṣuwar al-dhātiyyah*) of existents, the *āyahs* God's 'bringing together' or 'synthesis' (*jam'*) of things, the words (*al-kalimāt*) 'the essential realities of created beings' (*ḥaqā'iq al-makhlūqāt al-'ayniyyah*) and the letters (*al-ḥurūf*) several different things: the dotted letters represent the fixed entities or essences (*al-a'yān al-thābitah*), that is, the prototypes of existents that exist in the divine knowledge;[23] the five undotted letters that do not join to other letters (*alif, dāl, rā', wāw* and *lām*) represent the five 'requirements of perfection' (*muqtaḍayāt kamāliyyah*), which are the divine essence and the four key attributes of the divine self (life, knowledge, power and will); and the nine undotted letters that do join to other letters represent the five requirements of perfection and the four elements.[24] While the particulars of these correspondences need not concern us much here, these identifications do indicate that, in al-Jīlī's mind as in the minds of the earlier Ibn 'Arabian thinkers, the different elements that make up existence exist in parallel to and are represented by the different elements that make up the Qur'an, and vice versa. While this notion is expressed here in Sufi metaphysical terms, that is through the use of Ibn 'Arabian terms such as *al-aḥadiyyah*, *al-wujūd al-muṭlaq* and *al-a'yān al-thābitah*, it is ultimately grounded in the identification of the two forms of revelation or divine communication made by the Qur'an and elaborated upon by the Qur'anic exegetes. This reflects al-Jīlī's approach to the scriptures more generally, which, as we shall see, is to adopt the Qur'anic or traditional Islamic view and give it a Sufi metaphysical interpretation.

The revelation of the Qur'an to Muhammad

> The Real – May He be exalted – sent it [i.e. unqualified oneness] down (*anzalaha*) upon His prophet, Muhammad – May God bless him and grant him peace – so that he would be the locus of witnessing (*mashhadahu*) of His unqualified oneness among [created] beings. The meaning of this sending down (*al-inzāl*) is that the exalted, unqualified one reality (*al-ḥaqīqah al-aḥadiyyah al-muta'āliyyah*), in its dispersal (*dharāhā*), appeared in its perfection (*bi-kamālihā*) in his [i.e. Muhammad's] body (*fī jasadihi*). So it came down (*nazalat*) from its highest point (*awjihā*), despite the impossibility of [it] coming down and of ascending to it (*ma'a istiḥālat al-nuzūl wa-al-'urūj 'alayhā*). But since his body attained realization of all the divine realities (*taḥaqqaqa jasaduhu bi-jamī' al-ḥaqā'iq al-ilāhiyyah*), and since he was the one locus of manifestation of the names (*majlá al-asmā' al-wāḥid*), through his body, just has he was, through his ipseity (*bi-huwiyyatihi*), the locus of manifestation of unqualified oneness (*majlá al-aḥadiyyah*), and through his essence (*bi-dhātihi*), the essence itself (*'ayn al-dhāt*), for this reason he – May God bless him and grant him peace – said, 'He sent down the Qur'an to me as a single whole (*jumlatan wāḥidah*),' expressing his realization (*taḥqīq*) of all of that in a corporeal, total, universal way (*taḥqīqan dhātiyyan kulliyyan jismāniyyan*).[25]

This passage contains some very important insights into al-Jīlī's conception of revelation (both of the Qur'an and more generally) and his view of Muhammad. The concept of revelation is indicated here by the term *inzāl* and its verbal form *anzala*. This is the most common verb used for the revelation of scripture in the Qur'an, appearing on 188 occasions (though never as a verbal noun, the second form *tanzīl* being preferred). In keeping with its literal meaning of 'sending down', it is only ever used in the Qur'an to denote communication from God to man, and, in keeping with what we saw in the previous section, it is used of non-linguistic as well as linguistic forms of divine communication, that is, the revelation of divine 'signs' in creation as well as in scripture (see e.g. Q 2.57, 24.43, 30.49).[26] Al-Jīlī, who uses the term *anzala* to denote the revelation of all of the different scriptures treated in *al-Insān al-kāmil*, likewise seems to have both scriptural or linguistic revelation *and* the manifestation of the divine existence – that is, non-linguistic revelation – in mind when using the term. Indeed, in this instance the object of *anzala*, being grammatically feminine, cannot be the Qur'an, but must rather be *al-aḥadiyyah* (the unqualified oneness of the divine essence) or *al-dhāt* (the divine essence itself). *Inzāl*, then, appears to function here as a transitive counterpart to *tajallī*, that is, the key Ibn 'Arabian Sufi metaphysical concept of the 'manifestation' of the divine existence. This interpretation is supported by the fact that among the several other terms that al-Jīlī uses to denote the manifestation of the divine existence are *nuzūl* and *tanazzul*, which have the same root as *inzāl* and likewise denote 'going down'.[27] In fact, earlier in the book al-Jīlī uses these terms (as here) in the context of the manifestation of the divine essence at the level of *al-aḥadiyyah*: previously we saw his definition of *al-aḥadiyyah* as 'the first of the descents of the essence' (*awwal tanazzulāt al-dhāt*),[28] while elsewhere he says that *al-aḥadiyyah* is the level where the 'simple, pure essence (*al-dhāt al-sādhaj al-ṣarf*) descended (*nazalat*) from its simplicity and purity'.[29] The use of these terms in this way indicates that, in al-Jīlī's mind, the levels of existence are a vertical scheme: just as scriptures are sent *down* from God to creation, so too does the existence of the simple essence come *down* to the lower levels of existence.[30] Furthermore, as he sees it, these two processes are complementary, or perhaps even one and the same. Muhammad, in other words, receives not only the words of the Qur'an from God but also the manifestation of God's unqualified oneness. And because, as al-Jīlī indicates elsewhere,[31] the level of *al-aḥadiyyah* is also the level of pure, unqualified existence (*al-wujūd al-muṭlaq*), it also follows that, with the revelation of the Qur'an, this 'absolute existence' was also made manifest to – and within – Muhammad. This is a point that al-Jīlī makes explicitly in the chapter on the Mother of the Book (chapter thirty-three):

> So the Book (*al-kitāb*) that the Real – Glory be to Him – sent down upon the tongue of His Prophet – May God's blessings and peace be upon him – denotes the governing principles of absolute existence (*aḥkām al-wujūd al-muṭlaq*), which is one of the two aspects of the quiddity of the realities [i.e. the simple divine essence]. So knowledge of absolute existence (*ma'rifat al-wujūd al-muṭlaq*) is knowledge of the Book (*'ilm al-kitāb*).[32]

From all of this, we can see that al-Jīlī's conception of *inzāl* is of 'revelation' not only in the sense of God's revelation of scripture to humanity but also in the sense of God's 'unveiling' of Himself. As Naṣr Hāmid Abū Zayd has described the Ibn 'Arabian idea of revelation as manifestation: 'The divine language becomes manifest (*tatajallá*) – in the view of the Sufis – in all of existence; it is not limited to the Qur'anic discourse. It becomes manifest in all of existence, because existence is the words of God written on "the horizons" and the Qur'an is the words of God written in the codex.'[33] As discussed previously, such a notion can be viewed as an extension of the Qur'an-centred idea of linguistic and non-linguistic forms of revelation. The implication of this, as the last sentence of the passage from the chapter on the Mother of the Book indicates, is that to understand the world is to understand the Qur'an (and vice versa); indeed, it is to understand God Himself, for both the Qur'an and creation are a locus of His manifestation.

Having thus set out his conception of revelation, al-Jīlī goes on to explain what it means for Muhammad to receive the revelation/manifestation of *al-aḥadiyyah*. His view is summarized in the statement that Muhammad, in receiving *al-aḥadiyyah*, became the 'locus of witnessing' (*mashhad*) of that unqualified oneness within the phenomenal world. Al-Jīlī often uses the term *mashhad* in his writings to denote a place or instance where an individual attains a mystical vision or moment of 'witnessing' (*shuhūd*): in an important passage in the chapter on the Perfect Human, for instance, he says that he saw Muhammad appear in the form of his *shaykh*, al-Jabartī, and tells us that this was one of the *mashāhid* in which he witnessed the Prophet.[34] This might suggest that in describing Muhammad here as a *mashhad* of *al-aḥadiyyah*, al-Jīlī is indicating that advanced mystics such as himself are able to experience a vision of the divine at this level of existence by beholding the Prophet: as al-Farghānī (d. 699/1300) in his influential Ibn 'Arabian commentary on Ibn al-Fāriḍ's (d. 632/1234) *Tā'iyyah* puts it, 'The servant in whom [God] is manifest (*al-'abd al-mutajallá la-hu*) is a tool (*ālah*) for the perception of the manifested Real (*al-ḥaqq al-mutajallī*).'[35] This, I think, is one of al-Jīlī's intended meanings here: that Muhammad is a 'tool' for the Sufi realizer to access the divine unqualified oneness.

The other, complementary idea being expressed here is that Muhammad's receiving the manifestation of *al-aḥadiyyah* enables God *Himself* to witness His unqualified oneness become manifest within creation. This idea, that the Perfect Human – for that is what Muhammad is in al-Jīlī's view – is the locus in which God is able to witness Himself and the world, is a key one in Ibn 'Arabian Sufi metaphysics. In the famous opening passage of the first chapter of the *Fuṣūṣ*, Ibn 'Arabī describes the world as a mirror in which God can see himself, and identifies Adam, the first Perfect Human, as 'the very polishing of that mirror' (*'ayn jalā' tilk al-mir'āh*), who enables God to witness His own essence. Moreover, exploiting the fact that the Arabic term for 'human being' (*insān*) is also the word for 'pupil' of the eye, Ibn 'Arabī informs us that Adam was called a human being because 'through him, the Real gazes upon His creation (*yanẓur al-ḥaqq ilá khalqihi*), and has mercy upon them',[36] an idea that al-Jīlī in fact repeats almost word for word in *al-Insān al-kāmil*.[37] Similarly, one of the definitions given by Ibn 'Arabian Sufis for 'the Pole' (*al-quṭb*) – another name for the Perfect Human, and a role which al-Jīlī again identifies with Muhammad[38] – is that he is 'the place of the Real's gaze within the world' (*mawḍi' naẓar al-ḥaqq min al-'ālam*).[39] When al-Jīlī describes Muhammad as a *mashhad* of the unqualified oneness, then, he probably also has this role of the Perfect Human as a vehicle for *God's* vision of Himself and His creation in mind.

As al-Jīlī understands it, therefore, God reveals His unqualified oneness in the person of Muhammad so that He can see Himself and people can see Him. Moreover, he tells us here that Muhammad serves as a *mashhad* for God's unqualified oneness – and the rest of His names and attributes – in three ways: in his body (*jasad, jism*),[40] his 'ipseity' (*huwiyyah*) – which, by analogy with al-Jīlī's definition of the divine ipseity in chapter twenty-six,[41] we can understand as Muhammad's unseen, inner nature or identity – and in his essence (*dhāt*), which al-Jīlī here identifies in somewhat shocking terms with the divine essence itself (*'ayn al-dhāt*). As I have argued elsewhere, this statement, and the passage as a whole, conveys a highly exalted, almost divine conception of Muhammad. Muhammad, as al-Jīlī sees it, is not only a locus of divine manifestation in both his corporeal and non-corporeal aspects but also, in his essential nature – that is, what Ibn 'Arabian Sufis call 'the Muhammadan Reality' (*al-ḥaqīqah al-muḥammadiyyah*)[42] – identical to the divine essence, an idea that seems to shatter the normally unbreachable boundary between God's essence and His creation.[43] Significantly for the purposes of the present book, this exalted, quasi-divine status enjoyed by Muhammad is here connected to his being the recipient of the Qur'anic revelation. In receiving the Qur'an, in other words, Muhammad did not just become a vehicle for the propagation of the divine word to mankind, but also an embodiment or incarnation of the divine word and, in his essential nature, united with the divine essence itself.

While this might appear to be something of a new conception of prophethood or messengership, al-Jīlī does anchor his view in the wider Islamic tradition, grounding it in a hadith that states that the Qur'an was revealed to Muhammad 'as a single whole' (*jumlatan wāḥidah*). Interestingly, the apparent meaning of this hadith directly conflicts with what the Qur'an itself says about its own revelation, to the extent that the same language is used to denote two opposing positions: Qur'an 25.32 has the unbelievers asking why the Qur'an was not sent down as a single whole (*jumlatan wāḥidah*). Yet while the hadith quoted by al-Jīlī here is not canonical,[44] a similar idea is found in a widely quoted hadith reported on the authority of Ibn 'Abbās (d. 68/687), which al-Jīlī quotes later in the chapter, and according to which the Qur'an was revealed 'with a single push' (*daf'atan wāḥidatan*) to the lowest heaven, and then subsequently revealed in stages to Muhammad.[45] Al-Jīlī in fact goes further than this, however, for the hadith that he quotes indicates that the Qur'an was revealed all at once *to Muhammad*.[46] While the full significance of this notion will become clearer in the following sections, what matters here is that al-Jīlī connects the language of the hadith to the idea that Muhammad manifested the divine in a *comprehensive* way (*jumlatan* or *ijmālan*). In al-Jīlī's reading, therefore, the hadith indicates that Muhammad is the Perfect Human, the 'synthetic being' who is a perfect locus of divine manifestation; indeed, earlier in the book, al-Jīlī makes this connection clear: 'There is no one in the entirety of existence for whom being comprehensive (*al-jumlah*) is valid, except for the Perfect Human (*al-insān al-kāmil*), and [Muhammad] – Blessings and peace be upon him – alluded to this idea when he said, "He sent down the Qur'an to me as a single whole."'[47]

Al-Jīlī's quotation of this hadith in the present passage serves to bring us back from the discussion of Muhammad's nature to the consideration of the revelation of the Qur'an, to which this chapter is ostensibly devoted. More specifically, it indicates that, as suggested previously, these two topics are in fact interrelated, for Muhammad being a locus of manifestation for the unqualified oneness of God in his body and ipseity, and identical to the divine essence in his essence, clearly indicates something significant about the relationship between Muhammad and the Qur'an. Al-Jīlī's conception of the nature of this relationship can be expressed in the following way: if the Qur'an, as he indicated at the beginning of the chapter, is an expression of *al-dhāt* and *al-aḥadiyyah*, and if Muhammad's body and ipseity are loci of manifestation for *al-aḥadiyyah* and his essence is identical to *al-dhāt*, then it would seem to follow that Muhammad and the Qur'an are somehow identical, for they both manifest the same levels of divine existence.

Again, this idea, strange as it may seem, may in fact be taken as a Sufi metaphysical elaboration of a motif found in the wider Islamic tradition. Responding to a question about the Prophet's character, Muhammad's wife Aisha is believed to have said, 'His character was the Qur'an (*khuluquhu al-Qur'ān*)',[48] a statement that the Qur'anic exegetes connect to Qur'an 68.4: 'And truly you [i.e. Muhammad] have a great character (*khuluq 'aẓīm*).'[49] This tradition is found in classical Sufi literature,[50] and in the *Futūḥāt* Ibn 'Arabī uses it to make the same point that al-Jīlī is suggesting here, and in more explicit terms: 'It is as if the Qur'an,' he writes, 'had taken on a bodily form under the name of Muhammad b. 'Abd Allāh. . . . One who has not lived at the time of the Prophet but desires to see him, should contemplate the Qur'an for there is no difference between the act of contemplating it and the act of contemplating the Envoy of God.'[51] While al-Jīlī does not explicitly cite the saying of Aisha here, he does quote it in his *al-Kamālāt al-ilāhiyyah* to similar effect as Ibn 'Arabī: Aisha's statement, he says, is 'an allusion to the truth of [Muhammad's] realization of the divine perfections (*al-taḥaqquq bi-al-kamālāt al-ilāhiyyah*), because the Qur'an is simply an expression of the perfections of God'.[52] Al-Jīlī seems to be inviting the reader to draw the same conclusion in the passage of *al-Insān al-kāmil* under discussion, namely that, as the recipient of the divine revelation/manifestation that is the Qur'an, Muhammad is himself a locus of divine manifestation, which is to say that he is the Perfect Human.

All of this reflects al-Jīlī's more general Sufi metaphysical conception of revelation as a phenomenon that involves the levels of existence, the scriptures and human beings (specifically, the prophets or Perfect Humans). Each of these three categories, as loci of the divine manifestation, corresponds existentially with each of the others. The relevance of this key principle for our enquiry into al-Jīlī's views on sacred history is that it allows us to construct a series of corresponding hierarchies of the levels of existence, scriptures and prophets. At the top of these hierarchies stand, respectively, *al-aḥadiyyah*, the first and least qualified form of divine manifestation; the Qur'an, the scripture that expresses the divine essence in the most complete way; and Muhammad, the prophet or Perfect Human who, in his body, identity and essence, receives the most complete form of divine manifestation.

The two aspects of the Qur'an (i): *al-Qur'ān al-karīm* and *al-Qur'ān al-ḥakīm*

And this is what is expressed by 'The Generous Qur'an' (*al-Qur'ān al-karīm*), because He gave him [i.e. Muhammad] comprehensiveness (*al-jumlah*), which is [an act of] complete generosity (*al-karam al-tāmm*), because He spared nothing from it; rather, He poured forth (*afāḍa*) everything (*al-kull*) into it, out of the essential, divine generosity (*karaman ilāhiyyan dhātiyyan*).

As for 'The Wise Qur'an' (*al-Qur'ān al-ḥakīm*), it is the descent of the divine realities (*tanazzul al-ḥaqā'iq al-ilāhiyyah*) through the ascension (*'urūj*) of the servant up to the attainment of realization (*al-taḥaqquq*) of them in the essence, step by step, according to what is required by the divine wisdom (*al-ḥikmah al-ilāhiyyah*), of which [the realization of] the essence is a consequent. This is the only path to something [like this], for He does not permit the possibility that someone might attain realization of all the divine realities through his body from the first moment that he is brought into existence. However, he whose primordial nature (*fiṭrah*) is disposed towards divinity (*majbūlah 'alá al-ulūhiyyah*) rises up through them [i.e. the divine realities] and attains realization of them, according to what is unveiled (*yankashif*) to him of them, one [reality] after another, according to the divine ordering. And the Real has alluded to the explanation of that when He said: 'We have sent it down in stages (*nazzalnāhu tanzīlan*).' (17:106) This effect is neither cut off nor does it cease, rather the servant continues the ascent (*taraqqin*) in such a manner, and the Real continues with the manifestation (*tajallin*), since there is no way of exhausting that which does not end, because the Real in itself does not end.[53]

We have so far seen that, in al-Jīlī's view, God's sending down of the Qur'an to Muhammad constitutes the manifestation of His unqualified oneness within the Prophet. The Qur'an, therefore, represents the comprehensiveness, simplicity and unity of the divine essence at the level of *al-aḥadiyyah*. In this section, al-Jīlī both elaborates upon this idea and introduces a new element into his conception of the Qur'an, namely, that the revelation of the Qur'an constitutes the manifestation of the differentiated divine *attributes*, in addition to the manifestation of the comprehensive, simple essence.

These two aspects of the Qur'anic revelation are represented, as al-Jīlī sees it, in two of the different names by which the Qur'an is known, *al-Qur'ān al-karīm* and *al-Qur'ān al-ḥakīm*. Both of these are names that the Qur'an assigns to itself,[54] hence al-Jīlī's discussion here can be viewed as a Sufi metaphysical exegesis of those traditional Qur'anic terms. The adjectives *karīm* and *ḥakīm*, it should also be noted, are also among the attributes that the Qur'an assigns to God, meaning that the Qur'an (in its own self-understanding) 'reflects the attributes of the one who sent it down',[55] a notion that supports al-Jīlī's conception of revelation as the self-manifestation of God. Let us look, then, at how he integrates each of these names of the Qur'an into that conception.

The term *al-Qur'ān al-karīm* is generally understood by the exegetes and in the wider Islamic tradition to mean 'the Noble Qur'an': 'The Qur'ān is "noble"', writes the academic scholar of the Qur'an Mustansir Mir, summarizing the traditional interpretation, 'because it comes from a noble [i.e. divine] source, and, being noble, it deserves to be treated with reverence.'[56] The Qur'an exegete al-Qurṭubī (d. 671/1273) notes three different views on why the Qur'an is described as '*karīm*' – namely, because it is uncreated (*ghayr makhlūq*), because of what it contains by way of 'noble traits (*karīm al-akhlāq*) and the meanings of things' and because, 'He [i.e. God] declares the one who memorizes it to be noble (*yukarrim ḥāfiẓahu*) and the one who recites it to be great'.[57] *Karīm*, then, is generally taken to be synonymous with *'aẓīm*, 'great', 'magnificent'.[58] Al-Jīlī, however, seems to understand the term in the more particular sense of 'generous'. This secondary meaning of *karīm* goes back to the *Jāhiliyyah*, generosity being connected to nobility 'since', as Izutsu puts it, 'in the old Arab conception of human virtue, extravagant and unlimited generosity was the most conspicuous and concrete manifestation of a man's nobility'.[59] In the context of this passage, the generosity being spoken of is not that of a human being but of God, His generosity consisting in His not leaving anything out of the Qur'an. For al-Jīlī, therefore, the name *al-Qur'ān al-karīm* does not merely indicate the Qur'an's greatness, but more specifically points to its *comprehensive* nature,[60] an idea that he expresses using the key term *al-jumlah*. We have already seen this same term in the hadith that he quoted in the previous section, which he used to signify the comprehensive nature of Muhammad. This alerts us once again to the correspondences between the levels of existence, the scriptures and the prophets, for the divine essence at the level of unqualified oneness, the Qur'an and Muhammad, as al-Jīlī sees it, are all defined by comprehensiveness. These correspondences in turn reflect al-Jīlī's conception of revelation as a form of divine manifestation, a conception indicated here by his use of the term *afāḍa* – a term that connotes the 'emanation' (*fayḍ*) of the divine existence, a philosophical term sometimes used in Ibn 'Arabian Sufism as a synonym for or together with *tajallī*[61] – to denote God's revelation of the Generous Qur'an.

This Sufi metaphysical conception of revelation also applies to al-Jīlī's treatment of the term *al-Qur'ān al-ḥakīm*, as is indicated by his use of the term *tanazzul* – a term which, as already noted, is another synonym for *tajallī* – to denote the revelation of this aspect of the Qur'an. Yet, whereas the revelation of the Qur'an as *al-Qur'ān al-karīm* denoted the manifestation, emanation or descent of the *comprehensive* divine essence, the revelation of the Qur'an as *al-Qur'ān al-ḥakīm* denotes the descent of what al-Jīlī calls 'the divine realities' (*al-ḥaqā'iq al-ilāhiyyah*). This latter term generally indicates, in al-Jīlī's usage, the divine or higher levels of existence, that is, those levels that are associated with the divine names or attributes.[62] Indeed, when al-Jīlī tells us earlier in this chapter that Muhammad's body 'attained realization of all the divine realities' (*taḥaqqaqa jasaduhu bi-jamī' al-ḥaqā'iq al-ilāhiyyah*), he seems to be suggesting that Muhammad is a locus of manifestation of the divine names and attributes (as well as of the essence). What the Qur'an reveals as *al-Qur'ān al-ḥakīm* is not the comprehensive divine essence, therefore, but rather the specific divine names and attributes. The connection of this idea to the adjective *ḥakīm* is not immediately apparent. The majority of exegetes tend to interpret the term *al-ḥakīm* in *al-Qur'ān al-ḥakīm* to mean 'firmly established' (*muḥkam*), that is, clear and obvious, prone to no misinterpretation (as in the conventional interpretation of Qur'an 3.3).[63] Al-Jīlī's use of the term here may have something to do with the association made by Ibn 'Arabī in *Fuṣūṣ al-ḥikam* between the divine attributes and the different forms of 'wisdom' (*ḥikmah*) represented by 'words' of the prophets (e.g. the wisdom of divinity in the word of Adam, the wisdom of praiseworthiness in the word of Noah, the wisdom of unqualified oneness in the word of Hūd).[64]

The key distinction between the two names or aspects of the Qur'an leads to two further important distinctions, connected to the process through which the divine revelation or manifestation occurs, and the individual who receives it. Dealing first with the process of revelation, we have seen already that *al-Qur'ān al-karīm*, being an expression of the comprehensive essence, denotes the Qur'an that was revealed 'as a single whole' to Muhammad. Yet, al-Jīlī indicates in this passage that this is not the only way that the Qur'an was revealed, for he quotes a Qur'anic verse (17.106) that indicates, at least according to the dominant exegetical view, that the Qur'an was in fact revealed in piecemeal fashion, as in the traditional understanding of the process of revelation.[65] This *gradual* process of revelation is represented, then, by the name *al-Qur'ān al-ḥakīm*. This makes sense, if we remember that *al-Qur'ān al-ḥakīm* is an expression of the divine names and attributes, which, according to al-Jīlī's idea of the levels of existence, gradually appear as God descends through the levels of existence. In proposing that the Qur'an was revealed in two different ways to Muhammad in this way, moreover, al-Jīlī is able to capture the idea that Muhammad received the manifestation of *both* the utterly one and simple essence *and* the multiple, differentiated divine names and attributes, as would befit a true synthetic being or Perfect Human.

Moreover, the revelation of *al-Qur'ān al-ḥakīm* differs in another way from that of *al-Qur'ān al-karīm*, in that it involves not only the descent or manifestation of the divine names and attributes but also a corresponding 'ascent' (*'urūj*, *taraqqin*) of the individual through the divine levels of existence. This idea is in keeping with al-Jīlī's conception of the levels of existence not only as loci in which the divine existence becomes manifest, but as stations (*maqāmāt*) on the path to God. It suggests that revelation is not only a one-way, downward process (from God to man), but rather a two-way process involving human activity, presumably, the self-purifying activities of the Sufi path. As Nicholson puts it, for al-Jīlī, 'the ontological descent from the Absolute and the mystical ascent or return to the Absolute are really the same process looked at from different points of view'.[66] This idea, it should be noted, is not necessarily out of keeping with the conventional Islamic understanding of the process of revelation, for, in addition to receiving the 'downward' revelation of the Qur'an, the Prophet is believed to have experienced a revelatory 'ascension' (*mi'rāj*) through the heavens on his night journey.[67] Indeed, the etymological connection between *'urūj*, one of the terms that al-Jīlī uses here to denote the process of individual ascent through the divine realities, and *mi'rāj* suggests that he might have the story of the Prophet's ascension in mind here.

This being said, there also seems to be an indication here that individuals other than the Prophet are capable of undertaking this spiritual ascent and thereby receiving the revelation of *al-Qur'ān al-ḥakīm*. What indicates this is al-Jīlī's use here of the generic term *al-'abd*, meaning 'the servant' or most basically 'the (human) individual', and the phrase 'the one whose primordial nature is disposed towards divinity', to refer to the individual who ascends through the levels of existence. Given that al-Jīlī is normally very clear when he is talking about the Prophet – for instance, through his use of one of the common salutations – it is possible that these terms do not refer specifically to Muhammad.

Who, we might then ask, is capable of undergoing this ascent through the divine realities, or put another way, who is it that can receive the revelation of *al-Qur'ān al-ḥakīm*? The answer to this question lies in uncovering what al-Jīlī means by 'the one whose primordial nature is disposed towards divinity' (*fiṭratuhu majbūlah 'alá al-ulūhiyyah*). According to the Qur'an-centred view, the *fiṭrah* (primordial nature) of all human beings – indeed, of all creatures – is to be in a state of submission to God. Applying his Sufi metaphysical outlook to this idea, in the last chapter of *al-Insān al-kāmil* al-Jīlī states that all individuals are 'primordially disposed' (*mafṭūrūn, majbūlūn*) to the worship of God (*'ibādat Allāh*) by virtue of their 'original nature' (*al-aṣālah*).[68] Does this mean, then, that the primordial nature of all human beings is disposed towards divinity, and therefore that all humans can ascend through the divine realities and receive the revelation of *al-Qur'ān al-ḥakīm*? This is essentially the same question that al-Jīlī addresses in chapter sixty, namely, whether all humans are perfect. Al-Jīlī tells us in that chapter that while all individuals are perfect 'in potential' (*bi-al-quwwah*), nevertheless only certain people are capable of realizing and manifesting that perfection 'in actuality' (*bi-al-fi'l*).[69] The same, then, can be said here. While all individuals may have the potential to ascend through the divine realities, nevertheless only certain individuals possess, in Ibn 'Arabian terms, the requisite 'receptivity' (*qābiliyyah*) or 'preparedness' (*isti'dād*) to do so in actuality.[70] These latter individuals, we can assume, are what al-Jīlī calls 'the Perfect Ones' (*al-kummal*), the Perfect Humans other than Muhammad who stand below him in the hierarchy of perfection.

This notion that the Perfect Humans are capable of receiving the revelation of *al-Qur'ān al-ḥakīm* has important implications for our understanding of al-Jīlī's conception of revelation and sacred history. If the revelation of the Qur'an consists not only of *waḥy* and *tanzīl* in the traditional sense – that is, revelation of the divine word to Muhammad through the intermediary of the angel Gabriel[71] – but also of what al-Jīlī calls here *taḥqīq* and *kashf* – that is, the mystical 'realization' or 'unveiling' of the perfect Friends of God[72] – then it would seem to follow that the gates of revelation and prophethood are not closed with Muhammad, with the Qur'an continuing to be 'revealed' to the Perfect Ones, up to al-Jīlī's own time. In this case, sacred history, as al-Jīlī understands it, would be an ongoing phenomenon. This would fit with the Ibn 'Arabian notion of divine friendship or sainthood (*walāyah*) as a kind of 'general prophethood' (*nubuwwah 'āmmah*), which Ibn 'Arabī and his interpreters distinguish from the more specific 'legislative prophethood' (*nubuwwat al-tashrī'*) that is sealed with Muhammad.[73] Indeed, in the final chapter of *al-Insān al-kāmil*, al-Jīlī, adopting this Ibn 'Arabian notion, goes so far as to declare explicitly that those 'realizers' (*muḥaqqiqūn*) who have attained mystical 'proximity' (*al-qurbah*) to God acquire 'prophetic' or 'messenger' status:

> Those of the realisers who are limited [in their mission] to their own selves represent (*nāba 'an*) Muhammad at the station of prophethood (*maqām al-nubuwwah*), while those who guide [others] to God, like our perfect masters among the shaykhs, represent him at the station of messengership (*maqām al-risālah*). This religion will go on for as long as there is one of this group on the face of the earth, because they are the viceregents of Muhammad (*khulafā' Muḥammad*). . . . So they are prophets not Friends of God (*anbiyā' lā awliyā'*), by which is meant the prophethood of proximity, informing, and being connected to the divine (*nubuwwat al-qurb wa-al-i'lām wa-al-ḥukm al-ilāhī*), not the prophethood of legislation (*nubuwwat al-tashrī'*), since the prophethood of legislation was cut off with Muhammad. So they are informed of the knowledge of the prophets without an intermediary.[74]

While this Ibn 'Arabian idea of a post-Muhammadan form of prophethood would appear to conflict with the insistence, in the Qur'an-centred view of sacred history, on the finality of Muhammad's prophethood, it must also be remembered that, according to al-Jīlī's conception of the idea of the Perfect Human set out in chapter sixty, these 'prophets of proximity' are in fact merely forms or 'garments' in which the Muhammadan Reality becomes manifest.[75] This, as al-Jīlī explains in that chapter,[76] is what he means when he says that these post-Muhammadan prophets are 'viceregents' of Muhammad. In this way it can be said that, even if an individual other than Muhammad may be capable of receiving *al-Qur'ān al-ḥakīm*, it is still in a sense Muhammad – as the Muhammadan Reality manifested within that individual – who is the recipient of the Qur'anic revelation. Moreover, al-Jīlī suggests that it is only Muhammad who receives the revelation of the Qur'an as *al-Qur'ān al-karīm*, which is the more complete form of the Qur'an. Though his distinction between the two aspects of the Qur'an does lead him into what a mainstream Islamic perspective would view as dangerous waters, therefore, we can say that he still remains within the framework of the Qur'an-centred view of sacred history. For our purposes, meanwhile, with respect to our understanding of al-Jīlī's views on the relationship between Islam and other religions, it is notable that any inconsistency with the Qur'an-centred view of sacred history on his part concerns *post*-Muhammadan sacred history, not the pre-Muhammadan era of the earlier religious communities.

Though it is difficult for us to comprehend fully what al-Jīlī means when he talks about the different natures of *al-Qur'ān al-karīm* and *al-Qur'ān al-ḥakīm*, it should be emphasized that he is not talking about two different scriptures, but rather two different aspects of the same scripture, in accordance with the conventional Islamic view that the Qur'an 'possesses several aspects' (*dhū wujūh*).[77] This being the case, the fundamental role of the two different names is to show that the Qur'an represents both the unity and simplicity of the divine essence, on the one hand, and the multiplicity of the divine names and attributes, on the other hand. Al-Jīlī's rationale for highlighting the two different names, then, lies in his desire to draw attention to the comprehensive nature of the Qur'an, for true comprehensiveness entails not only being all-encompassing, like the divine essence, but also being detailed, like the divine names and attributes; as Martin Lings has put it from a similar Ibn 'Arabian perspective, 'The Qur'an is, like the world, at the same time one and multiple.'[78] In summary, therefore, al-Jīlī's discussion of these two names of the Qur'an – and of some of the Qur'an's other names later in this chapter and in the following chapter – ought to be placed within the context of his concern to show that the Qur'an, as the most comprehensive scripture, stands at the top of the hierarchy of scriptures, and that Muhammad, as its recipient, is the human being who most fully encompasses the divine manifestation.

The comprehensiveness of the Perfect Human

> So if you were to say, 'What is the benefit of him saying: "He sent down the Qur'an to me as a single whole"?' we would say, 'That [benefit] has two aspects. The first aspect is with respect to the effect (*al-ḥukm*), because the perfect servant (*al-'abd al-kāmil*), if God manifests Himself to Him through His Essence, is affected (*yuḥkam*) by what he witnesses (*yashhad*), which is that he is the whole (*jumlah*) of the essence that does not end, and that it [the essence] has descended upon him without leaving its locus (*maḥall*), which is its rank (*al-makānah*). The second aspect is with respect to the exhaustion of the remnants of humanness (*istīfā' baqāyāt al-bashariyyah*), and the disappearance of the traces of createdness (*iḍmiḥlāl al-rusūm al-khalqiyyah*), in their completeness, because of the appearance of the divine realities (*al-ḥaqā'iq al-ilāhiyyah*), through their [leaving their] effects (*āthār*) on every limb of the body (*kull 'aḍw min a'ḍā' al-jism*). So the comprehensiveness (*al-jumlah*) is connected to his saying [i.e. the hadith] according to this second aspect, and its meaning is the passing away of all of the defects of createdness (*dhahāb jumlat al-naqā'iṣ al-khalqiyyah*) through the attainment of realization of the divine realities (*al-taḥaqquq bi-al-ḥaqā'iq al-ilāhiyyah*).[79]

Al-Jīlī's conception of the Qur'an, as we have seen, centres upon his view that it is a comprehensive scripture – understood to mean that it is an expression of the divine essence and attributes – and, subsequent to that idea, upon his view that the recipient of the Qur'anic revelation – Muhammad, or, in the case of *al-Qur'ān al-ḥakīm*, the Perfect Human more generally – is a comprehensive being. In this section, al-Jīlī elaborates upon this connection between the comprehensiveness of the Qur'an and the comprehensiveness of the Perfect Human, through an explanation of the key term used to express the notion of comprehensiveness, namely, *al-jumlah*. As we saw earlier in the chapter, he draws this key term from a hadith in which Muhammad declares that he received the Qur'an 'as a single whole' (*jumlatan wāḥidah*); hence the section can be viewed as a kind of commentary on that uncanonical hadith.

There are two aspects, al-Jīlī tells us, to the comprehensiveness of the recipient of the Qur'anic revelation. How we understand the first aspect depends in part on how we interpret the key term *ḥukm*. This is a polysemic term that is often difficult to translate. In common usage, it most often denotes a 'category' or 'judgement'.[80] In Ibn 'Arabian Sufi literature, however, the term *aḥkām* is often used synonymously with *āthār*, *nisab* or *iḍāfāt* to denote the 'effects' or 'governing principles' of the divine names within the phenomenal world.[81] While it is possible to read the terms *ḥukm* and *yuḥkam* here as 'category' and 'categorize', we can do somewhat more with the meaning if we take the terms in their Ibn 'Arabian senses. If we read *ḥukm* as 'effect', then the implication of the hadith is that the individual who receives the revelation Qur'an 'as a single whole' bears the 'trace' or 'effect' of this revelation on his person. Since the Qur'an, as we have seen and as al-Jīlī again indicates here, represents the simplicity, comprehensiveness and everlastingness of the divine essence at the level of unqualified oneness, it follows that such an individual will similarly embody these traits, this being the 'effect' of the revelation. The point being made, then, is that not only does the recipient of the Qur'anic revelation 'witness' (*yashhad*) the comprehensive divine essence but he also becomes a locus for its manifestation, an idea that we saw developed in the earlier part of this chapter.

The second aspect of the comprehensiveness of the recipient of the Qur'anic revelation is not so much a different aspect but rather an elaboration upon the first. The revelation of the Qur'an as a single whole, al-Jīlī tells us, indicates the complete transformation of the recipient of the Qur'anic revelation, from a human to a quasi-divine being. According to my reading of the key terms used here, this transformation takes place – once again – at three interconnected levels: the ethical, the physical and the metaphysical. The first key expression used to signify this transformation is *istīfā' baqāyāt al-bashariyyah*.[82] The term *bashariyyah* is connected in al-Jīlī's usage, as in earlier Sufism,[83] with the notion that human nature is sinful and concupiscent: as he explains in chapter fifty, on the Holy Spirit, *bashariyyah* 'entails the sensual desires (*al-shahawāt*) upon which this [human] body (*jasad*) is based, and the things to which [his] nature (*ṭab'*) is accustomed', humanity's task being to pass beyond this 'base humanness' (*ḥaḍīḍ al-bashariyyah*) and attain a state of 'spirituality' (*rūḥiyyah*). At one level, then, the passing away of the *bashariyyah* of the recipient of the Qur'an denotes the *ethical* purification of that individual. This idea accords with the doctrine of the sinlessness or infallibility (*'iṣmah*) of the prophets; indeed, the dominant Sunni position in al-Jīlī's time was that the prophets were sinless from the moment that their prophetic missions began.[84] Al-Jīlī's view that, upon his receiving the Qur'anic revelation, the sinful human traits of the recipient are effaced, can therefore be viewed as an elaboration of that traditional Islamic idea.

In addition (and connected) to the transformation at the ethical level, the recipient of the Qur'anic revelation also appears to undergo a *physical* transformation. Aside from connoting man's sinful nature, *bashariyyah* is sometimes also connected to the physical aspect of man, in part due to its etymological association with the Arabic word for skin (*basharah*).[85] Al-Jīlī in fact defines *bashariyyah* in chapter fifty as 'the things that are entailed by [man's] form (*ṣūrah*)',[86] indicating that the sinful nature of man is connected to his corporeality. To say that the remnants of *bashariyyah* disappear from the recipient of the Qur'an, therefore, is also to suggest that his physical form undergoes a transformation. This is confirmed by the other phrases that al-Jīlī uses in this section. When he refers to *iḍmiḥlāl al-rusūm al-khalqiyyah*, for instance, he is apparently indicating the disappearance of the outward signs of the individual's createdness, that is, his human body, *rasm* denoting a physical mark or trace (*athar*).[87] When juxtaposed with al-Jīlī's indication earlier in the section that the 'effect' (*ḥukm*) of the divine essence leaves its mark on the recipient of the Qur'an, this would appear to indicate that his body ceases to be marked by human traits and instead is marked by the signs of divinity. This physical aspect of the transformation is made explicit and given greater definition by al-Jīlī's statement that the created traces that disappear from the recipient's body are replaced by the 'divine realities' (*al-ḥaqā'iq al-ilāhiyyah*) – a term that we have thus far interpreted as denoting the divine attributes – which leave their effects (*āthār*) on 'every limb of the body'. Once again, the use of a term denoting physical effects or traces underlines the physical aspect of the transformation being described here. The bodily members of the recipient of the Qur'anic revelation thus constitute loci for the manifestation of the divine attributes, a notion that is consistent with al-Jīlī's earlier discussion of how the Prophet's body becomes a locus of manifestation for the divine names, and with his broader conception of the Perfect Human's body parts as a microcosm for the higher levels of existence.

This physical transformation of the recipient of the Qur'anic revelation can be seen as an earthly reflection of a metaphysical transformation, which is to say, of a change in the recipient's essential nature. This metaphysical transformation is indicated by al-Jīlī's statement that 'all the defects of createdness' (*jumlat al-naqā'iṣ al-khalqiyyah*) pass away. While the term *naqā'iṣ* might well indicate ethical or even physical defects, it more basically connotes the absence of completeness or perfection, *naqṣ* being an antonym of *tamām* and *kamāl*.[88] What al-Jīlī seems to be implying, therefore, is the recipient's transformation from being an ordinary human being, with all the defects that accompany createdness, to being a Perfect Human (*insān kāmil*). In receiving the perfect and complete Qur'anic revelation, in other words, the individual becomes capable of realizing his own essential perfection and completeness. This realization of perfection is indicated by the Ibn 'Arabian phrase *al-taḥaqquq bi-al-ḥaqā'iq al-ilāhiyyah*, which is nearly identical to an above-quoted phrase that al-Jīlī uses in the *Kamālāt* in the context of Muhammad's identity with the Qur'an, and which denotes the highest stage of mystical attainment in Ibn 'Arabian Sufism; thus, in chapter fifty-eight of *al-Insān al-kāmil* ('On the Muhammadan Form'), for instance, al-Jīlī calls those who reach the seventh level of heaven, the highest level except for that reserved for Muhammad alone, 'the people who realize the divine realities' (*ahl al-taḥaqquq bi-al-ḥaqā'iq al-ilāhiyyah*).[89]

It remains for us to ask again whom al-Jīlī has in mind here. On the one hand, he again uses the generic term *'abd* – in this instance as part of the term *al-'abd al-kāmil* – to denote the individual who undergoes the transformation just described. This is a term sometimes used by Ibn 'Arabī for the advanced mystic or

Friend of God, particularly when discussing the famous hadith according to which God becomes the tongue, hearing, sight and so forth of the servant who draws near to him.[90] This would suggest that al-Jīlī here has in mind the 'perfect' Friends of God in general, rather than Muhammad in particular, which would be in keeping with his earlier indication that Perfect Humans other than Muhammad are capable of receiving the revelation of *al-Qur'ān al-ḥakīm*, and with his more general Ibn 'Arabian conception of the Perfect Humans or Friends of God as 'general' prophetic channels for continued communication between God and man, even after the sealing of legislative prophecy. On the other hand, Muhammad is obviously the messenger who receives the Qur'anic revelation; Muhammad is also the speaker of the hadith quoted here, on which this passage is effectively a commentary; and, as already noted, al-Jīlī's discussion here of the bodily transformation of the recipient of the Qur'anic revelation fits with his earlier statement that Muhammad's body (*jism*) was the locus for the manifestation of God's unqualified oneness. Furthermore, in the *Kamālāt*, a text describing Muhammad's embodiment of each of God's ninety-nine most beautiful names, al-Jīlī specifically links the transformation indicated here to Muhammad: 'There was no prophet among the prophets,' he writes, 'who did not manifest humanness (*al-bashariyyah*), with the exception of Muhammad, for his humanness was made non-existent (*ma'dūmah*), and there was no trace (*athar*) of it.'[91] The Prophet, he goes on to say, was marked by 'the absence of created remnants (*al-baqāyā al-khalqiyyah*) within him, in every respect, because of his realization of the perfections of the Real, in every respect', for God 'concealed his existence through His existence, and His perfection appeared within him without indwelling (*ḥulūl*) or adaptation [i.e. of God] (*takyīf*). So He appeared in the human form of the human organism (*nāsūt al-haykal al-insānī*), effacing the effects of humanity and humanness (*aḥkām al-insāniyyah al-bashariyyah*).'[92]

It therefore seems that, while the transformation from human to quasi-divine being is potentially attainable by other human beings, the archetypal – or perhaps the only – figure who has achieved this transformation is Muhammad. This fits with his insistence that the title of Perfect Human and all that goes with it only apply, properly speaking, to Muhammad, other individuals being perfect only by virtue of their attachment to the Prophet, the most perfect individual. If the other Perfect Humans do receive the Qur'anic revelation in some sense, therefore, then we can assume that they only do so in their capacity as loci in which the Muhammadan Reality appears, as suggested above. Underlying all of this is the centrality of Muhammad within al-Jīlī's Sufi metaphysics, a point that is obviously of great relevance to our understanding of his view of sacred history. Indeed, al-Jīlī's description of the effacement of Muhammad's humanness in this passage (and the passage quoted from the *Kamālāt*) seems to elevate the Prophet once again to quasi-divine status, to an extent not found in the earlier Ibn 'Arabian tradition or in the mainstream Islamic tradition.[93] Indeed, it is significant that where al-Jīlī does go beyond the conventional Muslim view, he does so in the context of his exaltation of Muhammad, a point that only goes to strengthen the reader's sense of the superiority of Muhammad and the Qur'an over the other prophets and scriptures in his thought.

The two aspects of the Qur'an (ii): Scriptural sources and other names

And a hadith has been related from the Prophet in which he says: 'He sent down the Qur'an with a single push (*daf'atan wāḥidatan*) to the heaven of the lower world (*samā' al-dunyā*), then the Real sent it down in divided-up *āyahs* after that.' This is the meaning of the hadith: the sending down of the Qur'an with a single push to the heaven of the lower world is an allusion to the essential realization (*al-taḥqīq al-dhātī*), and the descent of the divided-up *āyahs* is an allusion to the appearance of the traces (*āthār*) of the names and attributes, along with the ascent of the servant (*taraqqī al-'abd*) to the realization of the essence (*al-taḥqīq bi-al-dhāt*), in a gradual way (*shay'an fa-shay'an*).

And when He – May He be exalted – says: 'And We have given you seven oft-repeated [verses] (*sab'an min al-mathānī*) and the Great Qur'an (*al-Qur'ān al-'aẓīm*),' (Q 15:87) the Qur'an here denotes the totality (*jumlah*) of the essence, not from the perspective of the descent (*al-nuzūl*), nor from the perspective of the [high] rank (*al-makānah*), but from the perspective of the absolute, essential utter oneness (*muṭlaq al-aḥadiyyah al-dhātiyyah*), which is the absolute ipseity (*muṭlaq al-huwiyyah*) that synthesizes all the stages, attributes, affairs, and perspectives (*al-marātib wa-al-ṣifāt wa-al-shu'ūn wa-al-i'tibārāt*), and which is expressed as 'the simple essence along with the totality of the perfections' (*al-dhāt al-sādhaj ma'a jumlat al-kamālāt*). For this reason he attached the word 'great', because of this greatness. And the seven oft-repeated [verses] are an expression of that which appeared upon him in his bodily existence (*wujūdihi al-jasadī*), through his realization (*al-taḥaqquq*) of the seven attributes (*al-sab' al-mathānī*).

And when He – May He be exalted – says: 'The All-Merciful (*al-raḥmān*): He taught the Qur'an,' (55:1-2) it is an allusion to the fact that the servant, when the All-Merciful manifests Himself to him, finds a merciful enjoyment (*lidhdhah raḥmāniyyah*) within himself, and acquires by this enjoyment knowledge of the essence (*ma'rifat al-dhāt*), and so achieves realization of the realities of the attributes. So the one who taught him the Qur'an was the All-Merciful, and were this not the case, there would be no way to reach the essence without the manifestation of the All-Merciful, which is an expression of the totality of the names and attributes (*jumlat al-asmā' wa-al-ṣifāt*), since the Real – May He be exalted – does not teach except by way of His names and His attributes.[94]

This long passage, with which the chapter on the Qur'an concludes, recapitulates much of what we have seen in the preceding sections of the chapter. In particular, al-Jīlī here again goes over the idea that there are two aspects of the Qur'anic revelation, namely, the revelation or manifestation of God's essence at the level of unqualified oneness, and the revelation or manifestation of God's names and attributes, and the corresponding notion that the nature of the recipient of the Qur'anic revelation is determined by these different forms of revelation. What sets this section apart is that al-Jīlī identifies some more names of the Qur'an that denote these two different types of divine manifestation, and grounds the idea in a number of scriptural passages.

The first such scriptural passage is a hadith that, as already mentioned, is reported on the authority of Ibn 'Abbās. This hadith, or variants of it, is commonly used in the Qur'anic exegetical literature to indicate the idea that the Qur'an was sent down as a single whole from the Preserved Tablet (*al-lawḥ al-maḥfūẓ*) to the lowest heaven on the Night of Power (*laylat al-qadr*), and then revealed in stages to Muhammad, in the lower world, over a period of between twenty and twenty-five years.[95] Al-Jīlī exploits this traditional notion of a two-stage process of the Qur'anic revelation – the first as a complete whole, the second in gradual stages – for his own Sufi metaphysical notion of how the Qur'an represents two different aspects of the divine manifestation, namely, the manifestation of the essence and the manifestation of the names and attributes. Al-Jīlī tells us that the first part of the hadith, about the Qur'an being revealed 'with a single push' (*daf'atan wāḥidatan*), indicates what he terms *al-taḥqīq al-dhātī*,[96] a term that denotes the attainment of knowledge of the divine essence,[97] an accomplishment that constitutes the human response to the manifestation of the essence (*al-tajallī al-dhātī*). It can therefore be said that al-Jīlī understands the term *daf'atan wāḥidatan* to be synonymous with the aforementioned *jumlatan wāḥidah*, for both denote the manifestation of the divine essence to and within the recipient of the Qur'anic revelation, that is, Muhammad. Taking the correspondences further, it can also be said that the first part of the hadith denotes the revelation of what al-Jīlī earlier called *al-Qur'ān al-karīm*. By contrast, the second part of the hadith, which tells of how the Qur'an was revealed to Muhammad in 'divided-up verses' (*āyāt muqaṭṭa'āt*), denotes the manifestation of the differentiated divine names and attributes within Muhammad (or the Perfect Human more generally). The correspondence between this idea and the point al-Jīlī made earlier in the chapter is indicated by his use of the term *āthār*, a term that we have already come across (along with its synonyms, in the Ibn 'Arabian lexicon, *aḥkām* and *rusūm*) in the context of al-Jīlī's description of the physical effect that the manifestation of the divine names and attributes had on the body of Muhammad. The correspondence is further reinforced by al-Jīlī's reference to the 'ascent' (*taraqqī*) of the recipient of this Qur'anic revelation, a notion that we saw in his discussion of the revelation of *al-Qur'ān al-ḥakīm*, the form of revelation that represents the manifestations of the divine names and attributes. While the first part of the hadith denotes the revelation of *al-Qur'ān al-karīm*, therefore, the second part evidently denotes that of *al-Qur'ān al-ḥakīm*.

The hadith just discussed is not the only scriptural source, as al-Jīlī sees it, for his idea of the two aspects of the Qur'an, nor are *al-Qur'ān al-karīm* and *al-Qur'ān al-ḥakīm* the only two names for those different aspects. Al-Jīlī also cites Qur'an 15.87 here, which apparently refers to two forms of revelation – or perhaps, two aspects of the same form of revelation – given to Muhammad, called *sab'an min al-mathānī* or *al-sab' al-mathānī* and *al-Qur'ān al-'aẓīm*. In their commentaries on this verse, the majority of exegetes take these terms to denote the same thing.[98] Yet there is some disagreement on what this single thing is, which centres upon the different ways of understanding the term *sab'an min al-mathānī*. There are three principal views, namely, that it denotes: the seven verses of the *Fātiḥah*, the opening *sūrah* of the Qur'an; the seven longest *sūrahs* of the Qur'an (*al-sabʿ al-ṭuwal/ṭiwāl*); or the Qur'an as a whole, which is said to be made up of seven different kinds of passage (commands, prohibitions, declarations of good news, warnings, examples, enumerations of blessings and information about former ages).[99] Al-Jīlī, working on the Ibn 'Arabian principle that every letter and word of the Qur'an has some special significance, does not go along with the view that the two terms denote the same thing. As he reads it, the term *al-Qur'ān al-ʿaẓīm* denotes the Qur'an as a whole, specifically, in its capacity as a comprehensive embodiment of the simple divine essence (*al-dhāt al-sādhaj*); indeed, this point is made explicitly in chapter twenty-four of *al-Insān al-kāmil* ('On the Divine Hearing') when he writes, 'The Great Qur'an (*al-Qur'ān al-ʿaẓīm*) is the essence (*al-dhāt*).'[100] In this regard, *al-Qur'ān al-ʿaẓīm* is synonymous for al-Jīlī with *al-Qur'ān al-karīm*, a correspondence that is underlined by his use of the term *jumlah* once again here, and by his reference again to how this aspect of the Qur'an represents the manifestation of *al-aḥadiyyah*.

As for *al-sabʿ al-mathānī*, al-Jīlī's understanding of the term emerges most fully from the opening of the chapter on the *Fātiḥah* (chapter forty) of *al-Insān al-kāmil*: 'Know that the Opening of the Book (*Fātiḥat al-kitāb*)', he writes, 'is the seven oft-repeated verses (*al-sabʿ al-mathānī*), which are the seven attributes of the [divine] self (*ṣifāt al-nafsiyyah*), which are life, knowledge, will, power, hearing, sight and speech.'[101] At the exoteric level, it can therefore be said, *al-sabʿ al-mathānī* denotes the *Fātiḥah*, while at the esoteric level it denotes the seven attributes of the divine self.[102] These two levels of meaning are also present in the passage under discussion here: exoterically, the term denotes a form of revelation that was given to Muhammad, yet, from an esoteric Sufi metaphysical perspective, this act of revelation denotes the manifestation of the seven attributes of the divine self within the Prophet. This being the case, *al-sabʿ al-mathānī* is synonymous with *al-Qur'ān al-ḥakīm*, a correspondence underlined by his repetition here of the notion that this form of revelation leaves its mark on the recipient's bodily existence (*wujūdihi al-jasadī*), and his use again of the term *taḥaqquq* to denote the realization experienced by the individual who receives this revelation.

Al-Jīlī's interpretation of Qur'an 15.87 reflects his more general exegetical approach, which is to read his Sufi metaphysical ideas out of/into select Qur'anic verses or hadiths. It also reflects what may be his debt to earlier interpreters working in the Ibn 'Arabian tradition, or at least, the existence of a shared Ibn 'Arabian perspective on this verse. For instance, al-Qāshānī, in his commentary on this verse, similarly identifies the 'seven oft-repeated' with 'the seven attributes (*al-ṣifāt al-sabʿ*) that were affirmed of God – May He be exalted – which are: life, knowledge, power, will, hearing, sight, and speech' – that is, what al-Jīlī calls the 'attributes of the self'. Furthermore, al-Qāshānī goes on to explain that the term *al-mathānī* denotes how 'the affirmation [of these attributes] was repeated for you [i.e. Muhammad], first, at the station of the heart's existence, at the moment of your taking on His traits (*ʿind takhalluqika bi-akhlāqihi*) and being qualified by His attributes (*wa-ittiṣāfika bi-awṣāfihi*), so they were for you; and second, at the station of endurance (*al-baqā'*) in the Real existence, after the annihilation in the divine unity (*al-fanā' fī al-tawḥīd*)'.[103] Like al-Jīlī, then, al-Qāshānī not only identifies the term *al-sab' al-mathānī* with the seven attributes of the divine self but also views the revelation of these seven verses to Muhammad as an indication of Muhammad becoming a locus for the manifestation of these attributes. And the similarities do not end here, for al-Qāshānī subsequently glosses *al-Qur'ān al-'aẓīm* as 'the essence that synthesizes all the attributes' (*al-dhāt al-jāmi'ah li-jamī' al-ṣifāt*),[104] in anticipation of al-Jīlī's interpretation of the term as 'the simple essence with the totality of the perfections' (*al-dhāt al-sādhaj ma'a jumlat al-kamālāt*). Nor was al-Qāshānī the only Ibn 'Arabian thinker prior to al-Jīlī to interpret the verse in this way. Muhammad Wafā' (d. 760/1359), the eponym of the Egyptian Wafā'iyyah *ṭarīqah* who lived just after al-Qāshānī and was influenced by Ibn 'Arabī, puts forward a very similar interpretation in a treatise titled *Nafā'is al-'irfān* (*The Gems of Gnosticism*).[105] While we cannot say for certain, in the present state of our knowledge, whether al-Jīlī had read al-Qāshānī's Qur'anic commentary or Muhammad Wafā's treatise, the correspondence between these three thinkers' interpretations of Qur'an 15.87 should remind us that, though many of al-Jīlī's ideas and interpretations may appear original to us, this may be as much a product of our unfamiliarity with the literature that al-Jīlī was immersed in as it is an indication of genuine originality.

The final scriptural passage cited in this section is Qur'an 55.1-2. This pair of verses is normally taken in its apparent sense to mean that God taught Muhammad the Qur'an, the use of the divine name *al-raḥmān* sometimes being connected in the *tafsīr* tradition to the idea that God's revelation of the Qur'an was an act of mercy (*raḥmah*).[106] Al-Jīlī, however, interpreting it through the prism of his Sufi metaphysics, reads the verse as an insight into the relationship between the two aspects of the Qur'an. Simply put, in his interpretation, one has to first receive the manifestation of the divine names and attributes, that is, the revelation of *al-Qur'ān al-ḥakīm* or *al-sab' al-mathānī*, before one receives the manifestation of the divine essence, that is, the revelation of *al-Qur'ān al-karīm* or *al-Qur'ān al-'aẓīm*. This is an idea that appears on several occasions earlier in *al-Insān al-kāmil*.[107] To understand how al-Jīlī connects it to Qur'an 55.1-2, we have to go back to his definition of *al-raḥmāniyyah*. As we saw in Chapter 1, al-Jīlī defines *al-raḥmāniyyah* as the level of 'making the realities of the names and attributes appear (*al-ẓuhūr bi-ḥaqā'iq al-asmā' wa-al-ṣifāt*)',[108] a definition connected to the Ibn 'Arabian idea of 'universal mercy' – the notion that God gives phenomenal existence to things out of mercy (*raḥmah*), and through His 'All-Merciful breath' (*al-nafas al-raḥmānī*).[109] It is on account of *al-raḥmāniyyah*'s role in the manifestation of the names and attributes, then, that al-Jīlī can here define the name *al-raḥmān* as an expression of 'the totality of the names and attributes (*jumlat al-asmā' wa-al-ṣifāt*)'.[110] Returning to Qur'an 55.1-2, if we understand the name *al-raḥmān* to denote the divine names and attributes, and the term *al-Qur'ān* to denote the divine essence (as al-Jīlī defined it at the beginning of this chapter), then we get the meaning, 'The divine names and attributes taught [Muhammad, or mankind] the divine essence';[111] hence, al-Jīlī is able to draw from these Qur'anic verses the idea that one can only reach the essence by going *through* the names and attributes, or, it might be said, one can only receive the revelation of *al-Qur'ān al-karīm* if one has first received the revelation of *al-Qur'ān al-ḥakīm*.

Throughout this chapter, we have seen how al-Jīlī refers to the two aspects of the Qur'an using a number of different names. Before concluding, let us briefly consider one final name of the Qur'an that fits into this twofold conception, namely, the Furqan (*al-Furqān*), to which al-Jīlī in fact devotes a separate chapter of *al-Insān al-kāmil* (chapter thirty-five). From a root connoting separation and distinction, the term *al-Furqān* is used in the Qur'an in various ways: sometimes it denotes the Qur'an itself (see e.g. Q 25.01, 2.185), sometimes the Torah (see Q 2.53, 21.48), while at others it apparently refers to that which distinguishes the saved community of believers from the unbelievers (see e.g. Q 8.41, where, according to the dominant interpretation, it refers to the battle of Badr).[112] These interpretations are related, for they all connote that which distinguishes truth from falsehood.[113] *Al-Furqān* was commonly held to be one of the most significant names of the Qur'an.[114] As such, it does not come as a surprise that al-Jīlī displays considerable interest in the name here.

Al-Jīlī's understanding of the name, and how it fits into his notion of the two aspects of the Qur'an, emerges from the opening of chapter thirty-five. He opens the chapter with a poem, which begins: 'The attributes of God (*ṣifāt Allāh*) are a *furqān*, while the essence of God (*dhāt Allāh*) is a *qur'ān*.'[115] He elaborates on this in the opening lines of the prose section that follows the poem:

> Know that the Furqan is an expression of the reality of the names and attributes (*'ibārah 'an al-asmā' wa-al-ṣifāt*), in their different varieties (*'alá ikhtilāf tanawwu'ātihā*). From its perspective, every attribute and name is distinguished (*tatamayyaz*) from the others, so distinction (*al-farq*) occurs in the self of the Real, with respect to His most beautiful names and His attributes.[116]

He goes on to describe in more detail how the divine names and attributes are different from one another and, related to this, how some are better than others. While the details of these distinctions and hierarchies do not concern us here, it is clear from this that the name *al-Furqān* corresponds with those names of the Qur'an that point to God's names and attributes, that is, *al-Qur'ān al-ḥakīm* and *al-sab' al-mathānī*, while the name *al-Qur'ān*, when taken without qualification, indicates, like the names *al-Qur'ān al-karīm* and *al-Qur'ān al-'aẓīm*, the divine essence. *Al-Qur'ān*, in other words, is the name for the comprehensive aspect of the Qur'an, and *al-Furqān* is the name for the detailed aspect – associations that are also found in the works of Ibn 'Arabī.[117] In terms of al-Jīlī's scheme of the levels of existence, meanwhile, it can be said that *al-Qur'ān* represents *al-aḥadiyyah*, while *al-Furqān* represents *al-wāḥidiyyah*; indeed, as we saw in Chapter 1, al-Jīlī actually defines *al-wāḥidiyyah* as the 'differentiation' (*furqān*) of the divine essence. As with the other pairs of names, when taken together they indicate the Qur'an's status as the most comprehensive form of scripture, for it embodies both the divine essence and attributes.

By way of summing up the correspondences indicated by al-Jīlī between the different names of the Qur'an and the different aspects of God across this chapter, we can draw the following table (Table 2):

Table 2 The two aspects of the Qur'an

Comprehensiveness	The Essence	Unqualified Oneness	The Qur'an	The Generous Qur'an	The Great Qur'an
(*al-jumlah*)	(*al-dhāt*)	(*al-aḥadiyyah*)	(*al-Qur'ān*)	(*al-Qur'ān al-karīm*)	(*al-Qur'ān al-'aẓīm*)
Distinction	The Names and Attributes	Qualified Oneness / All-Mercifulness	The Furqan	The Wise Qur'an	The Seven Oft-Repeated
(*al-tafṣīl*)	(*al-asmā' wa-al-ṣifāt*)	(*al-wāḥidiyyah / al-raḥmāniyyah*)	(*al-Furqān*)	(*al-Qur'ān al-ḥakīm*)	(*al-sab' al-mathānī*)

Overarching all of the elements in Table 2 are God – of whom all of the elements constitute manifestations – and His Prophet, Muhammad – in whom all of the elements are manifest. In this respect, we find that al-Jīlī's discussion of scripture ultimately leads us back to the key points within his Sufi metaphysics, namely, the existence of multiplicity within unity and unity within multiplicity; the nature of God as both simple – in the 'unqualified oneness' of His essence – and qualified – in the 'qualified oneness' of His names and attributes; and the nature of the Perfect Human, Muhammad, as a comprehensive being who unifies the one and the many, the simple and the qualified, and the divine and the created.

Conclusion

Al-Jīlī's chapter on the Qur'an reveals much about his general conception of revelation. The Qur'an, as he sees it, is not merely a 'book' in the conventional sense; its revelation is also an expression of God's manifestation in the 'book' of the phenomenal world, its different names representing different aspects of God. Furthermore, the revelation of the Qur'an to Muhammad is an indication that Muhammad is the perfect locus for this divine manifestation, followed by those perfect individuals who embody the Muhammadan Reality. The chapter therefore constitutes an elaboration of al-Jīlī's key Sufi metaphysical ideas of universal theophany and the Perfect Human, expressed in terms of the Qur'anic revelation. This tendency of al-Jīlī's to use the scriptures as a 'way in' to his broader Sufi metaphysics can be seen throughout the chapters under discussion in this book.

This is not to say, however, that the Qur'an, in al-Jīlī's view, functions merely as a symbol for something else, with no intrinsic significance of his own. As he sees it, the revelation of the Qur'an to Muhammad is the central event in the course of history, constituting the moment when God revealed Himself most fully to His creation and when man correspondingly attained his fullest perfection. The chapter therefore not only deals with the general ideas of universal theophany and the Perfect Human at an abstract metaphysical level but also indicates the unique place of the Qur'an and Muhammad at the level of sacred history. If we were to try to sum up the nature of this uniqueness, we could say that it lies in the comprehensiveness or perfection of the Qur'an and Muhammad, for they both constitute a comprehensive manifestation of God's essence and His names and attributes.

Throughout this chapter, al-Jīlī flirts with ideas that might well be described, from a traditional Islamic perspective, as heterodox. This is particularly true of his depiction of Muhammad, whom he describes in such exalted terms as to almost blur the boundary between divinity and humanity. This can be seen in his identification of Muhammad's essence with the divine essence, of Muhammad's body as the locus of manifestation for God's unqualified oneness, and of Muhammad with the Qur'an. Yet for the purposes of the present book what is most important is that the overall view of sacred history that al-Jīlī puts forward here is in keeping with the Qur'an-centred view, even if it is expressed in Sufi metaphysical terms. For al-Jīlī, the Qur'an, being an expression of the divine essence at the level of unqualified oneness, constitutes the most complete form of divine manifestation, while Muhammad, being the recipient of the manifestation of the divine essence, constitutes the archetypal Perfect Human. These ideas can be seen as Sufi metaphysical elaborations of the Qur'an-centred view that the Qur'an is the best of scriptures and Muhammad the best of messengers. They provide the reference point for al-Jīlī's conception of the other scriptures and prophets, which, as we shall see in the following chapters, he deems to be inferior to the Qur'an and Muhammad, even if they also represent forms of divine manifestation. Insofar as al-Jīlī views Muhammad in highly exalted, almost divine terms, then, this only goes to reinforce the reader's sense of the ultimate superiority of Muhammad and his scripture over the other prophets and scriptures, and ultimately, therefore, of the superiority of the Islamic religion over the other faiths.

4

The Torah

Having begun his presentation of the scriptures with the Qur'an, in chapter thirty-six of *al-Insān al-kāmil* al-Jīlī moves back in time, presenting us with his understanding of the Torah (*al-Tawrāh*), 'the first book', in the words of al-Shahrastānī, 'to be sent down from heaven'.[1] The Qur'an mentions the Torah by name on eighteen occasions, all of them traditionally dated to the Medinan period, that is, subsequent to Muhammad's encounter with the Jews of that city.[2] There are also several references, from both periods of revelation, to the 'Book' (*al-kitāb*) that Moses received (see e.g. Q 2.53, 2.87, 6.154). Other terms used in apparent reference to the Torah (or at least to scriptures given to Moses) include the Furqan (*al-furqān*) (see Q 2.53, 21.48),[3] a term which, as we saw in the previous chapter, is elsewhere applied to the Qur'an itself (see Q 25.01, 2.185), 'the scrolls' (*al-ṣuḥuf*) (see Q 53.36-37, 87.19)[4] and, in the context of Moses' retreat on Mount Sinai, 'the tablets' (*al-alwāḥ*) (see Q 7.145), a term which as we shall see is central to al-Jīlī's conception of the Torah. The name *al-Tawrāh* itself is often mentioned together with the Gospel (*al-Injīl*) (see e.g. Q 3.3, 3.48, 3.65), these being the scriptures of the oft-mentioned 'People of the Book' (*ahl al-kitāb*) and the Gospel being presented as a confirmation of the Torah (see e.g. Q 3.50, 5.46).

As we saw in Chapter 2, the Qur'anic and post-Qur'anic view of both the Torah and the Gospel is ambivalent. On the one hand, they are said to have been 'sent down' (*anzala*) by God; are understood to exist within the same archetypal, heavenly book (*umm al-kitāb, al-lawḥ al-mahfūẓ*) as the Qur'an, which confirms the message contained in them (see Q 3.3, 26.196, 29.47); and are said to be 'guidance and light' (*hudá wa-nūr*) (see e.g. Q 5.44, 6.91). On the other hand, the Qur'an portrays the Jews and Christians as having not properly observed (see e.g. Q 2.85, 62.5, 5.44, 5.65–6), concealed (see Q 3.187, 6.91) or tampered (see e.g. Q 2.75-9; 4.46; 5.13) in some way with the true content of the revelations of Moses and Jesus, and in this way proposes that the Torah and Gospel that are presently in the possession of the Jews and Christians are different from the true revelations given by God to Moses and Jesus, and presents itself as an abrogating confirmation of the earlier scriptures.[5]

As noted in Chapter 2, this Qur'anic attitude towards the Torah was adopted and often used in the post-Qur'anic Sunni Islamic tradition as the basis for polemic against Judaism and the Jews. More specifically, according to Hava Lazarus-Yafeh, four 'somewhat contradictory and overlapping arguments' used by medieval Muslim polemicists against the Torah can be identified, all but one of which (the third argument) are based upon the Qur'an: (i) *taḥrīf*, the allegation that the Jews had falsified the true scripture revealed to them by Moses; (ii) *naskh*, the idea that the Qur'an had abrogated the Torah; (iii) absence of *tawātur*, that is, the failure of the Jews to reliably document the transmission of the Torah; and (iv) Muslim biblical exegesis, whereby prophecies of Muhammad's coming were read out of the Torah.[6]

As we shall see, some of these arguments, and the underlying and widespread idea in the Qur'an-centred view of sacred history that the Torah is both a genuine and yet imperfect and in some places false scripture, provide the overall framework for al-Jīlī's conception of the Torah. That being said, he is not writing polemic here, and we shall see that his Sufi metaphysical perspective leads him to adopt a relatively charitable, and at times even positive view of the Torah, Moses and the Jews, albeit within the wider context of the Qur'an-centred view's ambivalence towards the Torah, and his own insistence on the superiority of the Qur'an, Muhammad and the Muslims over the other scriptures, prophets and religious communities.

The revelation and propagation of the Torah

> God – May He be exalted – sent down (*anzala*) the Torah to Moses in nine tablets (*alwāḥ*), and commanded him to propagate (*yuballigh*) seven of them and to leave two tablets, because intellects (*al-'uqūl*) could scarcely accept (*taqbal*) what was in those two tablets. So had Moses revealed them (*abrazahumā*), what he had requested would have been destroyed, and not a single man would have believed him. So those two were particular (*makhṣūṣān*) to Moses – Peace be upon him – and not to anyone else among the people of that time (*ahl dhālik al-zamān*).[7]

Al-Jīlī begins by identifying two stages in the process by which the Torah was revealed. The first stage, signalled by the key term *anzala*, constitutes what might be called the 'vertical' dimension of revelation, that is, God's 'sending down' of the Torah to His prophet, Moses. As we have already seen, this is the term that the Qur'an most commonly uses for the revelation of the scriptures, both Qur'anic and pre-Qur'anic, including the Torah. As such, al-Jīlī's use of it here immediately establishes the Torah as a genuine divine revelation, as in the Qur'an-centred view. The second stage in the revelatory process, denoted by the key terms *yuballigh* and *abraza*, meanwhile, constitutes what might be called the 'horizontal' dimension of revelation, that is, Moses' proclamation of the divine revelation to his people (*qawm*), the Children of Israel. This is also a Qur'anic concept: in Qur'an 5.67, for instance, God instructs the Messenger (Muhammad) to 'propagate (*balligh*) what has been sent down (*unzila*) to you', and goes on to warn him, 'If you do not do that, then you will not have propagated His message (*mā ballaghta risālatahu*).' The same notion of the prophets' propagation (*tablīgh*) of the divine message (*al-risālah*) (which has been 'sent down') is also found in several other verses (see Q 7.62, 7.68, 33.39, 46.23). Al-Jīlī's notion of the two-stage revelation of the Torah, with Moses as the hinge between the two stages, can therefore be seen as an extrapolation of a Qur'anic notion.[8]

Yet while the Qur'an seems to imply that the message propagated by a messenger to his people is the *same* as that sent down to him by God, al-Jīlī here identifies an important distinction between what we might call the 'revealed Torah' and the 'propagated Torah'. This distinction centres upon the notion that the Torah is made up of 'tablets' (*alwāḥ*). This too is a Qur'anic idea (see Q 7.145), which is probably rooted in the biblical image of the 'tablets of stone' (*luḥōṯ hā'eḇen*) on which the Ten Commandments were written (see Exod. 24.12).[9] According to al-Jīlī's conception, the number of tablets differs between the revealed Torah and the propagated Torah, the former containing nine, and the latter only seven. The reason for this discrepancy lies in the exalted nature of the wisdom contained in the two tablets that God commanded Moses to keep to himself. This wisdom, al-Jīlī indicates, is too exalted for intellects (*al-'uqūl*) to comprehend, a sentiment that fits with the Ibn 'Arabian notion of the intellect as a limited (and limiting) tool of understanding,[10] and which therefore implies that the wisdom concerned can only be understood through supra-rational means, that is, mystical experience (*kashf*, etc.) or, as in the case of Moses, divine revelation (*waḥy*). Since Moses' people had not attained such insight, God commanded Moses not to propagate the two tablets, for fear that if he did so, no one would believe in his message.

Underlying all of this is the key Sufi metaphysical concept of completeness or perfection (*al-kamāl*). While the revealed Torah is complete (*kāmil*), and Moses, as the leading human – or, it might be said, the Perfect Human – of his age, possesses the requisite understanding to receive the complete Torah, the propagated Torah is incomplete (*nāqiṣ*), owing to the imperfect spiritual capacity of Moses' people. This places the Torah in an inferior position to the Qur'an, which, as was made clear in the previous chapter, is defined above all by its comprehensiveness and perfection, in al-Jīlī's view. Indeed, al-Jīlī's position here can be viewed as a Sufi metaphysical elaboration or reworking of the Qur'an-centred view that while the original message of the Torah is fully in keeping with the perfect message of the Qur'an, the actual scripture possessed by the Jews is defective, hence the need for further revelations in the form of first the Gospel and then the Qur'an. Where al-Jīlī differs from the standard interpretation is in ascribing this defectiveness not to the Jews' distortion of the meaning or text of their scripture (*taḥrīf*), but rather to God's instruction to Moses not to propagate all of the tablets that were revealed to him. In this way, it might be said that al-Jīlī adopts a more charitable stance towards the Jewish people, albeit while still indicating that their revealed scripture is incomplete vis-à-vis the Qur'an, and that this incompleteness of the revealed Torah was necessitated by their limited capacity for understanding.

If the rationale behind his identification of a discrepancy in the number of tablets of the revealed Torah and the propagated Torah is fairly clear, the source of al-Jīlī's view that the 'revealed Torah' consisted of nine tablets, and the 'propagated Torah' of seven is not so apparent. Again, his discussion of the number of tablets ought to be placed within the context of the wider post-Qur'anic tradition, for the Qur'anic exegetes also display an interest in this question in their commentaries on Qur'an 7.145. The commentary tradition is by no means unanimous on the number of tablets revealed to Moses, with most medieval commentators mentioning the existence of three different opinions, namely that the Torah consisted of ten, seven or two tablets.[11] Al-Jīlī's view that the propagated Torah consisted of seven tablets might therefore be taken as an affirmation of the second opinion. What, though, of his view that the revealed Torah consisted of nine tablets? While this view does not, as far as I know, appear in the major works of *tafsīr* written before al-Jīlī's time,[12] there is a precedent for it in the popular collection of 'tales of the prophets' (*qiṣaṣ al-anbiyā'*) made by al-Thaʿlabī (d. 427/1035/6), *Arā'is al-majālis*.[13] This might indicate that the nine tablets' motif has its origin in the so-called *Isrā'īliyyāt*, that is, the traditions of Jewish or Christian provenance that were incorporated into *qiṣaṣ al-anbiyā'*, though I have found no Jewish precedent for the motif. It is also possible that the nine tablets' motif is connected to the reference in Qur'an 17.101 to the 'nine signs' (*ayāt*) given to Moses. Though, in the context of that *sūrah*, this seems to refer to the plagues sent upon Egypt, this verse has also often been associated with Qur'an 7.145, and there is a hadith report in which Muhammad defines the nine signs as commandments revealed to Moses, thereby linking the verse to the tablets' motif.[14]

While these parallels may be suggestive, it is still not exactly clear how al-Jīlī could have derived from these earlier sources the idea that the revealed Torah consisted of nine tablets, and the propagated Torah of seven. We can, however, identify a couple of more direct precedents for his position. First, there is the following report attributed to Ibn Jurayj (d. 150/767), a scholar known for transmitting many *Isrā'īliyyāt*: 'It is reported that the tablets of Moses were nine. And two of them were removed (*rufiʿa*), and seven remained.'[15] This report is quoted by al-Suyūṭī (d. 911/1505: al-Suyūṭī lived after al-Jīlī, but preserved a lot of earlier material) in his commentary on Qur'an 7.150-151, in a passage that tells the story of Moses' anger on seeing the golden calf. This would suggest that the notion that the Torah originally consisted of nine tablets, but now consists only of seven, is connected to the biblical story of Moses breaking the (two) tablets out of anger on seeing that his people had made a golden calf the object of their worship (see Exod. 32.19).[16] While al-Jīlī makes no reference to the story of the golden calf here, it is possible that this story underlies his sense of the incompleteness of the propagated Torah and, specifically, his view that two of its tablets are missing. The second precedent, meanwhile, comes from the Ibn 'Arabian Sufi *tafsīr* of al-Qāshānī, a work that, as we saw in the previous chapter, al-Jīlī sometimes echoes. In his commentary on Qur'an 15.87, al-Qāshānī interprets the term *al-sabʿ al-mathānī* as a reference to the seven attributes (*al-sabʿ al-ṣifāt*) of the divine essence – or what al-Jīlī calls the attributes of the self (*al-ṣifāt al-nafsiyyah*) – an interpretation, it will be remembered, that al-Jīlī adopts in his chapter on the Qur'an. Significantly for our purposes here, al-Qāshānī goes on to say that Moses was given not seven but nine attributes – the other two being 'the heart' (*al-qalb*) and 'the spirit' (*al-rūḥ*) – owing to his attaining 'the station of The One Spoken To' (*maqām al-kalīm*).[17] Though there is no reference to the tablets in al-Qāshānī's passage, there is nevertheless a clear parallel with al-Jīlī's view that nine tablets were revealed to Moses and only seven to his people, a parallel reinforced by the fact that al-Jīlī, as we shall see presently, associates the tablets with certain divine attributes. While al-Jīlī's specific view that the Torah consists of nine tablets that were revealed to Moses, who was ordered to propagate only seven of them, seems to be without direct precedent (at least in the present state of our knowledge), nevertheless, we can see how he may have arrived at this view by weaving together various traditions from the exegetical and tales of the prophets' literature, and elaborating them in accordance with his Sufi metaphysical perspective.

The contents and material of the tablets

The tablets that he was commanded to propagate contained the knowledge of the first people and the last people (*'ulūm al-awwalīn wa-al-akhirīn*), with the exception of the knowledge (*'ilm*) of Muhammad – May God bless him and grant him peace – and the knowledge of Abraham, and the knowledge of Jesus – Peace be upon them – and the knowledge of the heirs of Muhammad (*warathat Muḥammad*). So the Torah did not include this, out of regard for the specialness (*khuṣūṣiyyatan*) of Muhammad and his heirs, and by way of honouring (*ikrāman*) Abraham and Jesus – Peace be upon them. And the tablets were made of stone marble (*ḥajar al-marmar*), by which I mean the seven tablets that Moses was commanded to propagate, in contrast to the two tablets, which were made of His light (*min nūrihi*). And for this reason their hearts hardened (*qasat qulūbuhum*), because the tablets were made of stone.

And all that the tablets contained was seven types of divine requirements (*al-muqtaḍayāt al-ilāhiyyah*), in accordance with the number of tablets. So the first tablet was light (*al-nūr*), and the second tablet was guidance (*al-hudá*). God – May He be exalted – said: 'We sent down the Torah containing guidance and light, through which the prophets could judge.' (Q 5:44) And the third tablet was wisdom (*al-ḥikmah*), and the fourth tablet was the faculties (*al-qiwá*), and the fifth tablet was judgment (*al-ḥukm*), and the sixth tablet was servanthood (*al-'ubūdiyyah*), and the seventh tablet was the clarification of the path of happiness from the path of misery (*wuḍūḥ ṭarīq al-sa'ādah min ṭarīq al-shaqāwah*), and making plain which of them is better. So these are the seven tablets that Moses – Peace be upon him – was commanded to propagate. As for the two tablets that were particular to Moses, the first tablet was the tablet of lordship (*lawḥ al-rubūbiyyah*), and the second tablet was the tablet of power (*lawḥ al-qudrah*).[18]

The Qur'an refers only very briefly and in very general terms to the contents of the tablets given to Moses, speaking of how God wrote an 'admonition' (*maw'iẓan*) and a 'detailed explanation' (*tafṣīlan*) of all things on them (see Q 7.145). In the post-Qur'anic Islamic tradition, it was commonly thought that the tablets contained some form of legal code,[19] while some commentators suggest that the tablets contained narrative as well as legal material.[20] We will look in more detail at al-Jīlī's understanding of the contents of the Torah later in the chapter. For now, let us consider how he categorizes the material contained in the propagated and revealed Torahs. The key terms in this regard are *'ilm*/*'ulūm* and *al-muqtaḍayāt al-ilāhiyyah*. With regard to the former, al-Jīlī indicates that the 'knowledge' contained in the propagated Torah was the knowledge possessed by 'the first people and the last people' (*al-awwalīn wa-al-ākhirīn*), a phrase that is usually used in Islamic literature in connection with the knowledge contained in the Qur'an, and which seems generally to denote the sum total of the knowledge acquired by all people in all ages, both in the past and the future.[21] According to a hadith cited by Ibn 'Arabī, it denotes the knowledge possessed by Muhammad, which, in Ibn 'Arabī's interpretation, is both inspired and comprehensive.[22] Al-Jīlī's use of the term here, then, would seem to indicate that the propagated Torah is a comprehensive scripture, like the Qur'an. However, this sense of the Torah's comprehensiveness is subsequently undermined by al-Jīlī's reference to various forms of *'ilm* that it does *not* contain, specifically, the knowledge possessed by Muhammad, Abraham, Jesus and Muhammad's 'heirs' (*warathah*) – by which he could mean either the Muslims generally, or those Muslim Perfect Humans or Friends of God who lived after Muhammad and embodied the Muhammadan Reality more specifically, in keeping with the common Sufi tendency – visible also in Ibn 'Arabian Sufism – to claim the status of 'heirs of the prophets' (*warathat al-anbiyā'*) for themselves.[23] This reference to *'ilm* that is missing from the Torah once again highlights the incompleteness of the propagated Torah when juxtaposed with the Qur'an. In this way, al-Jīlī's conception of the *'ulūm* contained in the propagated Torah reflects his broader stance towards that scripture, which is that it is a genuine, yet defective, form of divine revelation – a stance that is in keeping with the Qur'an-centred view.

While *'ulūm al-awwalīn wa-al-ākharīn* indicates a general and comprehensive kind of knowledge, the term *al-muqtaḍayāt al-ilāhiyyah* denotes something more specific. *Al-muqtaḍayāt* is a term that appears fairly regularly in al-Jīlī's thought, where it most often denotes the necessary corollaries of a particular existent's nature.[24] When qualified, as here, by the adjective *al-ilāhiyyah*, then, it indicates those things that are a necessary product of God's nature. This includes both the divine attributes and those properties of created beings that are necessitated by the nature of God. To take as examples the 'requirements' listed here, 'guidance' (*al-hudá*), 'wisdom' (*al-ḥikmah*) and 'judgement' (*al-ḥukm*) are all divine attributes, yet they are also things that man possesses, on account of the 'requirement' of the divine attributes to become manifest in the phenomenal world. Similarly, according to al-Jīlī's idea of the Perfect Human as a microcosm, man's 'faculties' (*al-qiwá*) are determined by God's nature,[25] while the 'servanthood' (*al-'ubūdiyyah*) of creation, as al-Jīlī understands it, is a necessarily corollary of the 'lordship' (*al-rubūbiyyah*) of God[26] – an idea that he adopts from Ibn 'Arabī.[27] While we shall look at the details of these divine requirements in more detail later in the chapter, what matters for now is that al-Jīlī's proposal that each of the seven tablets of the propagated Torah corresponds to a particular divine requirement means that the propagated Torah can tell us something about God's nature. Again, this is in keeping with the notion that the Torah is a genuine, divinely revealed scripture.

This being said, we cannot get away from the incompleteness of the propagated Torah. In this instance, this incompleteness is indicated by al-Jīlī's reference to the contents of the two additional tablets contained in the revealed Torah. These two tablets are also named after two of God's attributes, and particularly exalted attributes at that. *Al-rubūbiyyah*, according to his scheme, occupies the sixth level of existence, and indicates both the superiority of God over His creation (God being the one who is 'Lord'), and yet also the ontological connection (*nisbah*) between God and creation, on account of the dialectical relationship between the Lord and His servants, each of whom stand in mutual need of the other in order to be so called.[28] *Al-qudrah*, meanwhile, is one of the seven attributes of the divine self, and denotes God's power to bring things from non-existence into phenomenal existence.[29] In fact, as al-Jīlī sees it, these two attributes are connected, for God's power (*al-qudrah*) to bring things into existence enables His lordship (*al-rubūbiyyah*) to appear.[30] The tablets of *al-rubūbiyyah* and *al-qudrah* therefore tell us much about God and His relationship with His creation. For them to be kept back from the propagated Torah indicates the defectiveness of the Torah when it comes to revealing God's nature, and the incapacity of the Torah's audience, Moses' people, to comprehend these fundamental aspects of God's nature. In this sense, while the revealed Torah is relatively complete (though even then, it is not as complete as the Qur'an, which reveals God's nature at the level of *al-aḥadiyyah*, which is higher than the levels of *al-rubūbiyyah* and *al-qudrah* in al-Jīlī's scheme), the propagated Torah is an incomplete form of scripture.

The strong impression of ambivalence created here is further reinforced by al-Jīlī's discussion of the material from which the tablets were made. Again, his interest in this topic reflects the concerns of the Qur'anic exegetical tradition more broadly. As with the question of the material of the tablets, the Qur'anic commentators acknowledge that there are multiple views on the material of the tablets. Among the materials suggested are green emerald (*zumurrudah khaḍrā'*), chrysolite (*zabarjad*), wood (*kashab*), hard and solid rock (*ṣakhrah ṣammā'*) that God softened for Moses, and wood from the lote-tree of paradise (*sidrat al-muntahá*).[31] Though the commentators include multiple possibilities for the material of the tablets, al-Jīlī's view that the tablets of the propagated Torah were made of marble (*al-marmar*) does not appear to have much of a basis in the *tafsīr* tradition, which seems more inclined to identify the material of the tablets with a precious gemstone. Indeed, we find closer parallels to al-Jīlī's position in Jewish literature. As noted previously, the account in Exodus refers to the tablets on which the Ten Commandments were written as 'tablets of stone' (Exod. 24.12, 31.18), though in the rabbinic tradition this stone is commonly identified with the sapphire of God's throne.[32] Of more relevance for our purposes is a passage found in *Tiqūnei hā-Zohar*, a later appendix to the famous thirteenth-century CE Kabbalistic text, the *Zohar*.[33] According to the author of this text, there are two types of Torah, which correspond to the two sets of tablets received by Moses on Mt Sinai. 'The first set of tablets', in the words of the scholar of Jewish mysticism Elliot R. Wolfson, 'are associated . . . with the pure marble stones, *avnei shayish ṭahor*, mentioned in the warning that R. Akiva offers his colleagues in the legend of the four rabbis who entered Pardes.'[34] This is a reference to an enigmatic saying of Rabbi Akiva (d. 137 CE), one of the founding figures of the mishnaic tradition, in which the rabbi warns his audience not to confuse the 'pure marble stones' with water.[35] For the author of *Tiqūnei hā-Zohar*, the original marble tablets come from the Tree of Life, and are superior to the legalistic second set of tablets, which come from the Tree of Knowledge.[36] There is perhaps a parallel here with al-Jīlī's distinction between the revealed Torah and the inferior propagated Torah, although while the Jewish author views the marble in positive terms, as the material of the original set of tablets, al-Jīlī, as we shall see presently, views it more negatively as the hard – and therefore non-spiritual – material of the limited propagated Torah. Yet this is not the only parallel between al-Jīlī's conception of the tablets and medieval Jewish mystical conceptions. In a similar yet different vein to the author of the *Tiqūnei*, the eminent Saragossan Kabbalist Abraham Abulafia (d. 1291 CE), as the noted scholar of Kabbalah Moshe Idel puts it, 'believes that the word LḤVTh (*luḥot* – tablets) is a homonym, i.e., a term that has both inner and outer, esoteric and exoteric implications'.[37] With recourse to letter mysticism and numerology, Abulafia explains in his *Sefer hā-ḥeshek* the esoteric implications of the tablets of stone: 'Now the numerical value of ShNY LḤVTh 'BhNYM (shene luḥot 'avanim – the two tablets of stone) = 891, which is identical with 'BNY ShYSh THVR ('avne shayish tahor – stones of pure marble), and they denote YẒR TVB VYẒR R' (yeẓer tov ve-yeẓer ra' – the good and evil inclinations).'[38] Though the exact signification of this kind of esoteric letter mysticism is difficult to grasp, 'it is clear . . . beyond doubt,' Idel concludes, 'that Abulafia equates the two tablets of stone with the stones of pure marble [of the saying of Rabbi Akiva] and with the good and evil inclinations'.[39] While there is no indication that al-Jīlī was familiar with these Jewish mystical texts, and while it is clear that his concerns and views on the Torah are different from those of the Jewish mystical theorists, the parallels between his position and the positions of the Jewish thinkers reflect a shared 'mystical' approach to questions such as the material of the tablets, and might even suggest an ultimately common source, perhaps mediated through the legendary Islamic material of Jewish origin known as *Isrā'īliyyāt*.[40]

Whatever the source for al-Jīlī's position, its significance lies in what the stone marble represents, namely, the hardening of the Children of Israel's hearts. This is a Qur'anic motif with biblical roots: in the Hebrew Bible, the motif occurs most prominently with respect to Pharaoh's refusal to free Moses' people (see Exod. 4.21, 7.13-14, 8.15-32), while in the New Testament Jesus refers to the hardness of Moses' people's hearts to explain the permissibility of divorce in Jewish law (Mark 10:5), and Paul uses the motif to explain the Children of Israel's inability to comprehend the message of Moses and the failure of Jews in his own time to acknowledge Jesus as the Messiah (2 Cor. 3.14).[41] The Qur'an links the hardening of the hearts of Moses' people to their idolatry in the golden calf episode: 'Then your hearts were hardened (*qasat qulūbukum*) after that. They were like stone (*ka-al-ḥajārah*), or even harder (*aw ashadd quswatan*).' (Q 2.74) Similarly, Qur'an 57.16 connects the motif to the Children of Israel's breaking of the covenant: the believers are advised not to become 'like those who were previously given the book (*al-ladhīna uwtū al-kitāb min qabl*), whose hearts were hardened with the passing of the ages (*fa-ṭāla 'alayhim al-amad fa-qasat qulūbuhum*), many of whom were those who do bad (*fāsiqūn*)'. The Qur'anic exegetes tend to link the hardening of the hearts motif to the recalcitrance, moral degeneracy and lack of knowledge of the Children of Israel.[42] In his commentary on Qur'an 2.74, for instance, al-Qurṭubī says that the phrase 'your hearts hardened' denotes how the Children of Israel were 'devoid of adherence and submission to the signs of God (*khulūwhā min al-inābah wa-al-idh'ān li-ayāt Allāh*)'.[43] This definition seems particularly to denote the Children of Israel's non-adherence to revelation (the 'signs' of God), an association that has biblical antecedents (see e.g. Zech. 7.12). The Sufi exegetes, meanwhile, tend to link the phrase to attachment to bodily desires, lack of knowledge and distance from God. Thus al-Qāshānī explains the same verse: '"Your hearts hardened," because many bodily pleasures and matters clung to them (*bi-kathrat mubāsharat al-umūr wa-al-lidhdhāt al-badaniyyah*), and because they were clothed in the attributes of the lower self (*mulābasat al-ṣifāt al-nafsānī*),'[44] while the comparison with stone, he explains, denotes how their hearts 'have not been imprinted with knowledge (*'adam ta'aththurihā bi-al-naqsh al-'ilmī*).'[45]

All of these notions probably underlie al-Jīlī's conception of the hardening of the Children of Israel's hearts. Based on what he says about their inability to comprehend the contents of the two tablets reserved for Moses, it seems that he primarily understands the hardening of hearts motif in terms of Moses' people's limited capacity to comprehend the divine wisdom. In Ibn 'Arabian terms, it might be said that their hard hearts represent their lack of 'preparedness' (*isti'dād*) to receive and comprehend the divine revelation in its fullness. This lack of spiritual or cognitive receptivity is connected to their being trapped in the material world, which is here represented by the stone marble, one of the hardest material substances. The two additional tablets contained in the revealed Torah, by contrast, are made of light (*al-nūr*), an immaterial substance and one of the attributes of the divine essence in al-Jīlī's scheme, and which therefore represents access to the higher, divine (and immaterial) levels of existence.[46] Since Moses was not commanded to propagate these two tablets of light, however, his people do not have such access. In sum, therefore, like his views on the number of tablets and their contents, al-Jīlī's conception of the material of the tablets reflects the ambivalent stance that he takes towards the Torah and the Children of Israel.

The superiority of Muhammad, his revelation and his religion

> Thus none of Moses' people became perfect (*lam yukmal aḥad min qawm Mūsá*), because he was not commanded to reveal (*ibrāz*) [all of] the nine tablets. So none of his people became perfect after him, nor did any of his people inherit from him (*lam yarithhu*). This was unlike how it was with Muhammad – May God bless him and grant him peace – who did not leave out anything, but rather propagated it [all] to us (*ballaghahu ilaynā*). God – May He be exalted – said, 'We have left nothing out of the book.' (Q 6:38) And He said, 'And We have set out everything in detail.' (Q 17:12) For this reason his religious community was the best of religious communities (*millatuhu khayr al-milal*), and he abrogated, with his religion, all religions (*wa-nasakha bi-dīnihi jamī' al-adyān*), because he was given all that they were given, and added (*zāda*) to that that which they were not given. So their religions were abrogated (*fa-nusikhat adyānuhum*) due to their incompleteness (*li-naqṣihā*), while his religion became known for its perfection (*shahara dīnuhu bi-kamālihi*). God – May He be exalted – said, 'Today I have perfected (*akmaltu*) for you your religion and completed (*atmamtu*) for you My favour.' (Q 5:3) And He did not send down this verse to a prophet other than Muhammad. If He had sent it down to anyone [else], that person would have been the Seal of Prophets (*khātam al-nabiyyīn*). But that is only valid for Muhammad – May God bless him and grant him peace – so it was sent down to him. So he was the Seal of Prophets, because he did not omit any form of wisdom (*ḥikmah*), guidance (*hudá*), knowledge (*'ilm*) or mystery (*sirr*), but indicated and alluded to [all] of them, in accordance with what was fitting for the prophets [to reveal] of that mystery. . . . So he left no entry point (*madkhal*) for anyone, and was unique (*istaqalla*) in the matter, and sealed prophecy (*khatama al-nubuwwah*), because he left out nothing that was needed, but rather brought it [all]. And none of the Perfect Ones (*al-kummal*) who came after him found anything worthy of indicating that Muhammad had not

> already indicated. So such a Perfect One follows him (*yatbaʿuhu*), as he indicated, and becomes a follower (*tābiʿ*) [of his]. So the category of legislative prophethood (*nubuwwat al-tashrīʿ*) was cut off after him, and Muhammad was the Seal of Prophets, because he brought perfection, while no one else had brought that.[47]

This passage gives us a clear and direct insight into al-Jīlī's view of the relationship between Islam and other religions. The passage hinges upon the key dichotomy between perfection or completeness and imperfection. As we have already seen, for al-Jīlī, the propagated Torah is incomplete, since it is missing two of the tablets of the revealed Torah. Here al-Jīlī invites the reader to extrapolate from that idea the notion that the religion (*dīn*) in which the Torah is held sacred, that is, Judaism, and the religious community (*millah*) who hold it sacred, that is, the Jews or the Children of Israel, are similarly imperfect. He reinforces this point, moreover, by contrasting the imperfection of the revelation, religion and religious community of Moses – and, indeed, of all pre-Muhammadan prophets – with the *perfection* of the revelation, religion and religious community of Muhammad.

In keeping with the centrality of the completeness–incompleteness dichotomy, the most important key terms of this passage are those of the root *k-m-l*. As we know, the concept of *kamāl* lies at the heart of al-Jīlī's Sufi metaphysics, denoting in particular the perfection or completeness of the Perfect Human, a perfection that resides in his being a perfect locus for the manifestation of all of the divine names and attributes, a being that synthesizes all of the levels of existence, and a microcosm of the larger cosmos. When al-Jīlī says here then that none of Moses' people became perfect after him, he seems to be suggesting, on the one hand, that Moses was a Perfect Human,[48] and on the other hand, that none of the Jews can be considered Perfect Humans like him. This interpretation is supported by al-Jīlī's subsequent statement that none of Moses' people inherited (*yarith*) from him, since the 'heir' (*wārith*) of Muhammad denotes in al-Jīlī's Ibn ʿArabian lexicon the post-Muhammadan (Muslim) Friend of God.[49] Here we see al-Jīlī's ambivalent stance towards the Torah and the Jews integrated into his Sufi metaphysics, and specifically, into his idea of the Perfect Human. The implication seems to be that the station of Perfect Human is accessible only to those within the fold of Islam.[50] This position, it should be noted, is consistent with what appears to be the earlier Ibn ʿArabian view: the noted commentator on the *Fuṣūṣ* al-Jandī, for instance, in his discussion of the knowledge of God's 'greatest name', a knowledge that he declares to be limited to the Perfect Humans, writes:

> This badge of honour (*ʿalam*) that we have mentioned [i.e. knowledge of God's greatest name] was denied (*muḥarram*) to all religious communities prior to [the coming of] our Prophet. It was denied to all religious communities prior to ours, because the perfect human reality (*al-ḥaqīqah al-insāniyyah al-kamāliyyah*) had not yet appeared in its most perfect form. Rather, it had only appeared in accordance with the receptivity (*qābiliyyah*) of the perfect one of that age. But when the meaning and form of the [greatest] name were discovered, through the [coming into] existence of the Messenger of God, God allowed it – by which I mean, the meaning of the greatest name – to be known within his religious

> community, which is 'the best community sent out to mankind' [Q 3:110], by way of honouring our Prophet.[51]

For the Ibn 'Arabian Sufis, al-Jīlī included, therefore, human perfection is only attainable within the fold of Islam, and this is due to the fact that it was only with the coming of Muhammad, the most perfect of the Perfect Humans, that a model of true perfection appeared within the phenomenal world.

While the Torah, Judaism and the Jews – along with all other earlier scriptures, religions and religious communities – are marked by imperfection (*naqṣ*), therefore, the Qur'an, Islam and the Muslims are, by contrast, marked by perfection (*kamāl*). We have already seen this idea elaborated in metaphysical terms, with respect to the perfection of the Qur'an as a representation of both the divine essence and attributes. Here, al-Jīlī grounds it in the Qur'an and in a number of key notions within the Qur'an-centred view of sacred history. The scriptural basis for the notion of the perfection of Muhammad's revelation and religion, as al-Jīlī sees it, consists in three Qur'anic verses (Q 5.3, 6.38 and 17.12) that, according to the most common interpretation, denote the completeness of the Qur'an, and the perfection and supremacy of the Islamic religion more generally.[52] Verse 5.3 is particularly significant for al-Jīlī, it seems, because of the use of verbs of the two key roots – *k-m-l* and *t-m-m* – denoting perfection and completeness.

The perfection of the revelation and religion of Muhammad indicated by the Qur'an has a number of important corollaries for the relationship between Islam and other religions. First, it means that the Muslims, because they have the best scripture and the best religion, are the best religious community, an idea here indicated by the term *khayr al-milal*. Both this term and the idea behind it are also Qur'anic, for the term evokes the statement in Qur'an 3.110: 'You are the best community (*khayr ummah*) sent out to mankind.' Indeed, the Qur'anic term *khayr ummah* was often recast in the post-Qur'anic Islamic tradition as *khayr al-umam*,[53] a term that is synonymous with *khayr al-milal* and which al-Jīlī uses in the final chapter of the book to make the same point being made here.[54] Al-Jīlī's explicit declaration of the superiority of the Muslims over other religious communities here and (as we shall see in the conclusion) in that final chapter is a clear sign of his commitment to the Qur'an-centred view sacred history. This is a commitment, moreover, which he shares with Ibn 'Arabī, who had also used the *khayr al-umam/milal* motif and, like al-Jīlī, connected it to the comprehensiveness of the scripture received by Muhammad.[55]

Second, and following on from the first point, al-Jīlī clearly states that the perfection of Muhammad's revelation and religion mean that they *abrogate* all previous revelations and religions. Again, al-Jīlī's use of the key term *naskh* reflects his commitment to the Qur'an-centred view. While the Qur'an uses the term *naskh* in reference to Qur'anic verses that abrogate other Qur'anic verses (see e.g. Q 2.106), as noted earlier in this chapter the term and concept were transposed by medieval Muslim writers into the different context of interreligious polemic.[56] As discussed in Chapter 2, in this polemical context, *naskh* denotes how previous revelations and religious laws (particularly those of the Jews and Christians), though appropriate for their time and place, have been abrogated by the revelation and religious law of Muhammad. And though this is not the Qur'anic denotation of *naskh*, nevertheless this idea can be read out of the Qur'an (see e.g. Q 13.38).[57] While al-Jīlī's primary aim is not a polemical one here, nevertheless, his use of the concept of *naskh* to denote this same idea reflects how, like the Muslim interreligious polemicists, he views sacred history in terms of Islam's supersession of previous religions. Again, this is a view that he inherits from Ibn 'Arabī, who, as we saw in Chapter 2 (for instance, in the passage comparing Islam and the other religions to the sun and the stars), also uses the language of abrogation in the context of the relationship between the revelation received by Muhammad and those received by the earlier prophets.

Third, al-Jīlī indicates that, since the Qur'an is complete, there is no need for further scriptural revelation after it. This means in turn that Muhammad is the final messenger, an idea denoted here by the terms *khātam al-nabiyyīn* and *khatm al-nubuwwah*. The former is another Qur'anic term (see Q 33.40), which is conventionally interpreted to mean that Muhammad is both the last and the best prophet and messenger.[58] Taken together with *naskh*, the idea of the sealing of prophetood indicates that Muhammad is superior both to all who came before him and all who come after him, for the earlier prophets and the post-Muhammadan Friends of God – or what Ibn 'Arabian Sufis call the 'general prophets' – are or will be imperfect vis-à-vis his perfection.

Al-Jīlī's use of the concept of *khatm al-nubuwwah* again reflects his commitment to the Qur'an-centred view of sacred history. However, his Ibn 'Arabian Sufi metaphysical perspective also leads him, as we know, to develop this concept in what might be considered an unconventional or heterodox direction. As was indicated in the previous chapter, al-Jīlī adopts Ibn 'Arabī's notion that what is sealed with Muhammad is specifically *legislative* prophethood (*nubuwwat al-tashrī'*), that is, prophethood that involves the prophet receiving a new religious law (as well as the esoteric truth), while so-called general prophethood (*nubuwwah 'āmmah*) – or what al-Jīlī calls 'the prophethood of proximity, informing, and being connected to the divine' – which involves receiving and propagating the esoteric truth but not a new scripture or religious law, continues among the *awliyā'* or Perfect Humans.[59] Al-Jīlī refers to this idea here, indicating that the category (*ḥukm*) relevant to the discussion of the sealing of prophecy is that of *nubuwwat al-tashrī'*, in this way leaving open the possibility that a non-legislative prophet might come after Muhammad. Such would be the status of the post-Muhammadan Friends of God or 'Perfect Ones'. In this sense, al-Jīlī's position, like Ibn 'Arabī's, does differ somewhat from the Qur'an-centred view, which stresses the absolute finality of Muhammad's prophethood. At the same time, however, al-Jīlī also makes clear that the post-Muhammadan 'prophet' is not so much a prophet in his own right as he is a 'follower' (*tābi'*) of Muhammad. This term seems to be meant to imply not chronological succession, but succession in terms of being a representative (*nā'ib*) or viceregent (*khalīfah*) of Muhammad, terms which, as we have seen, al-Jīlī uses in chapter sixty to denote how the 'Perfect Ones' are embodiments of the Muhammadan Reality.[60] From this perspective, Muhammad remains the final prophet in al-Jīlī's conception, for the later 'prophets' are only prophets by virtue of their being loci in which Muhammad becomes manifest. While, from a non-Ibn 'Arabian perspective, the orthodoxy of this idea might be suspect – and Ibn 'Arabī's ideas about *walāyah* were indeed one of the major sources of his noted opponent Ibn Taymiyyah's criticisms of his Sufi metaphysics[61] – its appearance here does not take away from the fact that, in al-Jīlī's view, the Qur'an is the best of scriptures and Muhammad the best of messengers. It is this idea, as this section demonstrates, that governs his view of the Torah, for if the Qur'an is the most perfect scripture, the Torah must necessarily be imperfect.

Jesus' abrogation of Moses' religion and the errors of Jesus' people

So if Moses – Peace be upon him – had been commanded to propagate the two tablets that were particular to him, He would not have sent Jesus after him, because Jesus propagated the mystery (*sirr*) of those two tablets to his people. For this reason, from his first step, Jesus revealed the [divine] power (*al-qudrah*) and lordship (*al-rubūbiyyah*), namely [through] his speech in the cradle. And he cured the blind man, and brought the dead to life. And he abrogated (*nasakha*) the religion of Moses, because he brought what Moses had not brought. But when he revealed the effects of that, his people fell into error (*ḍalla*) after him, and they worshipped him (*'abadūhu*), and said, 'He is the third of three (*thālith thalāthah*),' (Q 5:73), and 'He is the Father, the Mother and the Son.' They called these the three hypostases (*al-aqānīm al-thalāthah*), and his people split into sects (*iftaraqū*) over that. Some of them say that he is the Son of God (*ibn Allāh*), and they are called the Melkites (*al-mulkāniyyah*) among his people. And others say that he is God (*Allāh*) who has come down (*nazala*) and taken the son of Adam, and returned, meaning that he took on the form of Adam (*taṣawwara bi-ṣūrat Ādam*), then returned to his exalted nature (*ta'ālīhi*). And they are called the Jacobites (*al-ya'āqibah*) among Jesus' people. And others say that God, in Himself, is an expression of three – a Father, who is the Holy Spirit (*al-rūḥ al-quds*), a Mother, who is Mary, and a Son, who is Jesus – Peace be upon him.

But Jesus purified himself (*nazzaha . . . nafsahu*) of that which his people believed. For they believed in God's unqualified comparability (*muṭlaq al-tashbīh*), without acknowledging God's incomparability (*al-tanzīh*), which is not worthy of God.

And the knowledge that Jesus brought was an addition (*ziyādah*) to what was in the Torah, namely the mystery of lordship and power. He revealed this, and for this reason his people became unbelievers (*kafara*), because 'the disclosure (*ifshā'*) of the mystery of lordship is unbelief (*kufr*)'. If Jesus had concealed (*satara*) this knowledge, and propagated it to his people in coverings (*qushūr*), expressions (*'ibārāt*) and lines of allusions (*suṭūr ishārāt*), as our prophet did, his people would not have fallen into error (*ḍallū*) after him. What was needed for the subsequent perfection of religion (*kamāl al-dīn*) was the knowledge of divinity and the essence that the Prophet brought in the Furqan and Qur'an, which we have already discussed in relation to the essence and attributes. And God synthesized (*jama'a*) that in a single verse, which was, 'There is nothing like Him; He is the All-Hearing, the All-Seeing', (Q 42:11) where 'There is nothing like Him' is connected to the essence, and 'He is the All-Hearing, the All-Seeing' is connected to the attributes.[62]

Having indicated the deficiency of the Torah vis-à-vis the Qur'an – and therefore of Judaism and the Jewish people vis-à-vis Islam and the Muslims – al-Jīlī here sets out the deficiency of the message of Moses relative to that of *Jesus*. This time, it is the relationship between the Torah and the Gospel that is defined by abrogation (*naskh*) (in this instance, of the former by the latter), an idea that is ultimately of Late Antique Christian origin.[63] In Islamic thought, according to Yohanan Friedmann, 'There is some divergence of opinion whether it was Islam that abrogated both Judaism and Christianity, or first Christianity abrogated Judaism and then Islam abrogated Christianity.'[64] The spirit of the latter view, which al-Jīlī puts forward here and which is supported by Sunni authorities like al-Qurṭubī,[65] is embodied in Qur'an 5.82, which describes the Jews and the polytheists as 'the most inimical of people (*ashadd al-nās ʿadāwatan*) towards those who believe', and the Christians as 'the nearest of them in love (*aqrabahum mawaddatan*) for those who believe'.

Al-Jīlī's basis for proposing that Jesus' religion abrogated that of Moses is not this Qur'anic verse, however, but rather the Qur'anic motifs of Jesus' miracle working, specifically, his speaking in the cradle (see Q 3.46, 5.110, 19.29), and his healing the blind and the leper and reviving the dead (see Q 3.49). These motifs, which are ultimately rooted in the canonical and apocryphal Gospels,[66] form a key part of presentations of Jesus in the Islamic tales of the prophets and other post-Qur'anic literature,[67] including Ibn ʿArabī's chapter on Jesus in the *Fuṣūṣ*.[68] Significantly for our purposes, they also appear in several places in *al-Insān al-kāmil* as examples of the miraculous, God-like powers of the Perfect Human.[69] More specifically, al-Jīlī indicates here that these miracles of Jesus constitute his manifestation of the divine attributes of power (*qudrah*) and lordship (*al-rubūbiyyah*). The rationale behind this is that, if *qudrah*, as indicated in Chapter 1, constitutes, for al-Jīlī, God's power to bring things from non-existence into existence, and *rubūbiyyah* denotes both God's power over creation and the link between God and creation, then Jesus' miracle working can be viewed as a manifestation of that divine power and of that connection between God and creation. As Sahl Tustarī puts it in his Sufi Qur'an commentary, then, 'Whoever denies the signs (*ayāt*) [i.e. miracles (*karāmāt*)] of God's Friends denies the power (*qudrah*) of God, because it is God's power that makes His signs appear through His Friends, not they who make them appear themselves.'[70]

The significance of this idea here is that *al-qudrah* and *al-rubūbiyyah*, as we saw previously, are the names of the two tablets of the 'revealed Torah' that Moses was commanded not to propagate to his people. By revealing these two divine attributes *through his miracles*, then, Jesus effectively propagated the two 'missing' tablets of the revealed Torah and the mysteries that God commanded Moses to conceal from his people; hence, al-Jīlī tells us here that Jesus brought an 'addition' (*ziyādah*) to the Torah. Jesus' revelation, therefore, is more complete than Moses', and therefore abrogates it, prior to its own abrogation by the revelation of Muhammad.

This being said, as al-Jīlī sees it, just because a particular revelation is more complete than another it does not necessarily follow that the people to whom it is propagated will get closer to the truth. We saw previously the idea that, if Moses had propagated the complete revealed Torah to his people, then not a single person would have believed him, indicating that the completeness of a revelation can potentially lead people *away* from the truth, if they do not possess the requisite spiritual or cognitive capacity to bear its contents. This, in fact, is how al-Jīlī views the situation of the Christians, who, he indicates here, were led into error (*ḍalāl*) and unbelief (*kufr*) on account of their inability to comprehend the mysteries of divine power and lordship that Jesus revealed to them. Such error and unbelief consist specifically in the Christians' false doctrines of the Trinity and Incarnation. Since al-Jīlī puts forward a detailed critique of these doctrines in his chapter on the Gospel, which we will look at in Chapter 6, we shall not linger on this point here, nor look at his treatment in this chapter of the Qur'anic narrative of God's interrogation of Jesus (see Q 5.116-119), which he also repeats in the chapter on the Gospel. For now, let us briefly consider what his discussion of the doctrines of the Trinity and Incarnation here reveal about his knowledge of Christianity and his overall view of sacred history.

Al-Jīlī displays some limited knowledge of Christian doctrine and terminology here. There is much truth to his claim that the source of the Christian schisms can be found in different interpretations of the Trinity and the Incarnation. It was disagreements over Christology and the Trinity that led, for instance, to the first seven Ecumenical Councils and their rejection of various Christological 'heresies'.[71] In his use of the technical term *aqānīm* to denote the hypostases or persons of the Trinity, meanwhile, al-Jīlī displays some knowledge of Arabic Christian theological vocabulary,[72] a knowledge that was fairly typical of medieval Muslim thinkers who wrote on Christianity.[73] Likewise, al-Jīlī's discussion of the Christological doctrines of the three Christian denominations mentioned here – the Melkites, Jacobites and an unnamed group – indicates that he had some awareness of internal Christian theological debates and sectarian divisions – again, as was typical of educated medieval Muslim thinkers.

This being said, his discussion also features several misunderstandings of the precise nature of these divisions and fails to capture the essential differences between the denominations. Thus, he defines the Melkite position as the belief that Jesus was the Son of God (*ibn Allāh*), yet this term is used by all of the major Christian denominations, whatever the differences of interpretation between them. Furthermore, this definition does not reflect any awareness on al-Jīlī's part of the Melkites' adherence to Chalcedonian orthodoxy, that is, the Dyophysite doctrine of Christ 'as one person in two perfect natures, divine and human'.[74] Likewise, his definition of the Jacobite position does not really capture the fact of their adherence to the anti-Chalcedonian, Miaphysite or Monophysite doctrine of 'one nature of God the Word incarnate' adopted by Jacob Baradeus (d. 578 CE) and his followers.[75] Rather, al-Jīlī's statement that, according to the Jacobites, God 'took on the form of Adam' (*taṣawwara bi-ṣūrat Ādam*) echoes his own Sufi metaphysical conception of the ability of the Muhammadan Reality 'to take on every form' (*taṣawwur bi-kull ṣūrah*).[76] Similarly, his definition of the Trinitarian doctrine of the unnamed group, whom we might expect to be the Nestorians, given that the three Christian denominations most often identified by medieval Muslim authors are the Nestorians, the Jacobites and the Melkites,[77] bears little relation to the characteristic Nestorian emphasis on the distinction between Christ's divine and human natures.[78] Rather, al-Jīlī's notion that this group professes a Trinity of the Holy Spirit, Mary and Jesus is probably drawn from the Qur'anic presentation of Christian doctrine (and the medieval Muslim exegetes' interpretation of that Qur'anic presentation), as I shall argue in Chapter 6. While al-Jīlī's discussion of the different Christological and Trinitarian doctrines of the different Christian denominations therefore reflects a degree of interest in and awareness of Christianity as a living and internally diverse theological tradition, nevertheless it also displays the limitations of his knowledge of that tradition. Indeed, it seems likely that everything he says here is based upon the common knowledge available to him as an educated medieval Muslim, rather than a direct engagement with Christian texts or individuals, or indeed with Islamic anti-Christian polemical texts, which tend to be more informed about the Christologies of the different Christian denominations present in the Islamic world.[79]

More significant, for our purposes, than the question of how much al-Jīlī knew about actual Christian doctrine is the question of how his understanding of Christian doctrine affected his understanding of sacred history. The passage under discussion indicates that he views the doctrines of the Trinity and Incarnation, in all of their various interpretations, as signs of error (*ḍalāl*) and, even more seriously, unbelief (*kufr*). This is the conventional Islamic view, grounded in the Qur'an, which states that those who say that God is Jesus, son of Mary and that God is 'the third of three' – generally taken to mean those who believe in the Incarnation and the Trinity – are unbelievers (*kafara*) (see Q 5.17, 5.73).[80] As we shall see in detail in Chapter 6, however, al-Jīlī's understanding of the Christians' error and unbelief is somewhat different to the conventional medieval Muslim view. In his view, the Christians' major mistakes consisted in their *confinement* of the (unlimitable) divine manifestation to Jesus alone, and their failure to balance their declaration of God's comparability to creation (specifically, to Jesus) (*tashbīh*) with a recognition of God's incomparability (*tanzīh*). These mistakes, he indicates here, were the consequence of Jesus' revealing openly the mysteries of lordship and divine power. According to a popular Sufi saying that al-Jīlī cites here, 'The disclosure of the mystery of lordship is an act of unbelief (*kufr*).'[81] There is perhaps an implicit criticism of Jesus here, for it was his miracle working, according to al-Jīlī, that led the Christians to identify with him with God, and therefore to fall into the error of unqualified *tashbīh*. Such an idea, in fact, is an echo of Ibn 'Arabī's position in the *Fuṣūṣ*, where, in the chapter on Jesus, he appears to indicate that it was Jesus' miraculous raising of the dead that led the Christians to view him mistakenly as God.[82] Nevertheless, al-Jīlī, mindful of the sinlessness and perfection of the prophets, is also careful to declare that Jesus 'purified himself' of the false Christian doctrine and, in a passage not included in our translation and which is echoed in the chapter on the Gospel, that the Christians 'erred on account of their understanding (*mafhūm*), and their understanding was not [Jesus'] intention (*murād*).'[83]

The synthesis of *tanzīh* and *tashbīh* – that is, the need to balance a recognition of God's incomparability to creation with a recognition of His comparability to or immanence within creation – is a key Ibn 'Arabian idea, and one that al-Jīlī advocates in several places in *al-Insān al-kāmil* and elsewhere.[84] When it is applied to sacred history, as here, the following narrative emerges. First, the Jews emphasized *tanzīh* at the expense of *tashbīh*, because the propagated Torah was missing the two tablets that revealed the *tashbīhī* aspect of God's relationship with creation, that is, the tablet of divine power (which contained the mystery of the manifestation of the divine power within the miracle-working Perfect Humans) and the tablet of lordship (which contained the mystery of God and creation's mutual need for one another). This deficiency of the Torah necessitated the revelation of the Gospel to Jesus, who was tasked with revealing the truth of *tashbīh* through his miracles, and who in this way abrogated the revelation of Moses. Nevertheless, because Jesus revealed the truth of *tashbīh* openly, his people, who did not possess the requisite understanding or spiritual preparedness to comprehend this truth, were led astray, adopting the other extreme to that of the Jews, namely unqualified *tashbīh*. This in turn necessitated the revelation of the Qur'an to Muhammad, to restore the balance of *tashbīh* and *tanzīh* and thereby abrogate the (now falsified) religion of Jesus.

This restoration of the balance between *tashbīh* and *tanzīh* has been achieved, al-Jīlī indicates here, thanks to the way in which the Qur'an addresses its listeners, specifically, through its allusive language, such that it can only be fully understood by those who are able to comprehend the truths of both *tashbīh* and *tanzīh*. This is a point that will be developed in the following section. Moreover, the Qur'an leads its audience to profess the synthesis of *tashbīh* and *tanzīh* because, as we saw in the previous chapter, it represents both the incomparable divine essence (*al-dhāt*) (as *al-Qur'ān*, *al-Qur'ān al-karīm* and *al-Qur'ān al-'aẓīm*) and the comparable divine names and attributes (as *al-Furqān*, *al-Qur'ān al-ḥakīm* and *al-sab' al-mathānī*) – here denoted by the term *al-ulūhiyyah*, the level of existence that contains all of the names and attributes.[85] Finally, al-Jīlī states that the Qur'an's synthesis of *tashbīh* and *tanzīh* is also indicated by verse 42.11 of the Qur'an: 'There is nothing like Him, and He is the All-Hearing, the All-Seeing.' This verse is often used by Ibn 'Arabī for the same purpose, the first half of the verse denoting, in his reading, the incomparability of God (*tanzīh*) with respect to His essence, and the second half, which mentions two of God's names, denoting His comparability (*tashbīh*), which pertains to His attributes.[86] Al-Jīlī, who was certainly familiar with this Ibn 'Arabian interpretation,[87] has the same idea in mind here.

All of this resonates with the conventional Islamic notion that Islam constitutes a middle path between the excesses of Judaism and Christianity, an idea that is often grounded in Qur'an 2.143, which sets up the Muslim community as a 'middle community' (*ummatan wasaṭan*) between the extremes of the earlier two communities.[88] The only difference here is that al-Jīlī expresses this notion of 'middle-ness' or moderation (*wasaṭiyyah*) in Sufi metaphysical terms. Indeed, this moderation can also be framed in terms of his key Sufi metaphysical concept of comprehensiveness. Unlike the revelations of Moses and Jesus, in other words, the revelation of Muhammad advocates the comprehensive synthesis of *tanzīh* and *tashbīh*, the position that Ibn 'Arabian Sufis know to be true. Indeed, this is an elaboration of Ibn 'Arabī's own position, for, as Izutsu has put it, 'according to Ibn 'Arabī, the ideal combination of *tanzīh* and *tashbīh* was achieved only in Islam'.[89] It is in this light that al-Jīlī can write here of the 'perfection of [Muhammad's] religion' (*kamāl al-dīn*), in contrast to the implied 'imperfection' of the earlier religions. It is this principle, as we have already seen and will continue to see in this book, which underlies al-Jīlī's view of sacred history and governs his view of the superiority of the Qur'an over the other scriptures, Muhammad over the other prophets and Islam over the other religions.

Moses' and Muhammad's concealment of the mystery of lordship

If Moses had propagated what Jesus had propagated to his people, his people would have accused him (*yattahimūnahu*) of [unjustly] killing (*qatl*) Pharaoh. For he [i.e. Pharaoh] had said, 'I am your lord the most exalted', (Q 79:24) and the disclosure of the mystery of lordship gives nothing but what Pharaoh claimed. But Pharaoh did not possess that by way of realization (*bi-ṭarīq al-taḥqīq*), so Moses fought him (*qātalahu*) and was victorious over him. So if Moses had revealed anything of the knowledge of lordship in the Torah, his people would have become unbelievers (*kafara*) and accused him for fighting (*muqātalat*) Pharaoh.

So God commanded him to conceal (*katm*) that, just as He commanded our Prophet Muhammad – May God bless him and grant him peace – to conceal (*katm*) things that others could not comprehend, according to the hadith transmitted from him, in which he said: 'On the night that I was made to travel by night (*usriya bī*) I was given three forms of knowledge (*'ulūm*): a form of knowledge that I was obliged to conceal (*katm*), a form of knowledge that I chose to propagate (*tablīgh*), and a form of knowledge that I was commanded to propagate.' The form of knowledge that he was commanded to propagate was the knowledge of the religious laws (*'ilm al-sharā'i'*), and the form of knowledge that he chose to propagate was the knowledge of the realities (*'ilm al-ḥaqā'iq*), and the knowledge that he was obliged to conceal was [that of] the divine mysteries (*al-asrār al-ilāhiyyah*). God has deposited (*awda'a*) all of that in the Qur'an. That which he was commanded to propagate is apparent (*ẓāhir*), and that which he chose to propagate is hidden (*bāṭin*), for he says, 'We shall show them Our signs on the horizons and in their selves, until it is clear to them that it is the truth/the Real (*al-ḥaqq*)', (Q 41:53) and 'We only created the heavens and the earth and what is between them for the truth/the Real (*al-ḥaqq*)', (Q 46:3) and 'He has subjugated for you all that is in the heavens and on earth, from Himself', (Q 45:13) and 'I breathed into him of My spirit' (Q 15:29, 38:72). In all of this there is an aspect that points to the realities (*al-ḥaqā'iq*), and an aspect that points to the religious laws (*al-sharā'i'*). It is as if it were wrapped up like a coil (*al-taḥayyuz*), for whoever's understanding was divine (*ilāhiyyan*), had that propagated to him, and whoever's understanding was not at that level and who was among those who, if they had been surprised by the realities, would have denied them (*ankarahā*), did not have that propagated to him, lest it would lead to his falling into error (*ḍalālatihi*) and misery (*shaqāwatihi*).

And the form of knowledge that he was obliged to conceal was deposited (*muwda'*) in the Qur'an, needing esoteric interpretation (*ta'wīl*) due to the obscurity of the concealment (*li-ghumūḍ katmihi*). This [form of knowledge] is only known by the one who has first been elevated to (*ashrafa 'alá*) the same form of knowledge, by way of divine unveiling (*al-kashf al-ilāhī*), then hears (*sama'a*) the Qur'an after that, for he knows the place where God deposited some of the knowledge that the Prophet – May God bless him and grant him peace – was obliged to conceal. And there is an allusion to this when He says, 'Only God knows

> its esoteric interpretation (*ta'wīlahu*)' (Q 3:7). According to the reading of those who stop here, the one who understands its esoteric interpretation in himself is the one called God, so understand![90]

While Jesus, as we saw in the previous section, disclosed the mystery of lordship to his people, causing them to fall into error, al-Jīlī here emphasizes that both Moses and Muhammad concealed that mystery. He uses the same key term, *katm*, for the actions of both prophets. This term, which is an antonym of the term used earlier for Jesus' disclosure of the mystery (*ifshā'*), is from the same root as *kitmān*, an important term in the various branches of Shi'i Islamic thought, in particular, where it is used as a near synonym for *taqiyyah*, the principle of dissimulation in the profession of one's beliefs for the sake of self-preservation and the protection of the mysteries from the uninitiated.[91] Both of these aspects of *katm*/*kitmān* are also found in Sufi thought;[92] indeed, Ibn Taymiyyah goes so far as to define Sufism as 'the concealment of meanings/ideas' (*kitmān al-ma'ānī*).[93] Both are of relevance here. Moses' *katm* of the mystery of lordship, al-Jīlī indicates, was motivated by the fact that, if he had revealed that mystery, his people would have criticized him for fighting and unjustly killing Pharaoh, the idea being that, if they had known that the Lord becomes manifest in man, they would then have accepted Pharaoh's claim to be Lord (*rabb*), and hence would have condemned Moses for his opposition to him. While this apparently blasphemous Pharaonic claim to lordship notoriously *does* have a certain truth to it from an Ibn 'Arabian perspective, in the sense that, in accordance with the idea of universal theophany, all individuals are loci for the divine manifestation,[94] nevertheless properly speaking (as Ibn 'Arabī himself indicates) it is untrue, for Pharaoh did not attain 'realization' (*taḥqīq*) of the mystery of lordship himself.[95] In other words, Pharaoh was not a complete locus for the manifestation of the divine lordship, for he was not a true 'realizer' (*muḥaqqiq*) – the station of *taḥqīq*, in al-Jīlī's view, being the preserve of the Perfect Humans.[96] Pharaoh's claim to lordship, therefore, *was* a blasphemous claim, in the way that the claim of a true Perfect Human would not have been. In concealing the mystery of lordship, therefore, Moses both protected himself from the accusations of his people and protected his people from falling into what would be, even from an Ibn 'Arabian perspective, a blasphemous error. Similar motivations, as we shall see presently, are at work in Muhammad's propagation and concealment of aspects of the Qur'an.

While both Moses and Muhammad conceal the divine mysteries, however, the nature of their *katm* is different. As we have seen, according to al-Jīlī Moses was given nine tablets of the Torah, and ordered to propagate seven and conceal two of them, meaning that the propagated Torah was incomplete. Muhammad's propagation and concealment of the knowledge contained in the Qur'an, al-Jīlī explains here, works in a different way. Based on a hadith about Muhammad's night journey (*al-isrā'*) that appears not to be canonical, al-Jīlī identifies three levels of knowledge (*'ilm*) contained in the Qur'an. At the most exoteric, apparent (*ẓāhir*) level, the Qur'an contains knowledge pertaining to religious laws (*'ilm al-sharā'i'*), which Muhammad was commanded to propagate, presumably because such laws are universal, which is to say that they apply to all of mankind. At the esoteric, hidden (*bāṭin*) level, the Qur'an contains knowledge pertaining to what al-Jīlī calls 'the realities' (*'ilm al-ḥaqā'iq*), which

Muhammad chose to propagate. While this is a polysemic term, al-Jīlī generally uses the term *ḥaqā'iq* to denote the true nature of things, and more specifically the true nature of the higher levels of existence and the divine names and attributes; hence, *'ilm al-ḥaqā'iq* can be understood to mean genuine Sufi metaphysical knowledge.[97] In keeping with the dominant Sufi view that the Qur'an contains both an exoteric and esoteric level of meaning,[98] al-Jīlī in this way identifies *ẓāhir* and *bāṭin* aspects of the Qur'an. The Qur'anic verses quoted here (Q 41.53, 46.3, 45.13 and 15.29/38.72) exemplify these two levels of meaning. At the exoteric level, they denote God's power and majesty over His creation (Q 41.53, 46.3), and His granting of life and favour to man (Q 45.13, 15.29/38.72),[99] truths that underpin the universal religious laws. At the esoteric level, they appear to denote the fundamental Sufi metaphysical truths of universal theophany and the Perfect Human, as al-Jīlī indicates in his interpretations of some of these verses elsewhere in the book (including, as we shall see, in his chapter on the Gospel).[100] These are interpretations that he shares with other Sufi authors, including Ibn 'Arabī.[101]

While the *ẓāhir* meaning is universal, this *bāṭin* meaning, as al-Jīlī sees it, is accessible only to certain spiritually and cognitively advanced individuals, for it is 'wrapped up like a coil'. The rationale behind this 'wrapping up' (*taḥayyuz*) of the inner meaning of the Qur'an, he indicates, is similar to the rationale behind Moses' concealment of the two tablets, namely, self-preservation and the protection of the uninitiated. Thus al-Jīlī explains that the *ḥaqā'iq* are hidden in the Qur'an to prevent those who do not possess sufficient 'understanding' (*fahm*) – or, in Ibn 'Arabian terms, lack the required 'preparedness' (*isti'dād*) – from explicitly denying or stating their disapproval (*inkār*) of those metaphysical truths. One aim of hiding some truths in the Qur'an, then, is to preserve the Qur'an and Muhammad – and those who understand its inner truths – from slander. The other aim, al-Jīlī states explicitly here, is to protect those who do *not* understand those truths from falling into 'error' (*ḍalālah*) and 'misery' (*shaqāwah*). These terms, which are both Qur'anic, carry soteriological significance: *shaqāwah*, in al-Jīlī's Qur'an-centred usage, is usually the state of those condemned to hell, as opposed to *sa'ādah*, the state of those in paradise,[102] while *ḍalāl* can generally denote 'a state of perdition', that is, the erroneous path that leads to the 'misery' of damnation.[103] The function of these key terms here seems to be to establish an implicit contrast between the Muslims and the Christians. While Muhammad hides certain metaphysical truths to protect his people from the error that leads to the hellfire and the misery experienced by its inhabitants, so al-Jīlī's argument goes, Jesus reveals them openly, thereby exposing his people to such a terrible fate. In other words, the Muslims are spared the punishment of hell, on account of the way in which the metaphysical truths are hidden in the Qur'an, while the Christians enjoy no such protection. As we shall see, this hierarchy of soteriological outcomes – salvation for the Muslims, punishment for others – is repeated and further expanded upon in the final chapter of *al-Insān al-kāmil*, though, as we shall also see, the sense that non-Muslims are punished is also somewhat mitigated, both in that final chapter and in the chapter on the Gospel, by the Ibn 'Arabian idea of universal mercy. The apparent exclusivism of his soteriology in the passage under discussion, however, further reinforces our sense of his belief in the superiority of Islam.

To return to the topic of Muhammad's concealment of the divine mysteries, we find that in al-Jīlī's scheme Muhammad was also given a third type of knowledge, which lies on a plane even deeper than the *bāṭin* level, namely that of the 'divine mysteries' (*al-asrār al-ilāhiyyyah*). Significantly, al-Jīlī tells us that these mysteries *are* deposited (*muwdaʿ*) in the Qur'an, only in an 'obscure' way (*ghumūḍ*), such that they can only be drawn out of the Qur'an via esoteric or figurative interpretation (*ta'wīl*). In contrast to the mysteries revealed to Moses, therefore, those revealed to Muhammad are in fact contained in the scripture that he propagated to his people. This means that, unlike the case with the propagated Torah, Muhammad's concealment of the mysteries revealed to him does *not* take away from the completeness of the Qur'an, which, as we know, is a key notion within al-Jīlī's conception of the Qur'an. Thus while none of Moses' people, as al-Jīlī stated previously, are able to attain perfection, on account of the incompleteness of their scripture, the same does not apply to Muhammad's people, who are able to know the divine mysteries from the Qur'an, provided that they are capable of undertaking *ta'wīl*. Muslims, it therefore appears, are capable of becoming Perfect Humans, whereas Jews are not. As for the Christians, they were exposed to the mysteries, yet they were *too* exposed, and, what is more, they were incapable of *ta'wīl*; hence, like the Jews, they too cannot become Perfect Humans, and are, moreover, apparently condemned to the misery of damnation.

Al-Jīlī's notion that certain Muslims are able to uncover the divine mysteries deposited in the Qur'an via *ta'wīl* poses the question of what he means exactly by the term *ta'wīl*, and who is able to undertake it. *Ta'wīl* is a Qur'anic term; in the scriptural context, it most often denotes 'explanation or interpretation of a dream or an event' (see e.g. Q 12.6, 12.21, 12.36, 12.37).[104] It was generally used in the first Islamic centuries, and sometimes in the medieval period, as a synonym for *tafsīr*, that is, a commentary on or interpretation of the Qur'an, yet it also acquired another technical meaning in Shīʿī, Sufi and philosophical thought, namely, the uncovering of the inner, hidden (*bāṭin*) meaning of the Qur'an.[105] Judging by what al-Jīlī says here, for him *ta'wīl* denotes the uncovering of a level of meaning even deeper than the *bāṭin* level, namely that of what he calls the 'divine mysteries' (*al-asrār al-ilāhiyyah*).

As al-Jīlī sees it, the uncovering of these mysteries in the Qur'an can only be undertaken by those who have *already* attained access to those divine mysteries via what he calls 'divine unveiling' (*al-kashf al-ilāhī*), a term generally used by al-Jīlī and other Ibn ʿArabian Sufis to denote the divinely given and quasi-prophetic experiential knowledge attained by those, such as himself, who have reached the summit of the Sufi path.[106] This suggests, on the one hand, that the esoteric interpretation of the Qur'an is merely a confirmatory process for the spiritually advanced individual, rather than the initial source of that individual's knowledge of the divine mysteries. On the other hand, it also indicates that the knowledge attained via *kashf* is in perfect harmony with the Qur'an, a point that al-Jīlī explicitly makes earlier in the book, and which reinforces our sense of the Qur'an-centredness of al-Jīlī's Ibn ʿArabian Sufism.[107] Al-Jīlī's position, it might be said, represents the Sufi counterpart to the position of the Aristotelian philosophers, most famously advocated by Ibn Rushd (d. 595/1198),[108] that the inner meaning of scripture accords with the truths arrived at via demonstrative reasoning (*burhān*) – the difference being that, from al-Jīlī's Ibn ʿArabian standpoint, the secret meaning of scripture accords with the truths arrived at via mystical experience (*kashf*), not rational thought. Just as, for Ibn Rushd, the discovery of the inner meaning of scripture is the preserve of the philosophers, for al-Jīlī, similarly, access to the divine mysteries is the preserve of spiritually advanced Sufis. Indeed, undertaking his own *ta'wīl* of Qur'an 3.7, which states that only God knows the *ta'wīl* of the Qur'an, al-Jīlī declares that *ta'wīl* can only be undertaken by 'the one called God' (*al-musammá bi-Allāh*), by which he seems to mean those individuals who are loci of manifestation for the name *Allāh* and all the other divine names that come under that name. If this is the correct interpretation of al-Jīlī's use of the verse, then this would mean that only the Perfect Humans, who are the loci of manifestation for all of God's names, can properly undertake *ta'wīl* and access the deepest layer of knowledge contained in the Qur'an.

It is possible to identify certain precursors and parallels in earlier Sufi literature for al-Jīlī's conception of the levels of knowledge contained in the Qur'an. Most notably, there is the widespread tradition that the Qur'an contains four levels of meaning – usually, the apparent (*ẓāhir*), hidden (*bāṭin*), normative (*ḥadd*) and anagogical (*maṭla'/muṭṭala'*). This tradition, which is variously attributed to the Shi'i Imams 'Alī (d. 40/661) and Ja'far al-Ṣādiq (d. 148/765), the famous early exegete Ibn 'Abbās, or the Prophet himself, is found in the most important early works of Sufi *tafsīr*, including the commentaries of Sahl Tustarī and al-Sulamī (d. 412/1021),[109] in classical Sufi manuals like 'Umar al-Suhrawardī's (d. 632/1234) *'Awārif al-ma'ārif*,[110] and is cited by Ibn 'Arabī in the *Futūḥāt*,[111] and so would have been known to al-Jīlī. As we have seen, however, al-Jīlī identifies three, not four, levels, and here too we can find precedents in earlier Sufi literature: Hujwīrī (d. 465/1072), for instance, cites a tradition according to which there are three kinds of knowledge: knowledge *of* God, which is the knowledge possessed by the prophets; knowledge *from* God, which is the knowledge given by the religious law; and knowledge *with* God, which is the Sufi 'science of stations and the path and the degrees of the Friends of God.'[112] One could map this on to al-Jīlī's scheme, where 'knowledge from God' denotes the 'knowledge of the religious laws' (*'ilm al-sharā'i'*), 'knowledge with God' denotes the 'knowledge of the realities' (*'ilm al-ḥaqā'iq*) and 'knowledge of God' denotes the knowledge of the 'divine mysteries' (*al-asrār al-ilāhiyyah*).

A more direct influence, however, might be Ibn 'Arabī's scheme of the levels of knowledge set out in the introduction to the *Futūḥāt*. Like al-Jīlī, Ibn 'Arabī identifies three levels of knowledge, namely 'theoretical, intellectual knowledge' (*al-'ilm al-'aqlī al-naẓarī*), which is based upon a fallible type of discursive thought (*fikr*); 'knowledge of states' (*'ilm al-aḥwāl*), which is based upon direct sense perception; and 'knowledge of the mysteries (*'ilm al-asrār*), which is above the level of the intellect (*fawq ṭawr al-'aql*) and . . . is particular to the prophet and Friend of God'.[113] While Ibn 'Arabī does not explicitly connect these three levels of knowledge to the Qur'an, and while his 'intellectual knowledge' and 'knowledge of states' may not correspond exactly to al-Jīlī's 'knowledge of the religious laws' and 'knowledge of the realities', the fact that they both put forward a threefold scheme, with knowledge of the 'mysteries' at the deepest level, suggests that al-Jīlī may well have had in mind Ibn 'Arabī's scheme, with which he would have no doubt been familiar. As for his notion that only the Perfect Humans can undertake *ta'wīl* and so access the deepest mysteries of the Qur'an, al-Jīlī's interpretation of Qur'an 3.7 finds an earlier parallel in the interpretation of al-Qāshānī, who interprets the verse to mean, 'The knowers know through His [i.e. God's] knowledge (*al-'ālimūn ya'limūn bi-'ilmihi*)', implying, like al-Jīlī, that the perfect 'knowers' can undertake *ta'wīl* by virtue of their being loci for the divine manifestation.[114] More generally, it can be said that al-Jīlī's notion that there are different levels of knowledge – and therefore different levels of knowers – reflects the strongly hierarchical and elitist conception of knowledge and society that was widespread in pre-modern Islamic thought, not only among Sufis, but also among Muslim jurists, theologians and philosophers,[115] many of whom – including the aforementioned Ibn Rushd – also outlined threefold hierarchies of 'knowers'.[116] As in al-Jīlī's case, this elitism was usually connected to an esoteric approach to the (non-) disclosure of the highest forms of knowledge.[117]

Leaving aside parallels and possible sources of influence, what is most important for our purposes is that al-Jīlī's hierarchical and esoteric conception of knowledge pertains not only to the distinctions between *Muslims* – in terms of their ability to interpret the Qur'an and to access its different levels of meaning – but also to the distinctions between the *scriptures* – in terms of the levels of knowledge that they contain – and the different religious communities – in terms of their ability to access and correctly interpret the knowledge contained in their respective scriptures. Unlike the Torah, the Qur'an that Muhammad propagated to his people contains the divine mysteries. And while the Gospel *does* contain certain divine mysteries, the Christians are unable to comprehend those mysteries, and so fall into error and unbelief. By contrast, the divine mysteries in the Qur'an are concealed in such a way that those Muslims who cannot comprehend them do not realize that they are there, and so do not fall into error and unbelief, while those Muslims who *do* possess the requisite spiritual capacity – that is, the advanced Sufis and/or Perfect Humans – are able to identify them within and read them out of the Qur'an, through *kashf*-based *ta'wīl*. In this way, al-Jīlī's ideas about *ta'wīl* and the levels of knowledge once again emphasize the superiority of the Qur'an and the Muslims over the other scriptures and religious communities.

The metaphysical meaning of the Torah

Know that the Torah is an expression of the manifestations of the attributive names (*al-asmā' al-ṣifātiyyah*), which is the appearance of the Real – Glory be to Him and may He be exalted – in the loci of the Real's manifestation (*al-maẓāhir al-ḥaqqiyyah*), for the Real – May He be exalted – set up the names as guides (*adillah*) to His attributes, and made His attributes a guide (*dalīl*) to His essence in His loci of manifestation and in His appearance within His creation through the names and attributes. Nothing else is possible, because creatures were fashioned (*fuṭirū*) in accordance with simplicity (*'alá al-sadhājah*), so creation is empty of all the divine meanings. Nevertheless it is like a white garment on which is printed that which it receives (*mā yuqābiluhu*). So it is called the Real, through these names, so that they [i.e. the names] would be guides to His attributes for people, and so that people would know through them the attributes of the Real.

> Then the people of the Real (*ahl al-ḥaqq*) were guided to Him, so they were like a mirror (*mir'āh*) to those names, and the names appeared within them, as did the attributes, and they witnessed (*shāhadū*) themselves in terms of the essential names (*al-asmā' al-dhātiyyah*) and the divine attributes that were imprinted on them. So when they call upon God – May He be exalted – they are the ones called upon by this name. And this is the meaning of Torah, for the linguistic meaning of Torahness (*al-tawriyyah*) / 'double entendre' (*al-tawriyah*) is 'carrying the meaning to the further of its two significations' (*ḥaml al-ma'ná alá ab'ad al-mafhūmayn*).[118]

As we saw in the previous chapter and will see in more detail in the forthcoming chapters, each of the scriptures, as al-Jīlī sees it, represents a metaphysical truth, specifically, a certain type of divine manifestation. The Torah, he tells us here, represents the manifestation of what he calls 'the attributive names' (*al-asmā' al-ṣifātiyyah*). As we know, central to al-Jīlī's Sufi metaphysics are the traditional theological categories of God's essence, attributes and names. In al-Jīlī's view, there is a hierarchy among these three elements of the Godhead.[119] He indicates in this passage that within this hierarchy, the lower elements point to the higher ones, or as he puts it here they are a 'guide' to or 'proof' of (*dalīl 'alá*) that aspect of God that lies above them in the hierarchy of the divine existence.[120] This notion helps us to understand that what al-Jīlī means by *al-asmā' al-ṣifātiyyah* are those divine names that 'guide' us to the divine attributes. The term might therefore be taken to mean all of the divine names, since all of God's names are an expression of a particular attribute (*Allāh* being an expression of *al-ulūhiyyah*, *al-raḥmān* of *raḥmah* or *al-raḥmāniyyah*, and so on); indeed, in the chapter on the Psalms, as we shall see in Chapter 5, al-Jīlī describes the Torah as 'an expression of the manifestations of the totality of the names of the attributes' (*tajalliyyāt jumlat asmā' al-ṣifāt*).[121] However, the term *al-asmā' al-ṣifātiyyah* also has a more technical sense, which seems to be relevant here, and which we can identify if we take into consideration what he means by the term 'the essential names' (*al-asmā' al-dhātiyyah*), which he also uses here. Elsewhere in *al-Insān al-kāmil* al-Jīlī indicates that the term 'the essential names and attributes' (*al-asmā' wa-al-ṣifāt al-dhātiyyah*) is used for those divine names and attributes, such as *Allāh*, *al-ḥaqq*, *al-aḥad*, *al-wāḥid* and so forth, which can only be attributed to the divine essence.[122] The essential names, in other words, are guides to the divine essence, or to those attributes that can only be used when speaking about the divine essence. Returning to the meaning of *al-asmā' al-ṣifātiyyah*, then, it can therefore be said that this term denotes those names that guide us to the *non-essential* attributes of God. In other words, it denotes all those names other than the names of the essence, and comes lower in the hierarchy than that latter category of names. In terms of the levels of existence, it represents the divine levels – here signified by the term *al-maẓāhir al-ḥaqqiyyah* – of *al-raḥmāniyyah* and below, that is, those levels *beneath* those that describe God's essence (*al-ulūhiyyah*, *al-aḥad*, *al-wāḥidiyyah*).

As we shall see in the following two chapters, this distinction between the attributive and the essential names is relevant for al-Jīlī's notion of a hierarchy of scriptures, for while the Torah, as he explains here, is an expression of the manifestations of *al-asmā' al-ṣifātiyyah*, the Gospel, as we shall see, is an expression of the manifestations of *al-asmāʾ al-dhātiyyah*. This means that the Gospel is a more complete expression of God's nature than the Torah, an idea that accords with what we have already seen in this chapter regarding the relative completeness of the two scriptures (since the Gospel contains those mysteries that Moses was ordered to keep out of the propagated Torah, and thereby abrogates it). The Qur'an, meanwhile, as an expression of the unqualified oneness of the essence, stands above both scriptures in the hierarchy. In this way, we can see how the hierarchy within the divine essence, names and attributes is mirrored in the hierarchy of scriptures, and therefore how al-Jīlī's Sufi metaphysical ideas (here, the idea of universal theophany and of the levels of existence) lead him to a position that is consistent with the Qur'an-centred view of sacred history.

Furthermore, in addition to telling us something about God's nature, al-Jīlī also indicates here that the Torah reveals the true nature of man. As already indicated, although man is primordially perfect, according to al-Jīlī, only the Perfect Humans realize this perfection in actuality.[123] He refers again to this idea here, only, instead of using the term *al-insān al-kāmil* or *al-kummal*, he refers to 'the people of the Real' (*ahl al-ḥaqq*). This term, along with the synonymous 'the people of God' (*ahl Allāh*), is used by Ibn 'Arabī 'to refer to the highest of God's friends', that is, the Perfect Humans.[124] Both Ibn 'Arabī and al-Jīlī derive the term from the *ḥadīth qudsī*: 'The people of the Qur'an are the people of God and His elect (*ahl al-Qur'ān ahl Allāh wa-khāṣṣatuhu*).'[125] According to al-Jīlī's interpretation of this hadith, which he puts forward in chapter 21 of *al-Insān al-kāmil*, the term *ahl Allāh* refers to 'His servants who are singled out for His essence' (*'ibādihi al-makhṣūṣīn bi-dhātihi*), that is, those individuals who are able to know, and receive the manifestation of, the divine essence (as well as the divine names and attributes).[126] As we saw in the previous chapter, the receipt of the manifestation of the essence is the privilege of the Perfect Human (specifically, Muhammad and those in whom the Muhammadan Reality becomes manifest); hence, we can say that the terms *ahl Allāh* and *ahl al-ḥaqq* are synonymous with *al-kummal*.

This being said, al-Jīlī here seems to be referring to a different class of Perfect Humans than in chapter 21. While there he discussed how the 'people of God' are loci for the manifestation of the divine essence, here he mentions only that they are loci for the manifestation of the divine *names and attributes*. They are, he says, 'mirrors' for the divine names;[127] they have the divine names and attributes 'imprinted' on them;[128] and they are 'called by' the divine names. While the Perfect Human's becoming a locus for the manifestation of the divine names and attributes is a central part of al-Jīlī's idea of the Perfect Human, nevertheless it is not the only part, for the archetypal Perfect Human, Muhammad, is also – as we saw in the previous chapter – a locus for the manifestation of the divine essence. As such, the 'Perfect Humans' who are guided to God by the Torah seem to be at a level below the utterly perfect level of Muhammad.

Here we hit again upon the difference in rank between the Qur'an, Muhammad and his people, on the one hand, and the Torah, Moses and his people, on the other. In the aforementioned chapter 21, al-Jīlī goes on to identify *ahl Allāh* with 'the Muhammadan people of the essence' (*al-dhātiyyīn al-Muḥammadiyyīn*). Such people, he explains, hear the recitation of the complete Qur'an, which, as we saw in the previous chapter, represents the divine essence, and are at 'the station of the Beloved' (*maqām al-ḥabīb*), that is, the station of Muhammad, the Beloved of God (*ḥabīb Allāh*). Below them in the hierarchy, he continues, are those he calls 'the Mosaic people of the self' (*al-nafsiyyūn al-mūsawiyyūn*). These people, he explains, hear only the recitation of the *Furqan*, which, as we saw in the introduction to this chapter, is one of the Qur'anic names of the Torah (see Q 2.53, 21.48), and which, as we saw in the previous chapter, also represents for al-Jīlī the differentiated aspect of the divine essence, that is, the essence that is qualified by names and attributes, also known as the level of *al-wāḥidiyyah*. This latter group are at 'the station of the One Spoken To' (*maqām al-kalīm*), that is, the station of Moses.[129] This clarifies the distinction implied in the passage under discussion: while the 'Muhammadan' Perfect Humans are loci of manifestation for the divine essence, the 'Mosaic' Perfect Humans are loci of manifestation for the divine names and attributes. This distinction, we might conclude, is a consequence of the different metaphysical significations of the Qur'an and the Torah, for while the former is an expression of the divine essence (as well as of the names and attributes), the latter is an expression of the divine attributes alone. So although the Torah does reveal the perfect nature of man, it does not reveal man's perfection to the same extent as the Qur'an does. Once again, therefore, al-Jīlī presents us with a subtle, Sufi metaphysical conception of the superiority of the Qur'an, Muhammad and his 'heirs' over the Torah, Moses and his heirs.

Al-Jīlī's insistence on the superiority of the Qur'an over the Torah should not, however, obscure the important point that, in his view, the Torah points us towards fundamental metaphysical truths. Al-Jīlī links this aspect of the Torah to the etymology of the term *al-Tawrāh*. This term, he notes, is etymologically and orthographically connected to the term *tawriyah*, the verbal noun of the second form of *w-r-y*.[130] This is a technical term in Arabic rhetoric that roughly corresponds to the concept of 'double entendre'.[131] For al-Jīlī, then, the very concept of 'Torahness' (*al-tawriyyah*), which is orthographically indistinguishable from *al-tawriyah*, signifies the presence of a twofold meaning, that is, both an outer, exoteric (*ẓāhir*) and an inner, esoteric (*bāṭin*) sense. In his understanding, as we saw in the previous section, the esoteric sense of scripture involves knowledge of 'the realities' (*al-ḥaqā'iq*), which can be taken to include the metaphysical truths of universal theophany and the Perfect Human. It would therefore seem that the Torah, since it signifies the existence of a hidden sense, contains these truths. While this type of etymological analysis is reminiscent of Ibn 'Arabī, whose propensity to explore the etymologies of key terms in order to come up with esoteric interpretations is well known,[132] precursors for al-Jīlī's interpretation can in fact be found in conventional *tafsīr*. Al-Qurṭubī, for instance, writes, 'It is said that *al-Tawrāh* is taken from *al-tawriyah*, which is the intimation of a thing and the concealment of something else (*al-ta'rīḍ bi-al-shay' wa-al-kitmān li-ghayrihi*); for most of the Torah was intimations (*ta'ārīḍ*) and indications (*talwīḥāt*), without clear statement or clarification.'[133] Nevertheless, al-Qurṭubī and the other major exegetes prefer another etymological interpretation of *al-Tawrāh*, connecting it to the verb *wará* (to kindle),[134] an interpretation that fits with the Qur'anic assertion that the Torah is guidance and light (see e.g. Q 5.44, 6.91). Furthermore, al-Jīlī's interpretation does appear to be original (as far as I am aware) insofar as he connects the etymology of *al-Tawrāh* to the notion that it contains hidden metaphysical truths. This notion reflects al-Jīlī's more general view that the Torah and the other scriptures recognized in the Qur'an-centred view of history genuinely point to the truth, albeit to lower levels of completeness than the Qur'an itself.

The contents of the tablets of the propagated Torah

Al-Jīlī concludes the chapter with a discussion of the contents of the seven tablets of the propagated Torah. For reasons of space and clarity, I have not translated this section in full, but have summarized what al-Jīlī says about the contents of each of the tablets into key bullet points, under which I have presented my analysis. Before we look at the contents of the seven tablets, it should be noted that, for al-Jīlī, the name of each of the tablets derives from the subject that 'dominates' (*ghalaba*) that particular tablet, meaning that other, secondary subjects are also included. He draws a direct comparison between this aspect of the Torah and the names of the *sūrahs* of the Qur'an, and in so doing indicates that the Torah and the Qur'an are analogous forms of revelation. This sense of analogy between Qur'an and Torah is reinforced, as we shall see, by his discussion of the contents of the tablets.

1) The tablet of light (*lawḥ al-nūr*)
   - An ascription of qualified oneness (*al-wāḥidiyyah*) and singularity (*al-ifrād*) to the Real, by way of an unqualified declaration of incomparability (*al-tanzīh al-muṭlaq*);
   - A declaration of what the Real possesses that distinguishes Him (*yatamayyaz*) from creation; a reference to the lordship (*rubūbiyyah*) and power (*qudrah*) of the Real, along with all of His most beautiful names and exalted attributes, all in terms of what the Real deserves due to His exaltedness (*ta'ālī*) and incomparability (*al-tanzīh*).[135]

Al-Jīlī's identification of the first tablet of the propagated Torah as the tablet of 'light' should be understood in the context of the repeated assertion in the Qur'an that the Torah is 'guidance and light'. While the classical Qur'anic exegetes tend to interpret the 'light' in this phrase as an indication of the Torah's 'clarification' of religious laws,[136] as al-Jīlī understands it, this 'light' represents God's incomparability and transcendence.[137] Indeed, in keeping with this interpretation, in the chapter of *al-Insān al-kāmil* devoted to *tanzīh* (chapter ten), al-Jīlī illustrates God's incomparability to creation with reference to a hadith, according to which, when the Prophet was asked if he had seen God, he replied, 'Light is what I see' (*nūr anná arāhu*).[138] Similarly, in the chapter on *tashbīh* (chapter eleven), he interprets the phrase 'light upon light' from the famous Light Verse of the Qur'an (Q 24.35) as a reference to the 'two lights' of *tashbīh* and *tanzīh*.[139] And, finally, it might also be noted that al-Jīlī includes the divine name 'the Light' (*nūr*) among God's 'essential names and attributes'.[140] Light, then, is an important symbol of God's incomparability and transcendence for al-Jīlī, as it is for Ibn 'Arabī.[141]

Al-Jīlī's assertion that the first tablet of the Torah encourages the 'unqualified profession of divine incomparability' (*al-tanzīh al-muṭlaq*) is significant because it sets up a direct contrast with the position of the Christians, who, so al-Jīlī indicated earlier in the chapter, hold to the 'unqualified profession of divine comparability' (*muṭlaq al-tashbīh*).[142] Al-Jīlī is therefore alluding here to the aforementioned idea that Judaism and Christianity represent two extremes – respectively, the extremes of *tanzīh* and *tashbīh* – in contrast to the middle position represented by (properly understood) Islam (the synthesis of *tanzīh* and *tashbīh*). Al-Jīlī's identification of the transcendence of God as the dominant aspect of the Torah is perhaps a distant echo of the biblical accounts (taken up by the Qur'an) of God's interactions with Moses, which stress the awe-inducing majesty and transcendence of God even while they describe His appearance to Moses (see e.g. Exodus 3, 19, 34). Other biblical passages – for example, the assertion that God 'dwells in thick darkness' and that the heavens and the earth cannot contain Him (1 Kings 8) – reinforce this sense of divine transcendence, which was carried over into Jewish theological and legal thought.[143]

Also of interest here is al-Jīlī's assertion that this tablet reveals God's lordship (*rubūbiyyah*) and power (*qudrah*), for as we saw previously, it was the tablets containing the mysteries of lordship and power that Moses was commanded *not* to propagate to his people. While this might appear to be a contradiction, what al-Jīlī may be indicating here is that the propagated Torah points to God's lordship and power (for instance, by describing Him as 'Lord' and 'powerful'), but does not reveal the deeper metaphysical truth that these divine attributes are manifested in His creatures. This is another way of expressing the idea that the propagated Torah directs people towards *tanzīh*, at the expense of *tashbīh*.

2) The tablet of guidance (*lawḥ al-hudá*)
    - Divine reports to Himself (*ikhbārāt ilāhiyyah li-nafsihi*); forms of knowledge acquired by taste (*'ulūm dhawqiyyah*); the inspirational light in the hearts of the believers (*al-nūr al-ilhāmī fī qulūb al-mu'minīn*) – for light is essentially an inspirational, existential mystery (*sirr wujūdī ilhāmī*) that awes the servants of God; it is the light of the divine attraction (*nūr al-jadhb al-ilāhī*) in which the gnostic (*al-'ārif*) ascends to the exalted loci of witnessing (*yataraqqī ilá al-manāẓir al-'uliyah*) on the divine path (*al-ṭarīq al-ilāhī*); an expression of the return of the divine light that was sent down, within the human body, to its locus and place (*rujū' al-nūr al-ilāhī al-munazzal fī al-haykal al-insānī ilá maḥallihi wa-makānihi*) – for guidance is an expression of the oneness of the path (*aḥadiyyat al-ṭarīq*) to the most advanced station and the most radiant level, where there is no 'where' (*ḥayth lā ḥayth*), found by the one who receives that light;
    - The science of unveiling the conditions of religious communities (*'ilm al-kashf 'an aḥwāl al-milal*), and reports about those who came before and will come after them;
    - Knowledge of the [world of] dominion (*'ilm al-malakūt*) – which is the world of spirits (*'ālam al-arwāḥ*); and knowledge of the [world of] sovereignty (*al-jabarūt*), which is the world that governs the world of spirits, that is, the presence of the holy (*ḥadrat al-quds*);
    - Knowledge of the intermediate state (*'ilm al-barzakh*); a reminder (*dhikr*) of the resurrection (*al-qiyāmah*), the [final] hour (*al-sā'ah*), the scale (*al-mīzān*),

the holding to account (*al-ḥisāb*), the garden [of paradise] (*al-jannah*), and the fire [of hell] (*al-nār*);

- Reports about an assembly of angels (*jam' min al-malā'ikah*);
- Knowledge of the mysteries (*'ilm al-asrār*) deposited in the forms (*al-ashkāl*), and things like that, through their knowledge (*ma'rifah*) of which the Children of Israel did what they did and performed those miracles (*al-karāmāt*) that they performed.[144]

As with the previous tablet, al-Jīlī's identification of the second tablet as the tablet of guidance ought to be understood with reference to the Qur'anic description of the Torah as 'guidance and light', this being another indication of the Qur'an-centredness of al-Jīlī's view of the Torah. The 'guidance' contained within it consists of various forms of knowledge (*'ulūm*). The first is what we can call 'mystical knowledge': *hudá*, in this sense, denotes guidance back to the presence of God, in keeping with al-Jīlī's notion that the manifestation (*tajallī*) or descent (*tanazzul*) of God into the world is met by a corresponding ascent (*taraqqī*) of man to God. The mystical quality of this return to God is indicated by al-Jīlī's use of several important Sufi technical terms with strong mystical connotations, such as *dhawq*,[145] *ilhām*,[146] *jadhb*,[147] *manẓar*,[148] *ṭarīq*[149] and *ḥayth lā ḥayth*.[150] The presence of this mystical knowledge in the Torah means that the Torah, if properly interpreted, can serve as a mystical guidebook. This accords with al-Jīlī's view, outlined in the previous section, that the Torah points to the fundamental metaphysical truths of universal theophany and the Perfect Human (even if it does not fully encompass them in its propagated form). It certainly reflects the more positive dimension of his view of the Torah, given his belief that mystical attainment constitutes the highest form of religious experience and the surest path to knowledge.

The second form of knowledge contained in the tablet of guidance is what might be called 'historical knowledge'; specifically, knowledge pertaining to past and future *milal*. This latter term is used in the Qur'an (see e.g. Q 2.120, 2.130, 7.89, 16.23) and the Islamic tradition (particularly in doxographical works) to denote religious communities.[151] It is in this sense that al-Jīlī uses the term in the final chapter of *al-Insān al-kāmil*, in which he identifies ten basic religious communities (which he variously calls *milal*, *adyān*, *ṭawā'if* and *umam*), including the dualists (*al-thānawiyyah*), the Zoroastrians (*al-majūs*) and the Brahmans (*barāhimah*), as well as the Jews, Christians and Muslims,[152] and it is this meaning that he probably has in mind here. Al-Jīlī's proposal that the Torah contains knowledge about past and future nations might be taken as a distant echo of the biblical 'table of nations' (Genesis 10), where *milal* would be the equivalent of the Hebrew *gōyīm*.[153] If this were the case, then it would indicate that he had at least some awareness of the contents of the canonical Torah. However, it seems much more likely that al-Jīlī's reference to the historical knowledge of the Torah derives from his conception of the Qur'an, the archetypal scripture, for the language that he uses here echoes that of a hadith about the Qur'an: 'The Book of God contains information (*naba'*) about those before and after you (*man qablakum wa-ba'dakum*)'.[154] This tendency to model his presentation of the contents of the Torah on the Qur'an appears on several occasions in this section, and reflects not only the

Qur'an-centredness of his approach but also his sense that the different scriptures are essentially different manifestations of the same phenomenon.

The third type of knowledge contained in this tablet is what might be called 'metaphysical knowledge', for it pertains to realms beyond the phenomenal world. The terms *al-malakūt* and *al-jabarūt* are found, respectively, in the Qur'an (see Q 6.75, 7.185, 23.88, 26.83) and hadith. They are used (along with *al-mulk*) in the various strands of Islamic metaphysical thought influenced by Neoplatonism, including the Ibn 'Arabian Sufi metaphysical tradition, to denote the different planes of existence.[155] Thus Ibn 'Arabī's commentator al-Qayṣarī, for instance, in setting out his conception of the five divine presences (*ḥaḍarāt*), associates the third presence, that of 'the unseen to which something has been added' (*ḥaḍrat al-ghayb al-muḍāf*), with 'the world of the spirits of dominion and sovereignty' (*'ālam al-arwāḥ al-jabarūtiyyah wa-al-malakūtiyyah*) on the one hand – which is the world that is closer to 'the absolute unseen' (*al-ghayb al-muṭlaq*), being 'the world of pure intellects and souls' (*'ālam al-'uqūl wa-al-nufūs al-mujarradah*) – and on the other, to 'the world of archetypal images' (*'ālam al-mithāl*) – which, he tells us, is synonymous with *'ālam al-malakūt*. He associates the presence of 'the absolutely visible' (*al-shahādah al-muṭlaq*), meanwhile, with *'ālam al-mulk*.[156] As can be seen here, al-Jīlī uses the terms *al-jabarūt* and *al-malakūt* in a similar way, that is, to denote different degrees within the intangible, unseen realm. Indeed, later in *al-Insān al-kāmil*, he identifies *'ālam al-malakūt*, like al-Qayṣarī, as one of the two kinds of unseen realms (*al-ghayb*), specifically, that which is 'set out in detail in the world of man' (*mufaṣṣilan fī 'ālam al-insān*).[157] The significance of this is that it suggests that the Torah contains knowledge of this unseen, metaphysical realm, again reflecting his notion that the Torah contains metaphysical wisdom. Furthermore, since *al-malakūt* is a Qur'anic term and the notion of the different worlds is read out of the Qur'an, it also reflects, once again, his tendency to model his view of the Torah on the Qur'an.[158]

The fourth type of knowledge contained in the tablet of guidance pertains to eschatology and soteriology. The key terms used here – *al-barzakh*, *al-qiyāmah*, *al-sā'ah*, *al-mīzān*, *al-ḥisāb*, *al-jannah* and *al-nār* – are all Qur'anic concepts relating to the final judgement, and form a key part of conventional Islamic eschatological doctrine.[159] The use of the term 'reminder' (*dhikr*) in this context (among other contexts) is also Qur'anic.[160] Though the actual Hebrew Bible does contain eschatological information (see e.g. Deuteronomy 28–31, Isaiah), biblical eschatology relates more to judgement upon this earth than in the next world, and in light of al-Jīlī's use of Qur'anic eschatological terminology, it seems that he is again modelling his view of the contents of the Torah on the Qur'an.

The assignation of knowledge about some of the angels to the tablet of guidance fits with al-Jīlī's earlier discussion of the metaphysical knowledge contained in this tablet, for *'ālam al-malakūt* is usually thought of as the realm of (most of) the angels (while *'ālam al-jabarūt* is sometimes said to be the realm of the elect among the angels).[161] Angels appear on several occasions in the actual Torah (see e.g. Gen. 16.7, 16.9-11, 19.1, 22.11, 28.12; Exod. 33.2), where they are referred to by the term *mal'ākhīm*, the Hebrew cognate of the Arabic word *malā'ikah*, which al-Jīlī uses here. Again, however, it is likely that al-Jīlī's model is the Qur'an, in which the angels also appear on many (roughly ninety) occasions.[162]

The 'knowledge of the mysteries deposited in the forms' is probably the most enigmatic type of knowledge that al-Jīlī identifies in the tablet of guidance. Its presence in the propagated Torah would again seem to contradict al-Jīlī's earlier claim that Moses was commanded to conceal the divine 'mysteries' of lordship and power by not propagating two of the tablets of the revealed Torah. This is especially the case given that, as we saw previously, al-Jīlī connects these mysteries to Jesus' ability to perform miracles, yet here suggests that, on account of the presence of certain unidentified mysteries in the propagated Torah, the Children of Israel were also able to perform miracles. In order to reconcile what al-Jīlī says here with what he says earlier in the chapter, we must presume that the 'mysteries' contained in this tablet are lesser mysteries than those contained in the two concealed tablets. This is perfectly conceivable, given that, according to al-Jīlī's Sufi metaphysics, God has deposited a particular mystery (*sirr*) or 'subtle reality' (*laṭīfah*) in every individual, which is that person's 'defined portion' (*muḥtadd*) of the divine perfection and the vehicle through which, if he is capable, he returns to God.[163] While Moses' people may not know the mysteries of lordship or divine power, therefore, nevertheless they do possess mysteries within their 'forms', and these mysteries connect them to God. This aspect of the Torah, then, is connected to the mystical knowledge that is also contained by the tablet of guidance. It reflects another tendency of al-Jīlī's, namely, his desire to read his own Sufi metaphysics into the Torah (and the other scriptures) – this Sufi metaphysics, of course, being identical, in his view, to the knowledge contained in the Qur'an.

3) The tablet of wisdom (*lawḥ al-ḥikmah*)
   - Knowledge of the method of intellectual wayfaring (*al-sulūk al-'ilmī*), by way of the [divine] manifestation (*al-tajallī*) and tasting (*al-dhawq*) in the divine holy precincts (*al-ḥaẓā'ir al-qudsiyyah al-ilāhiyyah*), such as the taking off of the two sandals (*khal' al-na'layn*), the ascent of Sinai (*tarāqī al-ṭawr*), conversing with the tree (*mukālamat al-shajarah*) and the vision of the fire (*ru'yat al-nār*) in the dark night – for all of these are divine mysteries (*asrār ilāhiyyāt*);
   - Astronomy (*'ilm al-falak wa-al-hay'ah*), arithmetic (*al-ḥisāb*), botany/dendrology (*'ilm al-ashjār*), geology (*'ilm al-aḥjār*), etc.
   - Whoever among the Children of Israel masters these sciences is called a monk (*rāhib*), which in their language (*lughah*) denotes the God-conscious man (*al-muta'allih*) who has abandoned the lower world out of desire for his Master (*al-tārik li-dunyāhu al-rāghib fī mawlāhu*).[164]

Al-Jīlī's identification of the third tablet of the propagated Torah as the tablet of 'wisdom' (*al-ḥikmah*) can be understood with reference to the Qur'an's tendency to pair the various scriptures with *ḥikmah* (see e.g. Q 2.231, 3.48);[165] indeed, he also associates *ḥikmah* with the Qur'an (as we saw in the previous chapter), and with the Psalms (as we shall see in the next).[166]

Like the previous tablet, the tablet of wisdom contains various forms of knowledge. Again like the previous tablet, the most prominent form of knowledge set out here is connected to mystical guidance, as can be seen from al-Jīlī's use of the Sufi terms *sulūk*, *tajallī* and *dhawq*. Interestingly, al-Jīlī qualifies the type of mystical 'wayfaring' explained in this tablet as 'intellectual' (*'ilmī*), a reflection perhaps of how Ibn 'Arabian Sufis view mystical experience as a cognitive exercise as much as (or more than) an ecstatic state.[167] Also of interest here is that al-Jīlī links the mystical guidance contained in this tablet to the Qur'anic accounts of Moses' conversations with God on Mount Sinai (see Q 7.142-143) and in the 'fire' or burning tree (see Q 20.9-16, 28.29-30), through his use of the language and imagery of those Qur'anic passages. Moses thus emerges here, as he does elsewhere in *al-Insān al-kāmil*,[168] as a kind of model mystic, an idea for which precedents can be found in earlier Sufi literature, in which Moses, in the words of Paul Nwyia, became 'the prototype of the mystic, called to enter into the mystery of God'.[169] Although Moses is also often depicted as a mystic in Jewish and Christian literature (often with reference, similarly, to the biblical story of his entry into the divine presence on Mount Sinai),[170] al-Jīlī's view ought, therefore, to be understood primarily with reference to this motif within the Sufi tradition, his own interpretation of the Qur'anic passages and his more general Sufi metaphysics.

Along with mystical wisdom, this tablet also contains what might be called scientific wisdom. This is in keeping with one of the standard usages of the term *ḥikmah*, which can mean philosophy (in the technical sense of *falsafah*) or science as well as generic 'wisdom'.[171] The sciences listed here were all part of the medieval Islamic scientific tradition,[172] with which al-Jīlī would likely have been familiar; hence, their inclusion in his conception of the Torah once again can be said to reflect his own knowledge, interests and view on what forms of learning are valuable.

Al-Jīlī's statement that the individual who has acquired the mystical and scientific wisdom associated with this tablet is called a 'monk', which he defines, using a term also found in the work of Ibn 'Arabī and his interpreters,[173] as someone who has renounced the world and 'turned their attention to God' (or even, 'become God-like') (*muta'allih*), comes as something of a surprise. *Ḥakīm* (sage), or else a more usual Sufi metaphysical term for the advanced individual, such as *'ārif* or *muḥaqqiq*, might have been more expected; indeed, among medieval Yemenite Jews (the Jewish community with which al-Jīlī was probably most familiar), the term *al-ḥukamā'* was used 'as a collective name for all who engaged in legitimate speculation', that is, 'speculation concerning *al-wujūd*'.[174] *Rāhib* is a particularly unusual choice in this context, in fact, since it is a word specifically associated with Christian monks or renunciants.[175] Al-Jīlī's use of *rāhib* here seems to be dictated by his belief that it is a term used in Hebrew, the language of the Children of Israel. It is possible that he has the Hebrew word *rabī* (rabbi) in mind. It is also possible that, following the suggestion of the early Qur'anic exegete Muqātil (d. 150/767), he understands the term to indicate, generically, '*al-mujtahidīn fī dīnihim*, the believers who make an effort to practice their religion with zeal'.[176] What is clear is that, by connecting the acquisition of the wisdom of this tablet to the renunciation of the world and concentration on (or imitation of) God, al-Jīlī again presents the Torah in light of his own Sufi position.[177]

4) The tablet of the faculties (*lawḥ al-qiwá*)
    - Knowledge of the sending down of the forms of wisdom (*'ilm al-tanzīlāt al-ḥikamiyyah*), into the human faculties (*al-qiwá al-bashariyyah*). This is a form of knowledge acquired by taste (*'ilm al-adhwāq, amr dhawqī*). Whoever of the Children of Israel obtains it is a rabbi (*ḥabr/ḥibr*), being at the level of the heirs of Moses (*martabat warathat Mūsá*). Most of what is in this tablet consists of symbols (*rumūz*), parables (*amthāl*) and allusions (*ishārāt*), which God established in the Torah so that the divine forms of wisdom (*al-ḥikam al-ilāhiyyah*) would be established in the human faculties. God indicated this when He said to John, '"O John, take the book with [all your] might (*bi-quwwah*)," and We gave him wisdom (*al-ḥikam*) while he was still a boy.' (Q 29.12) This 'taking with might' is only for those who know wisdom (*al-ḥikmah*) and have been guided (*ihtadá*) to the divine light (*al-nūr al-ilāhiyyah*); hence, it is for the elect (*al-khawāṣṣ*), not the masses (*al-'awāmm*).
    - The knowledge of signs (*'ilm al-sīmiyyā'*) and of the method of exalted magic (*al-siḥr al-'ālī*), which is similar to miracles (*karāmāt*), and is so called because it takes place without any tool (*adawiyyah*) or deed (*'amal*) or utterance (*talaffuẓ*), but merely through the magical faculties (*al-qiwá al-siḥriyyah*) in man. Things that are only possible in the imagination (*al-khayāl*) appear to be sensible (*maḥsūs*) and perceptible (*mashhūd*) to the senses. 'I myself', says al-Jīlī, 'fell upon that while on the path of monotheism (*'alá ṭarīq al-tawḥīd*). Had I wanted to take on any form in existence, I could have done so, and had I wanted to do anything, I could have done it, but I knew that it was destructive (*muhlik*), so I abandoned it.'[178]

Like the names of the previous three tablets, the name of the fourth tablet is drawn from the Qur'an. While the term *qiwá* does not itself appear in the Qur'an, nevertheless its singular form, *quwwah*, does appear on thirty occasions, with reference to the 'strength' or 'power' of both God and man. Al-Jīlī in fact grounds the name *lawḥ al-qiwá* and the idea to which it refers in one of these Qur'anic verses, specifically, a verse that relates to the prophet John (*Yaḥyá*), whose 'book', given that he was one of the Children of Israel and not himself a messenger who was given a scripture, would have been the Torah.

Again, the principal form of knowledge contained in this tablet, to which, as al-Jīlī sees it, that Qur'anic verse refers, can be classed as 'metaphysical knowledge'. The notion of 'the sending down of the forms of wisdom into the human faculties' should be understood as a reference to al-Jīlī's key Sufi metaphysical concept of the manifestation of the divine names and attributes within man. As we have seen, he uses the terms *inzāl* and *tanzīl* to denote not only the revelation of scripture but also the manifestation (*tajallī*) of the divine within the world, while the term *al-ḥikam* (*al-ilāhiyyah*) seems to be used here in the same sense as Ibn 'Arabī uses it in *Fuṣūṣ al-ḥikam*, that is, to denote the divine attributes. The notion that these attributes become manifest in the faculties (*qiwá*) of man, meanwhile, is spelled out in chapter twenty of *al-Insān al-kāmil*, where al-Jīlī lists all of man's faculties – for example, his spirit (*rūḥ*), intellect (*'aql*), thought (*fikr*), imagination (*khayāl*) and so forth – and explains that each of them is a 'copy' (*nuskhah*) of the divine perfection.[179] In this way, it can be said that the tablet of the faculties points towards the key Sufi metaphysical truth of the Perfect Human.

This truth, however, is not uncovered by everyone who reads or hears the Torah; indeed, al-Jīlī explicitly states that this truth is for the elite, not the masses. As with the previous tablets, al-Jīlī connects the metaphysical knowledge contained in the tablet of the faculties with mystical insight, explaining that only those who have attained such insight are able to understand the metaphysical truth contained in the tablet. As with the previous two tablets, this mystical insight is expressed via the term 'taste' (*dhawq*). Such repetition is a sign both of al-Jīlī's apparent belief in the possibility of a Torah-based mysticism, and of his privileging of mystical experience over other ways of knowing.

Where al-Jīlī indicated previously that the Children of Israel call the individual who acquires the forms of wisdom contained in *lawḥ al-ḥikmah* a *rāhib*, here he indicates that the individual who acquires the metaphysical knowledge contained in this tablet is called a *ḥabr*/*ḥibr*. This is the standard Arabic term for 'rabbi', and was also used by Arabic-speaking Jews as 'a synonym for educated men and scholars'.[180] As such, it might be deemed the Jewish equivalent of *ʿālim* (a religious scholar; pl. *ʿulamāʾ*). Al-Jīlī in fact seems to have this correspondence between the *aḥbār* and the *ʿulamāʾ* in mind, for he identifies the *aḥbār* as the 'heirs of Moses' (*warathat Mūsá*), a phrase that brings to mind the famous hadith, 'The scholars are the heirs of the prophets (*al-ʿulamāʾ warathat al-anbiyāʾ*).'[181] Significantly, while the religious scholars use this hadith in support of their own claim to be the only true interpreters of the prophetic legacy, Ibn ʿArabian Sufis like al-Jīlī, as already noted, take the term *al-ʿulamāʾ* in this hadith to be a reference to the *awliyāʾ* and mystics like themselves, whom they deem to be the true 'knowers'.[182] Something similar seems to be going on here: the *aḥbār*, as al-Jīlī sees it, are not the Jewish religious scholars (i.e. the rabbis), but rather those whom he elsewhere refers to as the 'Mosaic' (*mūsawī*) Friends of God. It is this latter group who are the true heirs of Moses and the 'elite' who are able to understand the symbols and allusions contained in this tablet, and so to comprehend the idea of the Perfect Human.

Turning back to the 'faculties' referred to in the name of this tablet, it is clear that they constitute not only those faculties of man that receive the manifestations of the divine attributes but also the magical powers of man.[183] Despite the condemnation of *siḥr* in the Qur'an and hadith,[184] belief in various kinds of magic and occult sciences seems to have been widespread among medieval Muslims, including many philosophically inclined intellectuals (e.g. the Brethren of Purity and Fakhr al-Dīn al-Rāzī),[185] and Sufi thinkers (e.g. the quasi-legendary Aḥmad al-Būnī [d. 622/1225 or 629/1232] and Ibn ʿArabī himself).[186] Given that magic and the occult were part of al-Jīlī's intellectual environment, therefore, it does not come as a great surprise that he includes magical knowledge among the contents of the Torah. He specifically mentions two forms of magic in this regard, which he calls *al-sīmiyyāʾ* and *al-siḥr al-ʿālī*. The former term is derived from the Greek *sēmeia*, meaning 'signs'. According to the classification of the different types of magic put forward by Ibn Khaldūn, the term was used by those whom he calls the 'later' Sufis – among whom he includes Ibn ʿArabī and his interpreters[187] –

to denote the esoteric 'science of letters' (*'ilm al-ḥurūf*).[188] Since al-Jīlī, like Ibn 'Arabī,[189] displays a particular interest in the science of letters and clearly believes in its efficacy,[190] and given his tendency to read his own views and preoccupations into the Torah, it seems likely that the science of letters is what he has in mind here.

As for *al-siḥr al-'ālī*, al-Jīlī indicates that the powers connected to it are like *karāmāt*, the term denoting the miracles of the *awliyā'* (as opposed to *mu'jizāt*, traditionally understood as the miracles of the prophets).[191] More specifically, the term denotes the capacity to cause what is usually possible only in the imagination (*al-khayāl*) to occur in the sensible world, which comes down to the ability to do anything one wants. Indeed, in chapter fourteen, on 'The Manifestation of the [Divine] Attributes' (*tajallī al-ṣifāt*), al-Jīlī informs us that both 'the miraculous powers of the People of Aspiration' (*taṣarrufāt ahl al-himam*) and 'exalted magic' issue from that kind of divine manifestation.[192] While the identification of exalted magic with the miraculous powers of the *awliyā'* would seem to fit with al-Jīlī's earlier indication that the wisdom contained in this tablet is the property of the *awliyā'* from among the Children of Israel, nevertheless it is significant that he says only that 'exalted magic' is 'like' (*yushbih*) the miracles of the Friends of God, which suggests that they are in fact not identical. Indeed, al-Jīlī's description of his own personal experience of this form of magic is characterized by a notable defensiveness – in particular, his instance that he encountered it 'while on the path of monotheism', and his profession to have abandoned it – and a sense of the dangers of this magic, summarized in his use of the strong term *muhlik* ('destructive', 'causing one to perish'). This defensive attitude may be a consequence of al-Jīlī's awareness of the condemnations of *siḥr* in the Qur'an and hadith, or of his awareness of the attacks launched by thinkers such as Ibn Khaldūn on Sufis like him for indulging in the occult sciences. Yet, his inclusion of this form of knowledge in the Torah, alongside other forms of knowledge that he evidently holds in high esteem, would suggest that he recognized magic as a potentially efficacious, if hazardous, activity.

5) The tablet of judgement (*lawḥ al-ḥukm*)
   - Commandments and prohibitions (*al-awāmir wa-al-nawāhī*) – which are what God imposed (*faraḍa*) on the Children of Israel, and that which He made forbidden (*ḥarrama*) for them. It contains the Mosaic legislation (*al-tashrī' al-mūsawī*), which the Jews built upon.[193]

In addition to the metaphysical, scientific and magical knowledge contained in the other tablets of the Torah, al-Jīlī also indicates here that the propagated Torah contains legal knowledge. Again, he expresses this idea in terms taken from the Qur'an and the Islamic tradition. The term *ḥukm* itself is used in the Qur'an to denote both God's 'individual ordinances and the whole of His dispensation'.[194] Similarly, the phrase *al-awāmir wa-al-nawāhī* reminds us of the Islamic principle of 'commanding the good and prohibiting evil' (*al-amr bi-al-ma'rūf wa-al-nahī 'an al-munkar*), which is derived from the Qur'an (see e.g. Q 3.110, 7.157, 9.67, 9.71).[195] The terms *faraḍa* (see e.g. Q 2.197, 24.1, 33.38, 33.50) and *ḥarrama* are likewise Qur'anic (see e.g. Q 2.173, 2.275, 5.72, 5.96), in which context their subject, like here, is God; and they were subsequently incorporated by the

Islamic legal tradition into the 'five legal categories' (*al-aḥkām al-khamsah*).[196] Finally, *al-tashrīʿ al-mūsawī* evokes the *sharīʿah* of Muhammad, though the term *al-tashrīʿ al-Muḥammadī* does not appear in pre-modern Islamic thought, legislation, properly speaking belonging to God alone.[197] Nevertheless, the terminological and conceptual parallels between Qur'an- and Torah-based law evoked here further strengthen the sense of analogy between the Qur'an and Torah, and between Islam and Judaism more generally.

Al-Jīlī's identification of legal content in the Torah fits with the conventional Islamic view that the tablets of the Torah contain legal regulations (*aḥkām*).[198] This, of course, is a genuine reflection of the contents of the actual Torah: the tablets that Moses brings down from Mount Sinai contain a legal code, the Ten Commandments (Exodus 20), while two of the five books of the Pentateuch, Leviticus and Deuteronomy, are primarily concerned with articulating the Mosaic Law. Furthermore, al-Jīlī's statement that the Jews 'built upon' (*baná ʿalá*) the law contained in the Torah suggests he may have been vaguely aware of the existence of the 'Oral Torah' codified in the Mishnah and Talmud, and the rabbinic literature that builds upon those sources. There may also be present here a subtle distinction between the 'Children of Israel', as the original recipients of the divine revelation, and the 'Jews', as the descendants of the original recipients of the Torah who added to – and perhaps corrupted – its original meaning through their interpretations of the Mosaic Law; in which case *taḥrīf* (*al-maʿná*) may be implied here. All that can be said for certain, however, is that al-Jīlī held what was a common view among medieval Muslims, namely that Judaism was a legalistic religious tradition.[199] In this regard, it is notable that while he here identifies legal content within the Torah, in the chapter on the Gospel he makes no mention of legal content in that scripture or of '*al-tashrīʿ al-ʿīsawī*'; indeed, in the final chapter of *al-Insān al-kāmil*, he states outright that 'Jesus . . . did not possess legislative prophethood (*nubuwwat al-tashrīʿ*).'[200] In this way, al-Jīlī indicates an awareness of the different status and function of law in Judaism and Christianity. Indeed, it is perhaps again implied here that, between the legalism of the Torah and Judaism and the permissiveness of the Gospel and Christianity, the Qur'an and Islam plot a middle course – an idea stated explicitly by other medieval Muslim authors.[201]

6) The tablet of servanthood (*lawḥ al-ʿubūdiyyah*)
   - Knowledge of the regulations (*al-aḥkām*) that are incumbent on creation, such as submissiveness (*al-dhillah*), neediness (*al-iftiqār*), fear (*al-khawf*) and humility (*al-khuḍūʿ*), such that he [i.e. Moses] said to his people: 'If one of you does an evil deed in recompense for an evil deed (*jāzá bi-al-sayyiʾah sayyiʾah*), then he has claimed what Pharaoh claimed of lordship, because the servant does not have the right (*al-ʿabd lā ḥaqqa lahu*).' It contains the mysteries of monotheism (*asrār al-tawḥīd*), submission (*al-taslīm*), putting one's trust in God (*al-tawakkul*), delegating one's affairs to God (*al-tafwīḍ*), satisfaction (*al-riḍā*), fear (*al-khawf*), hope (*al-rajāʾ*), desire (*al-raghbah*), renunciation (*al-zuhd*), turning to the Real (*al-tawajjuh ilá al-ḥaqq*), renouncing other than Him (*tark mā siwāhu*) and so forth.[202]

The sixth tablet of the propagated Torah contains what might be called 'pietistic knowledge', that is, knowledge of how man should act, in light of the transcendence of God set out in the first tablet, and the religious laws set out in the sixth. Words of the root *'-b-d* appear some 275 times in the Qur'an, invariably denoting man's worship of and servitude towards God;[203] hence, it can be said that the name and contents of this tablet are again based on a Qur'anic theme. Moreover, servanthood (*al-'ubūdiyyah*) is a key concept both in classical Sufism[204] and in Ibn 'Arabian Sufi metaphysics, where it serves as the human complement to divine lordship (*al-rubūbiyyah*).[205] Once again, therefore, al-Jīlī's view of the contents of the Torah seems to be determined by his own Sufi perspective. Indeed, the 'regulations' and 'mysteries' that he lists here are all among the stations (*maqāmāt*) and states (*aḥwāl*) of the mystical path outlined in the classical Sufi manuals, such as the *Risālah* of al-Qushayrī or 'Abd Allāh Anṣārī's (d. 481/1088) *Manāzil al-sā'irīn*. More particularly, they correspond to the practical virtues – the 'ways of acting' (*mu'āmalāt*) and 'morals' (*akhlāq*) – that are to be cultivated in the early stages of the Sufi path.[206] What al-Jīlī thus seems to be describing here, once again, is a Torah-based renunciant piety (*zuhd*), which might be considered the necessary precursor to the attainment of the mystical knowledge set out in the earlier tablets.

Al-Jīlī here sets up a contrast between this renunciant servanthood promoted by the Torah, and the arrogance of Pharaoh, who, as already noted, is said by the Qur'an to have claimed lordship (*al-rubūbiyyah*) for himself (see Q 79.24). There seems to be an allusion here to the idea discussed previously, namely that the mystery of lordship, the direct antonym of servanthood, is absent from the propagated Torah. Yet where before al-Jīlī indicated that this was a deficiency of the Torah, here he seems to have a positive regard for the Torah's valorization of human servanthood rather than human lordship, that is, its protection of the Children of Israel from falling into the excessive *tashbīh* professed by Pharaoh and later by the Christians (to whom, as we have seen, the mystery of lordship *was* revealed).

The contrast between the humility promoted by the Torah and the arrogance of Pharaoh is expressed via a statement that al-Jīlī attributes to Moses, in which Moses forbids his people to practise retaliatory justice. The idea seems to be that Pharaoh's claim to lordship leads him to act like the God of justice and majesty, that is, to punish wrongdoing with pain and torment. Those who act as humble servants, by contrast, leaving their affairs to God, put their trust in His ultimate punishment of the wrongdoers after death.[207] This idea in fact appears to directly contradict both the biblical *lex talionis* (Lev. 24.20; see also Exod. 21.24; Deut. 19.21) and the Qur'anic statement (Q 5.45) that God 'prescribed [in the Torah] for [the Children of Israel]: "Life for life, eye for eye, nose for nose, ear for ear, tooth for tooth, and for wounds retaliation (*al-qiṣāṣ*)."'[208] Yet, the saying that al-Jīlī attributes (without source) to Moses *does* have a Qur'anic basis; indeed, it is an almost direct quotation of the first part of Qur'an 42.40: 'The recompense for an evil deed is an evil deed like it (*jazā' sayyi'ah sayyi'ah mithluhā*): but whoever forgives and brings about reconciliation (*fa-man 'afā wa aṣlaḥa*) has a reward (*ajr*) from God, for He does not love the evildoers.' Al-Jīlī appears to have taken the message of the latter part of this verse, adapted the meaning of the first half of the verse by adding a negative particle, and put it into the mouth of Moses. The latter part of the aforementioned Qur'an 5.45, it should also be noted, similarly calls for clemency and conciliation. Once again, therefore, it seems that al-Jīlī is modelling his conception of the Torah on the Qur'an – at least as he interprets it, in accordance with his Ibn 'Arabian valorization of mercy. Furthermore, by transposing these Qur'anic affirmations of clemency onto the Torah, and by ignoring and contradicting the biblical and Qur'anic affirmations of the righteousness of retaliatory justice, he promotes Moses as a model of mercy and pious servanthood, and softens the harshness of the Torah and biblical law. Again, this is a reflection of his own Sufi metaphysical outlook: as we know, according to the Ibn 'Arabian Sufi metaphysical idea of 'universal mercy', the divine attribute of mercy is believed to underlie all of phenomenal existence, and the divine mercy to be superior to God's vengeance and wrath.

7) The tablet clarifying the path of happiness from the path of misery (*lawḥ wuḍūḥ ṭarīq al-sa'ādah min ṭarīq al-shaqāwah*)
   - The path to God (*al-ṭarīq ilá Allāh*); the clarification of the path of happiness from that of misery (*bayyana ṭarīq al-sa'ādah min al-shaqāwah*), and of what is appropriate (*awlá*) on the path of happiness and what is permitted (*jā'iz*) on it.
   - It was based on the contents of this tablet that Moses' people invented what they invented in their religion (*ibtada' qawm Mūsá mā ibtada'ū*), out of their own desires (*raghbatan*), and due to a monasticism that they invented (*rahbāniyyatan ibtada'ūhā*). They derived (*istakhrajū*) those [inventions] via their faculties of thought and their intellects (*bi-afkārihim wa-'uqūlihim*), not from the word of Moses (*kalām Mūsá*), indeed, [not] from the word of God (*kalām Allah*), for they did not take sufficient care over these things. If they were meant to have derived them from divine reports (*al-akhbār al-ilāhiyyah*) and divine unveiling (*al-kashf al-ilāhī*), God would have decreed (*qadara*) that for them, and if they were meant to have been able to take sufficient care God would have ordered them to do that, through the tongue of His prophet Moses. Moses opposed those things not out of ignorance (*jahlan*), but rather out of companionship for them (*rifqan bihim*). And since they invented those things, and did not take care of them, they were punished for them (*'uwqibū 'alayhā*).
   - Many sciences, including those connected to religions (*adyān*) and bodies (*abdān*).[209]

These are two possible levels on which the concepts of the 'path to God' and the 'path of happiness' – terms that probably denote the same thing here – can be understood. The first, more exoteric level relates to soteriology. As noted earlier in this chapter, al-Jīlī often uses the terms *sa'ādah* and *shaqāwah* to denote, respectively, the happiness of the inhabitants of paradise and the misery of the inhabitants of hell,[210] a usage that is based on the way in which those terms are employed in the Qur'an (see esp. Q 11.105-108) and hadith,[211] and which is a conventional one in Islamic thought.[212] In this sense, the term *ṭarīq al-sa'ādah* denotes the way to heaven, and this tablet would therefore inform the Children of Israel how to achieve salvation. This meaning would fit with the notion expressed earlier that the second tablet, the tablet of guidance, contains knowledge about the final judgement, as well as with the idea that the fifth tablet, the tablet of judgement, sets out the divine commandments and prohibitions, adherence to which is presumably a necessary condition for salvation. This implies that the Jews' *failure* to adhere to the path set out on this tablet, a failure which al-Jīlī makes clear here, means that they are punished (*ʿuwqibū*), and that this punishment consists in their being condemned to hell.[213] While al-Jīlī does not state this explicitly here, in the final chapter of the book, as already indicated, he does appear to argue that all non-Muslims, including Jews and Christians, will be condemned to hell. Such a view would be consistent with what seems to be the conventional medieval Islamic view,[214] a view grounded in such sources as the canonical hadith, 'By the one in whose hand is Muhammad's soul [i.e. God], every Jew or Christian of this community who hears me, [and then dies] without believing in what I was sent, will be among the people of the fire.'[215]

At the deeper, esoteric level, meanwhile, we find that in the final chapter of *al-Insān al-kāmil* al-Jīlī indicates that the happiness of paradise and the misery of hell, respectively, signify 'proximity' (*qurb*) to and 'distance' (*buʿd*) from God.[216] These are key terms in the technical lexicon of classical Sufism, where the former denotes the mystical state of being in God's presence, and the latter the state of being distant from that divine presence.[217] Indeed, for al-Jīlī, 'proximity' constitutes the seventh and final 'level' (*martabah*) of Islam, and those who reach it, as we have already seen, attain a station tantamount to that of prophethood itself.[218] In this sense, then, the path to happiness and the path to God denote not merely the path to salvation but also the path to an exalted form of divine communion. This meaning would fit with what al-Jīlī said previously about those tablets that contain mystical guidance, particularly the tablets of guidance and wisdom. If this is the intended meaning, then the Jews' *failure* to keep to the path set out on this tablet would imply that they fail to attain the mystical experience to which those other tablets refer to, an idea that would accord with his suggestion earlier in the chapter that none of Moses' people became perfect like him after him. It should be stressed that the two levels of meaning, the soteriological and the mystical, are not mutually exclusive; indeed, both are probably intended here, given the surrounding context of the soteriological and mystical knowledge contained in the other tablets.

Significantly, al-Jīlī introduces perhaps his first real criticism of Moses' people in his discussion of this tablet, proposing that they did not keep to the path laid out on this tablet, but rather 'invented' (*ibdtadaʿū*) certain things that were not based on the divine revelation. The term *ibdtadaʿū* connotes the generally pejorative legal–theological category of *bidʿah*,[219] a sign that al-Jīlī is adopting a condemnatory tone here.[220] Al-Jīlī does not give us much indication of what these things that the Children of Israel invented were, save for a reference to monasticism (*rahbāniyyah*) that echoes the language of the Qur'an,[221] which similarly condemns 'a monasticism that they invented (*rahbāniyyah ibtadaʿūhā*)' (Q 57.27). There is an important difference between the Qur'anic phrase and what al-Jīlī says here however, in that the people about whom the Qur'an appears to speak are the followers of *Jesus*, not of Moses, that is, the Christians rather than the Jews.[222] Al-Jīlī's ascription of monasticism to the Jews seems, therefore, to reflect a sense on his part that both the Jews and the Christians, being all originally Children of Israel, are one and the same, a tendency that is also reflected in his long digression on Christian doctrine earlier in the chapter. Furthermore, al-Jīlī's notion that Moses' people invented a form of monasticism fits with his earlier assertion that anyone of the Children of Israel who acquires the wisdom contained in the second tablet of the Torah is called a 'monk' (*rāhib*). Where in that context he seemed to be using the term in a neutral or even positive sense, however, here the tone is unambiguously negative, in keeping with the conventional medieval Muslim attitude to monasticism, as expressed in the Qur'anic verse just quoted and in the famous hadith, 'There is no monasticism in Islam' (*lā rahbaniyyah fī al-islām*); the monasticism of my community is jihad.'[223] Al-Jīlī's change of tone here perhaps indicates his desire, having spoken in rather positive terms about the Torah and the Children of Israel throughout his discussion of the contents of the tablets, to reaffirm the inferiority of the Jews vis-à-vis the Muslims.

While al-Jīlī does not tell us more about what the Children of Israel invented in their religion, the terms he uses to describe this process of 'invention' do tell us something important about the cause and nature of their errors. Rather than relying upon revelation (*kalām Allāh, kalām Mūsá, al-ikhbārāt al-ilāhiyyah*) or their own direct mystical experience (*al-kashf al-ilāhī*), the Children of Israel invented and 'derived' (*istakhrajū*) things via their intellects (*al-afkār, al-'uqūl*). Al-Jīlī is here making an epistemological statement, namely, that revealed knowledge (whether revealed in scripture or via mystical experience – as we saw previously, in al-Jīlī's view they lead to the same result) is superior to reason-based knowledge. This statement accords with his broader Ibn 'Arabian epistemological outlook: in the *Futūḥāt*, for instance, Ibn 'Arabī writes, 'If anyone wants entrance to God, let him abandon his reason and place before himself God's Law [i.e. revelation], for God does not accept delimitation (*taqyīd*), and reason is a delimitation',[224] while in the chapter of *al-Insān al-kāmil* on divinity, similarly, al-Jīlī declares that the nature of God 'is not known by way of the intellect (*lā yu'raf bi-ṭarīq al-'aql*), nor perceived by thought (*wa-lā yudrak bi-al-fikr*)', but rather via 'divine unveiling' (*al-kashf al-ilāhī*) and 'pure taste' (*al-dhawq al-maḥḍ*).[225] It is clear that al-Jīlī privileges these mystical ways of knowing over the rational methods of the theologians and philosophers. In this regard, it might be said that al-Jīlī has two groups in his sights here: the Jews, on the one hand, and the rationalist (Muslim) theologians and philosophers, on the other.

Though al-Jīlī does not use the term here or elsewhere in the chapter, it could be said that his notion that Moses' people deviated from the message of the Torah, preferring the conclusions of their own intellects to the original meaning of the revelation, constitutes his version of the Islamic polemical concept of *taḥrīf*, that is, the notion that the Jews somehow distorted their scripture. The concept of *taḥrīf*, as noted already, can refer both to distortion of the scriptural text itself (*taḥrīf al-naṣṣ*), which came to be the dominant view among medieval Muslim scholars (including Ibn 'Arabī),[226] and distortion of the meaning of the text (*taḥrīf al-ma'ná*), for instance through false interpretations.[227] Al-Jīlī's position would correspond to the latter view, which certain Sunni exegetes do take with respect to the Jews' distortion of scripture.[228] Whether or not he has the concept of *taḥrīf* in mind, al-Jīlī's position does seem to accord with what

Qur'an 57.27 goes on to say about monasticism – 'We did not prescribe it for them' – as well as with the general Qur'anic notion that the Jews, along with the Christians, have failed to properly adhere to their scriptures (see e.g. Q 2.85, 5.66), a notion which we know to be fundamental to the Qur'an-centred view of sacred history.

This leads to the question of *why* Moses' people lost sight of the need to adhere to the divine revelation. In answering this question, al-Jīlī takes care to absolve Moses of any guilt, denying that it was because of his ignorance (*jahl*) that Moses failed to prevent his people's error. Again, there is a parallel here with his treatment of the errors of the Christians, both earlier in this chapter and in the chapter on the Gospel, where, following the Qur'an, he insists on Jesus' 'purity' (*nazāhah*) or 'innocence' (*barā'ah*) of any wrongdoing.[229] This is perhaps an indication that al-Jīlī, in keeping with the conventional later-medieval Sunni position,[230] believed in the sinlessness (*'iṣmah*) of the prophets. And if Moses is not to blame, then nor, indeed, is free will; rather, al-Jīlī indicates that the Jews' innovations were determined by the divine 'decree' (*qadar*). His use of this latter term indicates that we are again dealing with a widespread Sunni theological concept, namely the principle of divine determinism (*al-qaḍā' wa-al-qadar*).[231] This notion, that it is God who leads people astray (and guides others to the truth), is drawn from the Qur'an (see e.g. Q 2.26, 7.186, 35.8),[232] and affirmed by the mainstream Sunni exegetes.[233] Al-Jīlī's espousal of it here therefore reflects, once again, his commitment to the Qur'anic paradigm.

By way of concluding our analysis of this section, it can be said that al-Jīlī's presentation of the contents of the Torah is evidently modelled on the Qur'an, on the one hand, and on his Sufi metaphysics (which constitutes the true meaning of the Qur'an), on the other. In taking the Qur'an as his model, he is following the conventional medieval Muslim tendency to conceive of the earlier scriptures in terms of the Qur'anic paradigm.[234] A similar tendency emerges from his discussion of Jewish ritual in the final chapter of *al-Insān al-kāmil*, where, as we shall see in the conclusion to this book, he names the Jewish *'ibādāt* after the pillars of Islam.[235] He views the Torah and Judaism, in other words, very much through an Islamic prism, rather than through direct engagement with the actual Torah or with actual Judaism. Again, this seems to be typical of most medieval Muslim authors,[236] who wrote mostly about an 'imagined' Torah,[237] rather than about the actual Jewish scripture. As for the impact of his Sufi metaphysics on his view of the Torah, this reflects what is surely a widespread tendency among exegetes, including those of a Sufi persuasion,[238] to interpret the contents of scripture in light of their own views, affiliations and preoccupations. In this case, this tendency manifests itself in the view that the Torah, as a genuine divine revelation, must contain the Sufi metaphysical ideas that, in al-Jīlī's view, constitute the truth, albeit with the proviso that its presentation of these ideas – and the Jewish understanding of them – is incomplete in comparison to the Qur'an.

Conclusion

Al-Jīlī's chapter on the Torah serves as a useful case study of how his Sufi metaphysical outlook determines his view of scripture, and of the pre-Qur'anic scriptures in particular.

His view of the Torah, Judaism and the Jews can best be described as ambivalent. On the one hand, the Torah constitutes a genuine revelation or, in Sufi metaphysical terms, 'manifestation' (*tajallī*) of an aspect of God, specifically, of His 'attributive names' (*al-asmāʾ al-ṣifātiyyah*). Furthermore, the seven tablets of the Torah that Moses was commanded to propagate to his people contain various forms of wisdom that, in al-Jīlī's world view, ought to be held in high regard, including theological, (Sufi) metaphysical, mystical, eschatological, historical, occult and scientific types of knowledge. Unlike the majority of medieval Muslim scholars who discuss the Torah, he does not explicitly indicate that the Jews have corrupted their scripture (*taḥrīf*), nor does he use terms such as *kufr* and *ḍalāl* to describe the Jews' theological position, as he does with the Christians, or cite the harsher Qur'anic passages on the Jews (e.g. 4.46, 5.41-42, 5.64). Indeed, on the contrary, at times he describes certain unnamed Children of Israel – particularly the intellectual and spiritual elite whom he calls the *ruhhāb* and *aḥbār* – in respectful and positive terms. Moses, meanwhile, though he is not discussed at the same length as Muhammad or Jesus are in the chapters on the Qur'an and the Gospel, emerges as a sinless figure who carried out God's commandments for the protection of the divine message and his own people, and as a model mystic. In Sufi metaphysical terms, then, Moses is a Perfect Human, even if al-Jīlī does not explicitly call him by this title, which after all belongs, properly speaking, to Muhammad alone.

This all being said, these relatively positive aspects of al-Jīlī's portrayal of the Torah and the Jews are counterbalanced by some more negative notions, which are also connected to al-Jīlī's Sufi metaphysics. So, while the Torah constitutes a form of divine manifestation, it is a less complete type of *tajallī* than the Gospel and the Qur'an, meaning that the Torah represents a lower level of existence than those scriptures. In keeping with this, al-Jīlī indicates that the 'propagated Torah', that is, the Torah that is in the Jews' possession, is an incomplete version of the Torah that was revealed to Moses, since it is missing two tablets that point towards two exalted divine mysteries, which Moses' people did not have the requisite spiritual capacity to comprehend. This incompleteness means that while the Torah correctly points to the incomparability and transcendence of God (*tanzīh*), it neglects to balance this perspective, as the Qur'an does and as Ibn 'Arabian Sufi metaphysics calls for, with that of God's comparability and immanence (*tashbīh*). This incompleteness of the Torah means that none of the Children of Israel after Moses were able to become Perfect Humans, and that, for the sake of the progress of sacred history, the revelation and law of Moses had to be abrogated by the more complete revelation of Jesus (which was in turn abrogated by the revelation of Muhammad). Finally, he indicates that the Jews have not even kept to their incomplete scripture, preferring the deductions of their own intellects to God's word – a kind of unspoken *taḥrīf al-ma'ná*. He indicates, moreover, that this is an error that will lead to their punishment in the afterlife and/or their inability to attain mystical proximity to God.

The ambivalence of al-Jīlī's view of the Torah and the Jews is in keeping with the ambivalent view of the wider medieval Islamic tradition, which can be summed up as the view that, while Moses was a genuine prophet and the Torah an originally genuine scripture, the Jews did not keep to this scripture, hence the revelation and religion of Moses were superseded by that of Muhammad. Al-Jīlī's discussion of the Torah, it can therefore be said, reflects his commitment to the Qur'an-centred view of sacred history. In addition to this, however, his view of the Torah is also determined by his Sufi metaphysical perspective, as can be seen, for instance, in his discussion of the Torah's contents, and in his conception of the Torah as an expression of a type of divine manifestation. These Sufi metaphysical notions make his view of the Torah rather distinctive. Their presence in a chapter ostensibly devoted to the Torah reflects the all-pervasiveness of al-Jīlī's Sufi metaphysical outlook within his writing, for, as al-Jīlī sees it, it is only through understanding the ideas of universal theophany, the levels of existence and the Perfect Human that one can understand the nature and significance of the Torah and the other scriptures. His position outlined here can, therefore, be described as a Sufi metaphysical version of the Qur'an-centred view of the Torah.

5

The Psalms

In chapter thirty-seven of *al-Insān al-kāmil*, al-Jīlī presents us with his conception of the Psalms (*al-Zabūr*), and of the prophet associated with that scripture, David (*Dāwūd*). The chapter also is partly devoted to Solomon (*Sulaymān*), who is closely associated with his father David in the Islamic tradition, just as he is in the biblical tradition. The Psalms is one of the few scriptures named by the Qur'an (see Q 4.163, 17.55, 21.105), and so takes its place among those scriptures universally recognized in Islam. Indeed, the Qur'an (Q 21.105) contains an 'explicit verbatim quotation' from the Psalms (Ps. 37.29), which establishes that the 'author' of the Psalms is the same as the divine author of the Qur'an and the other scriptures.[1] According to the Qur'anic conception, then, just as God revealed the Torah to Moses, the Gospel to Jesus and the Qur'an to Muhammad, so too did he reveal the Psalms to David. At the same time, it should be noted that the Psalms does not occupy so important a place in the Qur'an-centred view of sacred history as those other scriptures. All of this, we shall see, is reflected in al-Jīlī's presentation of the Psalms.

It seems likely that, just as he seems to have been unfamiliar with the actual Torah, al-Jīlī would have had little detailed knowledge of the biblical Psalms. While some Muslim scholars before him had some knowledge of some of the canonical Psalms,[2] the Cairene exegete al-Biqā'ī (d. 885/1480), who wrote after al-Jīlī's death and who stands out for his use of the Bible to interpret the Qur'an, seems to be the first Muslim scholar to display extensive knowledge of the biblical book of Psalms.[3] It appears that, prior to al-Biqā'ī, educated Muslims had a general conception of the Psalms as a book of pious sayings, prayers and admonitions that God had revealed to David, probably in Hebrew, and which was still being used in Jewish (and possibly Christian) liturgy.[4] For most Muslims up to al-Jīlī's time, then, the Psalms was, as David Vishanoff has put it, 'an imagined book',[5] that is, a scripture whose name they knew from the Qur'an, and of which they had a vague idea from discussions in post-Qur'anic literature and lore, yet of whose actual contents they had very little, if any, direct knowledge.[6] This was the intellectual context in which al-Jīlī developed his view of the Psalms.

'*Al-Zabūr*': the term and its meaning

Al-zabūr is a Syriac word (*lafẓah sūriyāniyyah*) that means 'the book' (*al-kitāb*). The Arabs (*al-'arab*) used it, with the result that God – Majestic and lofty is He –

> sent down (*anzala*) [the verse]: 'And all that they did is [noted down] in the *zubur*,' (Q 54:52) i.e. in the books (*fī al-kutub*).[7]

Al-Jīlī begins his chapter on the Psalms with a discussion of the origin and meaning of the term *al-zabūr*. In so doing, he adds his voice to a debate among Qur'anic exegetes over the meaning of this Qur'anic term. His position on this issue is largely in keeping with the dominant view of the Qur'anic exegetes, namely that the basic meaning of *al-zabūr* is 'the book' (*al-kitāb*), due to the etymological association of the root *z-b-r* with 'writing'.[8] Al-Jīlī adduces as evidence for this position Qur'an 54.52, where the plural form *al-zubur* is usually taken to mean the 'books' in which the deeds of humankind are recorded, rather than the book of Psalms.

Yet al-Jīlī also goes further than many of the exegetes in his analysis of the etymology of *al-zabūr*: in his view, it is an originally Syriac term (*lafẓah sūriyāniyyah*) that was Arabicized prior to the revelation of the Qur'an. In making this point, he is again contributing to a wider debate among Qur'anic exegetes, this time regarding whether the Qur'an contains foreign words. While, among the earliest exegetes, 'it was fully recognized and frankly admitted that there were numerous foreign words in the Qur'an',[9] later generations of commentators, under the impact of the Sunni doctrine of the uncreatedness of the Qur'an, tended to question this earlier judgement, the most widely adopted Muslim view ultimately being that foreign words in the Qur'an were limited to technical terms used in earlier revelations.[10] Such a view, indeed, had its adherents among the Ibn 'Arabian Sufis: al-Jandī, for instance, devotes several paragraphs of the first part of his commentary on the *Fuṣūṣ* to a refutation of the view that the divine name *Allāh* has a Hebrew origin.[11] Nevertheless, some medieval Sunni scholars, such as Ibn al-Jawzī (d. 597/1200/1), 'Abd al-Raḥmān al-Tha'labī (d. 875/1479) and al-Suyūṭī, adopted the view that the Qur'an *does* contain foreign words that had been Arabicized prior to the Qur'anic revelation. Al-Tha'labī, for instance, writes in his *tafsīr*, *Kitāb al-Jawāhīr*: 'The truth is that these words were foreign, but the Arabs made use of them and Arabicized them, so from this point of view they are Arabic.'[12] This seems to be the position taken by al-Jīlī here.

Among the foreign terms that exegetes found in the Qur'an were many of Syriac origin.[13] Among the eleven foreign languages in the Qur'an identified by al-Suyūṭī in his *al-Mutawakkilī*, for instance, is '*al-lughah al-sūriyāniyyah*'.[14] According to Arthur Jeffrey, Syriac is 'undoubtedly the most copious source of Qur'anic borrowings', which is unsurprising given that it was, at the time of the revelation of the Qur'an, 'the spoken language of those Christian communities best known to the Arabs'.[15] It is notable, however, that not all of the Qur'anic terms classified by al-Suyūṭī as Syriac are actually of Syriac origin. As Andrew Rippin notes,

> Goldziher has pointed out that *suriyānī* was frequently used by Muslim writers for anything ancient, time honoured, and consequently little understood. . . . It is thus clear that *suriyānī* in the writings of the Muslim exegetes may frequently have meant nothing more than that a word was of the old learned tongues and so more or less unintelligible to the ordinary person.[16]

Is it in this latter sense that al-Jīlī is using the term *lafẓah sūriyāniyyah* here? There is no evidence that al-Jīlī knew Syriac, and it is therefore highly unlikely that his identification of *al-Zabūr* as a Syriac word was a product of his own etymological research.[17] Equally, however, we do not need to go so far as to say that he is using the term 'Syriac' in the sense in which we say 'It's all Greek to me', that is, without intending any reference to the actual Syriac language. Rather, it seems likely that he identifies *al-zabūr* as Syriac because of the probable association of that language, in his mind and in medieval Islamic thought more broadly, with sacred scripture, for an educated Muslim of the medieval Middle East would in all probability have known Syriac to be the liturgical language of many of the Christian communities of the region. Indeed, as we shall see in the following chapter, al-Jīlī explicitly declares the Gospel, the scripture of the Christians, to have been revealed in Syriac. Moreover, while al-Suyūṭī does not include *al-zabūr* among his list of words of Syriac origin in the Qur'an,[18] and though the earlier historian al-Mas'ūdī (d. 345/956) suggests that the book was revealed in Hebrew,[19] it seems that the term *lughat al-zabūr* ('the language of the Psalms') was used in medieval times to denote the Syriac language.[20] If al-Jīlī believed that the Psalms was revealed in Syriac, therefore, then it would only have been a short move to the position that the Arabic word for 'the Psalms' was itself of Syriac origin.

Al-Jīlī's brief discussion of the origins and meaning of the term *al-zabūr* tells us something significant about his conception of scripture and sacred history. In acknowledging the presence of foreign words in the Qur'an, he implicitly recognizes its pre-history, that is, the story of God's engagement with other communities prior to the revelation of the Qur'an, through His revelation of different scriptures in different languages to different prophets, to be propagated to different peoples. At the same time, in noting that the word *al-zabūr* had been 'adopted' by the Arabs from Syriac, he might be said to be implying that these earlier revelations, and the languages in which they were revealed, were in a sense absorbed into the more complete Arabic Qur'an, in accordance with the Qur'an-centred view that the Qur'an abrogates the previous revelations by virtue of its greater completeness.

The revelation and propagation of the Psalms

> He [i.e. God] sent down (*anzala*) the Psalms to David in distinct, separate verses (*āyāt mufaṣṣalāt*), but he [i.e. David] only revealed (*yakhruj*) it to his people (*li-qawmihi*) as a single whole (*jumlatan wāḥidatan*), after God – May He be exalted – had completed (*akmala*) sending it down (*nuzūl*) to him.[21]

It is clear from the previous section that, when he writes of *al-zabūr*, al-Jīlī means the book of Psalms that God sent down to David. In this way, while acknowledging, at the beginning of the chapter, the polysemy of the term *zabūr* and its basic meaning of 'book', ultimately, he restricts it to this one meaning.

The key terms of this passage – *anzala/nuzūl, āyāt mufaṣṣalāt, qawm, jumlatan wāḥidatan, akmala* – concern the way in which God revealed the Psalms to David, and the way in which David, in turn, revealed it to his people. As noted previously, the term *anzala* is used in the Qur'an on multiple occasions to denote God's 'sending down' of scripture. It is used both of the Qur'an itself (e.g. Q 2.185, 12.2, 20.113) and of other scriptures, notably the Torah and the Gospel (e.g. Q 3.3). The Qur'an also uses the term *nazzala*, a different form of the same root, to denote the act of revelation, though this is used only of the sending down of the Qur'an (e.g. Q 17.82, 17.106, 25.1, 76.23) and not of the Torah and Gospel. The medieval Qur'anic exegetes make much of the use of the different terms *nazzala* and *anzala* for the different scriptures in Qur'an 3.3: 'He sent down (*nazzala*) upon you the Book [i.e. the Qur'an] in truth, confirming what came before it, and He sent down (*anzala*) the Torah and the Gospel.' The Mu'tazilite commentator al-Zamakhsharī, who is known for his concern with linguistic issues in the Qur'an, writes: If you say, 'Why is it said, "He sent down (*nazzala*) the Book," "and He sent down (*anzala*) the Torah and Gospel"?' I would say, 'Because the Qur'an came down in gradations (*munajjaman*), while the [other] two books came down all at once (*jumlatan*).'[22] On the one hand, this interpretation is apparently supported by verse 17.106, which is usually understood to mean, 'We have revealed it [the Qur'an] in stages (*nazzalnāhu tanzīlan*).' On the other hand, its validity is cast into doubt by the use of the term *anzala* in other verses to denote the revelation of the Qur'an, too. Moreover, in a hadith that al-Jīlī quotes in his chapter on the Qur'an, Muhammad is reported to have said, 'He sent down the Qur'an to me as a single whole (*anzala al-Qur'ān 'alayya jumlatan wāḥidatan*).'[23] In that chapter, as we have seen, al-Jīlī aims to resolve the tension in the question of how the Qur'an was revealed by making a distinction between what he calls 'the Generous Qur'an' (*al-Qur'ān al-karīm*) – which denotes how the Qur'an was revealed as a single whole – and 'the Wise Qur'ān' (*al-Qur'ān al-ḥakīm*) – which denotes how the Qur'an was revealed in separate verses and *sūrahs*, as stated in Qur'an 17.106.[24] An alternative solution adopted by certain exegetes, as we have also seen, was to say that the Qur'an was revealed from the Mother of the Book/Preserved Tablet to the lowest heaven (*samā' al-dunyā*) as a single whole, and then revealed to Muhammad in stages.

Al-Jīlī's discussion of how the Psalms was revealed ought to be viewed within the context of this debate. In this regard, it should be noted that the hadith he quotes in the chapter on the Qur'an matches almost word for word his description of the revelation of the Psalms to David. In al-Jīlī's view, then, the Psalms is in a sense analogous to the Qur'an by virtue of having been revealed both as a single, complete (*kāmil*) whole (by God to David), and then propagated in 'distinct, separate verses' (*āyāt mufaṣṣalāt*) (by David to his people). This analogy between the Psalms and the Qur'an is reinforced by his use of the term *āyāt mufaṣṣalāt*, which evokes the common word for the verses (*āyāt*) of the Qur'an. Just as earlier scholars such as al-Mas'ūdī and al-Qurṭubī drew an implicit parallel between the Psalms and the Qur'an by using the term *sūrah* to denote an individual psalm,[25] so too does al-Jīlī place the Psalms in a Qur'anic framework by his use of the term *āyah* for that purpose. As with his modelling the Torah on the Qur'an, this tendency to model the Psalms on the Islamic scripture reflects a more general medieval Muslim tendency to view the earlier scriptures as essentially analogous to the Qur'an.

The audience of the Psalms, in al-Jīlī's conception, is David's 'people' (*qawm*). His use of that term here reflects a conception of sacred history according to which each people (*qawm*) or community (*ummah*) possesses its own particular prophet(s) and revelation(s), a conception that is firmly Qur'an-centred (see e.g. Q 14.4), and which we also find in the other chapters of *al-Insān al-kāmil* on the scriptures. In the chapters on the Torah and the Gospel, al-Jīlī refers to Moses' people (*qawm Mūsá*),[26] Jesus' people (*qawm ʿĪsá*)[27] and Muhammad's people (*qawm Muḥammad*).[28] In those chapters, as well as in the final chapter of the book, al-Jīlī gives us to understand that by these terms he means, respectively, the Jews (*al-Yahūd*), the Christians (*al-Naṣārá*) and the Muslims (*al-Muslimīn, ahl al-Islām*).[29] Moses' people, Jesus' people and Muhammad's people, therefore, constitute, in his conception, three separate (religious) 'communities' (*milal, umam*).[30] In the case of David's people, however, al-Jīlī does not make it clear, either here or in the final chapter, who exactly they are and whether they constitute a separate religious community. This is a reflection of the Qur'an's own lack of specificity regarding the community to whom the Psalms was revealed and by whom it was held sacred. While the Torah of Moses is firmly associated with the Jews, and the Gospel of Jesus with the Christians, the Psalms of David seems to occupy a kind of middle ground between the two religious communities. We can infer from the Qur'an (see Q 5.78) and from medieval Muslim authors' references to David as king of the Children of Israel that it was generally understood that David's people were the same as Moses' people, which is to say that they were the Jewish people. It seems likely that al-Jīlī shared this view, in which case it would appear that a single religious community, in his conception, could possess more than one prophet and scripture.[31] Nevertheless, his indeterminacy on the matter reflects the somewhat nebulous status of the Psalms in medieval Islamic thought.

David's attributes (i)

> David – Peace be upon him – was the loveliest of people in conversation (*alṭaf al-nās muḥāwaratan*) and the best of them in character traits (*wa-aḥsanahum shamāʾil*). When he recited the Psalms (*talā al-zabūr*), the animals (*al-ḥayawānāt*) – namely, the wild animals and the birds (*al-wuḥūsh wa-al-ṭuyūr*) – would stand around him. He was slender of body (*naḥīf al-badan*) and short of stature (*wa-qaṣīr al-qāmah*), but possessed great strength (*dhā quwwah shadīdah*). And he was well acquainted with the sciences in use in his time (*kathīr al-iṭṭilāʿ ʿalá al-ʿulūm al-mustaʿamalah fī zamānihi*).[32]

Though chapter thirty-seven of *al-Insān al-kāmil* is ostensibly devoted to the Psalms, al-Jīlī also provides the reader with a fairly detailed and self-contained depiction of David and a discussion of some of the issues pertaining to him in Islamic literature. As in the case of his treatment of the Psalms, his view of David is anchored in the Qur'an and post-Qur'anic literature. This is particularly true in the case of his presentation of David's attributes.

The key terms used by al-Jīlī in describing David's attributes can be divided into three categories, namely, (a) his moral qualities – *aḥsanahum shamā'il*, (b) his physical attributes, including his beautiful voice – *alṭaf al-nās muḥāwaratan, talā al-zabūr, naḥīf al-badan wa-qaṣīr al-qāmah, dhā quwwah shadīdah*; (c) and his learning and knowledge – *kathīr al-iṭṭilāʿ ʿalá al-ʿulūm al-mustaʿamalah fī zamānihi*. Taken together, they produce a portrait of David as a kind of ideal man: morally upright, physically strong and remarkably learned. In this regard, it is noteworthy that the term al-Jīlī uses for David's qualities – *shamā'il* – comes from a root that is associated with comprehensiveness,[33] and is, moreover, a term that is often used in the Islamic tradition to denote the qualities of Muhammad.[34] The implication, perhaps, is that David is a Perfect Human (*insān kāmil*), who brings together the various (divine) attributes in himself – though this is never explicitly spelled out in this chapter or elsewhere in the book, just as it is never stated explicitly of any of the prophets other than Muhammad.

The style and structure of the passage, with its concise listing of key terms describing David's qualities, follow the pattern of the opening sections of the chapters on David in works of history (*tārīkh*) and prophetic tales (*qiṣaṣ al-anbiyā'*).[35] Furthermore, much of the specific information conveyed by al-Jīlī here is also found in those works (to a greater degree than can be said of al-Jīlī's treatment of the other prophets). Al-Jīlī's description of the loveliness of David's conversation, for instance, echoes the post-Qur'anic tradition that David possessed a uniquely beautiful voice,[36] while his reference to David's capacity to draw the animals to him with his voice is strongly reminiscent of, for example, al-Ṭabarī's description in his *Tārīkh*: 'When he recited the Psalms (*qaraʾa al-zabūr*), the wild animals (*al-wuḥūsh*) would cry out to him, until he took hold of them by the necks. And they would truly listen in silence.'[37] Similarly, Ibn Kathīr informs us,

> God had given him a great voice such as had not been given to anyone, so that when it rung out in the recitation of His book, the birds would stop in the air and come back, [drawn] by the vibration of his voice, and they would sing His praises along with him, whenever he sung praises, morning and evening.[38]

While the ultimate source for al-Jīlī's description of David may be the Qur'an (Q 21.79, 34.10), as well as *Isrāʾīliyyāt*-type traditions transmitted by early figures such as the Jewish convert to Islam Wahb b. Munabbih (d. 114/732),[39] it is possible that he drew directly on these famous works of *tārīkh* and *qiṣaṣ al-anbiyā'*. Likewise, when al-Jīlī describes David as *dhā quwwah shadīdah*, the ultimate source may be Qur'an 38.17, which describes David as 'the possessor of strength' (*dhā al-ayd*), yet it is also possible that al-Jīlī's understanding of this verse was mediated through a source such as al-Ṭabarī's *tafsīr*, where *dhā al-ayd* is glossed as *dhā al-quwwah*.[40] Aside from helping us build a picture of al-Jīlī's view of David, therefore, the passage gives us some insight into the possible sources of al-Jīlī's information and the literature and ideas of which he was aware. It is clear, moreover, that his depiction of David's attributes is in keeping with the common depiction of David in medieval Islamic literature.

This being said, al-Jīlī's notion that David possessed perfect knowledge of the sciences in use in his day does not appear to be an echo of earlier depictions. It is true that the Qur'an states that David and Solomon were given knowledge (*'ilm*) (Q 21.78-79, 27.15) – the same term that al-Jīlī uses here – and that David was commonly depicted in post-Qur'anic literature as a wise judge, among other roles.[41] Nevertheless, I have not come across any traditions stating that David was an expert in the Sufi metaphysical and rational sciences, which, as we shall see, al-Jīlī believes are contained in the Psalms, and therefore to be known to David. Again, the idea seems to be that David, as a perfect mystic, metaphysician and rational thinker, was a kind of Perfect Human.[42] This being said, al-Jīlī's point that David knew all of the sciences 'in use in his own time' also serves to *limit* David's knowledge to the knowledge of that time. There is perhaps an implication here that the Perfect Humans of later ages – in particular, Muhammad and his Muslim 'heirs' – were able to surpass David by virtue of possessing complete knowledge of the sciences of their own, more advanced ages – that is, the 'knowledge of the last and first things' mentioned in the title of al-Jīlī's book or the 'knowledge of the first people and the last people' mentioned in the chapter on the Torah. David, in other words, may be perfect, but he is still 'less perfect' than Muhammad, the archetypal Perfect Human.

The contents and hierarchy of the scriptures

> Know that in every book (*kitāb*) that He sent down to a prophet (*nabī*), He only put sciences (*'ulūm*) that were of the level of that prophet's knowledge of the divine wisdom (*ḥikmah ilāhiyyah*), so that the prophet would not be ignorant (*lā yajhal*) of that which he brought. For the books are distinguished (*yatamayyiz*) from one another in superiority (*al-afḍaliyyah*), to the degree that one messenger (*mursal*) is distinguished from another in the view of God – May He be exalted. For this reason, the Qur'an is the best of the books of God (*afḍal kutub Allāh*) – May He be exalted – which were sent down to his prophets (*anbiyā'*), because Muhammad was the best of the messengers (*afḍal al-mursalīn*). And if you say, 'One part of God's speech (*kalām Allāh*) has no superiority (*lā afḍaliyyah*) over another,' we would say, 'It has been reported in the hadith of the Prophet that he said, '*Sūrat al-Fātiḥah* is the best "sign" in the Qur'an (*afḍal āy al-Qur'ān*).'[43]

This passage deals with two interconnected topics, namely, the contents of scripture (in general) and the hierarchy of scriptures, and is therefore an important passage for our investigation of al-Jīlī's view of the scriptures. Both topics, as he sees it, are inextricably connected to prophecy: both the contents of the individual scriptures, and their order of superiority, follow on from the qualities of the prophet to whom they are revealed. Using the key terms of this passage, it can be said that, for al-Jīlī, the forms of knowledge or 'sciences' (*'ulūm*) contained in the scriptures (*al-kutub*) are determined by the level of knowledge (*'ilm*) of the prophets/messengers (*al-anbiyā'/al-mursalīn*) to whom they are revealed. The knowledge of the messengers, in turn, consists of their share of the divine wisdom (*ḥikmah ilāhiyyah*), by which al-Jīlī seems to mean, as we shall see, both Sufi metaphysical wisdom and rational scientific knowledge. Moreover, because different prophets possess different shares of the divine wisdom, there is a hierarchy of prophets. And because, as just noted, the contents of the scriptures are determined by the level of the prophets' knowledge, it follows that there is a hierarchy of scriptures as well. This sense of hierarchy is reflected in his repeated use here of terms such as *yatamayyiz*, *al-afḍaliyyah* and *afḍal* connoting uniqueness and superiority.

Al-Jīlī's position on the hierarchy of prophets and scriptures is founded on a conception of prophecy according to which prophets are distinguished according to the degree of their access to the divine wisdom. In suggesting that each prophet possesses a different type of divine wisdom – or the same divine wisdom but to a different degree – al-Jīlī seems to be following Ibn ʿArabī's conception of prophecy as outlined in his *Fuṣūṣ al-ḥikam*. The key idea of that major work of Ibn ʿArabī's is that the 'word' (*kalimah*) of each of the prophets represents a different type of divine wisdom (*ḥikmah*): for example, the wisdom of divinity (*ilāhiyyah*) in the case of Adam, transcendence (*ʿalawiyyah*) in the case of Moses and singularity (*fardiyyah*) in the case of Muhammad.[44] While Ibn ʿArabī does not fully bring out the implications of this idea for the hierarchy of prophets, nevertheless such a hierarchy is certainly in the background: the singularity of Muhammad, for instance, reflects his status as the best of prophets and 'most perfect' (*akmal*) being in the universe.[45] Al-Jīlī, in his role as an expounder and elaborator of Ibn ʿArabī's ideas, states this more explicitly: the Qur'an is the best of scriptures, because Muhammad is the best of messengers (*afḍal al-mursalīn*). This is a view (and expression), of course, that fully accords with the Qur'an-centred view of sacred history. Coming soon after al-Jīlī's description of David's qualities, its appearance here serves to reinforce the sense that, while David may have been the Perfect Human of his age, nevertheless the most perfect of the Perfect Humans – indeed, the one true Perfect Human of all ages – is Muhammad.

Al-Jīlī reinforces this sense of hierarchy among the scriptures and prophets through his contribution to another debate in the exegetical tradition and theological literature: namely, the question of whether one part of divine revelation can be said to be superior to another. Interestingly, by arguing that there *is* a hierarchy within the divine word, al-Jīlī is setting himself against what is apparently the majority opinion. Al-Ṭabarī, for instance, writes:

> It is not possible (*ghayr jā'iz*) for one thing in the Qur'an to be better (*khayr*) than another thing, because all of it is the speech of God (*kalām Allāh*), and it is not possible with regards to the attributes of God (*ṣifāt Allāh*) – May He be exalted – for it to be said that some of them are better than others (*baʿḍuhā khayr min baʿḍ*).[46]

Al-Ṭabarī's reasoning is similar to al-Jīlī's, even if, because of their different premises, they arrive at different conclusions. Whereas, for al-Jīlī (as shall be made clear presently) the hierarchy among the scriptures reflects how they represent manifestations of different kinds of divine names and attributes, which are themselves marked by hierarchy, for al-Ṭabarī, the absence of hierarchy among the divine attributes necessitates the absence of hierarchy within the divine revelation, which is all the 'speech' of God. Of course, al-Ṭabarī's argument concerns the Qur'an alone, not the hierarchy of scriptures: he and other medieval Muslim authors, as we saw in Chapter 2, would not argue with al-Jīlī's position that the Qur'an is superior to the other scriptures.

The basis for al-Jīlī's position is the hadith that he quotes regarding the superiority of the *Fātiḥah* over the rest of the Qur'an. While this particular hadith is not found in any of the six canonical books, hadiths on the superiority of the *Fātiḥah* do appear in the major collections;[47] hence, while the authenticity of the particular hadith he quotes may be doubtful, the idea that it expresses is a fairly conventional one in medieval Islamic thought.[48] His use of this idea in support of the view that, by analogy, there is a hierarchy of scriptures, with the Qur'an at the top, is typically idiosyncratic, creative and yet not without logic. For our purposes, its significance is that it helps al-Jīlī establish that there is a hierarchy of scriptures and prophets, within which David and the Psalms must fit. Though he is not drawn here on where David and the Psalms fit within this hierarchy (an issue that he clarifies later), it is evident from this passage that they rank below Muhammad and the Qur'an.

The contents of the Psalms

> Know that most of the Psalms consists of admonitions (*mawāʿiẓ*), and the remainder of it consists of praise of God (*thanāʾ ʿalá Allāh*), in accordance with how He is described in it. And there are no laws (*sharāʾiʿ*) within it, except for [in] specific verses (*āyāt makhṣūṣah*), but those admonitions and that praise contain abundant true, divine sciences (*ʿulūm jammah ilāhiyyah ḥaqīqiyyah*), and the sciences of absolute existence (*ʿulūm al-wujūd al-muṭlaq*), and the science of the manifestation of the Real – May He be exalted – within creation (*ʿilm tajallī al-ḥaqq taʿālá fī al-khalq*), and the science of dominion and administration (*ʿilm al-taskhīr wa-al-tadbīr*), and the science of the requirements of the realities of existents (*ʿilm mu qtaḍayāt ḥaqāʾiq al-mawjūdāt*), and the science of the receptacles and preparednesses (*ʿilm al-qawābil wa-al-istiʿdādāt*), and the biological sciences (*ʿilm al-ṭabīʿiyyāt*), and the mathematical sciences (*ʿilm al-riyāḍiyyāt*), and the science of logic (*ʿilm al-manṭiq*), and the science of viceregency (*ʿilm al-khilāfah*), and the science of philosophy (*ʿilm al-ḥikmah*), and the science of physiognomy (*ʿilm al-firāsah*), and other sciences. And all of those come consecutively (*bi-ṭarīq al-istitbāʿ*). Within it are things [said] by way of open expression (*al-taṣrīḥ*), which it is not harmful (*lā yaḍurr*) to reveal (*iẓhār*), and which do not lead to the unveiling of one of the mysteries of God (*kashf sirr min asrār Allāh*) – May He be exalted.[49]

Having set out the reason why the different scriptures contain different forms of knowledge (namely, the different levels of knowledge of the prophets who received them), al-Jīlī brings the discussion back to the Psalms, turning to the contents of that particular scripture. Most Muslim authors prior to al-Jīlī who dealt with the Psalms provide only a very brief summary of its contents, while only a handful of scholars – such as al-Yaʿqūbī (d. 284/897/8), Ibn Qutaybah (d. 276/889) and Ibn Ḥazm – quote from or paraphrase some of the canonical Psalms at length.[50] Though we cannot put al-Jīlī in the group of those scholars who quote from or had direct knowledge of the biblical book of Psalms, he does give a more detailed overview of the contents of the Psalms – as he sees it – than most other authors. Moreover, while some elements of his descriptive summary are clearly conventional, many of the others seem to be original to him.

To begin with those elements that are conventional, it is notable that the key terms of the opening sentence of the above passage are the same as or synonyms of the key terms used by earlier scholars such as al-Ṭabarī, al-Masʿūdī and al-Qurṭubī in their descriptions of the contents of the Psalms: *mawāʿiẓ*, *thanāʾ* and (*mā fīhī min*) *sharāʾiʿ*.[51] For al-Jīlī as for those earlier scholars, therefore, the Psalms are primarily a book of wisdom and praise, not of law, though he does add as an aside the unconventional view that certain 'verses' (*āyāt makhṣūṣah*) (note once more the use of the Qur'anic term) of the Psalms *do* contain legal prescriptions. It is possible, given that he has just been discussing the hierarchy of scriptures, that al-Jīlī views the relative absence of law in the Psalms as a deficiency vis-à-vis other scriptures, notably the Qur'an and the Torah. On the other hand, it is also possible that he views the Psalms as complementary to the legalistic Torah, in which case he would be acknowledging the relative (though still deficient, vis-à-vis the Qur'an) completeness of the scriptures of the Children of Israel.

Where al-Jīlī departs from the earlier scholars who provided overviews of the contents of the Psalms is in his description of the 'sciences' (*ʿulūm*) contained in the statements of praise and admonition in the Psalms. Indeed, the closest parallel to al-Jīlī's overview of the contents of the Psalms is in fact his description in the previous chapter of the various 'sciences' contained in the tablets of the Torah. In what follows I give brief explanations of the various sciences that, according to al-Jīlī, are contained in the Psalms, and of the technical terms used to denote them:

- ***ʿulūm jammah ilāhiyyah ḥaqīqiyyah*:** This is a very general term that could conceivably denote knowledge of, about, possessed by or given by God (*Allāh*, *al-ḥaqq*). The adjective *ilāhiyyah* picks up al-Jīlī's earlier use of the term *ḥikmah ilāhiyyah* to denote the knowledge possessed by the prophets. The second adjective, *ḥaqīqiyyah*, indicates that we are probably dealing with Sufi metaphysical knowledge; in the introduction to his *Marātib al-wujūd*, for instance, al-Jīlī refers to books in the Ibn ʿArabian Sufi metaphysical tradition as 'books of reality' (*kutub al-ḥaqīqah*),[52] while, in the chapter of *al-Insān al-kāmil* on the Torah, as we have seen, he identifies the second layer of knowledge in the Qur'an as 'knowledge of the realities' (*ʿilm al-ḥaqāʾiq*). The term as a whole therefore probably refers to Sufi metaphysical knowledge.
- ***ʿulūm al-wujūd al-muṭlaq***: *Al-wujūd al-muṭlaq* is one of the most important technical terms in the Sufi metaphysics of Ibn ʿArabī and his interpreters, in whose usage it denotes the utterly unlimited existence of God (in contrast to the limited existence [*al-wujūd al-muqayyad*] of creation).[53] Al-Jīlī uses it in much the same way: for him, it signifies the absolute existence of the divine essence at the level of unqualified oneness (*al-aḥadiyyah*).[54] The term *ʿulūm al-wujūd al-muṭlaq*, then, denotes metaphysical knowledge of the divine essence at its first level of manifestation. It can therefore be viewed as a subcategory of the *ʿulūm jammah ilāhiyyah ḥaqīqiyyah*.
- ***ʿilm tajallī al-ḥaqq taʿālá fī al-khalq***: This is another highly Ibn ʿArabian phrase and concept. Indeed, it denotes *the* key idea of Ibn ʿArabian Sufi metaphysics,

namely the idea of universal theophany, which, as noted in Chapter 1 of this book, is most often figured by the key term *tajallī*.

- ***ʿilm al-taskhīr wa-al-tadbīr***: *Al-taskhīr* and *al-tadbīr* are also technical terms in Ibn ʿArabian Sufi metaphysics, though they also appear in other genres of literature, notably political philosophy. The verb *sakhkhara* is used (twenty-two times) in the Qur'an to denote God's subjugation of created things (see e.g. Q 21.81). Significantly, it occurs in the context both of God's subjugation of the mountains and the birds such that they sing His praises with David (Q 21.79), and of God's subjugation of the wind such that it heeds Solomon's command (Q 38.36). Ibn ʿArabī uses the term *taskhīr* to denote the reciprocal effect that God and creation have upon one another.[55] Similarly, while *tadbīr* is used in political philosophy for the administration of the state, and in medicine for the administration of the body,[56] Ibn ʿArabī uses it in a metaphysical sense, to denote God's governing of the world.[57] All of these uses are probably in the background here. Thus *ʿilm al-taskhīr wa-al-tadbīr* denotes the science of political rule, because David was a worldly king; the science of God's governing of the world; and, it might further be suggested, the science of the Perfect Human's governing of the invisible and visible worlds on God's behalf.
- ***ʿilm muqtaḍayāt ḥaqāʾiq al-mawjūdāt***: Again, this term denotes a type of Sufi metaphysical knowledge. *Muqtaḍayāt* is not a term that Ibn ʿArabī uses especially often, but is found quite regularly in al-Jīlī's works (including, as we have seen, in his discussion of the Torah), where it denotes the 'requirements' associated with the nature of an existent, whether created or divine.[58] *Ḥaqāʾiq* is a key term in the Ibn ʿArabian tradition (as noted above), and in Islamic metaphysics more generally, where it has several possible (and related) meanings.[59] While al-Jīlī sometimes uses it merely as a synonym for *mawjūdāt*, that is, to denote things that exist,[60] the term *ḥaqāʾiq al-mawjūdāt* seems here to denote the inner natures, quiddities or essences (*māhiyyāt, dhawāt*) of existents. The term *ʿilm muqtaḍayāt ḥaqāʾiq al-mawjūdāt* therefore signifies knowledge of what is required by existents in their essential natures. In the case of the divine essence, this would be the requirement to make its existence manifest, and in the case of the essences of possible beings, the requirement to receive the divine manifestation and so acquire phenomenal existence. Once again, therefore, we are in the realm of Ibn ʿArabian Sufi metaphysics.
- ***ʿilm al-qawābil wa-al-istiʿdādāt***: Once more, *al-qawābil* and *al-istiʿdādāt* are technical terms in Ibn ʿArabian Sufi metaphysics. The term *qābil* and its plural *qawābil* are used to denote the passive aspect of the 'fixed entities' (*al-aʿyān al-thābitah*) – that is, the non-manifest prototypical forms – of phenomenal existents, which 'receive' their existence from God.[61] In a similar way, *istiʿdād*, a term and concept that has an Avicennian foundation,[62] signifies the capacity of existents to receive the divine manifestations.[63] The differences in the receptivities and preparednesses of the 'fixed entities' (*al-aʿyān al-thābitah*) of possible existents lead to multiplicity and hierarchy among created things; hence, these concepts are key to the Ibn ʿArabian explanation of the existence of multiplicity within a world of underlying ontological unity.

- ***'ilm al-ṭabī'iyyāt***: This appears to be the first of the sciences in the Psalms that is not directly connected to Sufi metaphysics. One of the 'rational' – that is, non-religious – sciences (*'ulūm 'aqliyyah*), in the schemes of Ibn Khaldūn and others who classified the sciences, the term *'ilm al-ṭabī'iyyāt* denotes the natural sciences or physics.[64] Among the topics covered by this term in medieval Islamic thought – as, for instance, in Ibn Sīnā's (d. 427/1037) philosophical compendium *Kitāb al-Shifā'* – are 'lectures on physics; the heaven and the world; generation and corruption; actions and passions; meteorological phenomena; the soul, plants; and the natures of animals'.[65] In keeping with this philosophical usage, when al-Jīlī uses terms of the root *t-b-'*, he most often has in mind matters connected to the lower world – that is the world of the four 'elements' (*al-ṭabā'i'*).[66] Its inclusion here may reflect the prominent motif of David's special connection to the animals.
- ***'ilm al-riyāḍiyyāt***: *Al-riyāḍiyyāt* denotes mathematics, another of the rational sciences.[67] According to Ibn Khaldūn, it includes such subjects as geometry, arithmetic, music and astronomy.[68] Its inclusion here may reflect the motif of David's beautiful voice – music, as just noted, being included in the mathematical sciences in medieval Islamic classifications of the sciences.[69]
- ***'ilm al-manṭiq***: *Al-manṭiq* is often used in Islamic thought to translate the Greek *logos*; hence *'ilm al-manṭiq* is logic, another of the rational sciences.[70] While the earlier Ash'arite *mutakallimūn* and, in particular, Ḥanbalīs such as Ibn Taymiyyah, adopted a sceptical attitude towards logic, a strong tradition of Aristotelian logic developed among *falāsifah* like al-Fārābī (d. 339/950/1) and Ibn Sīnā and those later Ash'arite theologians, such as Fakhr al-Dīn al-Rāzī, who came under the influence of philosophy, and from the thirteenth century logic was taught as part of the *madrasah* curriculum.[71] Its inclusion here, however, may also be connected to the Qur'anic tradition – discussed later in the chapter – that David and Solomon were taught 'the speech of the birds' (*manṭiq al-ṭayr*) (Q 27.16).
- ***'ilm al-khilāfah***: The term *khilāfah* is used in Islamic thought to denote how mankind is God's representative or 'viceregent' upon earth. This idea has a Qur'anic basis: in Qur'an 2.28, God says to the angels, in reference to Adam, 'I am placing a viceregent (*khalīfah*) on earth', while in Qur'an 38.26 He tells David, 'We have made you a viceregent on earth'. From early times, it seems, the concept of *khilāfah* was understood in both political and theological/metaphysical terms: the Umayyad caliphs were both rulers of the Islamic state and 'God's shadow on earth'.[72] Ibn 'Arabī, in his chapters on Adam and David in the *Fuṣūṣ*, focuses largely upon the metaphysical implications of the concept: for him, it denotes first and foremost how mankind is a locus for the divine manifestation.[73] This usage is picked up by al-Jīlī, who uses the term *khulafā'* (of Muhammad) for the Perfect Humans,[74] and defines the *khalīfah* as the individual who has 'achieved realization of His [i.e. God's] names and attributes' (*al-taḥaqquq bi-asmā'ihi wa-ṣifātihi*).[75] His inclusion of *'ilm al-khilāfah* among the contents of the Psalms is probably connected to the Qur'an's assignation of the title *khalīfah* to David, a title which, according to al-Jīlī's interpretation, denotes his status as a Perfect Human as well as a worldly ruler. In this regard, as a term used both in political thought and Sufi

metaphysics, *'ilm al-khilāfah* complements the aforementioned *'ilm al-taskhīr wa-al-tadbīr*.

- ***'ilm al-ḥikmah***: In medieval Islamic thought, *al-ḥikmah* can be a technical term meaning more than simply 'wisdom'. It is often used as a synonym for *falsafah*; indeed, some centuries before al-Jīlī's time it had come to replace that latter term as the most common term for the Neoplatonized Aristotelian philosophy of Ibn Sīnā and his interpreters.[76] Furthermore, as we have seen, the term is also used by both Ibn 'Arabī and al-Jīlī to denote the wisdom of the prophets, while Ibn 'Arabī's commentator al-Jandī links it to the Ibn 'Arabian idea of the levels of existence, defining 'wisdom' as 'knowledge of the realities of the levels (*marātib*) [of existence] and [the ability to] order (*tartīb*) objects of knowledge according to their levels'.[77] Given that the contents of the Psalms include both philosophical/scientific and Sufi metaphysical knowledge, it seems likely that *'ilm al-ḥikmah* is therefore meant to connote both of these senses, that is, both philosophical and Sufi metaphysical 'wisdom'.
- ***'ilm al-firāsah***: Physiognomy is the art of assessing a person's character based on his or her outward features. It was a practice of the ancient Greeks that was usually traced back to Hippocrates.[78] Physiognomic texts of supposedly Greek origin were translated into Arabic in the third/ninth century, after which the analogous pre-Islamic Arab practice known as *qiyāfah* was melded with Greek physiognomy to produce the science of *firāsah*, a discipline which produced a fairly considerable literature, including a work by the famous philosophical theologian Fakhr al-Dīn al-Rāzī.[79] In Sufi literature, *firāsah* is associated with mystical experience: 'In the usage of the wayfarers (*ahl al-sūluk*) [i.e. the Sufis], it is to come to know the unveiling of certainty and the direct vision of the mystery (*iṭṭilā' mukāshafat al-yaqīn wa-mu'āyanat al-sirr*)'.[80] Ibn 'Arabī, who devotes chapter 148 of the *Futūḥāt* to *'ilm al-firāsah*, uses the term in this way.[81] It therefore seems likely that the Sufi metaphysical usage is intended here.

The contents outlined by al-Jīlī seem far removed from both the contents of the canonical book of Psalms and from earlier Islamic conceptions of the contents of the Psalms. It is difficult to see how any of the Psalms contain information about physiognomy, for instance. His version of the Psalms, in other words, is very much an 'imagined book', imagined along the lines of his own Sufi metaphysical outlook, and in keeping with his knowledge of traditional motifs about David (his connection to the animals, his singing voice, his knowledge of the speech of the birds and his status as 'viceregent'). Like the Torah, therefore, al-Jīlī's Psalms is a repository of different kinds of truths, including both Sufi metaphysical truths, such as the idea of universal theophany and the Perfect Human, and various philosophical and occult sciences that an educated fourteenth-century Muslim like al-Jīlī would have studied and held in high esteem. As such, the Psalms is a fairly comprehensive guide to the truth, if interpreted in the correct way.

Nevertheless, it is not a *complete* repository of the sciences, for, as we have seen, it is relatively lacking in legal content, and so is less complete than both the Torah and the Qur'an. Moreover, several of the sciences that it contains, as we have seen, are specifically connected to David, the leading individual of the age – the implication perhaps being that the knowledge contained in the Psalms is *limited* to the sciences of David's time, as indicated in the previous section. In addition, in the final part of his description of the contents of the Psalms al-Jīlī indicates – via the key terms *al-taṣrīḥ* and *iẓhār* – that the sciences contained in the Psalms are expressed in an unambiguous and exoteric manner, so as not to cause harm (*lā yaḍurr*) to David's audience. This hypothetical 'harm', he indicates here, would consist in the revelation of the divine 'mysteries' (*kashf sirr min asrār Allāh*), that is, the deepest metaphysical truths according to al-Jīlī's threefold conception of the different types of knowledge contained in scripture presented in Chapter 4. The implication seems to be that, although the Psalms does point to some Sufi metaphysical and other truths, David's people, like Moses' and Jesus' peoples, were incapable of fully understanding those truths; hence, only those elements of Sufi metaphysical and philosophical wisdom that would not cause them to go astray were revealed in their scripture. Like the Torah, then, the Psalms is a veritable repository of wisdom, yet remains incomplete when compared to the Qur'an.

David's attributes (ii)

And David – Peace be upon Him – used to worship a lot (*kathīr al-'ibādah*), and knew the speech of the birds (*manṭiq al-ṭayr*) through divine unveiling (*bi-al-kashf al-ilāhī*), and would speak to them (*wa-yuḥaddithuhum*) through the divine power (*bi-al-quwwah al-ilāhiyyah*), and would send into their ears (*yuballigh fī ādhānihim*) whatever ideas (*al-ma'ānī*) he wanted, in whatever pronunciation (*lafẓ*) that He wished. It was not like what is claimed by those who have no knowledge (*ma'rifah*) of his state (*ḥāl*), who claim that he was speaking in the same language as the birds, claiming that it was pronounced in a conventional way (*muṣtalaḥ 'alayhi*). Rather, he understood the conversations of the birds (*aḥādīth al-ṭuyūr*) despite the difference in their sounds (*'alá ikhtilāf aṣwātihā*), and knew the ideas (*al-ma'ānī*) that those sounds indicated by way of divine unveiling (*bi-ṭarīq al-kashf al-ilāhī*), which was what [was meant when] his son Solomon said: 'We have been taught the speech of the birds (*'ullimna manṭiq al-ṭayr*).' (Q 27.16)

And he continued in that state (*ḥāl*), with the result that some claimed that the birds have a codified language (*lughah mawḍū'ah*) in which they speak to one another, and that David's understanding of that was with respect to his knowledge (*ma'rifah*) of that code (*waḍ'*). In fact, they only have sounds that they emit without possessing a code known (*waḍ' ma'lūm*) to them. However, if a state (*ḥāl*) comes upon them, a sound is emitted from them that the other birds understand by means of divine inspiration (*ilhāman ilāhiyyan*), because of the spiritual grace (*al-luṭf al-rūḥī*) that is within them. And if another state comes upon them, a sound like that is emitted from them, which is either the same or different, and it is understood by those among the birds, or by others who understand it, by means of divine inspiration (*ilhāman ilāhiyyan*). And if a sound came out of the other animals (*sā'ir al-ḥayawānāt*), David knew what the sound contained, by means

> of a divine, unveiled knowledge (*'ilman kashfiyyan ilāhiyyan*). If David wanted to speak to one of them, he spoke to it in the Syriac language if he wished, or in another of the animal sounds if he wished, and that animal would understand him through the divine power (*al-quwwah al-ilāhiyyah*) that God – May He be exalted – had given to David in his speech (*kalām*).[82]

Having begun to consider the Psalms per se, al-Jīlī here turns back to David. He treats two of David's key qualities in this passage, namely, his piety and his ability to understand the speech of the birds and converse with them. As can be seen, while he refers to David's piety with extreme concision, he discusses the issue of the speech of the birds at some length. Both of these attributes were key elements of the Qur'anic and the post-Qur'anic Islamic depictions of David.[83] Again, therefore, it can be said that al-Jīlī's depiction is in some senses conventional and Qur'an-centred. This is particularly true of his allusive reference to David's piety. The key term he uses – *kathīr al-'ibādah* – evokes the descriptions of David in the *tārīkh* and *qiṣaṣ al-anbiyā'* literature. In his *Tārīkh*, for instance, al-Ṭabarī quotes the statement of Qatādah ibn al-Nu'mān (d. 23/644), according to whom David 'was given strength in worship' (*quwwah fī al-'ibādah*).[84] According to Ibn Kathīr, meanwhile, 'David was the model (*al-muqtadá bihi*) in that time of someone who worshipped a lot (*kathrat al-'ibādah*).'[85] Perhaps surprisingly, however, al-Jīlī does not elaborate upon David's piety in the manner of other authors, particularly those Sufi authors such as the Persian Qur'an commentator Rashīd al-Dīn Maybudī (fl. early sixth/twelfth century) who depict David as a model of renunciation.[86] This is probably because al-Jīlī's primary goal here is not to instruct his readers in piety through the example of David, but rather to integrate David and the Psalms into his Sufi metaphysical conception of sacred history; hence, he shows a greater interest in those topics, such as David's knowledge of the speech of the birds and his viceregency, which have the potential to shed light on the Sufi metaphysical dimension of the figure of David.

How then, does al-Jīlī interpret the motif of the speech of the birds in such a way as to integrate it into his Sufi metaphysics? Again, it helps here to pay attention to the key terms he uses. These can be divided into three groups. The first group of terms simply denotes David's ability to understand the speech of the birds – *kāna ya'lam manṭiq al-ṭayr, kāna yafham aḥādīth al-ṭuyūr 'alá ikhtilāf aṣwātihā* – and to converse with them – *yuḥaddithuhum, yuballigh fī ādhānihim*. That David could understand the speech of the birds is, as already noted, part of the traditional Islamic view, being grounded, as al-Jīlī notes, in Qur'an 27.16. Al-Jīlī's use of the term *manṭiq al-ṭayr* follows that Qur'anic verse, and *aḥādīth al-ṭuyūr* appears to be a gloss on that term. Though the idea that David *understood* the speech of the birds is therefore a conventional one, less common is the slightly different idea, which is put forward by al-Jīlī here, that David could also *speak* to the birds in such a way that they could understand him. The Qur'an seems to imply that Solomon possessed this capacity, for in Qur'an 27.20-21 Solomon addresses the birds, and it may therefore follow, given that in Qur'an 27.16 Solomon describes how *both* he and David were taught the language of the birds, that this applies to David as well. Furthermore, it might be deduced from passages in the tales of the prophets and historical literature about the birds being drawn to the sound of David's voice that they understood the meaning of his speech.[87] Nevertheless, al-Jīlī appears to be unusual in spelling this out explicitly.

Connected to this group of key terms, moreover, is al-Jīlī's statement that David also understood the sounds that emerged from the animals other than the birds (*sā'ir al-ḥayawānāt*). In making this comment, al-Jīlī seems again to be contributing to a debate in the exegetical literature. In his commentary on Qur'an 27.16, al-Qurṭubī records the various positions within this debate. Qatādah ibn al-Nuʿmān and al-Shaʿbī (d. 103/723), he tells us, said that David's and Solomon's knowledge pertained to the speech of the birds in particular, while another group (*firqah*) held the following view:

> [His knowledge] applied to all of the animals, and he only mentioned the birds because they were a legion (*jund*) in the army of Solomon [see Q 27.17]. So, he singled them out for mention, because he conversed with them a lot (*li-kathrat mudākhalātihi*), and because [his speech] with the other animals was rare and not repeated in the way that it was repeated with the birds.[88]

It is likely that al-Jīlī would have been familiar with such debates and would therefore have been consciously contributing his voice to them. As is often the case with al-Jīlī, moreover, his contribution is made in an original way, that is, from his Sufi metaphysical perspective, as we shall see presently.

The second group of key terms relates to *how* David was able to converse with the birds. Al-Jīlī looks at this issue from his Ibn 'Arabian Sufi perspective, repeating a number of key terms again and again. David's understanding of the birds' speech, as al-Jīlī sees it, was a product of his *ḥāl*, a key term in the classical Sufi lexicon denoting the mystic's God-given spiritual state (in distinction from the spiritual 'station' [*maqam*], which is acquired through one's own effort).[89] Connected with this, al-Jīlī tells us that the conversation between David and the animals, and among the animals themselves, takes place through the divinely given, mystical powers denoted by the key terms *kashf*, *ilhām* and *quwwah*, which al-Jīlī repeats here a number of times. *Kashf*, as we have seen, is the term that al-Jīlī uses to denote a form of mystical experience that reveals knowledge of the divine mysteries,[90] and *ilhām* is sometimes used by him, as it is in Sufi literature more generally, with a similar sense.[91] It seems, then, that David's miraculous capacity to understand the speech of the birds is a result of such a mystical form of insight.[92] This fits with what we saw above, regarding David's knowledge of the Sufi metaphysical 'sciences' contained in the Psalms, a form of knowledge which is also derived from *kashf*.

The question of how David, the birds and the other animals were able to communicate with one another leads us onto the third and final group of terms, which relates to the *language* that they used. Once again, al-Jīlī seems here to be contributing to an ongoing debate in the exegetical literature. In this instance, the question is whether the birds possessed a 'codified' (*mawḍūʿah*) or 'conventional' (*muṣṭalaḥ ʿalayhi*) language. Al-Jīlī's response follows on from his earlier point: no, he says, the birds do not have a codified language; rather, they were able to understand the ideas or 'meanings' (*al-maʿānī*) denoted by the sounds made by one another through divine inspiration. For al-Jīlī, it seems, the mystical or miraculous nature of David's ability to communicate with the birds would be undermined if it were the case that the birds possessed a language with codified rules of grammar and syntax and a codified vocabulary, which David (and other humans) could learn. Indeed, because David's communication with the birds was divinely inspired, al-Jīlī explains, he could talk to the birds in whatever language he wished, that is, either in Syriac (which, based on al-Jīlī's earlier statement that *al-zabūr* is a Syriac word, he seems to think was David's mother tongue), or in any other tongue. Such are the miraculous powers of the prophets and the Perfect Humans.

The uniqueness of David's and Solomon's viceregency

> And this matter, which God – May He be exalted – gave to David and Solomon – Peace be upon them – was not limited or confined to them. Rather, it was a general matter (*amr ʿāmm*) among all of the viceregents (*al-khulafāʾ*) – by which I mean the greater viceregents (*al-khulafāʾ al-kubrá*). David and Solomon were only singled out (*ikhtaṣṣa*) by virtue of their manifestation (*al-ẓuhūr*) and public announcement (*al-taḥaddī*) of this. Nevertheless, each one of the Unique Ones (*afrād*) and the Poles (*aqṭāb*) possesses mastery (*al-taṣarruf*) over the whole of the existential kingdom (*al-mamlakah al-wujūdiyyah*), and each of them knows what trembles (*ikhtalaja*) day and night, besides the languages of the birds. Al-Shiblī – May God have mercy upon him – said, 'Were a black ant (*namlah suwdāʾ*) to crawl over a solid rock on a dark night, and I weren't to hear it (*lam asmaʿhā*), I would say, "I have been deceived or duped (*innī makhdūʿ aw mamkūr bihi*)."' And another person said, 'I wouldn't say, "and I weren't to feel it (*lam ashʿarhā*)," because it is not possible for it to crawl except through my power, since I am the one who moves it (*muḥarrikuhā*). So how could I say that I do not feel it, when I am the one who moves it?'[93]

Among the key elements of the Islamic conception of David is the idea that he was a viceregent (*khalīfah*) of God; indeed, as Ibn ʿArabī points out, David is the only figure explicitly referred to as God's viceregent in the Qur'an.[94] In the medieval exegetical tradition, David's viceregency was often linked to another aspect of his Qur'anic depiction, namely his kingship (*mulk*). Al-Jīlī's discussion of the viceregency follows directly on from his treatment of David's and Solomon's knowledge of the birds' speech, for this, it seems, is among the miraculous powers possessed by the viceregent. Once again, al-Jīlī's treatment of this topic consists of his grappling with a question. In this instance, the question concerns the generality or specificity of David's and Solomon's miraculous powers as viceregent.

What, we must first ask, does al-Jīlī mean by 'the viceregents'? In this passage he tells us that, when he uses the term *al-khulafāʾ*, he means 'the greater viceregents' (*al-khulafāʾ al-kubrá*). And among such 'greater viceregents' he includes those whom he calls the 'Unique Ones' (*al-afrād*) and the 'Poles' (*al-aqṭāb*). *Al-quṭb* is one of the names that al-Jīlī uses for the Perfect Human,[95] while the term *afrād* denotes those spiritually advanced individuals who have attained mystical 'realization' (*al-taḥqīq*),[96] which again is the privilege of the Perfect Humans. For Ibn ʿArabī, similarly, the *aqṭāb* and the *afrād* are those individuals at highest levels in the hierarchy of the Friends of God.[97] Since al-Jīlī, as we have seen, also uses the term *al-khulafā'* to denote the Perfect Humans,[98] it seems clear that what he means by *al-khulafā' al-kubrá* is the Perfect Humans or Friends of God,[99] as opposed to the *political* rulers known as caliphs, who would then be *al-khulafā' al-ṣughrá*.[100]

To return to the issue of the generality or specificity of David's and Solomon's powers, al-Jīlī first proposes that the miraculous powers possessed by David and Solomon were *not* unique to them, but were in fact a general matter (*amr 'āmm*) for the 'greater viceregents', that is the Perfect Humans. He reinforces this position by stating that *all* of the unique ones and poles possess 'mastery' (*taṣarruf*) over what he calls 'the existential kingdom' (*al-mamlakah al-wujūdiyyah*), in addition to knowing the language of the birds and all that occurs in the world. The key term *taṣarruf* – along with the related term *taṣrīf* – usually denotes in al-Jīlī's usage the quasi-divine, miraculous powers of the Friends of God or Perfect Humans. In his commentary on Ibn 'Arabī's *Futūḥāt*, for instance, al-Jīlī associates *taṣrīf* with the terms *karāmāt* and *kharq al-'ādah*, both of which are ordinarily used for miracles.[101] Similarly, he refers in chapter fourteen of *al-Insān al-kāmil* to 'the miraculous powers of the People of Aspiration' (*taṣarrufāt ahl al-himam*),[102] where the 'People of Aspiration' are to be understood as the Friends of God.[103] It would therefore appear that *all* of the Friends of God or Perfect Humans, and not just David and Solomon, are miracle workers. This is the force of the quotation from the famous Baghdadi Sufi al-Shiblī (d. 334/945) (and the anonymous commentator on al-Shiblī's statement). If an individual living in the post-prophetic era like al-Shiblī possessed the quasi-divine miraculous power to hear everything within the 'existential kingdom' (and if the anonymous commentator possessed the similarly miraculous power to 'move' all things), then it follows that Solomon and David were not the only 'viceregents'; rather, this status was also attainable by the later Friends of God or Perfect Humans.

In one respect, therefore, al-Jīlī's position is quite clear: David's and Solomon's viceregency was not unique, since all the Perfect Humans are miracle workers. However, al-Jīlī also wishes to argue that, on another level, David's and Solomon's viceregency *was* unique. They were 'singled out' (*ikhtaṣṣa*), he says, by virtue of their 'manifestation' (*al-ẓuhūr*) and 'public announcement' (*al-taḥaddī*) of their viceregency.[104] This is perhaps a reference to the fact that David and Solomon, unlike the other Perfect Humans, were worldly kings as well as prophets,[105] which is to say in al-Jīlī's terminology that they were 'lesser viceregents' as well as 'greater viceregents'. It was because of this, it seems, that they were able to fully manifest their spiritual powers in the phenomenal world, over which they had political as well as spiritual control, in contrast to the other Perfect Humans who, though certainly capable of performing miracles, govern the world while largely keeping out of sight. Because none of the other Perfect Humans were also worldly kings or publicly announced themselves as viceregents, therefore, in a certain respect it is true that David and Solomon *were* singled out by God.[106] Al-Jīlī, as is fairly typical of him (and of Ibn 'Arabian Sufi thinkers and mystics more generally), thus arrives at a kind of *coincidentia oppositorum*: on the one hand, all of the greater viceregents possess the miraculous power of *taṣarruf*, as demonstrated by the statements of Shiblī and the anonymous figure. On the other hand, he suggests, David and Solomon *did* enjoy a certain uniqueness in their viceregencies, since they were worldly kings who were able to reveal their powers openly.

Solomon's request for a unique form of kingship (i)

> And it has been reported about the Prophet, that he clung to the jinni, and wanted to tie it to the stone column of the mosque (*sāriyat al-masjid*). Then he recalled (*dhakara*) the supplicatory prayer (*du'ā'*) of Solomon, and left it. For he knew then that when Solomon had said, 'O Lord, grant me a kingship (*mulkan*) that is worthy of none after me, for You are the Giver of Gifts (*al-wahhāb*),' (Q 38:35) by this was only meant the public announcement (*al-taḥaddī*), and manifestation of (*al-ẓuhūr bi-*), this viceregency (*al-khilāfah*), which is not worthy of (*lā yanbaghī*) anyone after him in its completeness (*'alá al-kamāl*), though in certain things – but not others – the prophets manifested it, and the Friends of God (*al-awliyā'*) – May God be pleased with them – followed them in that.[107]

This section follows directly on from the last one, consisting of a more detailed explanation of *why* it is that David and Solomon possessed a unique type of viceregency. This explanation centres upon al-Jīlī's analysis of Qur'an 38.35, which tells of how Solomon requested a form of kingship (*mulk*) that was worthy of no one after him. Al-Jīlī first refers to what he calls this 'supplicatory prayer' (*du'ā'*) or 'request' (*da'wah*) of Solomon in the context of a story about the Prophet Muhammad. This story appears in the *Ṣaḥīḥayn* as well as in the *Musnad* of Aḥmad ibn Ḥanbal (d. 241/855).[108] Its relevance to the present discussion centres upon Muhammad's recollection of Solomon's request for a unique form of kinship. Al-Jīlī suggests that, in one respect, this request was answered: the uniqueness of Solomon's kingship, he says, repeating what he said earlier, consists in him publicly announcing (*al-taḥaddī*) and manifesting (*al-ẓuhūr bi-*) the viceregency, in his capacity as a prophet–king. At the same time, this should not be taken to mean that Solomon was the final viceregent: the prophets, including Muhammad, who came after him, and following them, the Friends of God, also possessed the divine viceregency, albeit not to the same degree of 'completeness' or 'perfection' (*kamāl*) as David and Solomon, who were both worldly kings and prophets. Such completeness, of course, should not be taken to imply that David and Solomon were more perfect than all of the other Perfect Humans, for we know that Muhammad is the 'most perfect' (*akmal*) Perfect Human in al-Jīlī's view. Rather, this completeness can be said to consist in their synthesis of both the worldly and metaphysical aspects of the role of viceregent or Perfect Human.

What, it might be asked, is the significance of the jinni in the story related by al-Jīlī? Why, in other words, does Muhammad's recollection of Solomon's request to God for a unique form of kingship cause him to leave the jinni that he was about to tie to the column of the mosque? In this regard, it is helpful to remember that, according to the Qur'an, the jinn are among those creatures – along with men and birds – who make up the legions (*junūd*) of Solomon (Q 27.17). This reflects Solomon's status as a worldly king who had sovereignty over the creatures of the phenomenal world, both human and animal. In letting the jinni go, therefore, Muhammad is signalling his acceptance of Solomon's unique worldly kingship, for no one after him can manifest such mundane power in such a complete way. Again, this should not be taken to imply that Muhammad was inferior to Solomon; indeed, it is notable that in the story Muhammad makes what amounts to a conscious choice to allow Solomon to retain his status as the final viceregent of his kind, the implication being that he was capable of tying the jinni to the column of the mosque had he so wished.

Notably, al-Jīlī's use of this story in this context is not original to him. In his chapter on Solomon in the *Fuṣūṣ*, Ibn 'Arabī cites the same story, interpreting it in the same way to make the same point, and using many of the same key terms. Solomon's kingship, Ibn 'Arabī says, was unique in that no one was worthy of 'manifesting it in the visible world' (*al-ẓuhūr bihi fī 'ālam al-shahādah*). He illustrates this point by telling the story of Muhammad and the jinni – or in his telling, 'the demon' (*al-'ifrīt*). The Prophet's recollection of Solomon's request (*da'wat Sulaymān*) and his abandonment of the demon, says Ibn 'Arabī, indicates that 'Muhammad did not manifest (*lam yaẓhar*) that which Solomon was made capable of and manifested'. In other words, while Solomon was a worldly king, Muhammad was not. Again, this is not to say that Muhammad's powers were inferior to Solomon's. Ibn 'Arabī makes it clear in this regard that 'Muhammad was given what Solomon was given', including 'mastery' (*al-taṣarruf*) over the demon, and only refrained from demonstrating those powers out of a sense of 'propriety' (*ta'addub*). Moreover, Ibn 'Arabī notes that Qur'an 38.35 refers to 'a kingship' (*mulkan*), not 'kingship' (*al-mulk*) per se. This leads him to conclude that Solomon's request was only for a 'certain type of kingship' (*mulkan mā*), in this way leaving open the possibility for others to be kings after him, albeit not in a manifest way, and not to the same degree of 'synthesis' (*majmū'*) of the mundane and the metaphysical.[109]

It seems likely, based on the correspondences between the positions taken by Ibn 'Arabī and al-Jīlī, their decision to draw upon the same story to illustrate their positions, and their use of some of the same key terms – for example, *al-ẓuhūr, al-taṣarruf* and, as we shall see, *ta'addaba* – that al-Jīlī is drawing directly upon this passage of the *Fuṣūṣ* here. Al-Jīlī's intended readers, it can be presumed, would have been expected to pick up on this correspondence. Ibn 'Arabī's passage can therefore be used to make more explicit some of the ideas that al-Jīlī states in a more ambiguous way. These include the idea that the uniqueness of Solomon's viceregency lies in its application to the phenomenal world, through his being a worldly king, and the notion that Muhammad, though he was not a king, nevertheless enjoyed the same powers as Solomon (and David).

The metaphysical meaning of the Psalms and the other scriptures

And know that the Psalms, in [the language of] allusion (*fī al-ishārah*) is an expression of (*'ibārah 'an*) the manifestations of the attributes of the [divine] acts (*tajalliyyāt ṣifāt al-af'āl*), while the Torah is instead an expression of (*'ibārah 'an*) the manifestations of the totality of the names of the attributes (*tajalliyyāt jumlat asmā ʾ al-ṣifāt*), and the Gospel is instead an expression of the manifestations of the names of the essence (*tajalliyyāt asmā ʾ al-dhāt*), and the Furqan is an expression of the manifestations of the totality of the attributes and names (*tajalliyyāt jumlat al-ṣifāt wa-al-al-asmā ʾ*), in an unrestricted way (*muṭlaqan*), pertaining to both those [names and attributes] of the essence and of the attributes (*al-dhātiyyah wa-al-ṣifātiyyah*), and the Qur ʾan is an expression of the pure essence (*al-dhāt al-maḥḍ*). We have already spoken about the Qur ʾan, the Furqan, and the Torah. The Psalms is an expression of the manifestations of the active attributes, so it is a detailed delineation (*tafṣīl*) of the divine, powerful, active differentiations (*al-tafārīʿ al-fiʿliyyah al-iqtidāriyyah al-ilāhiyyah*).[110]

This is one of the most significant sections of the chapter on the Psalms, and of the chapters on the scriptures more generally, since it shows clearly how al-Jīlī adopts the Qur'an-centred view of sacred history and the hierarchy of revelations, while recasting it in a Sufi metaphysical form.

In the Sufi lexicon, *ishārah* denotes the opposite type of speech to the aforementioned term *taṣrīḥ*.[111] While *taṣrīḥ* denotes a clear, unambiguous statement that is accessible to most people, *ishārah* signifies 'the esoteric language of the inexpressible mystical experience'.[112] In using the term here, then, al-Jīlī is indicating that there is a deeper, esoteric meaning to the Psalms and the other scriptures, and that he, as a spiritually and cognitively advanced Sufi, possesses knowledge of this deeper meaning. As we know from the previous chapters, the deeper meaning of the scriptures is that they represent or point to – the term he uses is *ʿibārah ʿan* ('an expression of') – a particular type of divine manifestation or revelation. This passage is helpful to us in that it summarizes the different types of divine manifestations that the different scriptures represent. Since the metaphysical meaning of the other scriptures are discussed at length in the other chapters of this book, let us concentrate here on al-Jīlī's conception of the metaphysical signification of the Psalms, before considering the broader implications of his Sufi metaphysical treatment of the scriptures for his conception of the hierarchy of scriptures.

The Psalms, al-Jīlī tells us, represents 'the attributes of the acts' (*ṣifāt al-afʿāl*). The term *ṣifāt al-afʿāl* goes back to early *kalām*. The Muʿtazilites made a distinction between the attributes of the essence (*ṣifāt al-dhāt*), which are 'those which Gods merits from all eternity, on account of his essence', and the attributes of the acts or active attributes (*ṣifāt al-afʿāl*), 'which He merits on account of His acts'.[113] The Ashʿarites, who conceived of the divine attributes in a different way to the Muʿtazilites, nevertheless kept the distinction: for them, the attributes of the essence 'are "things" which exist in God' – specifically, knowledge (*al-ʿilm*), life (*al-ḥayāt*), power (*al-qudrah*), will (*al-irādah*), speech (*al-kalām*), hearing (*al-samʿ*) and sight (*al-baṣar*) – while the attributes of the acts 'are produced by Him'.[114] The attributes of the acts therefore refer to 'what it is possible (not necessary) for God to do'.[115]

Al-Jīlī defines the attributes of the acts in a similar way, as those attributes which only have creation, and not God, as their object. One can say, for instance, that God creates existents, but not that He creates Himself; hence, the attribute of creation (*al-khalq*) is among *ṣifāt al-afʿāl*.[116] The same can be said of God's sustenance (*al-rizq*), decree (*al-qadr*), justice (*al-ʿadl*) and so forth.[117] These attributes, al-Jīlī tells us earlier in the book, appear at the level of kingship (*al-malikiyyah*),[118] which is the sixth or seventh of the forty levels of existence, depending on which version of his scheme one looks at.[119] In saying that the Psalms is an expression of the manifestations of the attributes of the divine acts, therefore, al-Jīlī seems to be suggesting that the Psalms embodies the divine manifestation at this level of existence. This fits with the fact that David, the recipient of the Psalms, was himself a king (*malik*).

In describing the Psalms as 'a detailed delineation of the divine, powerful, active differentiations', al-Jīlī indicates that the scripture provides a comprehensive summary of the different types of active attributes. However, in limiting the Psalms to the manifestation of the attributes of the divine *acts*, al-Jīlī also seems to suggest that it is a relatively limited form of divine revelation. In other words, the Psalms does not reveal the higher levels of the divine existence, specifically, lordship, all-mercifulness, divinity, qualified oneness and unqualified oneness. These levels of existence are only revealed in the other scriptures named here, which represent more exalted kinds of divine names and attributes. While, as we saw previously, the Psalms indicates Sufi metaphysical truths, nevertheless it does not itself point to the divine existence in its highest forms – an idea consistent with al-Jīlī's earlier indication that it only contains knowledge that does no harm to the spiritually uninitiated.

Turning now to the scriptures more generally, it is clear that al-Jīlī's Sufi metaphysical conception of the scriptures is the basis for his view on the hierarchy of the scriptures. As we can clearly see from the passage quoted here, the Qur'an/Furqan is the most exalted form of revelation, followed by the Gospel, then the Torah and finally the Psalms, on account of the different types of divine manifestations that they represent. Though al-Jīlī's explanation of the hierarchy of scriptures in this Sufi metaphysical way appears to be original to him, the hierarchy that he outlines is very much in keeping with the Qur'an-centred view of sacred history. In both the conventional Islamic view and al-Jīlī's conception, it is the Qur'an's comprehensiveness or completeness that marks it out as the best of scriptures, only in al-Jīlī's case this comprehensiveness is conceived in metaphysical terms, that is, in terms of the Qur'an being an expression of the all-comprehensive divine essence and, as the Furqan, of all of the divine names and attributes. His originality, then, such as it is, lies in the fact that he conceives of the hierarchy of scriptures in terms of his Ibn ʿArabian Sufi metaphysics, and not in a rejection of the conventional hierarchy.

David's viceregency

> For this reason [i.e. the Psalms being an expression of the attributes of the acts], David – Peace be upon him – was a viceregent over the world (*khalīfah ʿalá al-ʿālam*), for he made manifest the judgements (*ẓahara bi-al-aḥkām*) that were revealed to him in the Psalms (*uwḥiya ilayhi fī al-zabūr*). He journeyed over the unshakeable mountains (*yasīr al-jibāl al-rāsiyāt*), and softened the iron, and ruled over (*yaḥkum ʿalá*) different kinds of created things (*anwāʿ al-makhlūqāt*).[120]

As we have seen, there is a close connection in al-Jīlī's view between a scripture and the messenger who receives it, the knowledge contained in the scripture being determined by the messenger's knowledge. As such, it follows that the metaphysical meaning and contents of the Psalms, which al-Jīlī has just outlined, can tell us something about the nature of David, its recipient.

The most important key terms of this passage – *khalīfah 'alá al-'ālam*, *ẓahara bi-al-aḥkām*, *yaḥkum 'alá anwā' al-makhlūqāt* – are connected to David's role as ruler over the phenomenal world. The term 'viceregent over the world' echoes Qur'an 38.26, in which God declares that He has made David 'a viceregent upon earth' (*khalīfah fī al-arḍ*). The Qur'an connects this viceregency of David's to his responsibility and power of *ḥukm*, that is, his duty to 'judge [or, perhaps, to rule] between people according to the truth' (*fa-aḥkum bayn al-nās bi-al-ḥaqq*) (Q 38.22, 26). In both the Qur'anic phrase and the term used by al-Jīlī, the indication is that this duty is to be discharged in the lower world (*al-'ālam*, *al-arḍ*). Similarly, when al-Jīlī says here that David 'made manifest the judgments (*ẓahara bi-al-aḥkām*) that were revealed to him in the Psalms', a connection is made between David's viceregency and his power of *ḥukm*. Again, the notion that he 'manifested' this power of *ḥukm*, which picks up the idea that David's and Solomon's uniqueness consists in their 'manifestation' (*al-ẓuhūr bi-*) of the viceregency, indicates that David's rule is to be enacted in the phenomenal (*ẓāhir*) realm. The same idea also emerges from al-Jīlī's statement that David 'ruled over different kinds of created things (*yaḥkum 'alá anwā' al-makhlūqāt*)', which once again associates David's viceregency with the power of *ḥukm* over the phenomenal world – *al-makhlūqāt* denoting those beings within creation (*al-khalq*).

It is clear, therefore, that in this passage al-Jīlī is presenting the aspect of David as a worldly ruler. This is a perfectly conventional idea, in both the Islamic and the biblical traditions. What is unconventional, however, is that al-Jīlī links this idea to the metaphysical meaning of the Psalms. David is a viceregent with the power of *ḥukm* over the phenomenal world, he seems to be saying, because the revelation that he received was, in Sufi metaphysical terms, an expression of the attributes of the divine acts. As outlined before, among the examples of this type of divine attribute is the attribute of judgement (*al-ḥukm*), in addition to the attributes of mercy (*al-raḥmah*), creation (*al-khalq*), sustenance (*al-rizq*) and so forth. The implication seems to be that, because David received a scripture that embodies the manifestation of the active divine attributes, so too should he be considered a locus for the manifestation of those active attributes. It is this that explains the Qur'anic motifs connected to David's power, such as the iron being softened for him to make coats of mail (see Q 34.10-11, 21.79-80) (another motif that is extensively developed in the tales of the prophets and historical literature),[121] and especially his being a viceregent and king, since these motifs indicate his ability to manifest the divine attributes in the phenomenal world.

In this way, we can see how, for al-Jīlī, prophecy and scripture are two sides of the same coin: just as the scripture's contents are determined by the knowledge of the prophet who receives it, so too is the prophet's nature determined by the nature of the scripture that he receives. We saw this as well in Chapter 3: just as the Qur'an, in al-Jīlī's view, represents the absolute existence of the divine essence, so too is Muhammad, in his essence, 'the very nature of the [divine] essence (*'ayn al-dhāt*)'.[122] In relation to the Psalms, therefore, we can say that just as the book of Psalms is an expression of the attributes of the divine acts – which, as we saw previously, constitute the level of 'kingship' – so too is David a locus of manifestation of those attributes of the acts – that is, of the divine 'kingship'. In this way, the prophets, as well as the scriptures, are integrated into al-Jīlī's Sufi metaphysics of universal theophany.

David's superiority over Solomon

> Then Solomon inherited his kingship, for Solomon was David's heir (*wārith ʿan Dāwūd*), and David was an heir of the absolute Real (*wārithan ʿan al-ḥaqq al-muṭlaq*), and David was favoured (*fuḍḍila*), because the Real gave him viceregency at the beginning, and singled him out for being addressed, when he said, 'O David, We have made you a viceregent on the earth' (Q 38:26). And He did not make Solomon [a viceregent] until after he requested it, in a way that was restricted (*ʿalá nawʿ al-ḥaṣrah*). David knew that it was not possible that the viceregency be restricted to anyone in both its outward and inward senses (*ẓāhiran wa-bāṭin*), for the Real only gave it to him [in a restricted way] with respect to [his] outward manifestation [of it] (*min ḥayth al-ẓuhūr*).[123]

Throughout much of the chapter, al-Jīlī has presented David and Solomon as a pair, a presentation that accords with the Qur'anic depiction (e.g. the motif that both David and Solomon were taught the language of the birds). In this passage, however, he makes a distinction between the two prophet–kings, presenting David as the preferred prophet in God's eyes. This superiority of David is grounded in the two prophets' different kinds of 'inheritance' (*warāthah*), a term that in this context seems to be synonymous with *khilāfah*, which, as we have seen, denotes both worldly kingship (*mulk*) and divine friendship (*walāyah*).[124] While Solomon, as the Qur'an tells us (Q 27.16), is David's heir (*wārith ʿan Dāwūd*), David, according to al-Jīlī, is the 'heir of the absolute Real' (*wārith ʿan al-ḥaqq al-muṭlaq*), that is, of God Himself. This suggests that, for al-Jīlī, David should be considered a viceregent of God (*khalīfah ʿan Allāh*), and Solomon only a viceregent of God's messenger (*khalīfah ʿan rasūl Allāh*), that is, as the successor to David. In metaphysical terms, this would mean that David manifested the divine attributes of the acts in an unmediated way, while Solomon manifested them only insofar as he inherited these attributes from his father. David is therefore a more perfect locus of divine manifestation than Solomon, and therefore a 'more perfect' Perfect Human, a superiority expressed here through the contrast between David being a viceregent of the 'absolute' or 'unlimited' (*muṭlaq*) God, and Solomon being a viceregent in a 'restricted' way (*ʿalá nawʿ al-ḥaṣrah*).

Al-Jīlī's position is notable because it goes against what seems to be the dominant Islamic view. Solomon was generally believed to have surpassed David in knowledge and wisdom, a situation reflected in the fact that he succeeded, where David had tried and failed, in building the Temple in Jerusalem.[125] Al-Jīlī's view seems to stem from his close adherence to the text of the Qur'an, which, as already noted, explicitly refers only to David as a viceregent (Q 38.26). It may also be linked to al-Jīlī's sense of the significance of scripture: David, in other words, must have been superior to Solomon, by virtue of his having received the Psalms, meaning that, in addition to being a 'prophet' (*nabī*) and a 'Friend of God' (*walī*), David was also a 'messenger' (*rasūl*), while Solomon, who received no scripture of his own, was only a *nabī* and a *walī*. This superiority of David is reflected, as al-Jīlī sees it, in the two prophets' respective notions of the concept of viceregency. David, being a direct heir or viceregent of God, knew that the viceregency – that is, the viceregency belonging to the 'greater viceregent' or, as expressed here, the 'hidden viceregent' (*khalīfah bāṭin*) – could not be limited to a single individual. David, in other words, understood the ideas of universal theophany and the Perfect Human, a view that is in keeping with the notion that these ideas were among the 'sciences' contained in the Psalms. This understanding, however, was not shared by Solomon, hence his request for a unique type of viceregency or kingship. In the following section, al-Jīlī looks in more detail at this request, in order to explain why, from his Sufi metaphysical perspective, it is impossible for the viceregency to be restricted to David and Solomon.

Solomon's request for a unique form of kingship (ii)

Look at what He – May He be exalted – said, when it was related that Solomon said, 'O Lord, grant me a kingship (*mulkan*) that is worthy of none after me' (Q 38:35). He said in response, 'So We subjected for him the wind, to flow at his command, gently, wherever he directed' (Q 38:36). Then He enumerated the divine powers that were given to Solomon. But He did not say, 'So We gave him what he requested', since it is not possible to restrict it to one member of creation, because it is an exclusive possession of God's (*ikhtiṣāṣ ilāhī*). For wherever the Real appears in a locus of appearance (*maẓhar*), through His essence, that locus of appearance is the viceregent of God on earth (*khalīfat Allāh 'alá al-arḍ*).

This is what He referred to when He – May He be exalted – said, 'We have written in the Psalms, after the reminder (*dhikr*), that my righteous servants shall inherit the earth' (Q 21:105). He means: the righteous shall possess the divine inheritance (*al-warāthah al-ilāhiyyah*). And by 'the earth' here is meant the existential realities (*al-ḥaqā'iq al-wujūdiyyah*) that are contained within (*al-munḥasir bayn*) the loci of manifestation of the Real and the inner realities of created things (*al-majālī al-ḥaqqiyyah wa-al-ma'ānī al-khalqiyyah*). And this is what He referred to when He said, 'My earth is vast (*wāsi'ah*), therefore worship/serve Me' (Q 29.56).

But if you were to say that Solomon's petition was answered (*mustajābah*), in consideration of the fact that the greater kingdom (*al-mamlakah al-kubrá*) is worthy of no one after God, who is the reality of Solomon (*ḥaqīqat Sulaymān*), and so his petitionary prayer would have come true for him, you would be right. And if you were to say that Solomon's petition was not answered (*ghayr mustajābah*), in consideration of the viceregency not being limited to him, because it is also valid for the Poles (*al-aqṭāb*) and Unique Ones (*al-afrād*) [who came] after him, you would [also] be right.[126]

The key term in this passage is *maẓhar*. As we know, in al-Jīlī's Ibn 'Arabian Sufi metaphysics this term denotes how creation is a locus or 'theatre' for the divine manifestation. The term is also closely connected to the idea of the Perfect Human, who, being the locus of manifestation for the divine essence and all of the divine names and attributes, is the ideal *maẓhar*.[127] As al-Jīlī tells us here, every *maẓhar* is a viceregent of God. In the most general sense, this means that every existent is in fact a divine *khalīfah*, for according to the idea of universal theophany all beings are divine *maẓāhir*. For this reason, as al-Jīlī says, the viceregency cannot be restricted to any individual existent. In the more limited sense, it means that every Perfect Human is a divine *khalīfah*, for it is the Perfect Humans who are the ideal *maẓāhir*. Al-Jīlī links this point back to the Psalms by bringing into the discussion Qur'an 21.105, a verse notable for explicitly quoting from the biblical book of Psalms (Ps. 37.29). According to al-Jīlī's interpretation of this verse, the 'righteous servants' mentioned in the Psalms are the 'heirs' (*wurathā'*) of God, that is, the Perfect Humans or greater viceregents. This picks up al-Jīlī's designation of David in the previous section as an 'heir of the absolute Real' (*wārith 'an al-ḥaqq al-muṭlaq*). The inheritance of these divine 'heirs', meanwhile, consists of *al-ḥaqā'iq al-wujūdiyyah*, a term which would appear to denote all of existence. 'My righteous servants shall inherit the earth', then, means that God will go on becoming manifest in the Perfect Humans until, we are to presume, the end of time. While al-Jīlī is again engaging in a quasi-*tafsīr* here, his interpretation is different from the more common interpretation of the Qur'anic exegetes: while the latter tend to interpret the Psalms quotation in verse 21.105 to mean either that the Muslim *ummah* will take possession of the world or, more commonly, that the righteous will enter paradise,[128] al-Jīlī interprets it in accordance with his Sufi metaphysics. To return to Solomon's request in Qur'an 38.35, then, it is clear from all of this that in requesting that kingship or viceregency be limited to him, Solomon displays a misunderstanding of the key truths of universal theophany and the Perfect Human, for if to be a viceregent is to be a *maẓhar* of God, then these truths indicate that the viceregency can never be limited.

This being said, as is typical of a thinker in the Ibn 'Arabian tradition, al-Jīlī also indicates that there is another way of looking at the issue. We have already seen that, in a certain sense, David's and Solomon's viceregency *was* unique, by virtue of their being worldly rulers who were able to publicly announce and manifest their miraculous powers, in addition to their being prophets and Perfect Humans. Here al-Jīlī introduces a new idea into the discussion, which nevertheless follows on from his point that every *maẓhar* is a *khalīfah*. Because Solomon – like all Perfect Humans and, indeed, all created beings – is a locus of the divine manifestation, it can be said that God is his inner 'reality' (*ḥaqīqah*). And if Solomon stands in this way for God, then it follows that kingship or viceregency over the metaphysical realm – here referred to by the term *al-mamlakah al-kubrá* – *is* limited to him, in the sense that true kingship is limited to God – whom the Qur'an, it should be remembered, calls 'the possessor of kingship' (*mālik al-mulk*) (Q 3.26). While the ideas of universal theophany and the Perfect Human suggest that Solomon's request was not answered (a view that al-Jīlī in fact repeats immediately after this), they can therefore also lead us to the alternative view, namely that Solomon's request *was* answered. Again, in true Ibn 'Arabian fashion, and reflecting his more general tendency to take his key Sufi metaphysical ideas to their logical conclusions, even when those conclusions might appear to contradict one another, al-Jīlī here embraces the *coincidentia oppositorum*.

Muhammad's superiority over Solomon

> No one knows whether [Solomon's request] was valid (*ṣaḥḥa*) for him or not. And at this station, the Real – May He be exalted – informed us about his Friends (*awliyā'*), for He – May He be exalted – said, 'They did not measure God with His true measure' (Q 6:91), and 'Glory be to your Lord, the Lord of might (*rabb al-'izzah*), [who is] beyond that which they describe' (Q 37:180). So it [i.e. the limitation of viceregency] became impossible in this respect. For this reason the Greatest Sincere One (*al-ṣiddīq al-akbar*) said, 'Inability to perceive is itself a form of perception (*al-'ajz 'an dark al-idrāk idrāk*).' And [Muhammad] – peace and prayers be upon him – said, 'I cannot count Your praises. You are as You have praised Yourself.'
>
> So he [i.e. Muhammad] – May God bless him and grant him peace – showed propriety (*ta'addaba*) regarding the requesting of that which it is not possible to obtain, and acknowledged his inability (*al-'ajz*), due to [his acknowledgement of] the perfection of his Lord (*li-kamāl rabbihi*). And he – May prayers and peace be upon him – was more knowledgeable of his Lord than Solomon (*a'raf bi-rabbihi min Sulaymān*), because Solomon knew that which was finite (*mā yantahī*), and so requested that he obtain it, while Muhammad – May God bless him and grant him peace – knew that which was infinite (*mā lā yantahī*), and so showed propriety in not requesting to perceive that which is not perceived (*ṭalb idrāk mā lā yudrak*), by which I mean that he showed propriety, and so did not petition to obtain that, because of his knowledge that God – May He be exalted – would not give that to anyone, and [because of his knowledge] that there is a particularity within Him that pertains to the [divine] essence (*khuṣūṣiyyah fīhi dhātiyyah*), [a particularity] which God has exclusive possession of, to the exclusion of all of His creation. So distinguish between him whose knowledge of his Lord has a finite limit and him whose knowledge of his Lord has no limit and is infinite.[129]

We have already seen that Solomon's request for a unique form of viceregency is a reflection of his inferiority to David. Here al-Jīlī indicates that it is also a reflection of his inferiority to *Muhammad*, who as we know is the 'most perfect' Perfect Human in al-Jīlī's estimation. The superiority of Muhammad over Solomon is expressed in this passage via the key term *ta'addaba*, a term that indicates Muhammad's greater propriety (*adab*) in not requesting a unique form of viceregency (which was already alluded to in the story of Muhammad and the jinni). There is a certain irony here, in that, according to al-Jīlī's idea of the Perfect Human, Muhammad's viceregency *is* in fact unique and in one sense final. This being said, Muhammad's propriety in not requesting a special form of viceregency indicates a greater awareness on his part of the nature of God. We have seen how, in al-Jīlī's view, the divine essence is imperceptible, at least with regard to its inner nature at the very highest level of existence, a view in keeping with the dominant position in Ibn ʿArabian Sufi thought and in Islamic theology more generally. Al-Jīlī here quotes a pair of Qurʾanic verses in support of that view: Qurʾan 6.91, in al-Jīlī's esoteric interpretation, indicates that even the Friends of God or Perfect Humans are not able to fully fathom the nature of God,[130] while Qurʾan 37.180 indicates that God is beyond all description, and so by implication, beyond all knowledge.[131] This is further supported by the saying attributed to the first caliph Abū Bakr al-Siddīq (*ʿal-ṣiddīq al-akbarʾ*) (d. 13/634) quoted here, which is one of al-Jīlī's favourite sayings and, in his view, represents a truth realized only by those who have reached the end of the spiritual path.[132] One part of this truth is, again, the imperceptibility of the essence (*al-ʿajz ʿan idrāk*); indeed, the full version of the saying continues, 'and the search for His essence is unbelief and polytheism (*wa-al-baḥth ʿan dhātihi kufr wa-ishrāk*)'. The relevance of this to the unlimitability of the viceregency is that the essence is imperceptible because it is beyond limitation, and it is impossible to limit the representation or viceregency of something that is beyond limitation. The second part of the truth denoted by the saying of Abū Bakr's is that the realization of one's inability to perceive the essence itself constitutes a form of understanding – an Islamic reformulation of the Socratic notion that to know that one does not know is the highest form of knowledge.[133]

Returning to Muhammad's superiority over Solomon, then, we can see that Muhammad, by not making the request for a unique form of viceregency (again, recall the story of Muhammad and the jinni), and by thus not limiting the divine essence, showed that he possessed this exalted type of knowledge – a point that accords with al-Jīlī's idea, expressed in the chapter on the Qurʾan, that in receiving the Qurʾan Muhammad received the manifestation of the divine essence itself. This is what is meant, then, by Muhammad's 'propriety'. Solomon, on the other hand, made the request, thus demonstrating his belief that the essence could somehow be limited, and so demonstrating in turn his ignorance of his own ignorance. In this way, al-Jīlī strongly affirms the superiority of Muhammad over Solomon. The former shows propriety and knowledge of the infinite (i.e. the metaphysical/divine realm), while the latter shows impropriety and knowledge only of what is finite (i.e. the mundane realm over which he is king). This accords with al-Jīlī's view that Muhammad is the best of prophets and most perfect of the Perfect Humans, and perhaps is meant to serve as a corrective to any suggestion from the story of Muhammad and the jinni that Muhammad might in some way be inferior to Solomon.

Prophethood and divine friendship

> And at this station the Muhammadans among the Friends of God said what they said. So our master (*shaykhunā*) [Ibn ʿArabī] said of [i.e. quoted?] Shaykh ʿAbd al-Qādir al-Jīlānī [saying]: 'You, the assemblies of prophets, were given the title (*al-laqab*), and we were given that which you were not given.' The Imām Muḥyī al-Dīn Ibn ʿArabī transmitted this from him in *al-Futūḥāt al-Makkiyyah* with his chain of transmission. And the Friend of God (*al-walī*) Shaykh Abū al-Ghayth

> Ibn Jamīl – May God be pleased with him – said, 'We plunged into seas at the shores of which the prophets stopped.' Even if this discussion involves an element of allegorical interpretation (*ta'wīl*), our doctrine (*madhhab*) is that the prophet, in the unrestricted sense (*muṭlaq al-nabī*), is superior to the Friend of God, in the unrestricted sense (*muṭlaq al-walī*). And the discussion of prophethood and divine friendship will come in this book, God willing.[134]

Al-Jīlī concludes the chapter with a brief allusion to the question of the relationship between divine friendship or sainthood (*walāyah*) and prophecy (*nubuwwah*), a question related to what has gone before insofar as the Friends of God, in al-Jīlī's Ibn 'Arabian view, continue to manifest those miraculous powers that David and Solomon possessed.

Al-Jīlī alludes to the distinction between *walāyah* and *nubuwwah* by quoting a pair of statements attributed to two famous Sufis – or as he calls them, in emulation of Ibn 'Arabī, 'the Muhammadans among the Friends of God' (*al-muḥammadiyyūn min al-awliyā'*)[135] – 'Abd al-Qādir al-Jīlānī (d. 561/1166) and Abū al-Ghayth Ibn Jamīl (d. 651/1253). Both of these Sufis are important figures for al-Jīlī. He often refers, as here, to 'Abd al-Qādir as his *shaykh* or *sayyid*, a reflection of his adherence to the Jabartiyyah-Ahdaliyyah offshoot of the Qādiriyyah Sufi order,[136] although it is notable that his access to this saying of 'Abd al-Qādir's was via the *Futūḥāt*,[137] suggesting that his view of 'Abd al-Qādir was mediated through the writings of Ibn 'Arabī.[138] Ibn Jamīl's significance, meanwhile, derives from al-Jīlī's Yemeni environment, Ibn Jamīl being a 'semilegendary Sufi teacher and saint (*wali*) . . . , whom the popular Yemeni lore credits with spectacular ascetic feats and saintly miracles'.[139] In addition, the anti-Ibn 'Arabian Yemeni historian Ibn al-Ahdal associated Ibn Jamīl with the dissemination of Ibn 'Arabī's ideas in Yemen, though the accuracy of this view is questionable.[140] What we do know is that the utterance of Ibn Jamīl quoted here, which is in fact found in the writings of Ibn 'Arabī,[141] was important to the Ibn 'Arabian Sufis of Yemen: Aḥmad ibn al-Raddād (d. 821/1418), al-Jabartī's successor as *shaykh* of the Sufis of Zabid, wrote a Sufi metaphysical commentary on this saying, and al-Jīlī quotes it in several other places.[142]

The significance of the two statements lies in their apparent allusion to the superiority of the Friends of God over the prophets. The relationship between the *awliyā'* and the *anbiyā'*, or, more exactly, between *walāyah* and *nubuwwah*, is, as already noted, an important and controversial issue in Ibn 'Arabian Sufi metaphysics, and one that al-Jīlī elaborates upon in the final chapter of *al-Insān al-kāmil* (a discussion that he points to here).[143] The Ibn 'Arabian position, it will be remembered, is that, although legislative prophecy has been sealed by Muhammad, the post-Muhammadan *awliyā'* nevertheless possess a certain type of non-legislative 'general prophethood', for they maintain the channel of access to revelatory knowledge via their attainment of *kashf*. The sayings quoted here seem to go further than even this daring idea, however, in implying that the revelatory knowledge received by the Friends of God – the 'we' of both sayings – in fact goes *beyond* the knowledge given to certain prophets.

This is clearly controversial territory, and just the sort of thing that would expose an Ibn 'Arabian like al-Jīlī to the criticism of the anti-Ibn 'Arabian *'ulamā'*. This being said, al-Jīlī not only does not state this point explicitly but also makes it clear that, in his view, 'the prophet in an unrestricted sense (*muṭlaq al-nabī*)' – that is, the legislative prophet – 'is superior to the Friend of God in an unrestricted sense (*muṭlaq al-walī*)' – that is, the Friend of God who is not also a legislative prophet. This in fact is the standard Ibn 'Arabian view: according to Ibn 'Arabī, even though *walāyah* is superior to *nubuwwah*, the legislative prophet is superior to the ordinary Friend of God, because all legislative prophets are also *awliyā'*.[144] This is an idea that al-Jīlī repeats in the context of his discussion of the relationship between *walāyah* and *nubuwwah* in the final chapter.[145] The point, then, is not so much that the Friends of God are superior to the prophets, as that, insofar as the idea of universal theophany entails that the divine revelation/manifestation must continue after Solomon (and, indeed, after Muhammad), the Friends of God must have access to the same knowledge and powers as the prophets.

How, it might be asked, is all this related to David and the Psalms? Al-Jīlī has come a long way here from the stated topic of the chapter, reflecting how his primary concern is to integrate the scriptures and their associated prophets into his overall Sufi metaphysics. He therefore allows himself, somewhat like Ibn 'Arabī in the *Fuṣūṣ*, to be led in different directions by the flow of his argument. So the Psalms leads him into a discussion of David, which leads him in turn to discuss David's viceregency, which broadens into a discussion of Solomon's viceregency and request for uniqueness, which in turn leads onto *walāyah* and *nubuwwah*. All of these topics, then, seem to be interconnected in his mind. Sacred history and Sufi metaphysics, in other words, are fully integrated into one another.

Conclusion

We have seen that, while he engages with and draws upon the Qur'an and the post-Qur'anic Islamic tradition (particularly the tales of the prophets and historical literature), al-Jīlī's conception of the Psalms, David and Solomon is also conditioned by his Sufi metaphysics. The Psalms, in his view, is an expression of a particular type of divine manifestation – specifically, of the 'attributes of the divine acts' – and contains a number of forms of knowledge or 'sciences', many of which pertain to Sufi metaphysical topics. Similarly, when the Qur'an and the Islamic tradition say that David and Solomon were 'viceregents' and 'kings', this means that they were Perfect Humans who had the capacity, by virtue of their kingship, to demonstrate in the phenomenal world the divine attributes that were manifest within them. In this sense, they were unique among the Perfect Humans, even though the capacity to receive the divine manifestations could never be limited to them, owing to the universality of God's manifestation.

Does al-Jīlī's Sufi metaphysical conception of the Psalms, David and Solomon, it might be asked, lead him to take an original position, distinct from the wider Islamic tradition, on the place of the Psalms within sacred history? On the one hand, we have seen that the Psalms and David, as al-Jīlī sees it, are respectively a genuine expression of divine manifestation (*tajallī*) and a perfect locus of divine appearance (*maẓhar*), just like the other scriptures and prophets dealt with in *al-Insān al-kāmil*. The book of Psalms contains knowledge pertaining both to Sufi metaphysics and to the rational sciences. It is a book of wisdom, prayers and admonitions, which can therefore bring its audience – David's people, the Children of Israel – into a closer relationship with God. On the other hand, the Psalms constitutes a more limited type of divine manifestation than the Torah, the Gospel and the Qur'an, the active attributes being lower in the hierarchy of existence than those pertaining to God's self or essence, and it contains little legal material. Likewise, David and Solomon, though they are Perfect Humans and are in a sense unique in being able to announce their powers and make them manifest, are nevertheless less perfect than the archetypal Perfect Human, Muhammad. Indeed, Solomon seems to have fundamentally misunderstood the key truths of universal theophany and the Perfect Human. Certainly, his understanding is inferior to that of Muhammad – and, it seems, of al-Jīlī himself. In light of all of this, we can say that al-Jīlī's stance towards the Psalms, David and Solomon is ambivalent.

In taking this ambivalent stance towards the Psalms, David and Solomon, al-Jīlī ultimately does not depart from the overall framework provided by the Qur'an-centred view of sacred history, according to which the Psalms is one of the genuine divine scriptures, albeit one that is incomplete and has been superseded, and David and Solomon are two of the most important prophets, albeit prophets who are also imperfect and have also been superseded, eventually and most completely by Muhammad. Though he gives it a Sufi metaphysical form, al-Jīlī here still adheres to the Qur'an-centred view of the Psalms.

6

The Gospel

Chapter thirty-eight of *al-Insān al-kāmil*, the last chapter in the section on the scriptures, deals with the scripture of the Christians – the Gospel (*al-Injīl*) – and the prophet associated with that scripture, Jesus (*ʿĪsá*). As in previous chapters, al-Jīlī's treatment of the Gospel and of the Christians' interpretation of it is grounded in his Sufi metaphysics. The chapter therefore affords us another opportunity to consider his development of the key idea of that metaphysical system, namely, the idea of universal theophany, in the context of his discussion of the scriptures. As will be seen, this idea provides the grounds for al-Jīlī's assessment of Christian doctrine, leading him to both criticize the Christians for their failure to recognize the truth and yet identify a hidden truth concealed within Christian doctrine.

At the same time, and again as with the other scriptures, his discussion of the Gospel also proceeds within the conceptual framework provided by more conventional medieval Muslim views of the Gospel. According to the Qur'an-centred view of sacred history, the Christian scripture does not consist – as the Christians mistakenly imagine – of the four canonical Gospels and other books of the Christian New Testament, written by men under divine inspiration; rather, it is a single 'book' containing the word of God, mediated through His prophet Jesus, being viewed in an analogous way to the Torah, the Psalms and the Qur'an.[1] In addition, the conventional medieval Muslim view of the Gospel (like the Muslim view of the Torah) was heavily coloured by the concept of *taḥrīf*, that is, the idea that the Christians had somehow distorted the divine revelation given to them.[2]

At the heart of this concept of Christian *taḥrīf* is the critical Islamic attitude towards the fundamental Christian doctrines of the Trinity and Incarnation. This attitude is grounded in the Qur'an's assessment that the Christian teaching about Jesus is an affront to the unity of God (see Q 4.171, 5.17, 5.72-78, 5.116-117).[3] Medieval Muslim theologians developed this critique using logical arguments in polemical debates with Christians.[4] The Islamic Jesus, then, though he is a prophet held in high esteem, who is given the special titles 'Messiah' (*al-masīḥ*) (see Q 3.45, 4.157, 4.171, 4.172, etc.), 'Spirit of God' (*rūḥ Allāh*) (see Q 2.87, 2.253, 4.171, 5.110, etc.) and 'Word of God' (*kalimat Allāh*) (see Q 3.45, 4.171), among others,[5] is nevertheless a highly controversial figure.[6] Al-Jīlī's treatment of the Gospel, Jesus and the Christians, as we shall see, elaborates upon this Qur'anic assessment of Jesus and the Christians' views about him – and in particular upon the Qur'anic presentation and critique of the Incarnation and the Trinity. It is perhaps because these doctrines are closely tied to the Islamic charge that the Christians have distorted the true message of the Gospel that al-Jīlī concentrates upon them in a chapter ostensibly devoted to the Gospel. Indeed it is notable that while he devotes considerable attention to the Incarnation and the Trinity, al-Jīlī makes little or no mention in this chapter of many of the standard issues in Islamic discussions of Jesus and the Gospel, including the annunciation; Jesus' birth, titles, miracles, disciples, asceticism, crucifixion and ascension. This reflects the fact that al-Jīlī is not primarily engaged here in religious polemic; rather, his discussion of the Gospel constitutes a part of his broader presentation of his Qur'an-centred Sufi metaphysics.

The revelation and language(s) of the Gospel

> God sent down (*anzala*) the Gospel upon Jesus in the Syriac language (*bi-al-lughah al-suryāniyyah*), and it was recited (*quri'a*) in seventeen languages (*lughah*).[7]

The opening of the chapter establishes the Gospel, as in the Qur'an-centred view, as a scripture analogous to the Torah and the Qur'an, that is, as a single scripture that God revealed to a particular prophet in a particular language. The verb that al-Jīlī uses to denote God's revelation of the Gospel – *anzala* (*'alá*) – is the same as he uses to denote the revelation of those other scriptures, and as already noted in previous chapters, is also one of the verbs that the Qur'an most commonly uses to denote the revelation of scripture. Al-Jīlī's use of this verb with God as its subject therefore establishes that the Gospel, like the Qur'an, Torah and Psalms, is a genuine divine revelation, in accordance with the Qur'an-centred view.

In his chapters on the other scriptures, al-Jīlī made no mention of the language in which those scriptures were revealed. The Qur'an, of course, declares itself to be Arabic (see Q 12.2, 13.37, 16.103, etc.), and it can probably be assumed that al-Jīlī was aware that the Torah was a Hebrew scripture, and that he thought that the Psalms, as indicated in the previous chapter, were revealed in Syriac. What is the significance, then, of his explicit declaration that the Gospel was revealed to Jesus in Syriac and then recited in seventeen languages? Though the original language of the canonical Gospels was Greek, according to Sidney Griffith, 'Some early Muslim writers say that the original Gospel was written in Hebrew, or in Aramaic, both of them languages in use in the Jewish community at the time of Jesus.'[8] The historical Jesus, of course, was himself a native speaker of Aramaic, of which Syriac is a dialect. In some medieval Islamic literature, there indeed seems to be an assumption that Syriac was the original language of the Gospel,[9] and, soon after al-Jīlī, the noted Ibn 'Arabian Sufi of Herat 'Abd al-Raḥmān Jāmī (d. 898/1492) would similarly declare that the Gospel is God's speech in Syriac, just as the Qur'an is His speech in Arabic and the Torah His speech in Hebrew.[10] Al-Jīlī's declaration that the Gospel was revealed in Syriac is therefore not unique to him. I would suggest that it follows on from his adoption of the Qur'an-centred view of the Gospel as a 'book' analogous to the Qur'an: if Jesus spoke Aramaic or Syriac, then it would follow that the revelation that he received would have been in that language, just as the revelation received by Muhammad was in his native tongue, Arabic.

While al-Jīlī presents the Gospel in this respect in an analogous way to the Qur'an, the analogy breaks down with respect to his remark that the Gospel was recited (*quri'a*) in seventeen different languages. This implies that it was translated into sixteen languages, which are used – along with the original Syriac – by different Christian groups in their worship. According to the mainstream medieval Muslim view, the Qur'an cannot be translated: it is an Arabic Qur'an or else it is not the Qur'an.[11] It seems that, according to al-Jīlī, the same cannot be said of the Gospel. In the background here is perhaps the conventional idea that the Qur'an surpasses all other scriptures by virtue of the inimitability of its language (*iʿjāz al-Qur'ān*). As the prominent third-/ninth-century scholar Ibn Qutaybah put it, 'Unlike the Gospel, the Torah and the Psalms – which have all been translated into several languages – the Qur'an, in its stylistic perfection, cannot be rendered into any other language, which proves its miraculous nature.'[12] Similarly, in his critique of Christianity, the leading later Muʿtazilite theologian ʿAbd al-Jabbār connected the fact that the pre-Qur'anic scriptures had been translated to the doctrine of *taḥrīf* and the falsity of the Christian religion:

> The Hebrew language was abandoned [ʿAbd al-Jabbār thought that the Gospel was originally revealed in Hebrew], in order to enable [the Christians'] earthly authorities to introduce false doctrines and to cover up their lies and disguise the imposture committed by them to gain power, since those who spoke Hebrew were the People of the Book and the scholars of that time. So these persons changed the language or rather totally abandoned it, so that the scholars should not readily understand their doctrines and intentions and so be able to confuse them before their doctrine was firmly established and thus frustrate their aim. Thus they turned to other languages not spoken by Christ and his disciples, whose speakers are not People of the Book and are ignorant of God's books and laws, such as the Romans, Syrians, Persians, Indians, Armenians, and other barbarian-speaking nations. This was a means of confusing people and of covering up their imposture and achieving their desire of gaining the authority from those few who sought it through religion.[13]

By highlighting the Christian authorities' translation of the Gospel, therefore, al-Jīlī may be making a subtle point here about its confused and corrupt status and its inferiority to the untranslatable Qur'an.

What, we might wonder, are the seventeen languages in which al-Jīlī believed the Gospel to be recited? Other than the five ethnic–linguistic groups mentioned by ʿAbd al-Jabbār, I have not been able to find any source or parallel for this claim, nor does al-Jīlī suggest here or elsewhere which languages he has in mind. At a stretch, a connection could perhaps be made between the seventeen languages identified by al-Jīlī and the account in the book of Acts of how the Apostles spoke in tongues at Pentecost, which seems to list seventeen different geographical/ethnic identities (see Acts 2.7-11), implying, perhaps, that the Apostles spoke in each of these tongues. There is nothing to indicate, however, that al-Jīlī knew of this passage of the New Testament or traditions connected to it. Perhaps a more likely source is the *Isrāʾīliyyah* tradition on the crucifixion attributed to Wahb ibn Munnabih and quoted by ʿAbd al-Jabbār, according to which there were seventeen apostles 'who miraculously assumed the shape of Jesus, and one of them sacrificed himself'.[14] From the idea that there were seventeen apostles, it would be a short jump to the idea that the Gospel was recited in seventeen languages; indeed, such an idea could be harmonized with the account of the seventeen languages spoken by the Apostles at Pentecost. Regardless of where al-Jīlī got the idea from, his reference to the Gospel being recited in seventeen different languages, as well as his notion of the distinction between the Gospel and the Qur'an, demonstrates some awareness of the existence of a diversity of Christian communities (an awareness that we also saw in Chapter 4), and more generally of a lived Christianity (an awareness that is further revealed in his treatment of Christian rites in the final chapter of *al-Insān al-kāmil*).[15] Nevertheless, al-Jīlī does not elaborate upon this point here, instead devoting the rest of the chapter to a discussion of the theoretical place of the Gospel, Jesus and the Christians within his Sufi metaphysical conception of revelation and sacred history.

The opening of the Gospel

> The beginning of the Gospel is, 'In the name of the Father, the Mother, and the Son' (*bi-ism al-ab wa-al-umm wa-al-ibn*), just as the opening of the Qur'an is, 'In the name of God, the All-Merciful, the Compassionate'. His people (*qawmuhu*) took this phrase (*hādhā al-kalām*) in its apparent meaning (*'alá ẓāhirihi*), and so they thought (*ẓannū*) that the Father, the Mother, and the Son were an expression of the Spirit (*al-rūḥ*), Mary, and Jesus. So they then said, 'God is the third of three (*inna Allāh thālith thalāthah*).' And they did not know that what was intended by the Father was the name God (*Allāh*), and that by the Mother was intended the true nature of the essence (*kunh al-dhāt*), which is referred to as 'the quiddity of realities' (*māhiyyat al-ḥaqā'iq*), and by the Son was intended the book (*al-kitāb*), which is absolute existence (*al-wujūd al-muṭlaq*), because it is a branch and result of the quiddity of the true nature (*māhiyyat al-kunh*). God – May He be exalted – said, 'And with Him is the Mother of the Book (*umm al-kitāb*)', (Q 13:39) alluding to what has been mentioned. And this has been previously explained in its proper place.[16]

After opening the chapter with a more this-worldly focus on the languages in which the Gospel is recited, al-Jīlī moves quickly into more metaphysical territory. This passage[17] – and his overall conception of the Gospel – is grounded in what he understands to be the opening phrase of the Christian scripture. Again, an analogy is drawn – this time explicitly – between the Qur'an and the Gospel. Both scriptures, as al-Jīlī sees it, open with a *basmalah*, that is, with a formula in which the name of God is invoked. The *basmalah* of the Christian scripture, according to his conception, is a Trinitarian formula. Instead of the orthodox Christian Trinity of Father, Son and Holy Spirit, however, al-Jīlī presents us with a Trinity of Father, Mother and Son.[18] Furthermore, Jesus' people (*qawm*) – that is, the Christians – he tells us, make the mistake of taking this phrase in its 'apparent' (*ẓāhir*) sense, identifying the Father with the Spirit, the Mother with Mary and the Son with Jesus.

Al-Jīlī's description of the Christian Trinity probably derives from the Qur'anic account of the Trinitarian doctrine, which suggests that Jesus' people worship Jesus and his mother Mary 'as two gods besides God' (Q 5.116). This can be taken to mean that the Christians profess a Trinity of God, Mary and Jesus;[19] hence, Ibn Taymiyyah, for instance, notes that 'some of [the Christians] make Mary a god alongside God, just as they make Jesus a God'.[20] The Qur'an exegete al-Baghawī (d. 516/1122), similarly, tells us that a Christian sect that he calls 'al-Marqūsiyyah' (the Marcionites?) professed such a Trinity,[21] while the same commentator also relates a report according to which the Apostle Paul (who is often blamed in Islamic polemic for Christian *taḥrīf*),[22] 'taught Nestorius that Jesus, Mary, and God were three'.[23]

While there is a clear Qur'an-centred precedent for al-Jīlī's formulation of the Trinity as Father, Mother and Son, therefore, his suggestion that the Christians identify the Father with the Spirit is harder to interpret. It perhaps grows out of an awareness on his part that the Holy Spirit is a person of the Christian Trinity, and of the Nicaean formula that Jesus 'was conceived by the Holy Spirit'.[24] More immediately, it seems to be connected to the role of the divine spirit in the Qur'anic accounts of the conception of Jesus (see Q 21.91, 66.12). This becomes clearer if we look at Ibn 'Arabī's treatment of Jesus' conception in the opening to his chapter on Jesus in the *Fuṣūṣ*. There, Ibn 'Arabī tells of how Gabriel, 'the Trustworthy Spirit' (*al-rūḥ al-amīn*), 'took on the likeness of a created mortal before Mary (*tamaththala...li-Maryam basharan sawiyyan*)', with the result that 'she imagined that he wanted to have intercourse with her, and took refuge in God from him'. After Gabriel reassured her that he was a messenger of God who had come to bring her a son, Mary's chest was opened, 'desire flowed within [her]' (*fa-sarat al-shahwah fī Maryam*), and Gabriel 'breathed Jesus into her' (*fa-nafakha fīhā . . . 'Īsā*).[25] Ibn 'Arabī's retelling of the Qur'anic story in this way brings out the role of the Spirit – Gabriel – as the humanlike 'father' of Jesus in the Qur'anic account, a usage that seems to feed into al-Jīlī's conception of the Trinity here.[26]

Al-Jīlī's description of the Christian Trinity as Father, Mother and Son highlights the strong Qur'an-centredness of his approach. What the Qur'an apparently says about the Trinity, in other words, overrides all else, including any knowledge he might have had of actual Christian doctrine and practice, which would have made it clear to him that this is not the orthodox Christian Trinity. This Qur'an-centred approach is further underlined by his quotation of the formula that 'God is the third of three', which is cited in the Qur'an as an example of the Christians' *kufr* (Q 5.73).[27] Yet while the Qur'an criticizes the Christian doctrine of the Trinity on the grounds that it is incompatible with belief in the fundamental Qur'anic doctrine of the unity of God (see Q 4.171, 5.73), al-Jīlī's criticism is subtler and more metaphysically minded. The Christians' error, he proposes, consists in their reading the Trinitarian formula too literally. The phrase he uses to denote this literal type of interpretation – *akhada . . . 'alá ẓāhirihi* – implies that the Christians are too exoterically minded, being veiled from the deeper esoteric or hidden (*bāṭin*) truth represented by the Trinitarian formula.[28] This idea, it might be suggested, constitutes al-Jīlī's Sufi version of the traditional Islamic idea of the

Christians' distortion (*taḥrīf*) of their revelation, in a similar way to how his notion that the Jews 'invented' (*ibtadaʿū*) things in their religion via their intellects could be viewed as his Sufi version of the notion of the Jews' *taḥrīf* of the Torah. As in that context, his position here is not the more common medieval Muslim view that the Christians had falsified the text of the Gospel (*taḥrīf al-naṣṣ*), but rather that they had distorted the *meaning* of the scripture (*taḥrīf al-maʿná*), in this case by interpreting it overly literally.

Al-Jīlī's critique of the Christians on these grounds reflects how, to a certain degree, Christian doctrine here becomes in effect a foil for the elaboration of his own Sufi metaphysical position. In other words, by criticizing the Christians for limiting their interpretation of their scripture to its *ẓāhir* sense, al-Jīlī is indicating, in keeping with the dominant Sufi approach to the Qur'an, that scripture has a *bāṭin* as well as *ẓāhir* meaning; indeed, as we saw in Chapter 4, in Jīlī's view the Qur'an contains an even deeper level of meaning, namely that of the *asrār ilāhiyyah*. As we shall see later in the chapter, al-Jīlī compares the Christians in this regard to those whom he calls *ʿulamāʾ al-rusūm*, that is, the exoteric religious scholars, who are ignorant of those deeper truths that he, as a Sufi thinker, is able to access. In this way, his version of *taḥrīf* can be seen not only as a criticism of the Christians but also as the assertion of the superiority of his Sufi metaphysical conception of Islam, as part of an intra-Muslim argument against his non-Sufi scholarly opponents (again, just as his criticism of the Jews for deriving ideas with their intellects rather than sticking to their scripture could be seen as a veiled argument against rationalist Muslim theologians).

What, then, is the esoteric meaning of the Trinitarian formula that al-Jīlī believes the Christians have overlooked? Unsurprisingly, al-Jīlī's interpretation of the opening of the Gospel is grounded in his Sufi metaphysics. In his view, instead of the Spirit, Mary and Jesus, the three persons of the Trinity of the Gospel in fact represent different levels of existence. Indeed, they represent the three highest levels of existence in his scheme. So, the Mother denotes what he calls, among other names, 'the quiddity of the true nature of the essence' (*māhiyyat kunh al-dhāt*), that is, the simple divine essence in its utterly unknowable and unqualified state – the highest level of existence.[29] This brings to mind his similar identification of the Mother of the Book (*umm al-kitāb*) with the inner dimension of the essence.[30] For al-Jīlī, then, the Mother of the Trinity, like the Mother of the Book, stands for the 'mother' of existence, the source from which all of existence derives.

Following on from this, the Son, al-Jīlī tells us, represents not Jesus, but rather 'the Book' (*al-kitāb*). This identification can perhaps be seen within the context of the Qur'anic (and ultimately biblical) conception of Jesus as the Word of God (*kalimat Allāh*) (see Q 3.45, 4.171), for both terms suggest that the Son is a 'revelation' from God.[31] Relying on the same Qur'anic conception, Ibn ʿArabī draws a similar parallel in his chapter on Jesus in the *Fuṣūṣ* when he writes, 'Gabriel was transmitting (*nāqil*) the Word of God (*kalimat Allāh*) [i.e. Jesus] to Mary just as a messenger transmits the word of God to his community, for He says, "And His Word which He cast into Mary and a spirit from Him" (Q 4:171).'[32] According to al-Jīlī's Sufi metaphysical conception, however, the term *al-kitāb* also denotes – as we saw in Chapter 3 – 'absolute existence' (*al-wujūd al-muṭlaq*).[33] Put in terms of al-Jīlī's levels of existence, this is the level of 'unqualified oneness' (*al-aḥadiyyah*), the level at which the divine essence remains simple and unqualified, yet begins its process of manifestation by taking on qualification within itself.[34] The rationale of this association of the Son of the Trinity with the absolute existence of the unqualified essence seems to be that, just as an unborn son is latent within his mother, so too is the unlimited existence or unqualified oneness of God – the second-most simple level of existence – latent within His utterly simple essence – the first level. And just as the son subsequently emerges from the mother to be born into the world, so too, in al-Jīlī's Sufi metaphysics, does absolute existence emerge or 'descend' from the divine essence at the beginning of the process of divine manifestation.

Finally, the term 'Father', according to al-Jīlī, denotes not the Spirit (as he imagines the Christians to believe), but rather the divine name *Allāh*, which is to say, God at the level of 'divinity' (*al-ulūhiyyah*), the divine level that contains within it all the levels of existence. While the Mother of the Trinity denotes the divine essence in a state of total imperceptibility, and the Son the essence in its unqualified, unlimited existence, the Father represents the essence turned towards the phenomenal world. In this sense, the Father is 'lower' (*anzal*) in the hierarchy of existence than the other two persons of the Trinity, because it denotes the divine essence in a more qualified state. In suggesting this hierarchy of Mother, Son and Father, al-Jīlī is apparently reversing the orthodox Christian doctrine that the Father 'begets' the Son and the Spirit 'proceeds' from the Father (and, in the Latin West, from the Son).[35] As we know, however, al-Jīlī also suggests that, from another perspective, divinity is in fact the highest level of the divine existence, because it is God as *Allāh* who gives all levels of existence their reality.[36] From this perspective, it can be said that al-Jīlī's conception of the Father somewhat resembles the Christian conception, a resemblance that is superficially reinforced by his identification of the Father with *Allāh*. Nevertheless, any apparent resemblance between al-Jīlī's interpretation of the Trinity and the Christian view should not obscure the point that his treatment of the Trinity is based primarily on his Sufi metaphysics – in particular, his idea of the levels of existence – and the Qur'anic understanding of Christian doctrine, rather than on a direct engagement with actual Christian doctrine.[37]

In summary, the true, metaphysical Trinity, according to al-Jīlī's interpretation, consists of the simple divine essence (*al-dhāt al-maḥḍ/al-ṣarf/al-sādhaj*), the absolute existence (*al-wujūd al-muṭlaq*) or unqualified oneness (*al-aḥadiyyah*) of the divine essence, and the divinity (*al-ulūhiyyah*) of God. This, then, is the esoteric meaning of the opening of the Gospel, as well as of the Qur'anic verse (Q 13.39) that al-Jīlī quotes here: 'And with Him [i.e. *Allāh*, God at the level of divinity] is the Mother [i.e. *al-umm*, the simple divine essence] of the Book [i.e. *al-kitāb*, absolute existence, the unqualified oneness of the essence].' Al-Jīlī's metaphysical interpretation of the Christian Trinitarian formula, it should also be noted, parallels his metaphysical interpretation of the Islamic *basmalah* elsewhere in his writings.[38] This reflects how al-Jīlī's approach to scripture, whether the Qur'an or any of the pre-Qur'anic scriptures, is determined by his Sufi metaphysical perspective. Just as, in his metaphysical interpretation of the Islamic *basmalah*, he proposes that that formula denotes how all of reality issues from the divine essence,[39] so too does he here suggest that the Trinitarian formula with which the Gospel begins denotes how existence begins with the simple essence of God, and subsequently descends through the upper levels of the divine existence. In this way, we again can see how al-Jīlī uses the Gospel and Christian doctrine to elaborate his own Sufi metaphysical ideas and approach to scripture.

At the same time, there is also a sense in which he *is* engaging directly with (what he believes to be) Christian doctrine. As al-Jīlī sees it, by thinking that the Trinitarian formula refers to the Spirit, Mary and Jesus, the Christians make the mistake not so much of associating others with God, but rather, at the more metaphysical level, of possessing a *limited* understanding of the divine manifestations, the truth of which is revealed to them in their scripture if only they would interpret it correctly. By focusing only on the apparent meaning of the Trinitarian formula, the Christians overlook the fact that the Trinity points not to the three created beings that are apparently indicated, but rather to the highest metaphysical levels of the divine existence. In this way, they arrive merely at uncertain and limited 'supposition' (*ẓann*) – a term that, in Sufi usage, typically denotes knowledge that should be treated with suspicion and as uncertain – in (implied) contrast to the certain knowledge (*al-ʿilm al-yaqīn*) of the Sufi metaphysicians.[40]

Jesus' defence of himself and his people

Jesus referred to this [i.e. the true meaning of the Trinity] when he said, 'I only said to them that which You commanded me' (5:117) to propagate (*uballigh*) to them, which was this word (*hādhā al-kalām*). Then he said, '[I told them] to worship God, my Lord and your Lord.' So it is known that Jesus – Peace be upon him – did not limit himself (*lam yaqtaṣir*) to the apparent meaning of the Gospel (*ẓāhir al-Injīl*); rather, he added clarification and elucidation (*al-bayān wa-al-īḍāḥ*) by saying, 'to worship God, my Lord and your Lord', in order to refute their delusion (*mā tawahhamū*) that he, his mother (*ummuhu*), and the Spirit (*al-rūḥ*) were the Lord (*al-rabb*), and in order that Jesus would attain innocence (*al-barāʾah*) in the eyes of God, because he explained it to them.

[But] they did not stop at that which Jesus explained to them; rather, they believed in (*dhahabū ilá*) what they understood of (*mā fahimū min*) the word of God (*kalām Allāh*). So when Jesus said in response: 'I only said to them that which You commanded me', it was a way of excusing his people (*al-iʿtidhār li-qawmihi*). He meant, 'You are the One who sent them that word, which begins, "In the name of the Father, the Mother, and the Son". So, when I propagated Your word to them, they construed it (*ḥamalūhu*) in the way that it appeared to them (*ʿalá mā ẓahara lahum*). Do not blame them for that, because they [acted] in this regard in accordance with what they knew (*ʿalá mā ʿalimūhu*) of Your word.' Indeed, their polytheism is monotheism itself (*fa-shirkuhum ʿayn al-tawḥīd*), because they acted according to what they knew by virtue of the divine revelation in their selves (*bi-al-ikhbār al-ilāhī fī anfusihim*). Thus, they are like 'the *mujtahid* who undertakes *ijtihād* and errs (*akhṭaʾa*), but who still has a reward from his *ijtihād*'. So Jesus – Peace be upon him – excused (*iʿtadhara*) his people through that response to the Real when He asked him, "Did you say to people, 'Take me and my mother as two gods besides God'?"'[41]

The Qur'anic Jesus is a particularly contentious figure. The Qur'anic controversy surrounding Jesus, though it includes the question of the crucifixion, which the Qur'an seems to deny (see Q 4.157), centres principally upon the question of the divinity claimed by the Christians for him – that is, the doctrine of the Incarnation – and the related doctrine of the Trinity. Perhaps the key passage that deals with this question is Qur'an 5.116-119, which takes the form of what Tarif Khalidi has called 'an interrogation of Jesus by God'.[42] In this passage, and elsewhere in the Qur'an, Jesus, as Khalidi puts it, 'is deliberately made to distance himself from the doctrines that his community is said to hold of him', a unique task for a Qur'anic prophet.[43]

Because of the importance of this passage within the Qur'anic critique of Christian Christological doctrine, it is unsurprising that al-Jīlī uses it as a hook upon which to hang his views on the nature of Jesus and Christian doctrine; Ibn 'Arabī does something similar in his chapter on Jesus in the *Fuṣūṣ*.[44] Indeed, such is the extent to which this passage is interwoven into al-Jīlī's argument that it could be said that the greater part of this chapter (like Ibn 'Arabī's *faṣṣ* on Jesus) constitutes a quasi-*tafsīr* of that Qur'anic passage. According to al-Jīlī's interpretation of Qur'an 5.116-119, in defending himself against the charge that he told his people to worship him and his mother as gods, Jesus states that he only told them the 'word' or 'speech' (*kalām*) that God had commanded him to propagate to them. Since al-Jīlī used the term *kalām* a few lines above to refer to the Trinitarian formula, it is possible that he means here that Jesus claimed to have only taught his people the Trinitarian formula. It seems more likely, however, that the term denotes the original, true Gospel, which, as a genuine revelation analogous to the Qur'an, is the 'word' or 'speech' of God, and which opens, as al-Jīlī sees it, with that Trinitarian formula.

Like the Qur'an, al-Jīlī here seeks to absolve Jesus of responsibility for the errors of his people. While their understanding of the Trinitarian formula was limited to its apparent sense, Jesus 'did not limit himself (*lam yaqtaṣir*) to the apparent meaning of the Gospel (*ẓāhir al-Injīl*)'. The use of the terms *lam yaqtaṣir* and *ẓāhir al-Injīl* here sets up a direct contrast between the approach of Jesus and that of his people: while the Christians are led into 'delusion' (*wahm*) by their concentration only upon the *ẓāhir* meaning of the Trinity, Jesus, as a prophet cognizant of both the *ẓāhir* and *bāṭin* dimensions of revelation, suffered from no such limitations or delusions. Indeed, he offered his people 'clarification and elucidation' (*al-bayān wa-al-īḍāḥ*) of the inner metaphysical truth of the Trinitarian formula, when he instructed them to 'worship God, my Lord and your Lord'. This clarification, as al-Jīlī sees it, is a denial that the Trinity could possibly be true in its literal sense, that is, in the sense that Jesus, Mary and God are all gods.

The aim of Jesus' clarification of the meaning of the Trinitarian formula, al-Jīlī explains, was not only to guide his people back to the truth but also to absolve himself of any guilt for their error. Al-Jīlī's use of the term *al-barā'ah* in this regard conjures up the image of a court of law, in which God is sitting in judgement upon Jesus – an image that will recur in subsequent sections of the chapter, only with the Christians, rather than Jesus, in the dock. Al-Jīlī's concern to establish Jesus' innocence here echoes the discussion in Chapter 4 of Jesus' 'purification' of himself. This concern again reflects al-Jīlī's commitment to the Qur'anic framework: as well as presenting Jesus' self-defence in verses 115–19, the Qur'an also speaks of 'cleansing' (*muṭahhir*) him of the false doctrines of his followers (see Q 3.55).[45]

Yet, al-Jīlī appears to go further than the Qur'an in not only advocating the innocence of Jesus but also attempting to mitigate the errors of Jesus' *people*. To this end, he again repeats the idea that the error of Jesus' people resides in their stopping at the apparent meaning of the Trinitarian formula with which the Gospel opens. The Christians, he explains, did not take their doctrine of the Trinity from non-scriptural sources; rather, they 'believed in (*dhahabū ilá*) what they understood of (*mā fahimū min*) the word of God (*kalām Allāh*)', and adopted doctrines in accordance with 'what they knew (*'alá mā 'alimūhu*)' of the divine word and 'how it appeared to them' (*'alá mā ẓahara lahum*). Unlike the unbelievers, in other words, who turn away from the divine revelation (*al-ikhbār al-ilāhī*) given to them, the Christians accepted the revelation brought by Jesus and sincerely tried to understand it. Their error lay only in their inability to understand Jesus' explanation of the esoteric, metaphysical meaning of the Trinity – an inability that was the product not of insincerity or lack of effort but, we can assume, of their limited 'preparednesses' (*isti'dādāt*). For this reason, like the jurist who sincerely makes an independent legal judgement and errs, but is still rewarded (according to the hadith),[46] they deserved the reward given to sincere believers.

As the term *i'tidhār* used here indicates, al-Jīlī is here offering an 'excuse', put into the mouth of Jesus, for the Christians' false understanding of the Trinitarian doctrine. This, alongside the quotation of Jesus' injunction to God not to 'blame' his people for their profession of that doctrine, indicates that al-Jīlī is advocating a clement, understanding attitude towards the Christians here. Indeed, al-Jīlī seems to go further than merely offering an excuse for or attempting to mitigate the Christians' error, going so far as to equate the Christians' *shirk* – the ordinarily unforgiveable act of associating partners with God – with *tawḥīd*, that is, monotheism itself.[47] Such an idea ought to be understood in the context of his Sufi metaphysical idea of universal theophany. Elsewhere in *al-Insān al-kāmil* (as we shall see in the conclusion to this book), al-Jīlī adopts and elaborates upon Ibn 'Arabī's idea that because everything in existence, including idols and false gods, are loci for the divine manifestation, whatever one worships, one is in fact worshipping (an aspect of) God – that is, what I have called the idea of 'universal monotheism'. The relevance of this Ibn 'Arabian idea here is underlined by the remarkable similarity between al-Jīlī's statement about the *shirk* of the Christians being 'monotheism itself' (*'ayn al-tawḥīd*) and a verse written by another follower of Ibn 'Arabī's, the Persian poet Maḥmūd Shabistarī (d. 720/1340), who, in the section in his *Gulshan-i rāz* on idol-worship and Christianity writes, 'Since unbelief and religion are based upon existence (*chū kufr ū dīn qā'im bi-hastī*), monotheism is idol-worship itself (*tawḥīd 'ayn-i but-parastī*).'[48] Al-Jīlī's identification of the Christians' *shirk* with true monotheism is also somewhat reminiscent of Ibn 'Arabī's proposal, in his chapter on Jesus in the *Fuṣūṣ*, that the Qur'an ascribes *kufr* to the Christians (Q 5.17, 72) because – here he exploits the etymological association of the root *k-f-r* with the idea of 'covering up' or 'concealment' – they 'concealed (*satarū*) God, who gave life to the dead, in the human form of Jesus'.[49] Just as for Ibn 'Arabī the Christians' *kufr* is a sign of their belief in God, so too for al-Jīlī is their *shirk* in fact a sign of their monotheism.

Nevertheless, this should not be taken to mean that, in al-Jīlī's eyes, the 'monotheism' of the Christians is of equal merit to that of the Muslims, especially those who share al-Jīlī's Sufi metaphysical outlook. He is not claiming that the Christian doctrine of the Trinity is correct: he still describes belief in the Trinity as *shirk* – perhaps the gravest sin in Islam[50] – and elsewhere echoes the Qur'an in writing of the *kufr* of Jesus' people.[51] Nevertheless, his interpretation of Qur'an 5.117, a verse that does not appear on the surface to excuse the Christians or credit them with a sincere response to the divine revelation, does reveal a more charitable attitude towards the Christians than that displayed by the majority of Qur'an exegetes.[52] This, I would contend, is the result of him taking the Ibn 'Arabian Sufi metaphysical idea of universal theophany to its logical conclusion, namely that, while the Christians are undoubtedly in error and therefore of inferior standing to the Muslims, nevertheless their faith in and worship of the persons of the Trinity does in fact constitute, at the esoteric level, faith in and worship of forms in which God is manifest. In this sense, the Christian doctrine is monotheistic, even if the Christians themselves do not properly understand why it is so.

God's forgiveness of the Christians

For this reason he [i.e. Jesus] went on to say, 'If You forgive (*taghfir*) them, then You are the Mighty, the Wise (*al-'azīz al-ḥakīm*)' (Q 5:118). He did not say, 'If You punish them (*tu'adhdhibuhum*), then You are the Severe in Punishment (*shadīd al-'iqāb*)', or something like that. Rather, he mentioned forgiveness (*al-maghfirah*), requesting (*ṭalaban*) it for them from the Real, as a judgement (*ḥukman*) from Him that they had not departed from the truth/the Real (*lam yakhrujū min al-ḥaqq*), because the prophets (*al-anbiyā'*) – Peace and prayers be upon them – do not ask the Real – May He be exalted – for forgiveness for someone when they know that he deserves punishment (*yastaḥiqq al-'uqūbah*). God – May He be exalted – said, 'Abraham asked for his father's forgiveness (*istighfār*) only because of a promise he had made to him. But when it became clear to him that he was an enemy of God, he dissociated himself from him' (Q 9:114). All the prophets acted in this way.

So Jesus' request (*ṭalab*) for forgiveness (*al-maghfirah*) for his people [was made] in the knowledge that they deserved (*yastaḥiqqūn*) that, because they were in the right in their souls (*'alá al-ḥaqq fī anfusihim*), even though, in the reality of the matter (*'alá ḥaqīqat al-amr*), they were in the wrong (*'alá al-bāṭil*). For they were in the right in their belief (*mu'taqadihim*) that He is the one to whom their matter ultimately returns (*huwa al-ladhī ya'ūl ilayhi amruhum*), even if they were punished (*mu'āqabīn*) for their being in the wrong (*'alá bāṭilihim*), which is the reality of their matter. For this reason Jesus said, 'If You punish them' – and he spoke well (*aḥsana al-talaffuẓ*) when he said after that – 'then they are Your servants', (Q 5:118) meaning, they are worshipping You (*ya'budūnaka*), and are not being obstinate (*mu'ānidīn*), nor are they among those who have no master (*mawlá*), because it is the unbelievers (*al-kāfirīn*) who have no master. For they [i.e. Jesus' people] are, in reality (*'alá al-ḥaqīqah*), in the right (*muḥiqqūn*), because God – May He be exalted – is the reality of Jesus (*ḥaqīqat 'Īsá*), and the reality of

> his mother (*ḥaqīqat ummihi*), and the reality of the Holy Spirit (*ḥaqīqat al-rūḥ al-quds*), indeed, the reality of everything (*ḥaqīqat kull shay'*). This is the meaning of Jesus' – Peace be upon him – saying, 'then they are Your servants'. So Jesus testified (*shahida*) on their behalf that they were the servants of God (*'ibād Allāh*). Let this suffice as a testimony (*shahādah*) for them.[53]

The most important key terms of this passage – which continues al-Jīlī's commentary' on Qur'an 5.116-119 – concern forgiveness (*taghfir*, *al-maghfirah*, *istighfār*), on the one hand, and punishment (*tu'adhdhib*, *al-'iqāb*, *al-'uqūbah*), on the other. At the more exoteric level, these terms seem here to signify, respectively, salvation and damnation, that is, deliverance from or consignment to hell. The Qur'an often uses words of the root *gh-f-r* and *'-dh-b* (and, to a lesser extent, *'-q-b*) in this way (see e.g. Q 2.284, 5.18, 40.7). And while the term *'uqūbah* is more regularly used – in contrast to *'iqāb* – to denote punishment meted out to wrongdoers in this life,[54] nevertheless, because al-Jīlī is here discussing the intercession of the prophets on behalf of their communities, it seems likely that it is punishment in the afterlife that is meant here, the concept of prophetic intercession (*shafā'ah*) usually appearing in the context of the Day of Judgement.[55] If this interpretation is correct, then it follows that we are here dealing with soteriology, and that, at least at this level, Jesus is asking for his people to be spared the punishment of hell on account of the mitigating circumstances surrounding their mistaken beliefs about him and his mother. This being said, as we have seen in Chapter 4, there is also a more esoteric and metaphysical aspect to the divine 'punishment' and 'forgiveness'.

We saw in the chapter on the Torah that, in al-Jīlī's view, the Christians are not protected, as the Muslims are, from the 'misery' (*shaqāwah*) of hell, on account of their mistaken interpretation of Jesus' miracle working as a sign of his divinity. Here, too, he indicates at one point that the Christians are 'punished' (*mu'āqabīn*) for their 'false' (*bāṭil*) beliefs, and adds the seemingly conclusive remark that this is 'the reality of their matter'. From this angle, at least, al-Jīlī seems to be advocating a soteriologically exclusivist position vis-à-vis the Christians.

Yet this is by no means the whole picture. Indeed, in keeping with the more charitable attitude towards the Christians taken by al-Jīlī in his commentary on this extended Qur'anic passage, clemency is clearly the dominant tone of this section. Al-Jīlī notes, for instance, that Jesus would only have interceded for a people that 'deserved' (*yastaḥiqqūn*) forgiveness, in keeping with the general prophetic practice of only interceding for the deserving. Similarly, al-Jīlī draws attention to the fact that, while the Qur'anic Jesus connects the possibility of God's forgiveness of the Christians to two of His names (*al-'azīz* and *al-ḥakīm*),[56] he does not connect the possibility of God's punishment of them to a divine name such as 'the Severe in Punishment' (*shadīd al-'iqāb*),[57] the suggestion being that the forgiveness of Jesus' people, in being connected by the Qur'an to the divine names, is better than the option of punishing them. Likewise, al-Jīlī here juxtaposes those who 'worship' and 'serve' God (*'ibād Allāh*, *ya'budūnaka*) and are therefore 'in the right' (*muḥiqqūn*), and those who are 'obstinate' towards God (*mu'ānidīn*), who have no master (*al-ladhīna lā mawlá lahum*), and who are, in short, 'unbelievers' (*kāfirīn*). Noting Jesus' statement that his people are 'Your [i.e. God's] servants' (*'ibāduka*), al-Jīlī classifies the Christians among the former group. Al-Jīlī, it seems, takes this Qur'anic phrase as a reference to the underlying 'monotheism' of the Christian position, in keeping with his Ibn 'Arabian notion of universal monotheism discussed in the previous section. In so doing, in fact, he is directly following Ibn 'Arabī, who, in his quasi-commentary on this Qur'anic passage in the chapter on Jesus in the *Fuṣūṣ*, suggests that the Qur'an's use of the second-person *singular* pronominal suffix here is a sign that Jesus' people (potentially) worship the one and singular God.[58] Finally, in an apparent contradiction of his statement that the Christians' being in the wrong is 'the reality of the matter', al-Jīlī declares that the Christians are not merely in the right 'in their souls' – that is, from their own limited perspective – but are in fact right 'in reality' (*'alá al-ḥaqīqah*). This is because, seen from the perspective of the Sufi metaphysical ideas of universal theophany and universal monotheism – which, after all, is the 'true' perspective – God is the 'reality' (*ḥaqīqah*) of each of the three persons of the Trinity (just as, as we saw in the previous chapter, He is the 'reality' of Solomon), which is to say that they are all loci of the divine manifestation and so are, in one sense, worthy objects of worship.

The effect of all of this is to soften significantly the harsher, more exclusivist dimensions of al-Jīlī's soteriology – indeed, in stressing that the Christians are deserving of forgiveness, he appears here to be advocating an *inclusivist* soteriology – and to reinforce the reader's sense of the need to look upon the Christians' false doctrines with a charitable, more clement mindset. Yet, while this passage therefore serves as another good example of how al-Jīlī's Ibn 'Arabian Sufi metaphysical perspective can lead him to a more charitable view of Christianity, it should again be stressed that al-Jīlī is not proposing that the Christians, in professing the Trinity, have attained the truth in the same way that the Muslims, and especially the elite class of Sufi metaphysicians among them, have. There is still an ambivalence here, a sense that the Christians are 'in the wrong' and 'punished' as well as 'in the right' and 'forgiven', while in al-Jīlī's view, as we know, they remain incapable of comprehending the deeper meaning of the revelation given to them, such that they do not possess the full truth. This all being said, it is clear that the ideas of universal theophany and universal monotheism do lead al-Jīlī to interpret the Christian doctrine – and the relevant Qur'anic passage – in such a way as to argue that they deserve forgiveness.

Jesus' success in defending his people before God

> For this reason, God – May He be exalted – said immediately following this discussion: 'On this day, the truthful will benefit from their truthfulness (*yanfa' al-ṣādiqīn ṣidquhum*)' (Q 5:119) in the eyes of their Lord. This was an indication to Jesus – Peace be upon him – that he had achieved what he requested (*bi-injāz mā ṭalaba*). Its meaning is, 'Since they were truthful in their souls (*ṣādiqīn fī anfusihim*), due to their interpretation of My word (*li-ta'wīlihim kalāmī*) according to how it appeared to them (*'alá mā ẓahara lahum*) – even though they were opposed to the matter as it truly was – their benefit (*naf'uhum*) was with their Lord (*'inda rabbihim*), not with anyone other than Him.' This is because the judgement (*al-ḥukm*) that they were in error (*al-ḍalāl*), in our view, is the apparent aspect of

> the matter, in itself (*ẓāhir al-amr ʿalayhi fī nafsihi*), and for this they were punished (*ʿūqibū*). But since their final destination (*maʾāluhum*) consists in what they, [being] with God, will possess of the truth (*al-ḥaqq*) – which is their belief (*iʿtiqāduhum*), in their souls, in the reality of that (*ḥaqīqat dhālik*) – their sincerity (*ṣidq*) in that belief is their benefit with their Lord, with the result that the judgement (*ḥukm*) of them ends up at (*āla ilá*) the divine mercy (*al-raḥmah al-ilāhiyyah*). So, He manifested Himself (*tajallá*) within their souls, according to what they believed about Jesus. So it appeared to them (*ẓahara lahum*) that their doctrine (*muʿtaqad*) was true (*ḥaqqan*), from this perspective, and He manifested Himself to them through their doctrine, because He is in the thoughts (*ẓann*) of His servant.[59]

Al-Jīlī here rounds out his quasi-*tafsīr* of Qur'an 5.116-119 with a summary of the two different ways – the one negative, the other positive – in which the Christian doctrine concerning Jesus can be viewed. On the one hand, he declares, the Christians are in 'error' (*al-ḍalāl*). As we know, this is a Qur'anic term, signifying the opposite of being rightly guided (*al-hudá, al-rashād*),[60] and which is directly connected to both *shirk* (see e.g. Q 4.116) and *kufr* (see e.g. Q 4.136, 4.167), implying damnation after death. Al-Jīlī's reference here to the Christians' *ḍalāl* is therefore in keeping both with his earlier reference to their *shirk* and *kufr* and with the exegetes' traditional identification of the Christians with 'those who are in error' (*al-ḍāllīn*) mentioned in Qur'an 1.7.[61] According to al-Jīlī, the Christians' error derives, as we have already seen, from their superficial, exoteric interpretation – here referred to by the phrase *taʾwīluhum . . . ʿalá mā ẓahara lahum* – of the divine revelation. This interpretation led them to their erroneous belief (*iʿtiqād, muʿtaqad*) that Jesus – along with the other persons of the Trinity – was God, and for this apparently false belief they were 'punished' (*ʿūqibū*). As before, the term used for punishment here suggests punishment in the afterlife; indeed, in chapter fifty-eight, al-Jīlī explains that the inhabitants of hell are called 'the people of error' (*ahl al-ḍalāl*), a term that can be applied to the Christians, given their own 'error'.[62]

As in the previous passages, however, al-Jīlī indicates that such a condemnation of the Christians is only one of the two ways of assessing their doctrine. Moreover, once again, it is the less significant of the two ways; in the Sufi language that he uses here, it is merely the 'exoteric' (*ẓāhir*) aspect, rather than the deeper, 'esoteric' truth (*bāṭin, ḥaqīqah*) of the matter. That deeper truth, as indicated previously, allows us to look upon the Christians in a more positive light. In this instance, the more charitable assessment of the Christians is rooted in the language of Qur'an 5.119. In that verse, which comes immediately after God's interrogation of Jesus, God declares that the 'truthful' (*al-ṣādiqīn*) will acquire a 'benefit' (*nafʿ*) for their truthfulness. Al-Jīlī takes this to be a reference to Jesus' people, who, he thinks (as seen previously), were *sincere* in their interpretation of the divine revelation, and hence can be classified among *al-ṣādiqīn*. Indeed, sticking closely to the language of the Qur'anic verse, he suggests that the 'benefit' (*nafʿ*) that is due to the Christians consists in the very sincerity of their belief, the idea presumably being that the certitude or peace of mind that accompanies commitment to a particular doctrine is itself a divine blessing.

Again, there is also a soteriological dimension to this. While, at the exoteric level, punishment in the afterlife is the inevitable consequence of the Christians' error, if we focus – from the deeper, esoteric perspective – upon the 'truthfulness' (*ṣidq*) of their belief, then a different outcome emerges. Aside from the benefit accruing from their own sense of sincerity, their 'final destination' (*ma'āl*) consists in their being with God and knowing (at least a part of) the truth. And where earlier the 'judgement' (*ḥukm*) had been that they were in error and so worthy of punishment, now the judgement is that they will be brought back into 'the divine mercy' (*al-raḥmah al-ilāhiyyah*). On one level, this would appear to mean that Jesus' people are ultimately granted salvation, that is, entry to paradise or, at the least, deliverance from hell, for in several places the Qur'an describes how those admitted to paradise will experience the divine mercy (see e.g. Q 2.64, 2.218, 4.96, 4.175). Yet, according to al-Jīlī's Sufi metaphysical conception of 'salvation', the 'happiness' of paradise and the 'misery' of hell can also, respectively, signify, as we saw in Chapter 4, the Sufi concepts of 'proximity' (*qurb*) to and 'distance' (*bu'd*) from God. In keeping with this idea, al-Jīlī indicates here that the Christians' being brought into the divine mercy can also be understood to mean that God becomes manifest within them. Moreover, al-Jīlī connects this divine manifestation within Jesus' people to their doctrine of the Incarnation, his point apparently being that, because they are open to the possibility of God appearing in humanity, the Christians themselves are capable of becoming loci for the divine manifestation.

Al-Jīlī's position here is once again firmly grounded in his Ibn 'Arabian Sufi metaphysics. Mercy (*al-raḥmah*), as we know, is a key concept within Ibn 'Arabī's metaphysical system; according to the Ibn 'Arabian idea of 'universal mercy'; in fact, it constitutes both the origin and the *final destination* of all things. In the *Futūḥāt*, Ibn 'Arabī explains that God's mercy is 'attached' (*tulḥaq*) to the punished and that those in heaven will ultimately say that those in hell have been 'granted felicity' (*mun'amūn*),[63] while in the chapter on Hūd in the *Fuṣūṣ* he suggests that God will ultimately lead the damned to attain 'proximity itself' (*'ayn al-qurb*) or 'the felicity of proximity' (*na'īm al-qurb*), at which point 'what is called hell (*jahannam*) will vanish for them'.[64] In chapter fifty-eight of *al-Insān al-kāmil*, al-Jīlī echoes and elaborates upon this idea. Grounding his position, in true Ibn 'Arabian fashion, in the hadith, 'My mercy precedes My wrath', and in Qur'an 7.156, 'My mercy encompasses everything', he indicates that the punishment of the afterlife will not endure eternally:

> Therefore know that since the hellfire (*al-nār*) is something accidental to existence, it is permissible for it to pass away; indeed, anything else would be impossible. And its passing away means nothing other than that the burning (*al-iḥrāq*) will go away, and with the going away of the burning, its angels will go away, and with the going away of its angels, the angels of felicity (*malā'ikat al-na'īm*) will arrive, and with the arrival of the angels of felicity there will grow in its place the Jirjīr tree, which is green, and green is the most beautiful colour in paradise. So things will be overturned (*in'akasa*), such that that which was infernal (*jaḥīm*) will become felicitous (*na'īm*).[65]

Al-Jīlī's idea that the Christians will ultimately be embraced by the divine mercy can therefore be seen in the context of this adherence to the Ibn 'Arabian Sufi metaphysical principle of universal mercy, as well as to the similarly fundamental Ibn 'Arabian ideas of universal theophany and universal monotheism, which enable him to see the 'truth' hidden in the Christians' erroneous doctrine. Al-Jīlī's commitment to the Ibn 'Arabian principle of universal mercy gives us one way, too, of reconciling his apparently contradictory statements that the Christians will be both 'punished' and 'forgiven': they may well be punished but, like all others who are condemned to hell, their torment will not be eternal, but, thanks to the universality of the divine mercy, will ultimately give way to an experience of 'felicity'.

All this, it is true, could also be applied to any non-Muslim religious community; indeed, in both chapter fifty-eight and in the final chapter, as we shall see in the conclusion to this book, al-Jīlī indicates that the torment of the hellfire will 'pass away' from all of its inhabitants. Yet, there is also a sense here in which the Christians, as he sees it, are especially worthy of receiving the divine mercy. The reason for this is al-Jīlī's identification of a parallel between the Christian doctrines of the Trinity and Incarnation and his own Ibn 'Arabian Sufi metaphysics, for like the Sufi metaphysicians of the Ibn 'Arabī tradition, the Christians, he recognizes, are aware of the presence of the divine within the created world, and in particular within mankind. This is not to say that they fully comprehend the truth of universal theophany; as we shall see presently, al-Jīlī criticizes them for limiting their conception of the divine manifestation to Jesus and the other persons of the Trinity. Nevertheless, he does seem to demonstrate a particular sympathy for the Christian position here, a sympathy that is conditioned by his Sufi metaphysical perspective.[66] There is, for instance, a notable disparity between his interpretation of Qur'anic 5.119, and that put forward in non-Sufi *tafsīrs*, which tend to stress the innocence of Jesus while condemning the Christians for their false beliefs about him.[67] Al-Jīlī, by contrast, takes care to both demonstrate the innocence of Jesus and mitigate the errors of his people.

Al-Jīlī's position here does seem to represent a softening of the conventional medieval Muslim attitude towards the Christians, in particular with regard to their doctrines of the Trinity and Incarnation and the question of their ultimate fate. Again, however, this is not to say that he thinks Christianity to be on par with Islam. As will become clear, he remains within the framework of the Qur'an-centred view of sacred history, even if his Sufi metaphysical perspective may lead him to take the conventional medieval Islamic view in a more charitable direction.

The metaphysical meaning of the Gospel

The Gospel is an expression of the manifestations of the names of the essence (*tajalliyyāt asmā' al-dhāt*), meaning, the manifestations of the essence within His names (*tajalliyyāt al-dhāt fī asmā'ihi*), and among the aforementioned manifestations is the manifestation within the qualified oneness [of God] (*tajalliyyah fī al-wāḥidiyyah*), through which He appeared (*ẓahara*) to Jesus' people

> in Jesus, in Mary, and in the Holy Spirit. So, they witnessed (*shahidū*) the Real in each of these loci of manifestation (*fī kull maẓhar min hādhihi al-maẓāhir*).[68]

In the previous three chapters, we saw al-Jīlī outline his conception of the metaphysical meaning of the Qur'an, the Torah and the Psalms; that is, the way in which those scriptures represent the different aspects of the divine manifestation within creation. Here he applies this same idea to the Gospel, informing us that it represents the 'manifestations of the names of the essence' (*tajalliyyāt asmā' al-dhāt*). By 'the names of the essence' al-Jīlī means those names that are unique to God: these he lists earlier in the book as God (*Allāh*), the Unqualified One (*al-aḥad*), the Qualified One (*al-wāḥid*), the Unique One (*al-fard*), the Odd One (*al-watr*), the Everlasting (*al-ṣamad*), the All-Holy (*al-quddūs*), the Living (*al-ḥayy*), the Light (*al-nūr*) and the Real (*al-ḥaqq*).[69] Since *al-wāḥid* is one of the names of the essence, it follows that, as al-Jīlī indicates here, the divine manifestation at the level of *al-wāḥidiyyah* is among those manifestations represented by the Gospel. This is the level, it will be remembered, at which the divine essence begins to take on a degree of multiplicity within its unity, by virtue of the appearance here of the divine names and attributes.[70] In suggesting that this level of the divine existence is revealed in the Gospel, al-Jīlī indicates that the Gospel is a particularly exalted form of revelation, since the only levels above that of *al-wāḥidiyyah*, at least in one version of his scheme, are those of the 'unqualified oneness' (*al-aḥadiyyah*) or 'absolute existence' (*al-wujūd al-muṭlaq*) of the divine essence, and of the imperceptible, simple essence itself. This allows us to assign to the Gospel a place in the hierarchy of scriptures: while the Gospel is lower in the hierarchy than the Qur'an, which represents the divine manifestation at the higher level of *al-aḥadiyyah*, it is higher in the hierarchy than the Torah and the Psalms, which, as we saw in the previous chapters, represent the levels of *al-raḥmāniyyah* and *al-malikiyyah*, the fifth and sixth/seventh levels of existence, respectively. This hierarchy can also be expressed in terms of the divine essence, names and attributes, the divine essence (the Qur'an) being more exalted than the names of the essence (the Gospel), which in turn is more exalted than the names of the attributes (the Torah) and the attributes of the acts (the Psalms). This hierarchy is in keeping with the conventional Islamic notion of the abrogation of the Torah by the Gospel and of the Gospel, in turn, by the Qur'an, and reflects a view of sacred history in which things generally get better over time, until the revelation of the Qur'an, which cannot be bettered.

Al-Jīlī also makes a connection here between the Gospel's revelation of God as *al-wāḥid* – among the other names of the essence – and the Christian doctrine of the Trinity, which, as we have seen, is key to his understanding of the contents of the Christian revelation. As he sees it, it is at the level of *al-wāḥidiyyah* that God becomes manifest in the three persons of the Trinity. His reasoning here, we might suggest, is that since it is at this level that God begins to take on the names and attributes that He makes manifest in creation, *al-wāḥidiyyah* is therefore the source of the divine appearance within phenomenal forms, which is the truth represented by the doctrine of the Trinity. This idea can also be expressed in terms of al-Jīlī's idea of the Perfect Human. According to that idea, as we know, the Perfect Humans are those who manifest all of the divine names and attributes – that is, that aspect of the divine that appears at the level of *al-wāḥidiyyah*. In this sense, the Perfect Human – or at least those Perfect Humans other than Muhammad, who, as we saw in Chapter 3, also manifests the level of *al-aḥadiyyah* – can be viewed as the locus of manifestation of *al-wāḥidiyyah*.

The significance of all this is that, in explaining that God's qualified oneness appears in Jesus, Mary and the Holy Spirit, al-Jīlī seems to be implying that the persons of the Trinity are Perfect Humans, or, in the case of the Holy Spirit, perfect loci for the manifestation of the divine attributes. He spells this out, in fact, by describing the three persons of the Trinity as *maẓāhir*. As we know, this is a key term in Ibn 'Arabian Sufi metaphysics, denoting the created forms – and, in particular, the human beings – in which the divine names and attributes appear. Although, according to al-Jīlī's idea of universal theophany, all created forms are divine *maẓāhir*, in its fullest sense, as we saw in Chapter 5, the term applies to those created beings that receive all of the divine attributes and manifest them in their own attributes and actions – the Perfect Humans.[71] In using it here, al-Jīlī is acknowledging that the Christians truly witnessed the divine attributes in the phenomenal forms of Jesus, Mary and the Holy Spirit. Even if these three persons are not *identical* with God Himself, as the Christians would have it,[72] nevertheless they are genuine loci for the divine manifestation within creation. From the perspective of the Ibn 'Arabian idea of the Perfect Human, then, the Christians are right to think that God appears within the persons of the Trinity.

The Christians' mistake and error

> But even if they were in the right (*muḥiqqīn*) with respect to this manifestation (*tajallī*), nevertheless they were mistaken (*akhṭa'ū*) and erred (*ḍallū*). As for their mistake (*khaṭa'uhum*), it consisted in the fact that they believed (*dhahabū*), in this regard, in the confinement (*ḥaṣr*) of that to Jesus, Mary, and the Holy Spirit. And as for their error (*ḍalāluhum*), it consisted in the fact that they professed (*qālū bi-*) absolute incarnationism (*al-tajsīm al-muṭlaq*) and a divine comparability (*al-tashbīh*) that was limited to this qualified oneness (*al-muqayyad fī hādhihi al-wāḥidiyyah*). What they said by way of limitation (*al-taqyīd*) does not come under the category of it (*min ḥukmihā*) [i.e. of qualified oneness]. This was the source of their mistake and error. So understand![73]

While al-Jīlī, as we have seen, demonstrates a notable degree of sympathy for the Christians throughout much of this chapter, attempting to understand the ultimate truth of their doctrine of the Trinity from his Sufi metaphysical perspective and indicating that they will be embraced by divine mercy, so centred is his thought upon the Qur'an that he is ultimately bound to conclude that they are in some sense mistaken. The Qur'an, after all, is quite clear in its condemnation of the doctrine of the Trinity and of any suggestion that Jesus, Mary or any other created being should be taken as a god, a condemnation that was taken up and developed in the post-Qur'anic tradition. This passage makes it clear that al-Jīlī does not disagree with the Qur'an and the Islamic tradition that the Christians are mistaken in professing the Trinity and Incarnation. Nevertheless, his reasoning is somewhat different from the more conventional Islamic view.

Al-Jīlī divides the failings of Jesus' people into two categories: their 'mistake' (*khaṭa'*) and their 'error' (*ḍalāl*). The latter term, which we have already come across in this chapter and in the chapter on the Torah, is stronger than the former; or rather it seems more particularly to signify a religious error with potential soteriological consequences.[74] Thus in the hadith quoted previously, *khaṭa'* is used in the context of the erring – but still rewarded – *mujtahid*, while the term *ahl al-ḍalāl* is, by contrast, used by al-Jīlī to denote those condemned to hell.

The Christians' 'mistake' (*khaṭa'*), as al-Jīlī sees it, is to 'confine' (*ḥaṣr*) the manifestations of the divine attributes to the three persons of the Trinity. According to al-Jīlī's Ibn 'Arabian Sufi metaphysics, it will be remembered, God in His essence possesses 'absolute' – which is to say, unlimited – existence (*al-wujūd al-muṭlaq*), in contrast to the 'limited existence' (*al-wujūd al-muqayyad*) of creation. As such, it is a mistake to try to limit or restrict the divine in any way. 'Whoever limits Him (*qayyadahu*),' writes Ibn 'Arabī, 'denies Him (*ankarahu*) [i.e. His appearance] in that which he has limited Him.'[75] By trying to limit the unlimitable existence of the divine to three particular created forms (the persons of the Trinity), and in particular to Jesus (with the doctrine of the Incarnation) the Christians make such a mistake. In other words, because, according to the fundamental idea of al-Jīlī's Sufi metaphysics, the entirety of the phenomenal world is a locus for the divine manifestation, it is wrong to claim, as the Christians do, that the three persons of the Trinity are the *only* loci of divine manifestation. In this regard, al-Jīlī's stance towards Christian doctrine is again reminiscent of the position taken by Ibn 'Arabī and his earlier followers, a position summarized by Ibn Taymiyyah in the following way: 'They say, "The Christians only disbelieved (*kafarū*) insofar as they singled out (*khaṣṣaṣū*) the Messiah as God; if they had universalized (*'ammamū*) [this idea], they would not have been unbelievers."'[76] In the chapter on Jesus in the *Fuṣūṣ*, for example, Ibn 'Arabī indicates that the Christians 'deviated' (*'adalū*) by 'enclosing' (*taḍmīn*) the unlimitable divine reality within Jesus.[77] In his commentary on that passage from the *Fuṣūṣ*, meanwhile, the early commentator al-Jandī uses language that directly anticipates that of al-Jīlī. The Christian position, al-Jandī explains, 'entailed the confinement (*ḥaṣr*) of divinity (*al-ilāhiyyah*) to Jesus son of Mary'. In this way, he continues, those who said that Jesus is God 'limited (*ḥaddadū*) the divine identity and made it confined (*maḥṣūrah*) to a particular human form (*ṣūrah insāniyyah mu'ayyanah*), though it cannot be confined, for He possesses the identity of all things'. This means, says al-Jandī, again using terms that would later appear in al-Jīlī's chapter on the Gospel, that

> They united the [doctrine of] unbelief (*kufr*) that Jesus was God – for they concealed (*satarū*) the divine identity in Jesus – with the mistake (*khaṭa'*) that He is only within him – i.e. that that form and that form alone is Him, and nothing else, even though He is the essence of everything (*'ayn al-kull*), not in some respects, but absolutely (*muṭlaqan*), in His essence, without restriction or limitation (*ghayr qayd wa-iṭlāq*), as you know.[78]

That last phrase of al-Jandī's – 'as you know' – signals the centrality of the notion of the unlimitability (*iṭlāq*) of the divine existence to the idea of universal theophany, and to Ibn 'Arabian Sufi metaphysics more generally. In declaring that the Christians have made the 'mistake' of 'confining' the divine manifestation to Jesus, therefore, al-Jīlī, like Ibn 'Arabī and al-Jandī before him, is merely adhering to the basic principles of his Sufi metaphysical outlook.

Al-Jīlī's criticism of the Christians here reflects the distance between his Ibn 'Arabian Sufi metaphysical position and the Christian doctrines of the Trinity and Incarnation. Though his Ibn 'Arabian perspective leads him, as we have seen, to acknowledge that the Christians are correct to say that God appears in the three persons of the Trinity, nevertheless it also leads him to point out the limitations of the Christian position. To say, in other words, as the Christians do, that the three persons of the Trinity are the only locus of divine manifestation is, from al-Jīlī's Sufi metaphysical perspective, to fail to understand the fundamental truths of universal theophany and the Perfect Human (just as, from a Christian perspective, to say, as al-Jīlī does, that Jesus is only one of the many loci of the divine manifestation is to undermine the uniqueness of the Incarnation, the central event in the *Christian* view of sacred history). The fact that al-Jīlī's criticism of the Christian doctrine here is firmly rooted in his Ibn 'Arabian Sufi metaphysics is significant, in that it demonstrates that al-Jīlī's Sufi metaphysical perspective does not only or necessarily lead him to adopt a more sympathetic or charitable attitude to non-Muslim religions but can also be the source of his *criticisms* of the doctrines of those religions.

The Christians' 'error' (*ḍalāl*), meanwhile, is, in al-Jīlī's view, closely connected to their 'mistake'. In describing this error, al-Jīlī uses technical terms drawn from the discourse of *kalām*, namely, *tajsīm* and *tashbīh*. The former term is most commonly used in intra-Muslim theological debates on whether the Qur'an's assignation of body parts to God ought to be taken literally. It is generally a pejorative term used to denigrate those such as the early Shi'i theologians Hishām ibn al-Ḥakam (d. 179/795–6) and his student Yūnus b. 'Abd al-Raḥmān (d. 208/823),[79] who are said to have professed that God has or is a body (*jism*),[80] an idea rejected by both Mu'tazilites and Ash'arites.[81] Al-Jīlī's use of this term in his critique of the Christian doctrine of the Trinity is somewhat unusual. The terms more commonly used by Muslim theologians who wrote against the Trinity and Incarnation are *ittiḥād* (union) and *ḥulūl* (indwelling),[82] while Arab Christian theologians more often use terms such as *tajassud* and *ta'annus*.[83] Al-Jīlī's condemnation of the Christians for their 'absolute incarnationism' (*al-tajsīm al-muṭlaq*) therefore echoes not so much the theological polemics against Christianity as it does intra-Muslim polemic; indeed, later in the book, al-Jīlī stresses that the manifestation of God in man is 'on the condition of the divine incomparability, [for] He is exalted beyond incarnation (*al-tajsīm*) and representation (*al-tamthīl*)',[84] his intention apparently being to defend his Sufi metaphysical idea of the Perfect Human against those of his Muslim opponents who would charge him with identifying God and man. As in the conventional use of the term in *kalām*, the *tajsīm* of the Christians is perhaps connected here to a point made by al-Jīlī on several occasions in the course of the chapter, namely, the *limitation* of the Christians' literal reading of their scripture. In other words, just as the *mujassimūn* (anthropomorphists), in the Islamic theological context, are those who take the Qur'an's assignation of body parts to God too literally, so too might the Christians be deemed *mujassimīn* for believing that God is literally identical with the three persons of the Trinity.

The second term al-Jīlī uses to criticize the Christian doctrine of the Trinity – *tashbīh* – is also often used in *kalām* discourse, again in a pejorative sense, to attack those who assign created – particularly human – attributes to God.[85] For this reason, it is often paired, as here, with *tajsīm*. The theologians, both Mu'tazilite and Ash'arite, contrast it with *tanzīh*, a term which denotes the proper assertion of God's incomparability to creation. This pair of terms has a particular significance in the Sufi metaphysics of Ibn 'Arabī, who, as already noted, took an original stance on the issue, proposing the synthesis of *tanzīh* and *tashbīh*, a position that was adopted wholeheartedly by al-Jīlī. By attributing *tashbīh* to the Christians here (as he did in the chapter on the Torah),[86] therefore, al-Jīlī is again suggesting that they make the mistake of limiting themselves to only one half of the truth, by viewing God in terms of only one of His two fundamental aspects. In al-Jīlī's view, this is a serious mistake. Indeed, in his commentary on the *Futūḥāt*, he describes this kind of unadulterated *tashbīh* not only as a limitation of the divine but also as 'polytheism' (*shirk*) and 'dualism' (*tathniyah*),[87] while in his *Ghunyat arbāb al-sam'ā* he declares, 'The only thing forbidden (*mamnū'*) with respect to the divine is to declare Him comparable (*al-tashbīh*), for it is not permissible to compare the Real to anything.'[88] In this sense, by accusing the Christians of excessive *tashbīh*, al-Jīlī echoes the more conventional medieval Muslim view of the Trinity, which is to condemn it as *shirk*. At the same time, however, he makes the charges of *tashbīh* and *shirk* from his particular Ibn 'Arabian perspective.

The Christians' *tashbīh*, he also tells us, is 'limited to this qualified oneness' (*al-muqayyad fī hādhihi al-wāḥidiyyah*). The term *muqayyad* evokes the error of *taqyīd*, that is, the limitation of the absolute existence of God, a view condemned by Ibn 'Arabī and his followers.[89] The Christians' *tashbīh*, it seems, is limited by virtue of the fact that they consider God only at the level of unqualified oneness, to the exclusion of the higher levels of the divine existence. There is perhaps an implicit contrast being made here between the Gospel, which is a revelation limited to the level of *wāḥidiyyah*, and the Qur'an, which, as we have seen, al-Jīlī holds to be an expression of the higher level of *al-aḥadiyyah*. The Christians' error, therefore, could be said to be a consequence of the limited nature of their revelation. By manifesting the names of the divine essence, the Gospel leads the Christians to look upon God from the perspective of qualified oneness, that is, in His state of being qualified by names and attributes that, though strictly speaking unique to God, still invite comparison with creation. In focusing only on this aspect of the divine, the Christians are blinded by the all-consuming perspective of *tashbīh*, neglecting to balance this perspective with that of *tanzīh*.[90] The Muslims, by contrast, because their scripture reveals the divine essence in its unqualified state *and* the divine names and attributes, are able to look at God from the perspective of both *tanzīh* and *tashbīh* – on the condition that they share al-Jīlī's Ibn 'Arabian understanding of the Qur'an.

This being said, al-Jīlī also states that the Christians' *taqyīd* was not a determination (*ḥukm*) of *wāḥidiyyah*, which is to say that the revelation of the qualified oneness of God need not necessarily have led them into *tajsīm* and *tashbīh*. Similarly, in the following section, he states that the Christians' false doctrine of the Trinity was a result of their going against the true contents of their scripture. It can therefore also be argued that for al-Jīlī the Christians' error is a consequence not so much of the limitations of the Gospel – though it certainly *is* limited vis-à-vis the Qur'an – as of their mistaken or limited interpretation of that revelation. Such an argument would fit with what we saw earlier in the chapter regarding al-Jīlī's suggestion that the Christians' interpretation of the Gospel was limited to its *ẓāhir* meaning.

The true message of the Gospel, its appearance in the Qur'an and acceptance by the Muslims

> All that there is in the Gospel is that upon which is founded the divine revelation in human existence (*al-nāmūs al-lāhūtī fī al-wujūd al-nāsūtī*), which is the requirement of the appearance of the Real in creation (*muqtaḍá ẓuhūr al-ḥaqq fī al-khalq*). But when the Christians came to believe (*dhahabat*) what they believed, in terms of incarnationism (*al-tajsīm*) and confinement (*ḥaṣr*), this was in opposition to (*mukhālifan li-*) what is in the Gospel.
>
> So in reality, only the Muhammadans (*al-muḥammadiyyūn*) upheld what was in the Gospel, because the Gospel in its completeness (*bi-kamālihi*) is in a single verse of the Qur'an, which is when He – May He be exalted – said, 'And I breathed into him of My spirit (*wa-nafakhtu fīhi min rūḥī*)' (Q 15:29). And His spirit is none other than Him. This is God's – Glory be to Him and May He be exalted – announcement (*ikhbār*) of His appearance within Adam.
>
> Then He supported it [i.e. the verse] with, 'We shall show them Our signs on the horizons and in themselves, until it is clear to them that it is the truth/the Real (*al-ḥaqq*)' (Q 41:53). This means that the whole world (*jamīʿ al-ʿālam*), which is referred to by [the term] 'on the horizons and in themselves' is the Real (*al-ḥaqq*). Then He clarified it (*bayyana*) and stated it openly (*ṣaraḥa*) when He said with regard to Muhammad – May God bless him and grant him peace: 'Those who pledge allegiance to you only pledge allegiance to God' (Q 48:10), and when He said, 'Whoever obeys the messenger has obeyed God' (Q 4.80).
>
> So Muhammad's people were guided (*ihtadá*) by this to the reality of the matter (*ḥaqīqat al-amr*), and for this reason they did not confine (*lam yaḥṣirū*) the Real existence (*al-wujūd al-ḥaqqī*) to Adam alone, because the verse designated Adam alone. Rather, they acted with propriety (*taʾaddabū*), knowing (*ʿalimū*) that by Adam was meant every individual of this human race (*kull fard min afrād hādhā al-nawʿ al-insānī*), and witnessed the Real in every part of existence in its completeness (*fī jamīʿ ajzāʾ al-wujūd bi-kamālihi*), heeding the divine command (*imtithālan al-amr al-ilāhī*), which was that He said, 'until it is clear to them that it is the truth/the Real'. And so it was for Muhammad and the Muslims.[91]

This long passage gets to the heart of al-Jīlī's Sufi metaphysical view of the Gospel, the Christians and, more generally, the relationship between God and creation.

The Gospel, he explains, contains a single basic truth, which is summed up in the phrase *muqtaḍá ẓuhūr al-ḥaqq fī al-khalq*, that is, the necessity of God's manifestation within creation. This, of course, is the key Sufi metaphysical idea of universal theophany, expressed in its most basic terms. The Gospel, as al-Jīlī sees it, therefore contains a true expression of the underlying divine nature of reality, just as the earlier pre-Qur'anic scriptures had done. Moreover, this truth, he explains, is the basis for another idea, which is represented by the phrase *al-nāmūs al-lāhūtī fī al-wujūd al-nāsūtī*. Al-Jīlī uses the term *nāmūs* here and elsewhere in the book as a synonym for *tajallī* or *ẓuhūr* – that is, to denote the divine manifestation.[92] The terms *lāhūtī* and *nāsūtī*, though essentially synonymous here with (the perhaps more common) *ilāhī* ('divine') and *insānī* ('human'), carry a special significance in the context of a discussion of Christian doctrine. Medieval Muslim authors typically use the terms *lāhūt* and *nāsūt* in their descriptions of the Christian doctrine of the Incarnation, according to which, as they understand it, the *lāhūt* of God unites or mixes with, or inheres in, the *nāsūt* of Jesus.[93] The pair of terms also appears in the Sufi technical lexicon, having been first popularized, it seems, by al-Ḥallāj (d. 309/922),[94] and later adopted by Ibn 'Arabī.[95] Significantly, Ibn 'Arabī uses the terms in the chapter on Jesus in the *Fuṣūṣ* in the context of his exposition of the appearance of the divine spirit in man, perhaps indicating some awareness of the Christian resonance of the terms.[96] At the beginning of *al-Insān al-kāmil*, meanwhile, al-Jīlī describes Muhammad as 'the locus of the synthesis of the realities of the divine nature (*al-lāhūt*), and the source of the delicate aspects of human nature (*al-nāsūt*)',[97] indicating that these terms are connected, as he sees it, to the idea of the Perfect Human. Just as the phrase *muqtaḍá ẓuhūr al-ḥaqq fī al-khalq* stands for the idea of universal theophany, then, the phrase *al-nāmūs al-lāhūtī fī al-wujūd al-nāsūtī* stands for the idea of the Perfect Human. Both of these ideas, al-Jīlī appears to be suggesting, are contained in the Gospel.

If this is the case, then the source of the Christians' error would not be the Gospel, but rather, as suggested previously, their own false or limited interpretation of that scripture. Indeed, where before al-Jīlī indicated that their interpretation is confined to the apparent (*ẓāhir*) meaning of the revelation, here he goes further and explicitly states that Christian doctrine is actually 'opposed' (*mukhālifan*) to the contents of the Gospel. Specifically, what is opposed to the Gospel is their aforementioned 'incarnationism' (*tajsīm*) and 'confinement' (*ḥaṣr*) of God to the three persons of the Trinity. In other words, whereas the Gospel reveals that the divine (*al-ḥaqq, al-lāhūt*) is manifest in creation (*al-khalq*) – the idea of universal theophany – and, specifically, in humanity (*al-insān, al-nāsūt*) – the idea of the Perfect Human – the Christians make the mistake of claiming that God actually takes on a human body and of limiting the manifestation of the divine to Jesus and the other persons of the Trinity, thereby ignoring the metaphysical truth that the whole of creation is a divine *maẓhar*.

In contrast to the Christians' mistaken reading of their revelation, the Muslims – or as al-Jīlī calls them here, in keeping with his strong sense of the close connection between religious communities and their prophets, 'the Muhammadans' (*al-muḥammadiyyūn*)[98] – profess the true meaning of the Gospel, which is to say that they acknowledge the truths of universal theophany and the Perfect Human. This idea parallels the conventional medieval Muslim idea that the Christians have distorted or misinterpreted the true, original meaning of the Gospel, which is in perfect harmony with the Qur'an. As usual, however, al-Jīlī's reasoning here is somewhat different to the mainstream position. The Muslims' superior reading of the Gospel to the Christians', he explains, derives from the fact that the entire Gospel (*al-Injīl bi-kāmilihi*) is contained in a single *āyah* of the Qur'an. That *āyah* – Qur'an 15.29/38.72 (the wording is the same in both) – tells us that God breathed into Adam to give him life. This is in fact one of the key Qur'anic source texts for the Ibn 'Arabian idea expressed in the previously mentioned passage from the *Faṣṣ* on Jesus, namely that the divine spirit is the inner reality of mankind, or, put another way, that mankind is the perfect locus for the divine manifestation.[99] In identifying Qur'an 15.29/38.72 as the key Qur'anic 'announcement' (*ikhbār*) of the truths of universal theophany and the Perfect Human – an identification that he also makes elsewhere in *al-Insān al-kāmil* – al-Jīlī is again following Ibn 'Arabī's lead.[100]

Furthermore, by referring to Qur'an 15.29/38.72 in the context of his discussion of the Gospel, al-Jīlī calls to mind the similarity between the verse and those Qur'anic verses (Q 21.91, 66.12) that speak, using the same terminology, of how God breathed His spirit into Mary in order to conceive Jesus. It is notable in this regard that al-Jīlī identifies the verse describing God's breathing into Adam as the verse that summarizes the Gospel, rather than those verses that refer to God breathing into Mary. While the latter verses specifically indicate that God's spirit is the inner reality of *Jesus*, the former verse suggests more generally that God's spirit is the inner reality of the entirety of mankind, since Adam, as 'the father of mankind' (*abū al-bashar*), stands for mankind as a whole. This truth, he explains, is acknowledged by the Muslims, who recognize that what is meant by 'Adam' is 'every individual of this human race' (*kull fard min afrād hādhā al-naw' al-insānī*). The Muslims therefore do not make the same mistake as the Christians of restricting the manifestation of God to one particular individual, for they see God not only in Adam but also in 'every part of existence in its completeness' (*fī jamī' ajzā' al-wujūd bi-kamālihi*), which is to say that they recognize the metaphysical truths of universal theophany and the Perfect Human.

Al-Jīlī's claim that the entire message of the Gospel is contained in a single verse of the Qur'an clearly implies the superiority of the Qur'an over the Christian scripture. This is not to say, however, that verse 15.29 is the *only* Qur'anic proof for the Sufi metaphysical truths of universal theophany and the Perfect Human. In fact, says al-Jīlī, there are a number of Qur'anic verses that support and make evident the truth expressed in Qur'an 15.29. Specifically, he cites verses 41.53, 48.10 and 4.80. Qur'an 41.53 – 'We shall show them Our signs etc.' – is often quoted by Sufis, including Ibn 'Arabī, for the same purposes as al-Jīlī has here, namely, to denote the truth of universal theophany.[101] In his commentary on this verse, al-Jīlī stresses that it is the 'whole world' (*jamī' al-'ālam*) that is a divine manifestation, the point again being that the divine manifestation is not limited to Jesus or the three persons of the Trinity, but rather is universal. The other two verses that al-Jīlī cites here, meanwhile, indicate, according to his reading, that God became manifest in the person of Muhammad; or as he puts it in the final chapter in his explanation of the same two verses, 'He [i.e. God] established Muhammad in His own station (*aqāma Muḥammad maqām nafsihi*).'[102] As we know, in al-Jīlī's view, Muhammad is the archetypal Perfect Human. By citing these verses here, therefore, al-Jīlī seems to be indicating that the Christians are mistaken to imagine that their own prophet, Jesus, is the best of mankind and the only recipient of the divine manifestation, for in so doing they overlook both the primordial perfection of all human beings, and, what is more, the existence of a greater Perfect Human – Muhammad.[103]

Throughout this section, there is a clear sense of the superiority of the Muslims over the Christians. This is brought out by some of the key terms that al-Jīlī uses. While the Christians, as al-Jīlī declares on a number of occasions in this chapter, are in 'error' (*ḍalāl*), the Muslims are 'rightly guided' (*ihtadá*). While the Christians were earlier described as being 'in the wrong' (*'alá al-bāṭil*) 'in the reality of the matter' (*'alá ḥaqīqat al-amr*), the Muslims, by contrast, have arrived at 'the reality of the matter' (*ḥaqīqat al-amr*). While the Christians profess doctrines that deserve to be called by the pejorative terms *shirk*, *tashbīh* and *tajsīm*, the Muslims, by contrast, 'acted with propriety' (*ta'addabū*), 'heeding the divine command' (*imtithālan al-amr al-ilāhī*). Though al-Jīlī's Sufi metaphysical perspective, as we have seen over the course of the chapter, leads him to adopt a relatively charitable and sympathetic view of Christian doctrine, therefore, nevertheless there is no mistaking his sense of the superiority of the Muslims over the Christians. This superiority, as we have already seen, is a consequence partly of the greater completeness of the Qur'an vis-à-vis the Gospel, and partly of the Christians' more limited capacity to correctly interpret that scripture in accordance with fundamental Sufi metaphysical truths. As such, just as al-Jīlī's more charitable stance towards the Christians is a product of his Sufi metaphysical perspective, so too is his sense of the superiority of the Qur'an and the Muslims a corollary of his Sufi metaphysics.

Al-Jīlī's conception of what the Muslims believe about the universal divine manifestation, as expressed here, is clearly an idealized one. What he seems to mean is not that all Muslims believe that the entirety of creation is a manifestation of God – which would be an inaccurate statement, and one that would contradict what he says about the religious scholars further on – but rather that this is the true meaning of the Islamic message contained in the Qur'an, as his Qur'anic proof texts purport to show; hence, it is what true 'Muhammadans' profess. In this regard, it should be kept in mind that, although al-Jīlī is clearly concerned with the rights and wrongs of Christian doctrine in this chapter, his text is also directed at his fellow Muslims, and his primary goal here is to set out his Sufi metaphysics and the place of the various scriptures within that metaphysical system, rather than to engage in polemic against the Christians or any other non-Muslim group. This intra-Islamic dimension of al-Jīlī's discussion becomes clear in the concluding section of the chapter.

Guidance and error

> If a verse like this [i.e. Q 4:80] had been sent down (*unzilat*) in the Gospel, Jesus' people would have been guided (*ihtadá*) to that [i.e. the truth]. But it is not like that, because through every book that God – May He be exalted – sends down, He leads many into error (*yuḍill bihi kathīran*) and guides many others (*wa-yahdī*

bihi kathīran), just as He – Glory be to Him and May He be exalted – announced in the Qur'an.

Look at the scholars of external forms (*'ulamā' al-rusūm*), how they erred (*ḍallū*) in their interpretation (*ta'wīl*) of these two verses, believing what they believed (*fa-dhahabū ilá mā dhahabū ilayhi*) with regards to them. Even if what they believed contained an aspect of the truth (*wajhan min wujūh al-ḥaqq*), nevertheless principles (*uṣūl*) became established among them, by which they were distanced (*bu''idū*) from God and from knowing Him (*ma'rifatihi*). Meanwhile, the people of realities (*ahl al-ḥaqā'iq*) were guided (*ihtadá*) by these two [verses] to the knowledge of God (*ma'rifat Allāh*) – May He be exalted. So the same thing that guided some led others into error.

God – May He be exalted – said, 'Through it He leads many into error and guides many others, but through it He only leads astray those who do bad (*al-fāsiqīn*)' (Q 2:26). An egg is said to go bad (*fasaqat*) when it becomes rotten (*fasadat*), and is not fit for hatching. So, what is intended here is a people whose capacities to receive (*qawābil*) the divine manifestation (*al-tajallī al-ilāhī*) have rotted (*fasadat*), since they imagine that God – May He be exalted – does not appear in His creation (*lā yaẓhar fī khalqihi*). Indeed, He does not appear to them (*bal lā yaẓhar lahum*).

Then, since they found what was required by those principles of divine incomparability (*al-uṣūl al-tanzīhiyyah*), which He determines (*ḥakama*) through the divine essence (*bi-al-dhāt al-ilāhiyyah*), and since they abandoned essential matters (*al-umūr al-'ayniyyah*), they followed the governing attributes (*al-awṣāf al-ḥukmiyyah*). But they did not know that those governing attributes were, in their essence (*bi-'aynihā*), in a state of perfection (*'alá kamālihā*), due to this essential matter (*al-amr al-'aynī*) and the existence that is created and Real (*al-wujūd al-khalqī al-ḥaqqī*).[104]

Al-Jīlī here returns again to the question of the cause of the Christians' error. In this instance, he initially implies that it is the limitation of the Gospel that is to blame, given that it did not contain a verse like Qur'an 4.80, which explicitly establishes – as al-Jīlī sees it – the truth that God is manifest in the entirety of creation. At the same time, however, al-Jīlī adds an element to the discussion that he has not yet explicitly mentioned, namely the idea that the Christians' error was part of the divine plan, for whenever God sends down a scripture, He means by it to guide some and lead others astray. Al-Jīlī bases this idea on the Qur'anic statement (see Q 2.26, etc.) that it is God who guides the believers and leads the wrongdoers into error, a statement that appears to indicate that guidance and error are divinely ordained, that is to say, pre-determined. The Qur'an's stance on this point, however, is not perhaps as clear-cut as it may first appear, for in a coda to verse 2.26 it is said that God only leads astray those who do bad (*al-fāsiqīn*). This might be taken to suggest that God only leads astray those who are already sinners, in which case there would seem to be some element of free choice involved in the response to revelation.

As al-Jīlī understands it from his Sufi metaphysical perspective, the Qur'anic term *fāsiqīn* denotes not so much those who behave sinfully – though this is the exoteric meaning – as it does those individuals who have closed their hearts to God.[105]

Expressed, as it is here, in terms of his Ibn 'Arabian technical vocabulary, this means that their *qawābil* – that is, their 'receptivities' – are not sufficiently prepared to receive the divine manifestation. As we know, underlying this concept, and the related Ibn 'Arabian concept of 'preparedness' (*al-isti'dād*), is the idea that, although all individuals are inherently and potentially perfect, there is nevertheless a hierarchy among human beings with regard to their capacity to receive and manifest that perfection. Whether people's ability to manifest their inherent perfection is determined by God or by themselves is not clear from this passage, though it does seem from the writings of both Ibn 'Arabī and al-Jīlī that people's receptivities or preparednesses are dependent upon the particular 'mysteries' (*asrār*) or 'subtle reality' (*laṭā'if*) – that is, inner natures[106] – that God chooses for them.[107] In this sense, then, it can be said that those who do wrong – which is to say, those who are unreceptive to the possibility of the manifestation of God within themselves – only do wrong as a consequence of their God-given natures, as al-Jīlī understands it – an idea that fits with his earlier suggestion that the error of the Jews was a consequence of the divine decree (*qadar*).

Who are those, we might ask, who are incapable of receiving the divine manifestation within themselves? In one respect, given the context, al-Jīlī's target here is clearly the Christians. They are *fāsiqīn*, it might be said, because they are unreceptive to the possibility of God becoming manifest in creation, beyond the three persons of the Trinity. At the same time, al-Jīlī also explicitly directs his criticism here at those he calls 'the scholars of external forms' (*'ulamā' al-rusūm*). This is a pejorative term used by Ibn 'Arabī and other Sufis to refer to those religious scholars who concentrate only on the exoteric (*ẓāhir*) aspect of religion, at the expense of the esoteric (*bāṭin*) reality accessed by the Sufis themselves.[108] As Ibn 'Arabī's interpreter al-Qāshānī puts it in his lexicon of Sufi technical terms: 'The common people (*al-'āmmah*) are those who are limited in their knowledge (*iqtaṣarū 'ilmahum*) to the Law (*al-sharī'ah*), and their scholars are called "the scholars of external forms" (*'ulamā' al-rusūm*).'[109] Al-Jīlī is using the term here in the same pejorative sense.[110] Indeed, it seems that he is using the opportunity presented by his criticism of the Christians to damn the exoteric religious scholars by association, rather in the way that, in the chapter on the Torah, his criticism of the Jews' reason-based innovations in their religion contained an implied attack on the rationalist theologians and philosophers. In this regard, it is notable that when describing the approach of *'ulamā' al-rusūm*, he repeats many of the terms he has used over the course of the chapter in reference to the Christians. So, the scholars, like the Christians, are said to have 'erred' (*ḍallū*). This error, like the Christians' error, is a consequence of their limited interpretation (*ta'wīl*) of revelation (in this case, of Qur'an 48.10 and 4.80),[111] for like the Christians, it is implied, they are unable to progress beyond the apparent meaning of scripture. Their error is made manifest in their incorrect 'beliefs' (*dhahabū ilá mā dhahabū ilayhi*), which, like the Christian doctrines, nevertheless contain an element of truth (*wajhan min al-ḥaqq*).

The parallel that al-Jīlī implicitly draws between the Christians and the religious scholars brings into focus his view of the former. The error of the scholars, he tells us here, stands in contrast to the guidance attained by the 'people of realities' (*ahl al-ḥaqā'iq*), a term that denotes those who know the esoteric meaning of revelation – the level, as we saw in Chapter 4, that contains the 'realities' (*ḥaqā'iq*). We can say by analogy, therefore, that Christian doctrine, like the knowledge attained through exoteric religious scholarship, does not lead one to knowledge of the underlying reality of existence – that is, to the fundamental Sufi metaphysical truth that creation in its entirety is a locus for the divine manifestation. This is in keeping with what we have seen throughout this chapter. Likewise, just as it is said that the scholars have been 'distanced' (*bu"idū*) from God, so too can it be said that the doctrine of the Trinity also distances the Christians from Him, by limiting their conception of the manifestation of the Godhead to three particular forms. The overall impression given, then, is of a people sincerely striving to know God, yet who nevertheless fall well short of such knowledge.

This being said, it might also be said that the Christians, as al-Jīlī sees it, are in one sense *closer* to the truth than the exoteric scholars. While the latter, it is suggested, reject the very idea that God appears in creation, with the result that they are entirely veiled from seeing the divine manifestation, the Christians, by contrast, do at least acknowledge the fact of divine manifestation, even if they limit it to Jesus, Mary and the Holy Spirit. Whereas the Christians, as we have seen, are therefore guilty of professing a form of *tashbīh* – specifically, the doctrine of the Incarnation – that limits God to particular created forms, the scholars, by contrast, adopt what al-Jīlī calls 'the principles of divine incomparability' (*al-uṣūl al-tanzīhiyyah*). This is to say that they make a mistake that is antithetical to the Christians', namely, of professing (like the Jews) unadulterated *tanzīh*. They do so by focusing upon the divine attributes that relate to how God governs the world (*al-awṣāf al-ḥukmiyyah*), which thereby establish a clear distinction between God and His creation. In so doing, says al-Jīlī, they fail to realize the essential truth that God is in fact manifest in His creation, a truth which he here indicates by the phrase '*al-wujūd al-khalqī al-ḥaqqī*', which denotes that phenomenal existence is *both* created (*khalqī*) and divine (*ḥaqqī*). In light of this truth, the correct stance to take, as we have seen, is to profess both *tashbīh* and *tanzīh* simultaneously. By neglecting to bring together these two positions and instead professing one of the two extremes, both the Christians and the religious scholars fall into error.

Divine statements of the truth

> And the Real – Glory be to Him and may He be exalted – informed us about Himself in that regard in several places in His book (*kitābihi*), as when He said, 'So wherever you turn, there is the face of God' (Q 2:115), and when He said, '. . . and in your own selves; do you not see?' (Q 51:21) and when He said, 'We did not create the heavens and the earth and what is between them except through the truth/the Real' (Q 15:85), and when He said, 'And He subjected for you all that is in the heavens and on earth, from Him' (Q 45:12), and when he [i.e. Muhammad] – Prayers and peace be upon Him – said, 'God is the hearing, sight, hand, and tongue of the servant', and other examples like that, which are unlimited, so understand.[112]

Already in this chapter, al-Jīlī has provided several Qur'anic verses in support of his idea that God is manifest in man and creation. These, as we know, are the basic ideas of his Sufi metaphysics, and it is these ideas that the Christians only understand in a very limited way, and which the exoteric religious scholars utterly fail to grasp. In both cases, we have seen, it is those groups' limited or mistaken interpretation of the divine revelation that is the cause of their error.

Given the centrality of the Qur'an and divine revelation, more generally, both within al-Jīlī's Sufi metaphysics and within this chapter, it is not a surprise that the chapter concludes with some more scriptural texts that purportedly support his idea of universal theophany and, more particularly, of the Perfect Human. Thus, he quotes Qur'an 2.115, a favourite verse of Ibn 'Arabī and his followers, who view it as a clear statement of the presence of the divine throughout the phenomenal world.[113] The true meaning of this verse, al-Jīlī suggests earlier in the book, is realized by those who, unlike the Christians and the scholars, are able to synthesize the perspectives of *tanzīh* and *tashbīh*.[114]

In addition to Qur'an 2.115, al-Jīlī cites Qur'an 15.85 as another Qur'anic verse indicating the manifestation of God in all of creation. The other Qur'anic verses (Q 51.21, 45.12) cited here, along with the *ḥadīth qudsī* that he alludes to, indicate (according to al-Jīlī's interpretation) more specifically the manifestation of God in mankind, and thus provide scriptural support for his idea of the Perfect Human. Again, in quoting these particular verses in this context, al-Jīlī is following the example set by Ibn 'Arabī and his interpreters.[115] The *ḥadīth qudsī* mentioned here, meanwhile, is a favourite of many Sufi authors, Ibn 'Arabī included, for it evokes the manifestation of the divine attributes in the individual who has attained proximity to God through acts of devotion.[116] More specifically, this hadith indicates the manifestation of several of what al-Jīlī calls the attributes of the divine self (*al-ṣifāt/al-awṣāf al-nafsiyyah*) – specifically, hearing, sight, and speech – in those individuals who have attained perfection.[117]

It is notable that the chapter of *al-Insān al-kāmil* that is ostensibly devoted to the Gospel ends with a presentation of the Islamic scriptural proofs for al-Jīlī's ideas of universal theophany and the Perfect Human. This can be explained by the fact that these are the core ideas of the chapter, the book and al-Jīlī's thought more generally. The Gospel, like the other scriptures discussed here, therefore provides a window, not only into al-Jīlī's view of sacred history but also into his Sufi metaphysics.

Conclusion

We have seen how in chapter thirty-eight of *al-Insān al-kāmil*, al-Jīlī engages with and elaborates upon the Qur'an's and the post-Qur'anic tradition's evaluation of the Christians and their scripture, from his Sufi metaphysical perspective. Like the other scriptures discussed in this section of the book, the Gospel, as al-Jīlī sees it, is a genuine divine revelation. This means not only that it is a revealed book but also, in metaphysical terms, that it is an expression of a form of divine manifestation (*tajallī*). Indeed, it is an expression of the manifestation of the 'names of the divine essence' (*asmā' al-dhāt*) and the level of the divine 'qualified oneness' (*al-wāḥidiyyah*). This makes it a more complete form of revelation than the Torah and the Psalms, but a more limited form of revelation than the Qur'an. It indicates – to those who can understand it – the fundamental truth that God is manifest in His creation, even if it does not reveal the divine essence itself. At the same time, however, there is once again an ambivalence to al-Jīlī's view of the scripture concerned. As he sees it, the Gospel can also be viewed as the cause of a grave error on the part of Jesus' people, for the followers of Jesus, reading literally the Trinitarian formula with which it begins, came to take Jesus, Mary and the Holy Spirit as three gods. In keeping with the mainstream medieval Muslim view, al-Jīlī views this doctrine as *shirk*, and criticizes the Christians for declaring God to have been incarnate (*al-tajsīm*) and for comparing Him to His creation (*al-tashbīh*). Again, as in the conventional view, the fault for this lies primarily with the Christians themselves for their misreading of scripture, and not with Jesus, who taught them no such doctrines.

This, however, is only one side of al-Jīlī's assessment of Christian doctrine. Looking at it through the prism of his Ibn 'Arabian Sufi metaphysics, al-Jīlī acknowledges that there is a certain truth to the Christian position. Since the entirety of creation is a locus for the divine manifestation, it is correct, esoterically speaking, to say that God is manifest in Jesus, Mary and the Holy Spirit. And since the human being is the most perfect locus for the manifestation of the divine attributes, it is correct, esoterically speaking, to say that God appears within the world through man. Hence, from this perspective, it can be said that the Christians are monotheists and servants of God, who will be received into the mercy of God, whether in this life (through their attainment of 'proximity' [*qurb*] to God) or the next (through their salvation). Yet even from this perspective, it must still be acknowledged that the Christians are in error, for, as Ibn 'Arabī had already suggested, they make the mistake of *limiting* the divine manifestation to the three persons of the Trinity, and so ignore the basic Sufi metaphysical truth that God is manifest in all human beings and in all of creation. This basic truth, as al-Jīlī sees it, is expressed time and again in the Qur'an, which is much more comprehensive than the Gospel; indeed, it can even be said that the entire Gospel is contained in a single Qur'anic verse. In this sense, the Gospel, as already indicated, bears some responsibility for the Christians' error. While the Christians do not make the mistake made by the exoteric religious scholars, who see only the aspect of God that is incomparable to creation (*al-tanzīh*), nevertheless, being blinded by their *tajsīm* and *tashbīh*, they still fail to appreciate the complete picture. Hence it must be said that they are in error, even though they are, to a certain degree, also in the right.

Al-Jīlī's discussion in this chapter often veers into original and, from a more conventional medieval Islamic perspective, dangerous territory, particularly when he is discussing the hidden truth underlying Christian doctrine. Nevertheless, it is also clear that he maintains the superiority of Islam and the Qur'an – in both their ordinary and deeper metaphysical senses – over Christianity and the Gospel. We can therefore say that his Sufi metaphysical perspective leads him to adopt a relatively charitable attitude towards Christianity, yet that he remains within the framework of the Qur'an-centred view of sacred history, and that this adherence to the Qur'an-centred view is likewise consistent with, and in fact conditioned by, his Sufi metaphysics. These two aspects become clear in the final chapter of the book, where he declares that the Christians are 'nearer than the past communities to the Real' and 'nearer than others to the Muhammadans', implying both the relative exaltedness of Christianity and the ultimate superiority of Islam.[118] As we have seen, the respective places of these religious communities in the hierarchy of religions is largely a consequence, as al-Jīlī sees it, of the relative completeness of – and their interpretations of – their respective scriptures. Al-Jīlī assesses both of these matters through the prism of his Sufi metaphysics. Once again, therefore, we see that for al-Jīlī it is only through understanding the Sufi metaphysical ideas of universal theophany, the levels of existence and the Perfect Human, that one can understand the meaning of the Gospel and its place within sacred history.

Conclusion

The chapters of *al-Insān al-kāmil* on the Qur'an, Torah, Psalms and Gospel serve as a useful case study for anyone seeking to understand al-Jīlī's Ibn 'Arabian Sufi metaphysics and Ibn 'Arabian views on the scriptures, prophets and religions. As this book has tried to show, a close reading of these chapters gives us an insight into the key elements of both al-Jīlī's thought and into several important issues, such as how his Sufi metaphysics determines his view of sacred history, the relation of his thought to the Qur'an-centred view of sacred history and the relevance of these aspects of al-Jīlī's thought to his thinking on the relationship between Islam and other religions.

To begin with his Sufi metaphysics more generally, the chapters that we have looked at demonstrate that al-Jīlī's thought revolves around the three key Ibn 'Arabian Sufi metaphysical ideas of universal theophany, the levels of existence and the Perfect Human, as well as other related ideas like the ideas of universal monotheism and universal mercy. As we have seen, these Ibn 'Arabian ideas determine his view of scripture and prophecy. We have seen how, in accordance with al-Jīlī's idea of universal theophany, he believes that each of the scriptures constitutes a form of divine manifestation (*tajallī*). This means, in his interpretation, that each scripture is a 'revelation' not only in the narrow sense of being a book revealed by God but also in the broader sense that each is an 'unveiling' of God Himself. Thus the Qur'an is an unveiling of the divine essence, and the earlier scriptures of the various kinds of divine names and attributes. Connected to this, we have also seen how, in accordance with his idea of the levels of existence, al-Jīlī deems each of the scriptures to correspond to a particular level within the hierarchy of existence. Thus the Qur'an corresponds to the level of 'unqualified oneness' (*al-aḥadiyyah*), the Torah to the level of 'all-mercifulness' (*al-raḥmāniyyah*), the Psalms to the level of 'kingship' (*al-malikiyyah*), and the Gospel to the level of 'qualified oneness' (*al-wāḥidiyyah*). Furthermore, we have seen that he views the prophets Muhammad, Moses, David and Jesus, the recipients of these scriptures, as 'loci of manifestation' (*maẓāhir*) of these different types of divine manifestation and levels of existence. As loci of manifestation of the divine names and attributes (and, in the case of Muhammad, of the divine essence itself), the prophets can therefore be understood as Perfect Humans. Finally, we have seen that al-Jīlī's explication and interpretation of the contents of the scriptures, and the doctrines that are drawn from them, are also determined by his key Sufi metaphysical concepts and related Sufi ideas. This is true of his interpretation of Qur'anic verses, of his presentation of the 'sciences' contained in the Torah and the Psalms and of his analysis of the true meaning of the doctrine of the Trinity expressed in the Gospel. In each case, his discussion takes us back to the same key ideas, which provide a key to explaining the fundamental issue of the relationship between God and creation.

This tendency of al-Jīlī to view the scriptures and prophets through the prism of his Sufi metaphysics is reminiscent of Ibn 'Arabī, who similarly uses Qur'anic prophetic stories in his *Fuṣūṣ al-ḥikam* as gateways into a discussion of his Sufi metaphysical ideas. Equally, the three key Sufi metaphysical ideas that underlie al-Jīlī's view of the scriptures are highly Ibn 'Arabian. This deep influence of Ibn 'Arabī on a thinker living in Yemen 200 years after him can be taken as an indicator of the extent of Ibn 'Arabī's impact on the Sufi thought of the later Middle Ages – an influence that would only continue to grow over the following centuries, up until modern times. At the same time, however, it would be wrong to view al-Jīlī as merely a duplicator of Ibn 'Arabī's thought or a commentator on his work. Certainly, there are hints, in the work of al-Jīlī's Ibn 'Arabian predecessors, of the 'metaphysicalizing' way in which al-Jīlī understands the scriptures: for example, Ibn 'Arabī uses the term 'book'/'scripture' (*al-kitāb*) to denote 'every level of synthesis and inclusion' (*kull martabat jam' wa-ḍamm*), including the divine knowledge, Adam/man and existence/the world;[1] al-Qūnawī draws a tantalizing parallel between 'the universal divine books' (*kutub ilāhiyyah kulliyyah*) – that is, the Qur'an, Furqan, Torah, Psalms and Gospel – and the five divine 'presences' (*ḥaḍarāt*) (a concept closely related to the 'levels of existence');[2] and al-Qayṣarī, similarly, identifies the five 'presences' or 'worlds' (*'awālim*) as 'divine books' (*kutub ilāhiyyah*).[3] Yet, I have not come across a passage in Ibn 'Arabī's writings, or in the works of his interpreters, in which those earlier thinkers apply their Sufi metaphysics to the various scriptures in the same systematic, consistent and detailed fashion that we find in these chapters of *al-Insān al-kāmil*. Nor, as far as I know, do Ibn 'Arabī or his interpreters ever engage with such topics as the contents of the Torah or the Christian doctrine of the Trinity in such an in-depth way as does al-Jīlī. The present book, therefore, bears out the often-made claims that al-Jīlī is both an adherent of the Ibn 'Arabian tradition and yet also a more systematic writer than Ibn 'Arabī and a relatively independent-minded thinker, who develops the ideas of Ibn 'Arabī and his followers in new directions.[4]

While the chapters analysed here provide an overview of al-Jīlī's key Sufi metaphysical ideas and the relationship of his thought to Ibn 'Arabī's thought and the wider Ibn 'Arabian tradition, therefore, they also give us a clear and fascinating insight into the more specific issue of his views on sacred history. It is clear that, in line with the Qur'an-centred view of sacred history, al-Jīlī views the revelation of the Qur'an, Torah and Gospel as different examples of a single phenomenon. While in conventional, Qur'anic terms, the scriptures constitute different instances of God 'sending down' (*tanzīl*) the true message to one of His prophets, who are thereafter commanded to propagate this message to their people, in al-Jīlī's Sufi metaphysical reworking of the conventional view, as just noted, they constitute different types of 'manifestation' (*tajallī*) of the divine existence. The four recipients of these revelations, similarly, as loci of divine manifestation, also share in a similar kind of prophecy, as in the Qur'an-centred view.

At the same time, we are also able to draw out of al-Jīlī's discussion of the scriptures a hierarchy of scriptures, prophets and religions; indeed, al-Jīlī makes this hierarchy explicit on a number of occasions. The hierarchy is based on the principle that each of the scriptures represents a particular type of divine manifestation. Since, according to the Sufi metaphysical idea of the levels of existence, some of these manifestations are more complete than others, which is to say that they are fuller expressions of the divine names and attributes (or, in the case of the Qur'an, the divine essence), it follows that some of the scriptures are more complete than others. Significantly, we find that the hierarchy of scriptures, prophets and religions that emerges from al-Jīlī's discussion is fully in keeping with the Qur'an-centred view of sacred history, even if its Sufi metaphysical rationale is untypical. The Qur'an, as an expression of the divine essence and the level of 'unqualified oneness' (the third level of existence, yet the least qualified after the hidden aspect of the divine essence), stands at the top of the hierarchy of scriptures, followed by the Gospel, an expression of the names of the essence and the level of 'qualified oneness' (the fourth level), then the Torah, an expression of the names of the attributes and the level of 'all-mercifulness' (the fifth level), and finally the Psalms, an expression of the active attributes and the level of 'kingship' (the sixth or seventh level).

In accordance with this hierarchy of scriptures, Muhammad stands at the summit of the hierarchy of prophets, for as the recipient of the Qur'an he embodies the divine essence as well as all of the divine attributes, and is therefore the most perfect and comprehensive Perfect Human; indeed, his spiritual reality, known as the 'Muhammadan Reality' (*al-ḥaqīqah al-muḥammadiyyah*), seems not only to pervade the entirety of existence and the other 'Perfect Ones' but also to blur into the divine essence itself. As for Moses, David and Jesus, while al-Jīlī excuses them for the errors of their people, he nevertheless deems them to be lesser prophets and Perfect Humans than Muhammad, since the revelations or manifestations that they received were not as complete as the Qur'an, indicating that their knowledge was not as complete as his.[5] Indeed, although al-Jīlī suggests that these other prophets were Perfect Humans insofar as they were loci of manifestation of the divine names and attributes, he never actually applies the term *insān kāmil* to them, reflecting his view that this title, properly speaking, should only be used of Muhammad.

Finally, the superiority of the Qur'an and Muhammad means that, in al-Jīlī's view, Muhammad's people, the Muslims, are the best religious community, and his religion, Islam, the best of religions. So, while those spiritually and cognitively advanced Muslims who properly understand their scripture and their faith are able to synthesize, in true Ibn 'Arabian fashion, the perspectives of *tashbīh* and *tanzīḥ* (divine comparability and incomparability), the Jewish people are excessive in their *tanzīh*, while the Christians go to an extreme of *tashbīh*. When it comes to assessing the relative merits of the Jews and the Christians, just as the Gospel comes second in the hierarchy of scriptures, so too do the Christians come second in the hierarchy of religious communities, for though they have committed the error of limiting the divine manifestation to Jesus and the other persons of the Trinity, nevertheless, their mistaken doctrines of the Trinity and Incarnation serve the positive purpose of enabling them to recognize – at least partially – the key Sufi metaphysical truth that God becomes manifest in His creation, and in particular in mankind. The Jews, meanwhile, do not recognize this truth, since Moses was commanded not to propagate the two tablets of the Torah that contained the mysteries of 'lordship' (*rubūbiyyah*) and 'power' (*qudrah*), which point to God's appearance within mankind. Judaism and the Jews therefore come third, it seems, in the hierarchy of religions and religious communities.

The views that al-Jīlī puts forward on the different religions in the chapters on the scriptures are reaffirmed in the final chapter of *al-Insān al-kāmil* (chapter sixty-three), which is devoted to 'the different religions (*diyānāt*) and forms of worship (*'ibādāt*)'.[6] In that chapter, al-Jīlī identifies the existence of ten different religious communities (*ṭawā'if*, *milal*), namely: the idol-worshippers (*'abadat al-awthān*), who, he tells us, have created an image (*shakhṣ*, *ṣūrah*) of Adam out of stone, which they worship; the naturalists (*al-ṭabī'ī'ūn*), who worship the four elements (*al-ṭabā'i' al-arba'ah*); the philosophers (*al-falāsifah*), who worship the seven planets (*al-kawākib al-saba'ah*); the dualists (*al-thānawiyyah*), who worship light and darkness (*al-nūr wa-al-ẓulmah*); the Zoroastrians (*al-majūs*), who worship fire (*al-nār*); the 'fatalists' (*al-dahriyyūn*) or 'the godless' (*al-mulḥidūn*), who have abandoned worship, declaring that only fate (*al-dahr*) exists; the Brahmans (*barāhimah*), the first group from among 'the People of the Book' (*ahl al-kitāb*), who claim to follow the religion of Abraham (*dīn Ibrāhīm*) and to be descended from him, and who have 'a particular form of worship' (*'ibādah makhṣūṣah*); the Jews (*al-yahūd*), who are 'the Mosaics' (*al-mūsawiyyūn*); the Christians, who are 'the Jesuites' (*al-'īsawiyyūn*); and the Muslims, who are 'the Muhammadans' (*al-muḥammadiyyūn*).[7]

Although this final chapter, as we saw in Chapter 2, has been taken as evidence of al-Jīlī's religious pluralism, the view that he presents here of the nine non-Muslim religious communities is an ambivalent one. On the one hand, in accordance with the idea of universal monotheism, al-Jīlī indicates that each of these religious communities worships and serves a particular form of the one true God. All created beings, as he puts it at the beginning of the chapter, are 'fashioned (*majbūlūn*)' to worship God, being 'primordially disposed (*mafṭūrūn*) to this by virtue of their original nature (*al-aṣālah*)', such that 'there is nothing in existence that does not worship (*ya'bud*) God – May He be exalted – through its spiritual state (*bi-ḥālihi*), its speech (*maqālihi*) and its actions (*fi'ālihā*), indeed, through its essence and attributes (*bi-dhātihi wa-ṣifātihi*)'.[8] Applying this to the Jews and Christians (in whom, given his adherence to the Qur'an-centred view of sacred history, he is most interested), al-Jīlī declares that the Jews have five ritual practices: 'declaring the oneness of God (*tawḥīd Allāh*)', 'prayer (*ṣalāh*) twice a day', 'fasting (*al-ṣawm*) on the Day of Kinnūr (*yawm kinnūran*) [*sic*, i.e. Yom Kippur, the Day of Atonement]', 'going into seclusion (*al-i'tikāf*) on the Sabbath (*yawm al-sabt*)' and avoiding particular foods and drinks and celebrating certain festivals (*a'yād*).[9] Significantly, as with the analogy between the contents of the Torah and the Qur'an, there is an implied analogy here with Islamic ritual practice: the first of the three Jewish rites, for instance, immediately call to mind three of the five pillars of Islam. More significant still is al-Jīlī's suggestion that these Jewish rituals contain 'mysteries' (*asrār*), 'wisdom' (*ḥikmah*) and 'allusions' (*ishārāt*), terms that suggest that, understood esoterically, the Jewish rituals (like the 'sciences' contained in the Torah) point to Sufi metaphysical truths and lead the Jewish believer to worship the one God. In his analysis of Christian practice and doctrine, similarly, al-Jīlī applies the principles of universal monotheism. Like the Jewish rituals, Christian rituals like the Lenten fast, he indicates, point towards 'the mysteries of God' (*asrār Allāh*).[10] Similarly, echoing the more positive dimension of his discussion of the Trinity and Incarnation in the chapter on the Gospel, he declares that, on account of these doctrines, the Christians 'are the nearest of the past religious communities (*al-umam al-māḍiyyah*) to the truth/the Real (*al-ḥaqq*)' and 'nearer than others to the Muhammadans (*aqrab min ghayrhim ilá al-muḥammadiyyīn*), for whoever witnesses God in the human being (*man shahida Allāh fī al-insān*) witnesses Him more perfectly (*kāna shuhūduhu akmal*) than all of those who witness God within the different kinds of created beings (*anwā' al-makhlūqāt*)'.[11] Moreover, these more positive ideas about the ritual practices and religious doctrines of non-Muslims have soteriological ramifications. As in chapter fifty-eight (and as hinted at in the section on the scriptures), al-Jīlī puts forward a position that is conditioned by the idea of 'universal mercy': just as, for Ibn 'Arabī, the pain inflicted on those condemned to hell will eventually give way to mercy and 'felicity' (*ni'mah*), so too for al-Jīlī here, 'after the passing of the heavens and the earth . . . the cycle will turn upon [the damned], and they will return to the thing from which everything began, which is God – May He be exalted'.[12] As in the chapters on the scriptures, therefore, there is here a charitable dimension to al-Jīlī's view of the non-Muslim religions, both in his assessment of the underlying truth of their practices and doctrines, and in his assessment of the fate of their adherents in the life to come.

On the other hand, however, again as in the chapters on the scriptures, al-Jīlī also leaves the reader in little doubt as to the other religions' deficiency when compared to Islam. As in his chapter on the Gospel, for instance, he suggests that the Christians have made a mistake in limiting the divine manifestation to the persons of the Trinity: 'When they confined (*ḥaṣarū*) [divinity] to those three,' he writes, 'they fell (*nazalū*) from the level of those who declare God's oneness (*darajat al-muwaḥḥidīn*)',[13] a statement that apparently dilutes the inclusivity of al-Jīlī's declaration in chapter thirty-eight that the Christians' polytheism was 'monotheism (*tawḥīd*) itself'. Similarly, in the case of the Jews, while their rituals may point towards exalted Sufi metaphysical truths, 'the mysteries and [*sic* – 'of the'?] forms of worship of the people of Islam (*asrār wa-ta'abbudāt ahl al-islām*)', he informs us, are 'better (*afḍal*) than [the Jewish rituals] . . . for they brought together all of the separate [forms of worship] (*jama'at jamī' al-mutafarriqāt*)'. The Islamic rites, in other words, are marked, like the Islamic scripture, by *comprehensiveness*: 'There remained none of God's mysteries (*asrār Allāh*)', he writes, in this regard, 'that Muhammad – May God bless him and grant him peace – did not guide us to.' And this means unambiguously that 'his religion is the most complete/perfect of religions (*fa-dīnuhu akmal al-adyān*) and his religious community the best of communities (*wa-ummatuhu khayr al-umam*)'.[14] This explains al-Jīlī's explicitly stated reluctance to divulge the mysteries of the Jewish rituals, on account of his fear that 'ignorant' (*juhhāl*) Muslims would be enticed by those mysteries and so apostatize from Islam – a fear that only makes sense if Islam is indeed the superior religion in his view.[15] In keeping with this, after discussing the non-Muslim religions, al-Jīlī devotes the remainder of the chapter, which forms its major part, to an exposition of the seven different 'levels' (*marātib*) of spiritual attainment within Islam, and of the 'mysteries' (*asrār*) contained in the five pillars of Islam,[16] just as Ibn 'Arabī had done before him.[17] The implication of this discussion is that it is only through adhering to the superior Islamic doctrines and practising the superior Islamic rites that a person can obtain the 'proximity' (*al-qurbah*) to God that, so al-Jīlī tells us, is the last of the seven 'levels' of spiritual attainment within Islam.[18] Again, there are soteriological implications to all this. Although, as we have seen, al-Jīlī indicates that all will return to God and experience the 'felicity' of the divine mercy at the end of time, nevertheless he is clear that, prior to that far-off point, only the Muslims will be saved: 'Every one of the other religious communities (*umam*),' he tells us, 'that is opposed to [the Muslims], after the prophethood of Muhammad and his being sent with the message (*baʿthihi bi-al-risālah*), whoever they are, is in error (*ḍāllin*), wretched (*shaqīy*), and punished with the hellfire (*muʿadhdhab bi-al-nār*), just as God – May He be exalted – has informed us.'[19]

Al-Jīlī's discussion of the different religions and forms of worship in chapter sixty-three, therefore, supports and complements the message of the chapters on the scriptures. Though his Ibn ʿArabian notions of universal theophany, universal monotheism and universal mercy may lead him at times to adopt a more charitable view of the other religions, he is ultimately quite clear in his insistence on the superiority of the Qur'an, Muhammad, Islam and the Muslim community. Above all, this superiority is dictated by the comprehensiveness or completeness of the Islamic revelation and prophet. While the adherents of the other religions may worship a limited *form* of the one God, the Muslims – or at least those Muslims who properly understand Islam from a Sufi metaphysical perspective – worship God in His comprehensive perfection; hence, he declares, 'there are no [real] monotheists (*muwaḥḥid*), except the Muslims'.[20] This use of comprehensiveness as the decisive criterion for determining the superiority of Islam is significant, for it shows that al-Jīlī's commitment to the Qur'an-centred view of sacred history is governed not by the pressures of medieval Muslim society and his desire for self-preservation (as a Straussian reading might have it),[21] but rather by his Ibn ʿArabian Sufi metaphysics, in which the principle of perfection, completeness or comprehensiveness is key.

Let us then return, finally, to the idea that Ibn ʿArabian Sufism, and the Sufi thought of al-Jīlī in particular, is pluralist, inclusivist, universalist or ecumenical, and that it might serve as the basis for a more pluralist or inclusivist Islamic approach to religious difference in modern times, as the scholars whose views were discussed in Chapter 2 have argued. This idea is certainly well intentioned and potentially beneficial, and does, as this book has shown, have a textual basis in Ibn ʿArabian literature, which at times does appear to advocate a more charitable view of other religions, based on the Sufi metaphysical ideas of universal theophany, universal monotheism and universal mercy. As the seventeenth-century Ottoman intellectual Kātib Çelebī (also known as Ḥājjī Khalīfah) (d. 1068/1657) said of Ibn ʿArabī, 'In most of his works he stresses the gentler aspects of divinity rather than the sterner ones',[22] and the same could be said of al-Jīlī in *al-Insān al-kāmil*, where the divine attributes of beauty and mercy likewise tend to be brought to the foreground. Nevertheless, the 'pluralist' reading of Ibn ʿArabian Sufism advocated by some scholars ought also to be recognized for what it is: a modern interpretation of medieval thought, conditioned by contemporary concerns, and conducted by scholars working within or inspired by the Ibn ʿArabian Sufi tradition. Such a modern interpretation should not obscure the fact that, when viewed on its own terms – as in the present book – al-Jīlī's discussion of the scriptures reveals his close adherence to the Qur'an-centred view of sacred history and its notion of a hierarchy of scriptures, prophets and religions, where the Qur'an, Muhammad and Islam stand at the top. In the words of Nicholson, Islam remains for al-Jīlī 'the crown of religions'.[23] In this commitment to the Qur'an-centred view of sacred history, he was in agreement not only with Ibn 'Arabī but also with most Sufi thinkers prior to modern times.

Notes

Introduction

1 Al-Jīlī, *Al-Insān al-kāmil fī maʿrifat al-awākhir wa-al-awāʾil*, ed. Ṣ. ʿUwayḍah (Beirut: Dār al-Kutub al-ʿilmiyyah, 1997). This edition seems essentially to be a reprint of the two-volume Cairo edition used by Nicholson.

2 See F. Morrissey, *Sufism and the Perfect Human: From Ibn ʿArabī to al-Jīlī* (Abingdon: Routledge, 2020).

3 M. Lings, *What Is Sufism?* (London: George Allen & Unwin, 1975), 121.

4 J. Spencer Trimingham, *The Sufi Orders in Islam* (Oxford: Clarendon Press, 1971), 161, n. 4.

5 One sign of this is that Reza Shah-Kazemi, whose Sufi-inspired interpretation of the Qur'an's position on religious diversity (on which see further) accords in certain places with al-Jīlī's, makes no mention of al-Jīlī or the chapters on the scriptures in his work *The Other in the Light of the One: The Universality of the Qurʾān and Interfaith Dialogue* (Cambridge: Islamic Texts Society, 2006). As we shall see, those writers who have drawn upon al-Jīlī's treatment of other religions tend to focus on the last chapter of *al-Insān al-kāmil*, rather on the more in-depth treatment of sacred history given in the chapters on the scriptures.

6 Al-Jīlī, *De l'homme universel: extraits du livre* al-Insân al-kâmil, tr. Titus Burckardt (Alger: Messerschmitt; Lyon: P. Derain, 1952); al-Jīlī, *Universal Man*, tr. A. Culme-Seymour (Sherborne: Beshara Publications, 1983).

7 M. Smith, *Readings from the Mystics of Islam; Translations from the Arabic and Persian, Together with a Short Account of the History and Doctrines of Ṣūfism and Brief Biographical Notes on Each Ṣūfī Writer* (London: Luzac, 1950), 117–21.

8 H. Corbin, *Terre céleste et corps de résurrection, de l'Iran mazdéen à l'Iran shīʿite* (Paris: Buchet/Chastel, 1960), 233–50; H. Corbin, *Spiritual Body and Celestial Earth: From Mazdean Iran to Shīʿite Iran* (Princeton, NJ: Princeton University Press, 1977), 148–59.

9 See M. Iqbal, *The Development of Metaphysics in Persia: A Contribution to the History of Muslim Philosophy* (London: Luzac & Co., 1908), 116–31.

10 R. A. Nicholson, *Studies in Islamic Mysticism* (Richmond, Surrey: Curzon Press, 1921), 137–41.

11 See e.g. in this respect Lings, *What Is Sufism?* 121: 'Until recently most scholars were inclined to agree that Jīlī was the last great mystic of Islam.' A. ʿAfīfī, 'Ibn ʿArabī fī dirāsātī', in *Al-Kitāb al-tidhkārī: Muḥyiddīn Ibn ʿArabī fī al-dhikrā al-miʾwiyyah al-thāminah li-mīlādihi*, ed. I. Madhkūr (Cairo: Dār al-kitāb li l-ṭibāʿah wa l-nashr, 1969), 3–34, 26, where ʿAfīfī includes al-Jīlī among those Sufis 'who wrote on *waḥdat al-wujūd* . . . and took it to new, distant horizons demanded by the logic of the doctrine', and describes him as 'absolutely the most famous of these, and the one who came closest to originality and invention.'

12 In the realm of interreligious dialogue and debate, three possible approaches to other religions are often identified: 'exclusivism', 'inclusivism' and 'pluralism'. Simply put, exclusivism is the view that one's own religion is the one and only path to the truth and/or salvation; inclusivism is the view that, while one's own religion is the correct path to the truth and/or salvation, adherents of other religions can still be admitted to the truth and/or salvation; and pluralism is the view that there are multiple possible paths to the truth and/or salvation. This threefold typology was first set out by the Christian theologian Alan Race. See A. Race, *Christians and Religious Pluralism: Patterns in Christian Theology* (London: SCM Press, 1983).

13 Owing to its relevance to the subject of this book, I also bring into my analysis relevant passages from the last chapter (chapter sixty-three) of *al-Insān al-kāmil*, 'On all of the religions and forms of worship', and include a brief summary of the key ideas contained within this chapter in the conclusion to this book.

14 For these potential pitfalls of textual analysis, see Q. Skinner, 'Meaning and Understanding in the History of Ideas', *History and Idea* 8, no. 1 (1969), 3–53, esp. 3–38.

15 In adopting this method to the study of texts, I am particularly indebted to Michael Freeden's description (and advocacy) of the approach to the study of ideologies that is focused upon concepts, for which see M. Freeden, *Ideology: A Very Short Introduction* (Oxford: Oxford University Press, 2003), 48–55, as well as to Ronald Nettler's approach to the study of Ibn 'Arabī, as developed in R. Nettler, *Sufi Metaphysics and Qur'ānic Prophets: Ibn 'Arabī's Thought and Method in the* Fuṣūṣ al-ḥikam (Cambridge: Islamic Texts Society, 2003). Similar conceptual approaches to the study of Ibn 'Arabian thought can also be seen in S. M. N. Al-Attas, *The Mysticism of Ḥamzah Fanṣūrī* (PhD diss., School of Oriental and African Studies, 1966) (see esp. 13–15); T. Izutsu, *Sufism & Taoism: A Comparative Study of Key Philosophical Concepts* (Berkeley and London: University of California Press, 1984).

16 See S. al-Ḥakīm, *Ibn 'Arabī: mawlid lughah jadīdah* (Dandarah li-al-ṭabā'ah wa-al-nashr, 1991). For a useful lexicon of the technical terminology of Ibn 'Arabī and his followers, see S. al-Ḥakīm, *al-Mu'jam al-ṣūfī: al-ḥikmah fī ḥudūd al-kalimah* (Dandarah li-al-ṭabā'ah wa-al-nashr, 1981).

17 See G. Lipton, *Rethinking Ibn 'Arabi* (New York: Oxford University Press, 2018), esp. 5, 9, 24–54, 55–83.

Chapter 1

1 C. Addas, '"At the Distance of Two Bows' Length or Even Closer": The Figure of the Prophet in the Work of 'Abd al-Karīm al-Jīlī', pt. two, *Journal of the Muhyiddin Ibn 'Arabi Society* 46 (2009), 1–26, 1.

2 See R. Atlagh, 'Contribution à l'étude de la pensée mystique d'Ibn 'Arabī et son école à travers l'oeuvre de 'Abd al-Karīm al-Jīlī' (PhD diss., École pratique des hautes études, 2000). I thank Claudio Marzullo for helping me access this work.

3 See A. Knysh, *Ibn 'Arabi in the Later Islamic Tradition: The Making of a Polemical Image in Medieval Islam* (Albany, NY: State University of New York Press, 1999), 225–69; 'A. al-Ḥibshī, *al-Ṣūfiyyah wa-al-fuqahā' fī al-Yaman* (Sana'a: Tawzī' maktabat al-jīl al-jadīd, 1976), *passim*, esp. 95–167.

4 For a fuller discussion of al-Jīlī's life and historical context, and further references, see Morrissey, *Sufism and the Perfect Human*, 9–14.

5 For the definitive list of al-Jīlī's works, see Atlagh, *Contribution*, 26–8.

6 Al-Jīlī, *Sharḥ mushkilāt al-Futūḥāt al-Makkiyyah*, ed. Y. Ziedan (Cairo: Dār al-Amīn, 1999) (for the dream account, see p. 199); al-Jīlī, *Göttliche Vollkommenheit und die Stellung des Menschen: die Sichtweise ʿAbd al-Karīm al Ǧīlīs auf der Grundlage des 'Šarḥ muškilāt al-futūḥāt al-makkīya'*, tr. A. Al-Massri (Stuttgart: Deutsche Morganländische Gesellschaft, 1998); F. Morrissey, 'An Introduction to 'Abd al-Karīm al-Jīlī's Commentary on the *Futūḥāt*', *The Maghreb Review* 41, no. 4 (2016), 499–526. A commentary on Ibn 'Arabī's *Risālat al-anwār* has been attributed to al-Jīlī: al-Jīlī, *al-Isfār 'an Risālat al-anwār fī-mā yatajallá li-ahl al-dhikr min al-anwār*, ed. 'Ā. al-Kayyālī (Beirut: Dār al-Kutub al-'ilmiyyah, 2004). Ibn 'Arabī, *Journey to the Lord of Power: A Sufi Manual on Retreat*, tr. R. Harris (London and The Hague: East-West Publications, 1981). Since the author of the commentary mentions a vision he experienced in 889 AH [= 1484 CE] (p. 25 of the Arabic edition), however, it seems that this attribution is mistaken. Similarly, a commentary on Ibn 'Arabī's *Kitāb al-Tajalliyyāt* has also been attributed to al-Jīlī, and again, this attribution has been called into question. See M. Chodkiewicz, 'The Vision of God According to Ibn 'Arabi', *Prayer and Contemplation*, a special issue of the *Journal of the Muhyiddin Ibn 'Arabi Society* 14 (1993), 53–67, 60.

7 For this work, see R. Atlagh, 'LE POINT ET LA LIGNE: Explication de la Basmala par la science des lettres chez 'Abd al-Karīm al-Ǧīlī (m. 826 h.)', *Bulletin d'études orientales* 44, SCIENCES OCCULTES ET ISLAM (1992), 161–90; N. Lo Polito, "Abd al-Karīm al-Jīlī: Tawḥīd, Transcendence, and Immanence' (PhD diss., University of Birmingham, 2010), 138–270.

8 See al-Jīlī, *al-Nādirāt al-'ayniyyah li-'Abd al-Karīm al-Jīlī, ma'a sharḥ al-Nābulusī*, ed. Y. Ziedan (Cairo: Dār al-Amīn, 1999); al-Jīlī, *Ibdā' al-kitābah wa-kitābat al-'ibdā' ('ayn 'alá al-'ayniyyah: sharḥ mu'āṣir li-'ayniyyat al-imām al-ṣūfī 'Abd al-Karīm al-Jīlī)*, ed. S. al-Ḥakīm (Beirut: Dār al-Burāq, 2004).

9 Al-Jīlī, *al-Insān*; Nicholson, *Studies*, 77–142; M. Iqbal, 'The Doctrine of Absolute Unity as Expounded by Abdul Karim Jilani', in *Speeches, Writings and Statements of Iqbal*, in two volumes, ed. A. Shirwani (Lahore: Iqbal Academy Pakistan, 2015), 1:77–96.

10 Al-Jīlī, *al-Manāẓir al-ilāhiyyah*, ed. N. al-Ghunaymī (Cairo: Dār al-Manār, 1987).

11 See Atlagh, *Contribution*, 99–103, and the forthcoming doctoral thesis of Claudio Marzullo at the University of Naples.

12 Al-Jīlī, *al-Kamālāt al-ilāhiyyah fī al-ṣifāt al-muḥammadiyyah*, ed. S. ʿAbd al-Fattāḥ (Cairo: 'Ālam al-fikr, 1997); al-Jīlī, *I Nomi divini e il Profeta alla luce del sufismo*, tr. C. Marzullo (Turin: Il leone verde, 2015); Atlagh, *Contribution*, 93–8

13 See Y. Nabhānī, *Jawāhir al-biḥār fī faḍā'il al-nabī al-mukhtār*, in four volumes, ed. M. al-Ḍannāwī (Beirut: Dār al-Kutub al-'ilmiyyah, 1998), 1:1494–520; C. Addas, 'At the Distance'. This is the tenth part of al-Jīlī's huge work in forty parts, *al-Nāmūs al-a'ẓam wa-al-qāmūs al-aqdam fī ma'rifat qadr al-nabī*, the majority of which is lost.

14 Al-Jīlī, *Marātib al-wujūd wa-ḥaqīqat kull mawjūd* (Cairo: Maktabat al-Qāhirah, 1999); Atlagh, *Contribution*, 142–51.

15 It should be noted, however, that Atlagh (*Contribution*, 65) thinks that the division into two parts is a later editorial addition. For our purposes here what matters is that, while the subject matter of the whole book is unified, there is a progression in subject matter from the first half of the book to the second.

16 See e.g. Al-Attas, *Mysticism*, 53, 78, 81–2, 97.

17 See e.g. Lings, *What Is Sufism?*, 63–5; Shah-Kazemi, *The Other*, 74, 86, 96, 99; W. Chittick, *The Self-Disclosure of God: Principles of Ibn al-'Arabī's Cosmology* (Albany,

NY: State University of New York Press, 1998), 78–9; S. Murata, *Chinese Gleams of Sufi Light* (Albany, NY: State University of New York Press, 2000), 117. For al-Jīlī's articulation of this interpretation, see al-Jīlī, *al-Insān*, 266.

18 Al-Jīlī, *Sharḥ*, 126.

19 See al-Ḥakīm, *al-Mu'jam*, 257–69, 756–7.

20 Izutsu, *Sufism and Taoism*, 152.

21 See Ibn Khaldūn, *Muqaddimah*, in three vols, ed. by 'A. 'Abd al-Wāḥid Wāfī (Cairo: Dār Nahdat Miṣr li-al-nashr, 2014), 3:995; Ibn Khaldūn, *The Muqaddimah*, tr. F. Rosenthal (London: Routledge & Kegan Paul, 1958), 3: 89.

22 See Izutsu, *Sufism and Taoism*, 99–109; Chittick, *Self-Disclosure*, vii–xix; and see e.g. Ibn 'Arabī, *Fuṣūṣ*, 80–1: 'Do you not see that the created (*al-makhlūq*) manifests the attributes of the Real (*yaẓhar bi-ṣifāt al-ḥaqq*), from the first to the last, and all of them are real for it, just as the attributes of originated things are real for the Real?'

23 Ibn Khaldūn, *Shifā' al-sā'il wa-tahdhīb al-masā'il*, ed. M. al-Ḥāfiẓ (Damascus: Dār al-Fikr, 1996), 107 (my emphasis).

24 See W. Chittick, *The Sufi Path of Knowledge: Ibn al-'Arabi's Metaphysics of Imagination* (Albany, NY: State University of New York Press, 1989), 5, 35–6, 52; Chittick, *Self-Disclosure*, 74; Nettler, *Sufi Metaphysics*, 79, 159, 167.

25 Al-Jīlī, *Sharḥ*, 124.

26 See also Ibn Khaldūn, *Muqaddimah*, 3:995, where he refers to the Ibn 'Arabian concept of *marātib al-tajalliyyāt*.

27 See W. Chittick, 'The Five Divine Presences: From al-Qūnawī to al-Qayṣarī', *The Muslim World* 72, vol. 2 (1982), 107–28; al-Ḥakīm, *al-Mu'jam*, 323–7.

28 See in this regard the passage from the *Futūḥāt* quoted in Chittick, *Sufi Path of Knowledge*, 35: 'Once God has created the cosmos, we see that it possesses diverse levels (*marātib*) and realities (*ḥaqā'iq*). Each of these demands a specific relationship with the Real. . . . The divine names allow us to understand many realities of obvious diversity (*ikhtilāf*).' Another source of the diversity in the phenomenal world, to be discussed later on, is the differing 'preparednesses' (*isti'dādāt*) of the created existents.

29 Al-Jīlī, *Sharḥ*, 126. See also al-Ḥakīm, *al-Mu'jam*, 958–60.

30 There is some degree of overlap in what follows with Nicholson, *Studies*, 94–103. However, in his exposition of the main ideas of *al-Insān al-kāmil*, Nicholson does not lay such great emphasis on the concept of the levels of existence, nor does he always treat the levels in the same order as al-Jīlī, as I have tried to do. For other expositions of the highest levels of existence in al-Jīlī's thought, see Iqbal, *Development*, 116–31; Al-Attas, *Mysticism*, 120–1. For an exposition of all of the forty levels, as presented in *Marātib al-wujūd*, see Morrissey, *Sufism and the Perfect Human*, 37–40.

31 For the imperceptibility of the essence in the thought of Ibn 'Arabī and his leading interpreters prior to al-Jīlī, see Izutsu, *Sufism and Taoism*, 23–38; al-Farghānī, *Muntahá al-madārik fī sharḥ Tā'iyyat Ibn al-Fāriḍ*, in two vols, ed. 'Ā. al-Kayyālī (Beirut: Dār al-Kutub al-'ilmiyyah, 2007), 1:19.

32 This term is taken from a hadith, in which Muhammad is asked where God was before He created the world, and he responds, 'In a cloud (*fī 'amā'*).' It is recorded in Ibn Mājah, *Sunan Ibn Mājah*, in five volumes, ed. M. Naṣṣār (Beirut: Dār al-Kutub al-'ilmiyyah, 1998), 1:183–4 (no. 182); al-Tirmidhī, *al-Jāmi' al-kabīr*, in six volumes, ed. B. Ma'rūf (Beirut: Dār al-Gharb al-islāmī, 1998), 5:186 (no. 3109); Ibn Ḥanbal, *Musnad al-Imām Aḥmad Ibn Ḥanbal*, in eight volumes, ed. S. Majdhūb and M. Samārah (Beirut and Damascus: al-Maktab al-islāmī, 1993), 4:16 (no. 16169).

The term is used in a similar way by Ibn ʿArabī (see al-Ḥakīm, *al-Muʿjam*, 820–6; Chittick, *Sufi Path of Knowledge*, 125–30).

33 The term *ḥaqīqat al-ḥaqāʾiq* was earlier used by Ibn ʿArabī (see al-Ḥakīm, *al-Muʿjam*, 345).

34 For the standard distinction between *azal* and *abad*, see al-Tahānawī, *Kashshāf iṣṭilāḥāt al-funūn*, ed. L. ʿAbd al-Badīʿ, ʿA. Ḥusayn and A. Khūlī (Cairo: al-Muʾassasah al-Miṣrīyah al-ʿāmmah li-lta'līf wa-al-tarjamah wa-al-ṭibāʿah wa-al-nashr, 1963), 143: '[*Al-azal*] is the continuation of existence in the past (*dawām al-wujūd fī al-māḍ*), just as *al-abad* is its continuation in the future (*dawāmuhu fī al-mustaqbal*).'

35 *Qidm* and *ḥudūth* are typically presented as opposites in Islamic theology, the former being applied to God and denoting, like *azal*, anteriority (*masbūqiyyah*) to creation, and the latter being applied to creation (see Tahānawī, *Kashshāf*, 1305; R. Arnaldez, *EI*², s.v. 'Ḳidm').

36 The distinction between God and creation in terms of necessity and possibility is a typically Avicennian one. See J. McGinnis, *Avicenna* (New York; Oxford: Oxford University Press, 2009), 160–77. This terminology was adopted by Ibn ʿArabī and his interpreters (see Izutsu, *Sufism and Taoism*, 166–8; Chittick, *Sufi Path of Knowledge*, 80–2). Al-Jīlī uses it occasionally in *al-Insān al-kāmil* (see e.g. al-Jīlī, *al-Insān*, 42–3).

37 See al-Jīlī, *al-Insān*, chapter one, 26–9, and chapter nine, 55–8.

38 Cf. al-Jīlī, *Marātib al-wujūd*, 74–5, where the second level is said to be occupied by 'unqualified oneness' or 'absolute existence'.

39 For *wājib al-wujūd*, see A. M. Goichon, *Lexique de la langue philosophique d'Ibn Sīnā (Avicenne)* (Paris: Desclée de Brouwer, 1938), 417–18; McGinnis, *Avicenna*, 163–8. Once again, the term was taken on by Ibn ʿArabī and his interpreters (see e.g. Ibn ʿArabī, *Fuṣūṣ al-ḥikam*, ed. A. ʿAfīfī (Beirut: Dār al-Kitāb al-ʿArabī, 1946), 53; Izutsu, *Sufism and Taoism*, 167; Chittick, *Sufi Path of Knowledge*, 12; Todd, *Sufi Doctrine*, 88).

40 This was the typical Ibn ʿArabian view. See e.g. Chittick, *Sufi Path of Knowledge*, 302; al-Jandī, *Sharḥ Fuṣūṣ al-ḥikam*, ed. ʿĀ. al-Kayyālī (Beirut: Dār al-Kutub al-ʿilmiyyah, 2007), 40; W. Chittick, 'The Perfect Man as the Prototype of the Self in the Sufism of Jāmī', *Studia Islamica* 49 (1979), 135–57, 143; Al-Attas, *Mysticism*, 112, 120, where he notes that the sixteenth-century Sumatran Sufi thinker Ḥamzah Fanṣūrī's conception of the divine name Allāh 'must be regarded as identical with al-Jīlī's'.

41 See al-Jīlī, *al-Insān*, chapter two, 30–7, and chapter four, 42–7.

42 See Ibn ʿArabī, *Fuṣūṣ*, 105; al-Jandī, *Sharḥ*, 84; Chittick, *Sufi Path of Knowledge*, 337–8. For the concept of *aḥadiyyah* in Ibn ʿArabian thought, see al-Farghānī, *Muntahá*, 1:21; al-Jandī, *Sharḥ*, 84; Chittick, 'The Perfect Man', 146.

43 See al-Jīlī, *al-Insān*, chapter five, 47–8. See also ibid., 22, 49, 77.

44 See ibid., chapter six, 49–50.

45 See ibid., chapter twenty-six, 101–2. For this concept in the thought of Ibn ʿArabī and al-Qāshānī, see I. Lala, 'The Term 'Huwiyya' in Muḥyī al-Dīn ibn ʿArabī and ʿAbd al-Razzāq al-Qāshānī's Sufi Thought' (DPhil diss., University of Oxford, 2017), 79–218.

46 See al-Jīlī, *al-Insān*, chapter twenty-seven, 102–5.

47 See esp. Ibn ʿArabī, *Fuṣūṣ*, 177; Izutsu, *Sufism and Taoism*, 116–40; R. Nettler, 'Ibn ʿArabī's Notion of Allah's Mercy', *Israel Oriental Studies* 8 (1978), 219–29; Nettler, *Sufi Metaphysics*, 154–75; Chittick, *Sufi Path of Knowledge*, xv, 23, 130, 290–1; S. Murata, *The Tao of Islam: A Sourcebook on Gender Relationships in Islamic Thought* (Albany, NY: State University of New York, 1992), 55–6, 107–8, 206–8.

48 See al-Jīlī, *al-Insān*, chapter seven, 50–7. See also ibid., 38–41.

49 See e.g. Ibn ʿArabī, *Fuṣūṣ*, 81. This Ibn ʿArabian notion may in turn be rooted in the Avicennian concept of the 'relation' or 'addition' (*iḍāfah*), which Ibn Sīnā defines as 'the idea whose existence is in relation to another thing (*wujūduh bi-al-qiyās ilá shay' ākhar*), and which does not have existence without that other thing, like paternity (*al-ubuwwah*) in relation to sonhood (*al-bunuwwah*)' (quoted in Goichon, *Lexique*, 197).

50 In this regard, al-Jīlī declares in his *Sharḥ* on the *Futūḥāt* (p. 128): 'Were it not for the world, the names and attributes of the Real would not be known; and were it not for the names and attributes of the Real, the world would not have appeared.'

51 Compare Ibn ʿArabī's statement, 'Lordship is the relationship (*nisba*) of the He-ness [*al-huwiyyah*] to an entity, but the He-ness in Itself does not require any relationship' (quoted in Chittick, *Sufi Path of Knowledge*, 135).

52 See al-Jīlī, *al-Insān*, chapter eight, 53–4.

53 Ibn ʿArabī uses the term 'attributes of the self' to denote those attributes of an existent that, if they were taken away, the existent would no longer exist. See Ibn ʿArabī, *al-Futūḥāt al-makkiyyah*, in fourteen volumes, ed. U. Yaḥyá (Cairo: al-Hay'ah al-Miṣriyyah al-ʿāmmah li-al-kitāb, 1972–92) [hereafter, 'Ibn ʿArabī, *Futūḥāt*'], 3:334–5. In the *Mawāqif* of ʿAḍud al-Dīn al-Ījī (d. 756/1356), one of the most important handbooks of philosophical theology in late-medieval Islamic thought and a text that would therefore likely have been known to al-Jīlī, the *ṣifah nafsiyyah* is defined as 'that which originates in the essence itself'. See al-Ījī, *al-Mawāqif fī ʿilm al-kalām* (Beirut: ʿĀlam al-kutub, n.d.), 81.

54 See D. Gimaret, *EI²*, *s.v.* 'Ṣifa'; N. El-Bizri, 'God: Essence and attributes', *The Cambridge Companion to Classical Islamic Theology*, ed. T. Winter (Cambridge: Cambridge University Press, 2008), 121–40, 128. Jāmī (d. 898/1492), the Ibn ʿArabian Sufi of Herat who lived slightly later than al-Jīlī, calls them 'the attributes of perfection' (*al-ṣifāt al-kamāliyyah*), a term which al-Jīlī uses for those attributes that are both attributes of 'beauty' and 'majesty'. See Jāmī, *The Precious Pearl*, tr. N. Heer (Albany, NY: State University of New York Press, 1979), 59.

55 In *Marātib al-wujūd* al-Jīlī specifically identifies only four attributes of the self (life, knowledge, will and power), the remaining three being subsidiary to the primary four.

56 See al-Jīlī, *al-Insān*, chapter sixteen, 78–80. See also al-Jīlī, *Sharḥ*, 117–18.

57 Al-Jīlī is reacting here against statements such as that found in Ibn ʿArabī, *Fuṣūṣ*, 83–4, 131. For al-Jīlī's criticism of Ibn ʿArabī on this point, see also Al-Attas, *Mysticism*, 131–3. For ʿAbd al-Qādir al-Jazā'irī's (d. 1300/1883) defence of Ibn ʿArabī's position against al-Jīlī's criticism, see al-Jazā'irī, *al-Mawāqif al-rūḥiyyah wa-al-fuyūḍāt al-subūḥiyyah*, in two vols, ed. ʿĀ. al-Kayālī (Beirut: Dār al-kutub al-ʿilmiyyah, 2004), 1:228–9, 2:289.

58 See al-Jīlī, *al-Insān*, chapter seventeen, 81–3.

59 Al-Jīlī identifies the *Futūḥāt* as the place where Ibn ʿArabī makes this argument. For a discussion of this point, see M. Mahmoud, *Quest for Divinity: A Critical Examination of the Thought of Mahmud Muhammad Taha* (Syracuse, NY: Syracuse University Press, 2007), 111.

60 This may be a reference to Ibn ʿArabī's idea of the *aʿyān thābitah*, the prototypical forms or essences of existents that exist in God's knowledge prior to their being made manifest in the phenomenal world, for which see al-Ḥakīm, *al-Muʿjam*, 831–9. It should be noted, however, that in the very first line of the *Futūḥāt*, Ibn ʿArabī declares that God 'gave existence to things from non-existence (*min al-ʿadam*) and from the non-existence of it [i.e. of non-existence].' Ibn ʿArabī, *Futūḥāt*, 1:41. For

Ibn 'Arabī's use of terms *wujūd 'aynī* and *wujūd 'ilmī* in the sense indicated by al-Jīlī, see, respectively, Ibn 'Arabī, *Futūḥāt*, 1:208, 1:240, and F. Rundgren, 'The Preface of the *Futûhât al-Makkiyya*', in *Muhyiddin Ibn 'Arabi: A Commemorative Volume*, ed. S. Hirtenstein and M. Tiernan (Shaftesbury: Element for the Muhyiddin Ibn 'Arabi Society, 1993), 341.

61 See al-Jīlī, *al-Insān*, chapter nineteen, 86–7.

62 This statement also appears in the hadith (see Bukhārī, *Le recueil des traditions mahométanes*, in four volumes, ed. L. Krehl (Leiden: Brill, 1862), 4:470–1). This is also a key verse for Ibn 'Arabī (see Chittick, *Sufi Path of Knowledge*, 444, s.v. 'Be (*kun*)').

63 Al-Jīlī's distinction between these two forms of divine speech corresponds with Ibn 'Arabī's distinction between 'the creative command' (*al-amr al-takwīnī*), which all existents obey, and 'the prescriptive command' (*al-amr al-taklīfī*), that is, the command to follow the religious law, which some obey and others do not. For this distinction, see W. Chittick, *Imaginal Worlds: Ibn al-'Arabī and the Problem of Religious Diversity* (Albany, NY: State University of New York Press, 1994), 141–2.

64 See al-Jīlī, *al-Insān*, chapter twenty, 88–90.

65 Compare this to Ibn 'Arabī's notion (*Futūḥāt*, 4:114–15) that the spiritual realities (*ḥaqā'iq*, *laṭā'if*) of one (or more) of the prophets are revealed to 'those who attain' among the Friends of God (*al-wāṣilūn min al-awliyā'*), such that some Friends of God are 'Mosaic in their locus of witnessing' (*mūsawī al-mashhad*), others are 'Christic' (*'īsawī*) and so forth. See also al-Jandī, *Sharḥ*, 67: 'Every prophet has a Friend of God within this [Islamic] religious community. . . . So they are known by the people of realization as being, for instance, Muhammadan in their station, or Mosaic in their station, knowledge, and state, etc.'

66 See al-Jīlī, *al-Insān*, chapter twenty-one, 90–2.

67 See ibid., chapter twenty-two, 92–3.

68 See ibid., chapter twenty-three, 93–5.

69 See also al-Jīlī, *Sharḥ*, 140: 'the divine nature (*al-sha'n al-ilāhī*), such as it is, requires that the essence of the Necessary Existent be qualified by the qualities of perfection, majesty, and beauty' (*ma'nūtan bi-nu'ūt al-kamāl wa-al-jalāl wa-al-jamāl*). For the important distinction between the attributes of beauty and majesty in Ibn 'Arabian Sufism more generally, see Chittick, *Sufi Path of Knowledge*, 23–4; Murata, *Tao of Islam*, esp. 69ff. For the distinction in earlier Sufism, see I. Goldziher, *Die Richtungen der islamischen Koranauslegung* (Leiden: Brill, 1920), 210–11.

70 See esp. Ibn 'Arabī, *Fuṣūṣ*, 177; al-Jīlī, *al-Insān*, 183. The hadith is recorded in Bukhārī, *Le recuiel*, 2:303; 4:457; Muslim, *Ṣaḥīḥ Muslim*, eighteen vols in nine, ed. M. 'Abd al-Bāqī (Beirut: Dār al-kutub al-'ilmiyyah, 1995), 17:57 (no. 2791).

71 See al-Jīlī, *al-Insān*, chapter twenty-one, 95–9.

72 See ibid., 11.

73 See also ibid., 207: 'This chapter [chapter sixty, on the Perfect Human] is the basis (*'umdah*) of the [other] chapters of this book; indeed, the whole book, from beginning to end, is a commentary (*sharḥ*) on this chapter.'

74 See e.g. Ibn 'Arabī, *Fuṣūṣ*, 48, 55, 199; M. Takeshita, 'Ibn 'Arabī's Theory of the Perfect Man and Its Place in the History of Islamic Thought' (PhD diss., University of Chicago, 1987), 110; Tahānawī, *Kashshāf*, 281.

75 See Morrissey, *Sufism and the Perfect Human*.

76 See al-Jīlī, *al-Insān*, 89–90, 211–12.

77 See ibid., 207.

78 Ibid.

79 See ibid., 210.
80 Al-Jīlī, *Sharḥ*, 175.
81 See al-Jīlī, *al-Insān*, 213, where al-Jīlī indicates that there are three 'isthmuses' for the Perfect Human, followed by what he calls 'the conclusion' (*al-khitām*); al-Jīlī, *Sharḥ*, 93–9, where he discusses the seven 'stations of perfection'.
82 See al-Jīlī, *al-Insān*, 210.

Chapter 2

1 J. E. Lindsay, "Ali ibn 'Asakir as a Preserver of *Qisas al-Anbiya'*: The Case of David b. Jesse', *Studia Islamica* 82 (1996), 45–82, 53.
2 K. Cragg, *The Event of the Qur'ān: Islam in Its Scripture* (London: Allen & Unwin, 1971), 166.
3 As noted by scholars such as Jacques Waardenburg, Alexander Knysh and Shahab Ahmed, among others, we need to be careful about declaring a particular view to be representative of 'traditional', 'conventional', 'mainstream' or 'orthodox' Islamic opinion in a transhistorical and undifferentiated manner. See e.g. J. Waardenburg, *Muslims as Actors: Islamic Meanings and Muslim Interpretations in the Perspective of the Study of Religions* (Berlin and New York: Walter de Gruyter, 2007), esp. pt. one, chapters one and two; A. Knysh, '"Orthodoxy" and "Heresy" in Medieval Islam: An Essay in Reassessment', *The Muslim World* 53, no. 1 (1993), 48–67; S. Ahmed, *What Is Islam? The Importance of Being Islamic* (Princeton, NJ: Princeton University Press, 2016). Nevertheless, I think it possible to identify the existence of a common framework that provided the general contours for how medieval Muslims of different affiliations – but particularly Sunnis – thought about sacred history, and this is what I call 'the Qur'an-centred view'. Other Muslim views of sacred history, such as the cyclical theory of the Ismaili Shi'a, certainly did exist, however.
4 For the Qur'anic conception of these concepts, see esp. T. Izutsu, *God and Man in the Koran: Semantics of the Koranic Weltanschauung* (Tokyo: Keio Institute of Cultural and Linguistics Studies, 1964), 216ff.
5 See the famous hadith: 'There is no child who is not born according to the primordial nature (*'alá al-fiṭrah*). But then his parents make him a Jew (*yuhawwidānihi*), a Christian (*yunaṣirrānihi*) or a Zoroastrian (*yumajjisānihi*)', recorded in Bukhārī, *Le recueil*, 1:348; Muslim, *Ṣaḥīḥ*, 16:169–73 (no. 2658). See also Macdonald, *EI*[2], s.v. 'Fiṭra'; Hoover, *EI*[3], s.v. 'Fiṭra'.
6 See e.g. al-Zamakhsharī, *al-Kashshāf 'an ḥaqā'iq ghawāmiḍ al-tanzīl wa-'uyūn al-aqāwīl fī wujūh al-ta'wīl: wa-huwa tafsīr al-Qur'ān al-karīm*, in four vols (Beirut: Dār al-Kitāb al-'Arabī, 1947), 3:164–5 (Q 22.52); al-Maḥallī and al-Suyūṭī, *Tafsīr al-Jalālayn*, ed. Ṣ. Mubārakfūrī (Riyadh: al-Dār, 2002), 349 (Q 22.52). See also J. Horovitz, *EI*[1], s.v. 'Nabī'; A. J. Wensinck, *EI*[2], s.v. 'Rasūl'; M. Zahniser, *Encyclopaedia of the Qur'ān*, s.v. 'Messenger'; U. Rubin, *Encyclopaedia of the Qur'ān*, s.v. 'Prophets and Prophethood'.
7 Ibn Taymiyyah, *al-Jawāb al-ṣaḥīḥ li-man baddala dīn al-masīḥ*, four vols in one, ed. 'A. al-Madanī (Cairo: Maṭābi' al-Majd al-tijāriyyah, 1964), 1:210.
8 See A. H. Johns, 'Moses in the Qur'an: Finite and Infinite Dimensions of Prophecy', in *The Charles Strong Lectures: 1972-1984*, ed. R. Crotty (Leiden: Brill, 1987), 123–38; C. Schöck, *Encyclopaedia of the Qur'ān*, s.v. 'Moses'; Annabel Keeler, 'Moses from a Muslim Perspective', in *Abraham's Children: Jews, Christians and Muslims in*

Conversation, ed. R. Harries, N. Solomon and T. Winter (London; New York: T&T Clark, 2005), 55–66.

9 See H. Lazarus-Yafeh, *EI*², s.v. 'Tawrāt'; C. Adang, *Encyclopaedia of the Qur'ān*, s.v. 'Torah'; W. Saleh, 'The Hebrew Bible in Islam', in *The Cambridge Companion to the Hebrew Bible/Old Testament*, ed. S. B. Chapman and M. A. Sweeney (Cambridge: Cambridge University Press, 2016), 407–25.

10 See U. Rubin, *Encyclopaedia of the Qur'ān*, s.v. 'Jews and Judaism'.

11 See J.-L. Déclais, *David raconté par les musulmans* (Paris: Cerf, 1999).

12 See J. Horovitz [R. Firestone], *EI*², s.v. 'Zabūr'; A. Schippers, *Encyclopaedia of the Qur'ān*, s.v. 'Psalms'; W. Saleh, 'The Psalms in the Qur'an and the Islamic Tradition', in *The Oxford Handbook of the Psalms*, ed. W. P. Brown (Oxford: Oxford University Press, 2014), 281–96.

13 See e.g. Ibn Taymiyyah, *Majmū'ah al-Rasā'il al-kubrá*, in two vols. (Beirut: Dār Iḥyā' al-turāth al-'arabī, 1972), 1:197: 'As for the Psalms, David brought nothing different to the law (*sharī'ah*) of the Torah.'

14 See T. Khalidi, *The Muslim Jesus: Sayings and Stories in Islamic Literature* (Cambridge, MA; London: Harvard University Press, 2001); G. Parrinder, *Jesus in the Qur'an* (London: Oneworld, 2003); M. Siddiqui, *Christians, Muslims, & Jesus* (New Haven, CT and London: Yale University Press, 2013).

15 See C. de Vaux [G. Anawati], *EI*², s.v. 'Indjīl'; S. H. Griffith, *Encyclopaedia of the Qur'ān*, s.v. 'Gospel'.

16 See J. D. McAuliffe, *Qur'ānic Christians: An Analysis of Classical and Modern Exegesis* (Cambridge: Cambridge University Press, 1991); S. H. Griffith, *Encyclopaedia of the Qur'ān*, s.v. 'Christians and Christianity'.

17 See U. Rubin, *Encyclopaedia of the Qur'ān*, s.v. 'Muhammad'.

18 See A. T. Welch, R. Paret and J. D. Pearson, *EI*², s.v. 'Al-Ḳur'ān'.

19 See R. Wisnovsky, *Encyclopaedia of the Qur'ān*, s.v. 'Heavenly Book'.

20 Quoted in Ibn Taymiyyah, *Majmū'ah al-Rasā'il*, 1:197.

21 Ibn Ḥazm, *al-Faṣl fī al-milal wa-al-ahwā' wa-al-niḥal*, in five vols, ed. M. Ṣubayḥ (Cairo: Maktabat al-Salām al-'ālamiyyah, n.d.), 1:157.

22 Quoted in R. Tottoli, *Biblical Prophets in the Qur'ān and Muslim Literature* (Richmond: Curzon, 2002), 111.

23 Ibn Taymiyyah, *al-Jawāb al-ṣaḥīḥ*, 1:5.

24 See also the hadith quoted in Ibn Ḥazm, *al-Faṣl*, 1:160: 'Neither put your trust in the People of Scripture, nor deem them liars, but say, "We believe in what has been sent down to us and what has been sent down to you, and our God and your God is one."'

25 See e.g. the statement of the Jewish thinker Abraham Joshua Heschel (d. 1972) quoted in A. Race, *Making Sense of Religious Pluralism: Shaping Theology of Religions for our Times* (London: SPCK, 2013), 1: 'In this aeon diversity of religions is the will of God.' More recently, in February 2019 Pope Francis and the Grand Imam of al-Azhar Ahmed el-Tayeb signed a joint declaration stating, 'The pluralism and the diversity of religions, colour, sex, race and language are willed by God in His wisdom, through which He created human beings.' https://catholicherald.co.uk/news/2019/02/05/pope-signs-declaration-saying-god-wills-religions-pluralism-what-does-this-mean/ (accessed 10 February 2020)

26 Ibn Kathīr, *Tafsīr Ibn Kathīr*, ed. M. Khinn and M. Khinn (Beirut: Mu'assasat al-Risālah, 2000), 6.

27 See H. Lazarus-Yafeh (1992), *Intertwined Worlds; Medieval Islam and Bible Criticism* (Princeton, NJ: Princeton University Press, 1992), 19–35; H. Lazarus-Yafeh, *EI*², s.v.

'Taḥrīf'; C. Adang, *Muslim Writers on Judaism and the Bible: From Ibn Rabban to Ibn Hazm* (Leiden: Brill, 1996), 223–48; G. S. Reynolds, 'On the Qur'anic Accusation of Scriptural Falsification (*taḥrīf*) and Christian Anti-Jewish Polemic', *Journal of the American Oriental Society* 130 (2010), 189–202; al-Shahrastānī, *al-Milal wa-al-niḥal*, three vols in one, ed. A. F. Muḥammad (Beirut: Dār al-Kutub al-'ilmiyyah, 1992), 2:233.

28 See Reynolds, 'On the Qur'anic Accusation', 193.

29 See e.g. Ibn Rabban, *The Polemical Works of 'Alī al-Ṭabarī*, ed. R. Ebied and D. Thomas (Leiden and Boston: Brill, 2016), 65, n. 12; G. S. Reynolds, *A Muslim Theologian in a Sectarian Milieu:* 'Abd al-Jabbār *and the Critique of Christian Orgins* (Leiden: Brill, 2004), 84.

30 See al-Shahrastānī, *al-Milal wa-al-niḥal*, 2:252; J. Waardenburg, 'Muslim Studies of Other Religions: 2. The Medieval Period: 650-1500', in *Muslim Perceptions of Other Religions: A Historical Survey*, ed. J. Waardenburg (New York and Oxford: Oxford University Press, 1999), 18–69, 53.

31 See Reynolds, 'On the Qur'anic Accusation', 189; Reynolds, *A Muslim Theologian*, 84.

32 Reynolds, *A Muslim Theologian*, 84.

33 See S. M. Stern, "Abd al-Jabbār's Account of How Christ's Religion Was Falsified by the Adoption of Roman Customs', *Journal of the Theological Society* 19 (1958), 128–85; Reynolds, *A Muslim Theologian*, 85ff.

34 See Ibn Ḥazm, *al-Faṣl*, 1:93ff., 2:2ff.; Waardenburg, 'Muslim Studies of Other Religions', 53.

35 See e.g. Ibn Taymiyyah, *al-Jawāb al-ṣaḥīḥ*, 1:361: 'The majority (*jumhūr*) of the Muslims . . . say that some of their [i.e. the earlier scriptures'] words (*alfāẓ*) have been altered (*buddila*), just as many of their meanings (*ma'ānī*) have been altered.' See also Ibn Qayyim al-Jawziyyah, *Hidāyat al-ḥayārá fī ajwibat al-yahūd wa-al-naṣārá*, 311ff.; D. Schlosser, 'Ibn Qayyim al-Jawziyya's Attitude Toward Christianity in *Hidāyat al-ḥayārā fī ajwibat al-yahūd wal-naṣārā*', in *Islamic Theology, Philosophy and Law: Debating Ibn Taymiyya and Ibn Qayyim al-Jawziyya*, ed. B. Krawietz and G. Tamer (Berlin; Boston: Walter de Gruyter, 2013), 422–60, 453–4.

36 See e.g. al-Zamakhsharī, *al-Kashshāf*, 1:*nūn*; al-Shahrastānī, *al-Milal*, 2:229, 233; Ibn Taymiyyah, *al-Jawāb al-ṣaḥīḥ*, 3:299ff.; Ibn Qayyim al-Jawziyyah, 306–11, 316ff. See also Lazarus-Yafeh, *Intertwined Worlds*, 47–8; J. D. McAuliffe, 'The Prediction and Prefiguration of Muḥammad', in *Bible and Qur'ān: Essays in Scriptural Intertextuality*, ed. J. C. Reeves (Atlanta, GA: Society of Biblical Literature, 2003), 107–32; S. Schmidtke, 'The Muslim Reception of Biblical Materials: Ibn Qutayba and His *A'lām al-nubuwwa*', *Islam and Christian-Muslim Relations* 22, no. 3 (2011), 249–74.

37 See e.g. al-Shahrastānī, *al-Milal wa-al-niḥal*, 2:245, 254; Ibn Taymiyyah, *al-Jawāb al-ṣaḥīḥ*, 1:15, 18ff., 2:91; Ibn Qayyim al-Jawziyyah, *Hidāyat al-ḥayārá*, 492ff.

38 See e.g. Ibn Ḥazm, *al-Faṣl*, 1:141ff., esp. 143, where, discussing the 'fornication' (*zinā*) that the Bible attributes to David, Ibn Ḥazm declares 'a thousand thousand curses upon whoever attributes this to the prophets'. See also Lazarus-Yafeh, *Intertwined Worlds*, 32–5; Adang, *Muslim Writers*, 239–40.

39 See e.g. Ibn Ḥazm, *al-Faṣl*, 1:93ff.; Lazarus-Yafeh, *Intertwined Worlds*, 28–9.

40 See e.g. al-Shahrastānī, *al-Milal wa-al-niḥal*, 2:229–30.

41 Al-Ṭūfī, *Muslim Exegesis of the Bible in Medieval Cairo: Najm al-Dīn al-Ṭūfī's (d. 716/1316) Commentary on the Christian Scriptures*, ed. and tr. L. Demiri (Leiden: Brill, 2013), 101–2.

42 Ibn Taymiyyah, *al-Jawāb al-ṣaḥīḥ*, 1:9.

43 Al-Shahrastānī, *al-Milal wa-al-niḥal*, 2:230.
44 See Lazarus-Yafeh, *Intertwined Worlds*, 35–41; Adang, *Muslim Writers*, 192–222; J. Burton, *Encyclopaedia of the Qur'ān*, s.v. 'Abrogation'.
45 Ibn Taymiyyah, *Majmū'ah al-Rasā'il*, 197.
46 See al-Ash'arī, *The Theology of al-Ash'arī: The Arabic Texts of al-Ash'arī's Kitāb al-Luma' and Risālat Istiḥsān al-khawḍ fī 'ilm al-kalām*, ed. R. J. McCarthy (Beirut: Imprimerie catholique, 1953), 15 [Arabic text]; al-Qurṭubī, *al-Jāmi' li-aḥkām al-Qur'ān: tafsīr al-Qurṭubī*, twenty volumes in ten (Beirut: Dār al-Kitāb al-'Arabī, 1997), 1:30.
47 See e.g. al-Qurṭubī, *al-Jāmi'*, 6:60 (Q 5:3).
48 Ibn Khaldūn, *The Muqaddimah*, 2:438.
49 See Y. Friedmann, *Prophecy Continuous: Aspects of Aḥmadī Religious Thought and Its Medieval Background* (Berkeley, CA and London: University of California Press, 1989), 49–82; Rubin, *Encyclopaedia of the Qur'ān*, s.v. 'Muhammad'.
50 Al-Zamakhsharī, *al-Kashshāf*, 1:*nūn*.
51 Ibn Kathīr, *Tafsīr*, 1061 (Q 33.40).
52 Quoted in Tottoli, *Biblical Prophets*, 112. See also Ibn Khaldūn, *The Muqaddimah*, 2:439; Kātib Çelebī, *The Balance of Truth*, tr. G. L. Lewis (London: Allen and Unwin, 1957), 120.
53 See al-Zamakhsharī, *al-Kashshāf*, 3:544–55 (Q 33.40).
54 Ibn Kathīr, *Tafsīr*, 1061 (Q 33.40). See also ibid., 6; Ibn Taymiyyah, *al-Jawāb al-ṣaḥīḥ*, 1:2, 88ff.
55 See J. Schacht, *The Origins of Muhammadan Jurisprudence* (London: Oxford University Press, 1950), esp. 11–20. For the later-medieval period, see e.g. Ibn Kathīr, *Tafsīr*, 7.
56 Ibn Kathīr, *Tafsīr*, 642 (Q 10.47).
57 See e.g. Ibn Ḥazm, *al-Faṣl*, 1:93.
58 See e.g. al-Zamakhsharī, *al-Kashshāf*, 1:17 (Q 1.1); al-Qurṭubī, *al-Jāmi*, 1:194 (Q 1.1); Ibn Kathīr, *Tafsīr*, 27–8 (Q 1.1); Ibn Taymiyyah, *Majmū'ah al-Rasā'il*, 75.
59 Lazarus-Yafeh, *Intertwined Worlds*, 21.
60 See e.g. al-Sarrāj, *Kitāb al-Luma' fī al-taṣawwuf*, ed. R. A. Nicholson (Leiden: Brill, 1914), 15: 'And the knowledge of all of that [i.e. Sufism] is found in the Book of God and in the reports (*akhbār*) of the Messenger of God', and ibid., 16ff.; M. Chodkiewicz, *An Ocean Without a Shore: Ibn 'Arabî, the Book, and the Law*, tr. D. Streight (Albany, NY: State University of New York Press, 1993), 64, for Ibn 'Arabī's statement: 'All of that of which we speak in our sessions and in our writings proceeds from the Qur'ân and from its treasures.' Rūmī, *The Mathnawí of Jalálu'ddín Rúmí*, in eight volumes, ed. R. A. Nicholson (London: Luzac & Co., 1925–1940), 1:1, where Rūmī describes the *Mathnawī* as 'the unveiler of the Qur'an' (*kashshāf al-Qur'ān*).
61 See L. Massignon, *Essay on the Origins of the Technical Language of Islamic Mysticism*, tr. B. Clark (Notre Dame, IN: University of Notre Dame Press, 1997).
62 See e.g. A. Schimmel, *Mystical Dimensions of Islam* (Chapel Hill, NC: University of North Carolina Press, 1975), 25: 'The words of the Koran have formed the cornerstone for all mystical doctrines [of the Sufis].' C. Ernst, *Words of Ecstasy in Sufism* (Albany, NY: State University of New York Press, 1985), 1: 'Sufism is a mystical tradition that is Qur'anic and Muhammadan.' With regard to Ibn 'Arabī, in particular, Michel Chodkiewicz has argued that 'the work of the Shaykh al-Akbar . . . is in its entirety a Qur'ānic commentary.' Chodkiewicz, *Ocean*, 24. With respect to the *Fuṣūṣ*, in particular, Ralph Austin has made the point that 'it is mystical

exegesis . . . that is the dominant feature of this work'. Ibn 'Arabī, *The Bezels of Wisdom*, tr. R. W. J. Austin (Mahwah, NJ: Paulist Press, 1980), 18. And Ronald Nettler has likewise shown how 'Qur'ānic and traditional elements, in direct citation or in paraphrase, most often serve in the *Fuṣūṣ* as foundation and framework for explicating his metaphysics'. R. Nettler, *Sufi Metaphysics and Qur'ānic Prophets: Ibn 'Arabī's Thought and Method in the* Fuṣūṣ al-ḥikam (Cambridge: Islamic Texts Society, 2003), 14.

63 S. Tustarī, *Tafsīr al-Qur'ān al-'aẓīm*, ed. Ṭ. Sa'd and S. 'Alī (Cairo: Dār al-Ḥaram li-al-turāth, 2004), 241 (Q 43.4).

64 Y. Casewit, *The Mystics of al-Andalus: Ibn Barrajān and Islamic Thought in the Twelfth Century* (Cambridge: Cambridge University Press, 2018), 255.

65 For other passages where Ibn 'Arabī describes the Torah, Psalms and Gospel, along with the Qur'an, as the 'speech of God' see also Chittick, *Sufi Path of Knowledge*, 244; Jāmī, *Precious Pearl*, 62.

66 Ibn 'Arabī, *al-Futūḥāt al-Makkiyyah*, in four volumes (Egypt: Dār al-Kutub al-'arabiyyah al-kubrá, 1329 AH [1911]) [hereafter 'Ibn 'Arabī, *al-Futūḥāt al-Makkiyyah*'], 2:279–80; Lipton, *Rethinking*, 105.

67 See Casewit, *Mystics*, 248, 255ff.

68 Lipton, *Rethinking*, 112–13, quoting Ibn 'Arabī, *al-Futūḥāt al-Makkiyyah*, 3:351 [translation slightly modified].

69 Lipton, *Rethinking*, 11, quoting Ibn 'Arabī, *al-Futūḥāt al-Makkiyyah*, 1:145.

70 Tustarī, *Tafsīr*, 110. See also ibid., 96, 139, 153, 167, 207, 249, 262–3.

71 Al-Qushayrī, *Laṭā'if al-ishārāt: tafsīr Ṣūfī kāmil li-al-Qur'ān al-Karīm*, in four vols, ed. I. Basyūnī (Cairo: al-Hay'ah al-Miṣriyyah al-'āmmah li-al-kitāb, 2000), 2:353 (Q 17.55).

72 Lipton, *Rethinking*, 77. See e.g. Ibn 'Arabī, *al-Futūḥāt al-Makkiyyah*, 1:135.

73 Lipton, *Rethinking*, 76, quoting Ibn 'Arabī, *al-Futūḥāt al-Makkiyyah*, 1:135.

74 M. Chodkiewicz, *Seal of Saints: Prophethood and Sainthood in the Doctrine of Ibn 'Arabī*, tr. L. Sherrard (Cambridge: Islamic Texts Society, 1999), 80.

75 Al-Qāshānī, *Sharḥ 'alá Fuṣūṣ al-ḥikam* (Egypt: al-Maṭba'ah al-Yamaniyyah, n.d.), 6.

76 Al-Qushayrī, *Laṭā'if al-ishārāt*, 1:269–70 (Q 3.110).

77 Casewit, *Mystics*, 258.

78 Lipton, *Rethinking*, 5, and see esp. chapter two of that work, the argument of which is based in particular on chapter twelve of the *Futūḥāt*.

79 Ibn 'Arabī, *al-Futūḥāt al-Makkiyyah*, 3:153. This passage is quoted and discussed in R. A. Nicholson, *The Mystics of Islam* (London: G. Bell & Sons, 1914), 87–8; Chittick, *Imaginal Worlds*, 125; N. Keller, 'On the validity of all religions in the thought of ibn Al-'Arabi and Emir 'Abd al-Qadir: A letter to 'Abd al-Matin'; C.-A. Keller, 'Perceptions of Other Religions in Sufism', *Muslim Perceptions of Other Religions*, 181–94, 189; Lipton, *Rethinking*, 67–70.

80 Rāzī, *The Path of God's Bondsmen from Origin to Return* (Merṣād al-'ebād men al-mabdā' elā'l-ma'ād*): A Sufi Compendium*, tr. H. Algar (Delmar, NY: Caravan Books, 1982), 157–78.

81 See ibid., 163, 177.

82 Ibn 'Arabī, *Fuṣūṣ*, 72.

83 Al-Jandī, *Sharḥ*, 39.

84 See Ibn 'Arabī, *Fuṣūṣ*, 192.

85 Ibid., 195.

86 See ibid., 72, 192; Ahmed, *What Is Islam?*, 28.
87 See al-Jandī, *Sharḥ*, 71.
88 See Izutsu, *Sufism and Taoism*, 254.
89 For *al-qābiliyyah* and *al-isti'dād* in Ibn 'Arabian thought, see Chittick, *Sufi Path of Knowledge*, 91–4; Izutsu, *Sufism and Taoism*, 33–5; Jāmī, *Precious Pearl*, 59; Al-Attas, *Mysticism*, 75.
90 Ibn 'Arabī, *Fuṣūṣ*, 47.
91 Al-Jandī, *Sharḥ*, 84.
92 See, in this regard, the similar points made in Keller, 'Perceptions of Other Religions', 189; Lipton, *Rethinking*, 33.
93 See C. Addas, *The Quest for the Red Sulphur*, tr. D. Streight (Cambridge: Islamic Texts Society, 1993), 234–6; N. Abū Zayd, *Hākadhā takallama Ibn 'Arabī* (Casablanca; Beirut: Dār al-Thaqāfī al-'Arabī, 2006), 128–38; Keller, 'Perceptions of Other Religions', 189–90; Lipton, *Rethinking*, 55–8. Similarly, in 1691, the Ibn 'Arabian Sufi al-Nābulusī would write to the Ottoman Grand Vizier calling on him 'to follow a stricter policy towards the Christians of Serbia'. E. Sirriyeh, *Sufi Visionary of Ottoman Damascus: 'Abd al-Ghanī al-Nabulusī, 1641-1731* (Abingdon: RoutledgeCurzon, 2005), 91. Indeed, for al-Nābulusī, it is through paying the *jizyah*, and thereby acknowledging their divinely ordained place in the hierarchy of religious communities, that the Jews and Christians can gain 'happiness' (*sa'ādah*) in this life and, possibly, the next. See M. Winter, 'A Polemical Treatise by 'Abd al-Ġanī al-Nābulusī against a Turkish Scholar on the Religious Status of the Dimmīs', *Arabica* 35 (1988), 92–103, 93.
94 This particularly comes to the fore in Sufi poetry. See e.g. Ibn 'Arabī's famous lines on 'the religion of love': Ibn 'Arabī, in *The Tarjumān al-Ashwāq*, ed. and tr. R. A. Nicholson (Oriental Translation Fund, 1978), 67, poem XI, vv. 13–15; Rūmī, *Selected Poems from the Dīvāni Shamsi Tabrīz*, ed. and tr. R. A. Nicholson (Cambridge: Cambridge University Press, 1898), 124–7, poem XXXI; Rūmī, *The Mathnawí*, 2.1770; and the verses of Niẓām al-Dīn Awliyā' quoted in Ahmed, *What Is Islam?*, 203.
95 It is true that, in early Ottoman times certain heterodox Muslim thinkers, perhaps influenced by their (partial or incorrect) reading of Ibn 'Arabī, would suggest that the Christians were equal to the Muslims or even that Jesus was superior to Muhammad, yet these ideas were swiftly condemned by more mainstream Ibn 'Arabian thinkers, who insisted on the Qur'an-centred position that it was only Muhammad who united 'all the forms of perfection and all the signs of God'. See T. Winter, 'Ibn Kemāl (d. 940/1534) on Ibn 'Arabī's Hagiology', *Sufism and Theology*, ed. A. Shihadeh (Edinburgh: Edinburgh University Press, 2007), 137–57, 143–4.
96 See C. Ernst, *Sufism: An Introduction to the Mystical Tradition of Islam* (Boston and London: Shambhala, 2011), 8–18. The Anglican priest and missionary Henry Martyn (d. 1812), for instance, wrote of 'the creedless theopathy' of the 'Sufi school, the "Methodists of the East"', a statement that was included in the 1881 edition of the Oxford English Dictionary. See Massignon, *Essay*, xxiii; C. Padwick, *Henry Martyn: Confessor of the Faith* (London: Student Christian Movement, 1922), 269.
97 See e.g. H. A. R. Gibb and H. Bowen, *Islamic Society and the West: A Study of the Impact of Western Civilization on Moslem Culture in the Near East*, in two vols (London: Oxford University Press, 1957), 2:209: 'Ṣûfism is inclined to place all religions on a level.' M. Hodgson, *The Venture of Islam: Conscience and History in a World Civilization*, in three vols (Chicago, IL: University of Chicago Press, 1974), 1:410: 'Ṣûfîs increasingly tended to minimize differences among religious beliefs.

In contrast to the communalist exclusivity of most of the Piety-minded, they readily tended toward a universalistic viewpoint, looking less to a person's religious allegiance than to his spiritual and moral qualities in whatever guise they appeared.' J. van Ess, 'Tolerance and Pluralism in Islam', in *The Religion of the Other: Essays in Honour of Mohamed Talbi*, ed. M. Ben-Madani (London: Maghreb Publications, 2013), 27–32, 31: 'Open advocacy of tolerance and praise of pluralism can be found, as is well known, in Islamic mysticism.' See also the comment of a noted German historian of the Ottoman Empire: 'The substantially pantheistic character of the dervishes' beliefs enabled them to take a more liberal attitude toward non-Moslems and won them a certain affection even among the Christian subject population, so much so that Christians and Moslems occasionally joined in the cults of identical saints.' F. Babinger, *Mehmed the Conqueror and His Time*, tr. R. Manheim, ed. W. Hickman (Princeton, NJ: Princeton University Press, 1978), 413.

98 For a critical introduction to some of the major works and ideas of the thinkers associated with the Perennialist school and their connection to Islamic Studies, see C. Ernst, 'Traditionalism, The Perennial Philosophy, and Islamic Studies', *Middle East Studies Association Bulletin* 28, no. 2 (1994), 176–80. Ernst's student Gregory Lipton has carried forward this critique in his *Rethinking Ibn 'Arabi*. For a highly sympathetic account of the Perennialist school and its role in the study of Islam, written by a prominent adherent of that school, see S. H. Nasr, *Islam in the Modern World: Challenged by the West, Threatened by Fundamentalism, Keeping Faith with Tradition* (New York: Harper Collins, 2011), Appendix IV, 361–402. A similar perspective to that of the Perennialists is adopted by scholars connected to the Beshara school and the associated Muhyiddin Ibn 'Arabi Society, for which see S. Taji-Farouki, *Beshara and Ibn 'Arabi: A Movement of Sufi Spirituality in the Modern World* (Oxford: Anqa, 2007).

99 See T. Woerner-Powell, *Another Road to Damascus: An Integrative Approach to 'Abd al-Qādir al-Jazā'irī (1808-1883)* (Berlin: De Gruyter, 2017), 189–94.

100 See also in this regard the comment of the Austrian–Bosnian scholar Smail Balić (who was not, as far as I know, a Perennialist) in his entry on the seventeenth-century commentator on the *Fuṣūṣ* 'Abd Allāh al-Bosnawī (d. 1054/1544)]: 'They [Ibn 'Arabī, Ibn al-Fāriḍ, and al-Bosnawī] make no distinction between belief and unbelief. The decisive factor for them is love.' After quoting Ibn 'Arabī's famous lines on 'the religion of love', Balić concludes, "Abdī [al-Bosnawī] is committed to the religion of love. He is guided by it because love is his belief and his Islam. Therein lies the basis for understanding for tolerance and understanding for all the religions of the world.' S. Balić, *Das unbekannte Bosnien: Europas Brücke zur islamischen Welt* (Köln: Bölau, 1992), 223.

101 A. Knysh, *Sufism: A New History of Islamic Mysticism* (Princeton, NJ: Princeton University Press, 2018), 39.

102 Chittick, *Imaginal Worlds*, 11. For the Qur'an-centredness of Ibn 'Arabī's supposed affirmation of 'the validity of religions other than Islam', see also ibid., 4, 97; Chittick, *Sufi Path of Knowledge*, 171.

103 See Chittick, *Imaginal Worlds*, 125.

104 See ibid., 174–6. This language is Ibn 'Arabī's; it is related to his concept of the 'God created in the beliefs' (*al-ḥaqq/al-ilāh al-makhlūq fī al-i'tiqādāt*). See e.g. Ibn 'Arabī, *Fuṣūṣ*, 113: 'Take care not to be limited (*tataqayyad*) by a particular "knot" (*'aqd makhṣūṣ*) and to disbelieve (*takfir*) in that which is other than it, with the result that many good things escape you; indeed, with the result that knowledge of the matter as

it is escapes you.' For the concept of the 'God created in the beliefs', see Izutsu, *Sufism and Taoism*, 254; Nettler, *Sufi Metaphysics*, 126–30. Interestingly, Ibn 'Arabī's warning against becoming 'knotted' to a particular form of religious belief was already noticed by Goldziher (*Die Richtungen*, 184–5), who took it as a sign that the Sufis advocated 'indifference to confessional differences'.

105 See Chittick, *Imaginal Worlds*, preface, esp. 11. For Chittick's critique of the modern world, see W. Chittick, *Science of the Cosmos, Science of the Soul: The Pertinence of Islamic Cosmology in the Modern World* (Oxford: Oneworld, 2007).

106 Shah-Kazemi, *The Other in the Light of the One*, ix.

107 Ibid., xii.

108 Ibid., 140.

109 Ibid., 157.

110 See ibid., xix–xxv.

111 See ibid., chapter 4, 210–78. Hick defines pluralism in the following way: 'In its broadest terms, it is the belief that no one religion has a monopoly of the truth or of the life that leads to salvation.' J. Hick, 'Religious Pluralism and Islam', lecture delivered at the Institute for Islamic Culture and Thought, Tehran (February, 2005).

112 V. Cornell, 'Practical Sufism. An Akbarian Foundation for a Liberal Theology of Difference', *Journal of the Muhyiddin Ibn 'Arabi Society* 36 (2004), 59–84.

113 Cf. Nettler, *Sufi Metaphysics*, 128: 'The 'religious pluralism' of Ibn 'Arabī's outlook, as some have seen this notion, is not so much derived from any principle analogous to modern religious pluralism with its 'liberal' ideological and social foundation, but, rather, from the non-dualist ontology underlying Ibn 'Arabī's thought.

114 Cornell, 'Practical Sufism', 69–70.

115 S. Akkach, *Intimate Invocations: Al-Ghazzī's Biography of 'Abd al-Ghanī al-Nābulusī* (Leiden: Brill, 2012), 86–7.

116 On this debate and al-Nābulusī's treatise in defence of al-Jīlī, see, in addition to Akkach's treatment, L. Demiri, "Abd al-Ghanī l-Nābulusī: *al-Kashf wa-al-bayān 'an asrār al-adyān fī kitāb al-Insān al-kāmil wa-kāmil al-insān*', in *Christian-Muslim Relations: A Bibliographical History*, vol. 12, ed. D. Thomas and J. Chesworth (Leiden; Boston: Brill, 2018), 121–4; K. El-Rouayheb, *Islamic Intellectual History in the Seventeenth Century* (Cambridge: Cambridge University Press, 2015), 334.

117 S. Akkach, *'Abd al-Ghani al-Nabulusi: Islam and the Enlightenment* (Oxford: Oneworld, 2007), 107–8.

118 Ibid., 111–12.

119 Ibid., 112.

120 See N. Kermani, 'From Revelation to Interpretation: Nasr Hamid Abu Zayd and the Literary Study of the Qur'an', in *Modern Muslim Intellectuals and the Qur'an*, ed. S. Taji-Farouki (Oxford: Oxford University Press, 2004), 169–224.

121 See Abū Zayd, *Hākadhā*, Preface, 17–30; C. Ernst, 'Nasr Hamid Abu Zayd on Ibn 'Arabi and Modernity', *Journal of the Muhyiddin Ibn 'Arabi Society* 58 (2015), 1–16. For Abū Zayd's opposition to Salafism and what he calls the 'religious establishment', see N. H. Abū Zayd, *Critique of Religious Discourse*, tr. J. Wright (New Haven, CT: Yale University Press, 2018).

122 See Abū Zayd, *Hākadhā*, chapter three, 'The Limitations of Place and the Pressures of the Time', 123–62; ibid., 13–14.

123 Y. Ziedan, *al-Lāhūt al-'arabī wa-uṣūl al-'unf al-dīnī* (Cairo: Dār al-Shurūq, 2015), 18, 21.

124 Y. Ziedan, *Dawwāmāt al-tadayyun* (Cairo: Dār al-Shurūq, 2013), 240.

125 Ibid., 245–6.
126 Ziedan, *al-Lāhūt al-'arabī*.
127 The potential for misunderstanding and disagreement when the two perspectives are confused can be seen in Gerald Elmore's review of Ronald Nettler's *Sufi Metaphysics and Qur'ānic Prophets*. Though the latter work is explicitly framed as an attempt to understand Ibn 'Arabī's thought on its own terms, through a close reading of the *Fuṣūṣ*, Elmore unfairly takes Nettler to task for having 'missed a very good opportunity to show how potentially relevant Ibn al-'Arabī's "sufi metaphysics" can be today', a task that is clearly superfluous to Nettler's stated goal. G. Elmore, 'Review of *Sufi Metaphysics and Qur'ānic Prophets: Ibn 'Arabī's thought and method in the* Fuṣūṣ al-ḥikam', *Journal of Qur'anic Studies* 7, no. 1 (2005), 81–97, 93.
128 See e.g. Chittick, *Imaginal Worlds*, 125; Shah-Kazemi, *The Other*, 162, 185, 191, 214; Cornell, 'Practical Sufism', 69–70; Akkach, *'Abd al-Ghani*, 111; Abū Zayd, *Hākadhā*, 123–62.

Chapter 3

1 This being said, it is not the first chapter devoted to the topic of revelation: chapter thirty-three is on the Mother of the Book (*Umm al-kitāb*), the 'heavenly book' that is 'the source (*aṣl*) and totality (*jumla*) of all revelations, including the Qur'ān' (Wisnovsky, *Encyclopaedia of the Qur'ān*, s.v. 'Heavenly Book'). Though al-Jīlī's Sufi metaphysical treatment of this scriptural archetype serves to give context to his treatment of the Qur'an and the other scriptures, I have not dedicated a specific chapter to it here, because the focus of this book is al-Jīlī's treatment of the scriptures that were revealed to the prophets and subsequently propagated to their respective peoples.
2 For the Ibn 'Arabian idea of the Muhammadan Reality, see A. 'Afīfī, *The Mystical Philosophy of Muhyid Dín Ibnul 'Arabí* (Cambridge: The University Press, 1939), 66–101; al-Ḥakīm, *al-Mu'jam*, 347–9; Izutsu, *Sufism and Taoism*, 236–8; Morrissey, *Sufism and the Perfect Human*, 97–116.
3 See e.g. Ibn 'Arabī, *Fuṣūṣ*, 214; 'Afīfī, *Mystical Philosophy*, 73; Chodkiewicz, *Seal*, 50; Chittick, *Sufi Path of Knowledge*, 239–40; Chittick, *Self-Disclosure*, 154, 296.
4 Al-Jīlī, *al-Insān*, 116.
5 Ibid., 115.
6 For the issue of the createdness of the Qur'an in Islamic theology, see R. C. Martin, *Encyclopaedia of the Qur'ān*, s.v. 'Createdness of the Qur'ān'.
7 As we saw in Chapter 1, al-Jīlī also indicates that the divine essence is indescribable and hidden, at the same time as he suggests that it is describable and manifest (see al-Jīlī, *al-Insān*, 26–9), an apparent paradox that can be resolved if we recognize that he is talking about the divine essence at different levels of existence.
8 See also al-Jīlī, *al-Insān*, 42, where he makes the same connection between the Qur'an and unqualified oneness.
9 See al-Jīlī, *Marātib*, 17. For the Ibn 'Arabian key term *al-wujūd al-muṭlaq*, see 'Afīfī, *Mystical Philosophy*, 1–6; Izutsu, *Sufism and Taoism*, 35; al-Ḥakīm, *al-Mu'jam*, 1133; Nettler, *Sufi Metaphysics*, index, s.v. Wujūd al-Muṭlaq.
10 See al-Jīlī, *Marātib*, 15; al-Jīlī, *al-Insān*, 113.
11 Al-Jīlī, *al-Insān*, 47. See also ibid., 77.
12 Ibid., 113.

13 See Izutsu, *God and Man in the Koran*, 142–215; Abū Zayd (*Hākadhā*, 93) speaks in this regard of 'ontological language' (*al-lughah al-wujūdiyyah*).
14 See Izutsu, *God and Man*, 133–47; F. Rahman, *Major Themes of the Qur'ān* (Minneapolis, MN: Bibliotheca Islamica, 1989), 47–50; B. Abrahamov, *Encyclopaedia of the Qur'ān*, s.v. 'Signs'; D. Madigan, *Encyclopaedia of the Qur'ān*, s.v. 'Revelation and Inspiration'.
15 Rahman, *Major Themes*, 49.
16 A similar motif is found in Ismaili thought, which may be a source for the Ibn 'Arabian usage. See M. Ebstein, *Mysticism and Philosophy in al-Andalus: Ibn Masarra, Ibn al-'Arabī and the Ismā'īlī Tradition* (Leiden: Brill, 2014), esp. 41–51, 169–72, 217.
17 See Abū Zayd, *Hākadhā*, 100; al-Ḥakīm, *al-Mu'jam*, 951–2. See also N. H. Abū Zayd, *Falsafat al-ta'wīl: dirāsah fī ta'wīl al-Qur'ān 'ind Muḥyī al-dīn Ibn 'Arabī* (Beirut: Dār al-Tanwīr, 1983), 263–95.
18 See Ebstein, *Mystical Philosophy*, 53ff., citing *al-Futūḥāt al-Makkiyyah*, 2:385; Izutsu, *Sufism and Taoism*, 163.
19 See al-Ḥakīm, *al-Mu'jam*, 320.
20 Al-Qūnawī, *I'jāz al-bayān fī tafsīr umm al-Qur'ān*, ed. J. Āshtiyānī (Qom: Mu'assasah-yi Būstān-i Kitāb-i Qom, 1423 AH [= 2002]), 10.
21 Al-Qāshānī ['Ibn al-'Arabī'], *Tafsīr al-Qur'ān al-karīm*, in two volumes, ed. 'A. Muḥammad 'Alī (Beirut: Dār al-Kutub al-'ilmiyyah, 2001), 2:372 (Q 76.23).
22 S. H. Nasr, *An Introduction to Islamic Cosmological Doctrines: Conceptions of Nature and Methods Used for Its Study by the Ikhwān al-Ṣafā', al-Bīrūnī and Ibn Sīnā* (London: Thames and Hudson, 1978), 2, note 2.
23 For the Ibn 'Arabian concept of *al-a'yān al-thābitah*, see A. 'Afīfī, 'Al-A'yān al-thābitah' fī madhhab Ibn 'Arabī wa-'al-ma'dūmāt' fī madhhab al-Mu'tazilah', *Al-Kitāb al-tidhkārī*, 183–208; al-Ḥakīm, *al-Mu'jam*, 831–9; Izutsu, *Sufism and Taoism*, 159–96.
24 See al-Jīlī, *al-Insān*, 114.
25 Al-Jīlī, *al-Insān*, 116.
26 See Izutsu, *God and Man*, 153; S. Wild, 'We have sent down to thee the book with the truth': Spatial and temporal implications of the Qur'anic concepts of nuzūl, tanzīl, and 'inzāl', in *The Qur'an as Text*, ed. S. Wild (Leiden: Brill, 1996), 137–53, 146; Madigan, *Encyclopaedia of the Qur'ān*, s.v. 'Revelation and Inspiration'. According to the great jurist al-Shāfi'ī (d. 204/820), it is its being 'sent down' (*munazzal*) that makes a book revelation or scripture in the Qur'anic sense. See Friedmann, *Tolerance and Coercion*, 82.
27 Ibn 'Arabī also uses the term *tanazzul* in this way (see e.g. Ibn 'Arabī, *Futūḥāt*, 4:210, 4:212; Chittick, *Self-Disclosure*, 114), and his interpreters also employ *tanazzul* to the same effect (see Chittick, 'Five Divine Presences', 125, note 9). Similarly, at the very beginning of the *Fuṣūṣ* (47), Ibn 'Arabī describes God as 'the One who sent down (*munazzil*) the forms of wisdom (*al-ḥikam*) upon the hearts of his "words" [i.e. the prophets]', where the divine act of 'sending down' His wisdom denotes God's manifestation of His attributes within His prophets.
28 Al-Jīlī, *al-Insān*, 47.
29 Ibid., 77.
30 Compare in this regard al-Jandī, *Sharḥ*, 66: 'By *inzāl* is understood "the realization (*taḥaqquq*) of something from its highest to its lowest point", where "high" and "low" can refer either to space (*makān*) or status (*makānah*).' In the case of revelation, al-Jandī indicates, both senses are meant.

31 See al-Jīlī, *Marātib*, 17–18.
32 Al-Jīlī, *al-Insān*, 114.
33 Abū Zayd, *Hākadhā*, 91.
34 See al-Jīlī, *al-Insān*, 210.
35 Al-Farghānī, *Muntahá al-madārik*, 21.
36 Ibn 'Arabī, *Fuṣūṣ*, 49–50.
37 See al-Jīlī, *al-Insān*, 230.
38 See ibid., 210.
39 Ibn 'Arabī, *Futūḥāt*, 2:5; Chodkiewicz, *Seal*, 93. See also Morrissey, *Sufism and the Perfect Human*, 83–96.
40 Compare al-Jīlī, *Sharḥ*, 97, where he indicates that, at the seventh and final station of perfection, 'the sun of perfection appears on all of [the Perfect Human's] bodily limbs (*a'ḍāi'hi al-jismāniyyah*) . . . such that his body becomes a spirit'.
41 See al-Jīlī, *al-Insān*, 101.
42 For the synonymity of *dhāt Muḥammad* and *al-ḥaqīqah al-muḥammadiyyah*, see al-Jandī, *Sharḥ*, 96.
43 See Morrissey, *Sufism and the Perfect Human*, 97–116.
44 See V. Cornell, *Realm of the Saint: Power and Authority in Moroccan Sufism* (Austin, TX: University of Texas Press, 1998), 344, note 55.
45 See G. Böwering, 'The Scriptural "Senses" in Medieval Qur'an Exegesis', in *With Reverence for the Word: Medieval Scriptural Exegesis in Judaism, Christianity, and Islam*, ed. J. D. McAuliffe, B. Walfish and J. Goering (Oxford: Oxford University Press, 2003), 346–36, 349–50.
46 There is in fact a precedent for this notion in the Sufi tradition. Quoting the hadith related by Ibn 'Abbās, Sahl Tustarī (*Tafsīr*, 253 [Q 44.3]) explains that on the Night of Power God sent down the whole of the Qur'an to the lowest heaven *and* to 'the spirit of Muhammad' (*rūḥ muḥammad*).
47 Al-Jīlī, *al-Insān*, 98.
48 This tradition is recorded in *Muslim, Ṣaḥīḥ*, 6:23–6 (no. 746).
49 See e.g. al-Qurṭubī, *al-Jāmi'*, 18:198 (Q 68.4); Ibn Kathīr, *Tafsīr*, 1355 (Q 68.4).
50 See e.g. al-Sarrāj, *al-Luma'*, 95.
51 Quoted in Addas, 'At the Distance', 1:68; Chodkiewicz, *Ocean*, 71, note 38; Chittick, *Sufi Path of Knowledge*, 241–2; Lipton, *Rethinking*, 41. Ibn 'Arabī also uses the term 'little Qur'an' (*Qur'ān ṣaghīr*) to denote the Perfect Human, and in one instance even identifies himself with the Qur'an and the seven oft-repeated verses (*al-sab' al-mathānī*), that is, the *Fātiḥah*. See al-Ḥakīm, *al-Mu'jam*, 908; Abū Zayd, *Hākadhā*, 48–9.
52 See al-Jīlī, *al-Kamālāt*, 228.
53 Al-Jīlī, *al-Insān*, 116.
54 For *al-Qur'ān al-karīm*, see Q 56.77, as well as Q 27.29 ('*kitāb karīm*'). For *al-Qur'ān al-ḥakīm*, see Q 36.2, as well as Q 3.58 ('*al-dhikr al-ḥakīm*') and Q 31.2 ('*al-kitāb al-ḥakīm*').
55 M. Mir, *Encyclopaedia of the Qur'ān*, s.v. 'Names of the Qur'ān'.
56 Ibid.
57 Al-Qurṭubī, *al-Jāmi'*, 17:193 (Q 56.77).
58 See ibid.; Ibn Kathīr, *Tafsīr*, 1292 (Q 56.77).
59 Izutsu, *God and Man*, 43. See also T. Izutsu, *The Structure of the Ethical Terms in the Koran; A Study in Semantics* (Tokyo: Keio Institute of Cultural and Linguistics Studies, 1959), 76–9.

60 Al-Jīlī's interpretation of the name *al-Qur'ān al-karīm* may have a precursor in al-Qāshānī's commentary on Q 56.77, where he explains that the term denotes how the Qur'an is 'a comprehensive form of knowledge (*'ilm majmū'*), which has eternal nobility and honour (*karam wa-sharaf qadīm*) and a high value (*qadr rafī'*)'. Al-Qāshānī, *Tafsīr*, 2:296 (Q 56.77). The interpretations of both authors may be connected to the etymological association of the root *q-r-'* with 'gathering together' (see E. W. Lane, *Arabic-English Lexicon*, in two volumes, spl. S. Lane-Poole (Cambridge: Islamic Texts Society, 1984), 1:2502), an association exploited by Ibn 'Arabī (see *Fuṣūṣ*, 70).

61 See e.g. Ibn 'Arabī, *Fuṣūṣ*, 49.

62 See e.g. al-Jīlī, *al-Insān*, 212.

63 See e.g. al-Qurṭubī, *al-Jāmi'*, 15:10 (Q 36.2); Ibn Kathīr, *Tafsīr*, 632 (Q 10.1), 1104 (Q 36.2).

64 See Ibn 'Arabī, *Fuṣūṣ*, 57–8 and *passim*. Interestingly, al-Qāshānī understands the name *al-Qur'ān al-ḥakīm* to be an allusion to the Qur'an's – and Muhammad's – comprehensiveness, that is, in much the same way as al-Jīlī understands the name *al-Qur'ān al-karīm*. See al-Qāshānī, *Tafsīr*, 2:163 (Q 36.2).

65 For the exegetical association of the verb *nazzala* with the idea of revelation in stages, see al-Zamakhsharī, *al-Kashshāf*, 1:336 (Q 3.3).

66 Nicholson, *Studies*, 125–6.

67 See M. Sells, *Encyclopaedia of the Qur'ān*, s.v. 'Ascension'.

68 Al-Jīlī, *al-Insān*, 252.

69 Ibid., 207.

70 For these concepts, see Chittick, *Sufi Path of Knowledge*, 91–4; Izutsu, *Sufism and Taoism*, 33–5. For al-Jīlī's definition of them, see V. Hoffman, 'Annihilation in the Messenger of God: The Development of a Sufi Practice', *International Journal of Middle East Studies* 31, no. 3 (1999), 351–69, 355–6.

71 See Madigan, *Encyclopaedia of the Qur'ān*, s.v. 'Revelation and Inspiration'.

72 For Ibn 'Arabī's identification of the station of the Perfect Human (*maqām al-insān al-kāmil*) as the station of *taḥqīq*, see W. Chittick, 'The Central Point: Qūnawī's Role in the School of Ibn 'Arabī', *Journal of the Muhyiddin Ibn 'Arabi Society* 35 (2004), 25–45, 33.

73 For this notion, see Ibn 'Arabī, *Fuṣūṣ*, 62–4; Chodkiewicz, *Ocean*, 50–1, 114–15; Friedmann, *Prophecy Continuous*, 71–6; Nettler, *Sufi Metaphysics*, 142–5.

74 Al-Jīlī, *al-Insān*, 264–5.

75 See ibid., 210.

76 See ibid., 211.

77 See Böwering, 'The Scriptural "Senses"', 346; P. Nwyia, *Exégèse coranique et langage mystique; nouvel essai sur le lexique technique des mystiques musulmans* (Beirut: Dar el-Machreq, 1970), 109ff.

78 Lings, *What Is Sufism?*, 79. Earlier interpreters of Ibn 'Arabī also stress the comprehensiveness (*jam'*, *ijmāl*) of the Qur'an. See e.g. al-Qāshānī, *Tafsīr*, 1:90 [Q 2.185], 2:163 [Q 36.2]; al-Qūnawī, *I'jāz al-bayān*, 11: '[Muhammad's] speech was the most universal in its effect (*a'amm ḥukman*) and the revelations that reached him were the most all-encompassing (*a'ẓam iḥāṭatan*), and the most comprehensive in the knowledge they contained (*ajma' 'ilman*), due to his comprehension and encompassing of the effects of [all] the levels, so that nothing is beyond the effect of his station and his grasp.'

79 Al-Jīlī, *al-Insān*, 116–17.

80 See Lane, *Lexicon*, 1:617; J. Schacht, *EI*[2], s.v. 'Aḥkām'.
81 See Chittick, *Sufi Path of Knowledge*, 39.
82 Cf. the similar language used by 'Ayn al-Quḍāt al-Hamadānī (d. 525/1131) in reference to the Prophet, whom he describes as 'a soul purified of the fleshly human condition (*bashariyyat*) and beyond this world'. Quoted in L. Lewisohn, 'In Quest of Annihilation: Imaginalization and Mystical Death in the *Tamhīdāt* of 'Ayn al-Quḍāt al-Hamadhānī', in *The Heritage of Sufism: Classical Persian Sufism from Its Origins to Rumi (700-1300)*, ed. L. Lewisohn (Oxford: Oneworld Publications, 1999), 285–336, 325.
83 See e.g. Hujwīrī, *Kashf al-maḥjūb: The Oldest Persian Treatise on Ṣúfiism*, tr. R. A. Nicholson (Leiden: Brill, 1911), 32.
84 See W. Madelung, *EI*[2], s.v. "Iṣmah'.
85 See R. Berjak, 'Bashar', *The Qur'an: An Encyclopaedia*, ed. O. Leaman (London: Routledge, 2006), 115.
86 Al-Jīlī, *al-Insān*, 151.
87 See Lane, *Lexicon*, 1:1085.
88 See Lane, *Lexicon*, 1:2841–2.
89 See al-Jīlī, *al-Insān*, 193. See also Addas, 'At the Distance', 1:69. For Ibn 'Arabī's use of the term *taḥaqquq*, see Chittick, *Self-Disclosure*, xxiv.
90 See al-Ḥakīm, *al-Mu'jam*, 773–4.
91 Al-Jīlī, *al-Kamālāt*, 231.
92 Ibid., 232.
93 See in this regard Morrissey, *Sufism and the Perfect Human*, esp. 59–62.
94 Al-Jīlī, *al-Insān*, 117.
95 See e.g. al-Qurṭubī, *al-Jāmi'*, 20:120 (Q 97.1); Ibn Kathīr, *Tafsīr*, 1433 (Q 97.1); al-Suyūṭī, *al-Durr al-manthūr fī al-tafsīr al-ma'thūr: wa-huwa mukhtaṣar tafsīr Tarjumān al-Qur'ān*, in six vols (Beirut: Dār al-Kutub al-'ilmiyyah, 2011), 91–4; D. Madigan, *Encyclopaedia of the Qur'ān*, s.v. 'Preserved Tablet'; Böwering, 'The Scriptural "Senses"', 350.
96 In the same context, al-Qāshānī (*Tafsīr*, 2:418 [Q 97.1]) writes of *al-shuhūd al-dhātī.*
97 For al-Jīlī's use of the term *taḥqīq*, see e.g. al-Jīlī, *al-Insān*, 79–80, where he speaks of his attainment of 'a faith of realization' (*īmān taḥqīq*), which he links to *kashf*; and ibid., 94, where he describes his 'realization' that ice (which stands for creation) is nothing but water (which stands for God). For Ibn 'Arabī's use of the same term, see Chittick, *Self-Disclosure*, xxiv; Chittick, 'Central Point', 33.
98 See e.g. al-Qurṭubī, *al-Jāmi'*, 10:51–4 (Q 15.87); Ibn Kathīr, *Tafsīr*, 730 (Q 15.87). Some scholars, including al-Bukhārī (d. 256/870), however, understand *al-Qur'ān al-'aẓīm* to relate to the rest of the Qur'an. For this and other interpretations of the verse, see U. Rubin, *Encyclopaedia of the Qur'ān*, s.v. 'Oft-Repeated'.
99 See al-Qurṭubī, *al-Jāmi'*, 10:51–4 (Q 15.87); Ibn Kathīr, *Tafsīr*, 730 (Q 15.87); A. Yusuf Ali, *The Holy Qur-an: Text, Translation and Commentary* (New York: Hafner Pub. Co., 1946), 652, note 2008; Tahānawī, *Kashshāf*, 966–7; Rubin, *Encyclopaedia of the Qur'ān*, s.v. 'Oft-Repeated'.
100 Al-Jīlī, *al-Insān*, 91. Similarly, in *al-Kahf wa-al-raqī*m (Lo Polito, "Abd al-Karīm', 159/215), he identifies *al-Qur'ān al-'aẓīm* with 'the unseen essence' (*al-dhāt al-ghā'ib*) that Muhammad became identified with.
101 Al-Jīlī, *al-Insān*, 133.
102 For al-Jīlī's treatment of these attributes, see ibid., 78–93.
103 Al-Qāshānī, *Tafsīr*, 1:279 (Q 15.87).

104 Ibid.
105 See Addas, 'At the Distance', 2:9. Addas notes that she has 'never encountered an analogous interpretation in Ibn 'Arabī's writings that relates directly to the verse in question'. Ibn 'Arabī does, however, connect the verse, and specifically the term *al-Qur'ān al-'aẓīm*, to the notion that Muhammad's character was the Qur'an (see Chittick, *Sufi Path of Knowledge*, 241). For Muhammad Wafā' and the Wafā'iyyah, and the influence of Ibn 'Arabī upon them, see R. McGregor, *Sanctity and Mysticism in Medieval Egypt: The Wafā' Sufi Order and the Legacy of Ibn 'Arabī* (Albany, NY: State University of New York Press, 2004).
106 See e.g. Ibn Kathīr, *Tafsīr*, 1275 (Q 55.1).
107 See e.g. al-Jīlī, *al-Insān*, 21: 'There is no way to know the Real (*ma'rifat al-ḥaqq*) – Glory be to Him and may He be exalted – except through His names and attributes. For the servant witnesses Him (*yushāhiduhu*) initially in His names and attributes, in an absolute way (*muṭlaqan*), and then ascends (*yarqī*) to know the essence (*ma'rifat al-dhāt*), attaining realization [of it] (*muḥaqqiqan*).' See also ibid., 30: 'There is no way (*sabīl*) to know (*ma'rifat*) the Real – Glory be to Him and may He be exalted – except by way of His names.'
108 Ibid., 50.
109 See Izutsu, *Sufism and Taoism*, 116–40; Nettler, 'Ibn 'Arabī's Notion'.
110 Cf. al-Qāshānī, *Tafsīr*, 2:184 (Q 55.1-2).
111 See also al-Jīlī, *al-Insān*, 90, where he writes of the 'the All-Merciful's teaching of the Qur'an (*ta'līm al-raḥmān al-Qur'ān*)' to those who attain the manifestation of the essence.
112 See e.g. Ibn Kathīr, *Tafsīr*, 574 (Q 8.41).
113 See Ali, *Holy Qur-an*, 29, note 68 (Q 2.53), 73, note 192 (Q 2.185), 926, note 3053 (Q 25.01).
114 See Mir, *Encyclopaedia of the Qur'ān*, s.v. 'Names of the Qur'ān', 507–8.
115 Al-Jīlī, *al-Insān*, 117.
116 Ibid., 117–18.
117 See e.g. Ibn 'Arabī, *Fuṣūṣ*, 70; Chittick, *Sufi Path of Knowledge*, 364; al-Ḥakīm, *al-Mu'jam*, 908.

Chapter 4

1 Al-Shahrastānī, *al-Milal wa-al-niḥal*, 2:231.
2 Adang, *Encyclopaedia of the Qur'ān*, s.v. 'Torah'.
3 The modern Qur'an translator and commentator Abdullah Yusuf Ali (d. 1953) (*Holy Qur-an*, 29, note 68 [Q 2.53]) understands *al-kitāb* and *al-furqān* to denote two separate things given to Moses, respectively, 'the written Book' and 'other signs', though he acknowledges that other commentators conflate the two.
4 Again, 'Ali (*Holy Qur-an*, 1449, note 5110 [Q 53.36]) understands *al-ṣuḥuf* to be distinct from *al-Tawrāh*, believing it to refer to 'some other book or books now lost'.
5 See also Adang, *Encyclopaedia of the Qur'ān*, s.v. 'Torah'; Schöck, *Encyclopaedia of the Qur'ān*, s.v. 'Moses'; Rubin, *Encyclopaedia of the Qur'ān*, s.v. 'Jews and Judaism'; Saleh, 'Hebrew Bible'.
6 See Lazarus-Yafeh, *Intertwined Worlds*, 19–49. See also Waardenburg, 'Muslim Studies of Other Religions', 44; S. H. Griffith, *The Bible in Arabic: The Scriptures of*

the 'People of the Book' in the Language of Islam (Princeton, NJ: Princeton University Press, 2013), 176.

7 Al-Jīlī, *al-Insān*, 118–19.

8 In this regard, Mohammed Arkoun writes of how the Qur'an 'establishes an arena of communication between three grammatical persons, a *speaker* who articulates the discourse contained in the Heavenly Book; a first *addressee*, who transmits the message of the enunciation as an event of faith; and a second *addressee*, *al-nās* (the people), who constitute the group'. M. Arkoun, *Islam: To Reform or Subvert?* (London: Saqi Essentials, 2006), 64 [italics his].

9 Many Qur'anic commentators identify the term *alwāḥ* with the Torah as a whole, as al-Jīlī does here. See e.g. al-Qurṭubī, *al-Jāmi'*, 7:248 (Q 7.145); al-Maḥallī and al-Suyūṭī, *Tafsīr al-Jalālayn*, 177 (Q 7.145). At the same time, the Ten Commandments motif was not absent from discussions of the tablets in the *tafsīr* tradition.

10 See Izutsu, *Sufism and Taoism*, 31; Chittick, *Sufi Path of Knowledge*, 159, 337; F. Rosenthal, "Ibn 'Arabī between "Philosophy" and "Mysticism": 'Sūfism and Philosophy Are Neighbors and Visit Each Other'. *fa-inna at-taṣawwuf wa-t-tafalsuf yatajāwarāni wa-yatazāwarāni*', *Oriens* 31 (1988), 1-359-10; Ibn 'Arabī, *Futūḥāt*, 2:372–3, for his account of his meeting with Ibn Rushd; M. Rustom, 'Ibn 'Arabī's Letter to Fakhr al-Dīn al-Rāzī: A Study and Translation', *Journal of Islamic Studies* 25, no. 2 (2014), 113–37.

11 See e.g. al-Zamakhsharī, *al-Kashshāf*, 2:157 (Q 7.145); Ibn Kathīr, *Tafsīr*, 532 (Q 7.145).

12 The Ottoman commentator Ismā'īl Ḥaqqī (d. 1127/1725), who like al-Jīlī was a Sufi metaphysician in the Ibn 'Arabian tradition, also identifies nine tablets (see Ismā'īl Ḥaqqī, *Kitāb tafsīr al-Qur'ān al-musammá Rūḥ al-bayān* (Būlāq: al-Maṭbaʿah al-ʿāmirah, 1870), 1:340 [Q 7.145]).

13 See al-Tha'labī, *'Arā'is al-majālis fī qiṣaṣ al-anbiyā', or, 'Lives of the Prophets'*, tr. W. M. Brinner (Leiden: Brill, 2002), 336.

14 See W. M. Brinner, 'An Islamic Decalogue', in *Studies in Islamic and Judaic Traditions*, ed. W. M. Brinner and S. D. Ricks (Atlanta: Scholars Press, 1986), 67–84, 68–9.

15 See al-Suyūṭī, *al-Durr*, 3:236 (Q 7.150).

16 Other exegetes, it should be noted, also discuss this biblical theme, and connect it to the idea that the Torah in its present state is incomplete, often suggesting that as much as sixth-sevenths of the original Torah has been 'removed' (*rufi'a*). See e.g. al-Tha'labī, *al-Kashf wa-al-bayān al-ma'rūf bi-Tafsīr al-Tha'labī*, in ten volumes, ed. A. Ibn 'Āshūr (Beirut: Dār Iḥyā' al-turāth al-'arabī, 2002), 4:286 (Q 7.150); al-Qurṭubī, *al-Jāmi'*, 19:261 (Q 85.22). Abdullah Yusuf Ali (*Holy Qur-an*, 385, note 1116 [Q 7.150]), however, lays emphasis on the fact that the Qur'an, unlike the Old Testament, does not tell us that Moses broke the tablets in his anger.

17 See al-Qāshānī, *Tafsīr*, 1:379 (Q 15.87).

18 Al-Jīlī, *al-Insān*, 119.

19 See e.g. al-Ṭabarī, *Tafsīr al-Ṭabarī: al-musammá Jāmi' al-bayān fī ta'wīl al-Qur'ān*, in thirteen volumes (Beirut: Dār al-Kutub al-'ilmiyyah, 1999), 6.57–9 (Q 7.145); al-Zamakhsharī, *al-Kashshāf*, 2:158 (Q 7.145); al-Rāzī, *Mafātīḥ al-ghayb*, 14:246–7 (Q 7.145).

20 See e.g. al-Shahrastānī, *al-Milal wa-al-niḥal*, 2:231; Ibn Kathīr, *Tafsīr*, 492 (Q 7:145).

21 See e.g. al-Zarkashī, *al-Burhān fī 'ulūm al-Qur'ān*, in four vols (Cairo: Dār al-Turāth, 1984), 2:181–2.

22 See Ibn 'Arabī, *Futūḥāt*, 1:214: 'The Messenger of God said, "God struck with His hand between my shoulders, and I felt the coldness of His fingertips between my breasts, and I knew then the knowledge of the first people and the last people (*'ilm al-awwalīn wa-al-ākhirīn*)." Within this knowledge came everything that is known, thought of or sensed (*kull ma'lūm ma'qūl maḥsūs*), from those things that created beings perceive, though this is a form of knowledge that is not obtained by way of one of the sensory or spiritual faculties.' Though this wording of the hadith is not canonical, a variant is recorded in Tirmidhī, *al-Jāmi'*, 5:285 (no. 3235).

23 For the *awliyā'* as heirs of Muhammad in the Sufi metaphysics of Ibn 'Arabī, see al-Ḥakīm, *al-Mu'jam*, 1193–5; Chodkiewicz, *Ocean*, 47. In the introduction to the *Fuṣūṣ* (p. 48), Ibn 'Arabī declares himself to be a *wārith*, in the context of explaining that he received the book directly from the Prophet. The idea that the Sufis are the true heirs of the Prophets is already found in al-Sarrāj, *Kitāb al-Luma'*, 5. See also A. T. Karamustafa, *Sufism: The Formative Period* (Berkeley: University of California Press, 2007), 68.

24 See e.g. al-Jīlī, *al-Insān*, 90, 115, 119; al-Jīlī, *Sharḥ*, 118, 253.

25 See al-Jīlī, *al-Insān*, 89–90, 211–12.

26 See al-Jīlī, *al-Insān*, 53–5; al-Jīlī, *Marātib*, 20–1.

27 See e.g. Ibn 'Arabī, *Fuṣūṣ*, 90–4.

28 See al-Jīlī, *al-Insān*, 53–5, 68.

29 See ibid., 86–7.

30 See ibid., 86.

31 See e.g. al-Qurṭubī, *al-Jāmi'*, 7:248–9 (Q 7.145); al-Zamakhsharī, *al-Kashshāf*, 2:157–8 (Q 7.145); al-Maḥallī and al-Suyūṭī, *al-Jalālayn*, 177 (Q 7.145).

32 M. Berenbaum and F. Skolnik, *Encyclopaedia Judaica*, s.v. 'Tablets of the Law'.

33 It should be noted, however, that the *Zohar* itself contains the common rabbinic opinion that the tablets were made of sapphire. See D. C. Matt (tr.), *The Zohar*, in nine volumes (Stanford: Stanford University Press, 2004–2016), 4:470–1.

34 E. R. Wolfson, *Venturing Beyond – Law and Morality in Kabbalistic Mysticism* (New York: Oxford University Press, 2006), 273.

35 For the saying of Rabbi Akiva as it is quoted in the Babylonian Talmud, see M. D. Swartz, 'Jewish Visionary Tradition in Rabbinic Literature', in *The Cambridge Companion to the Talmud and Rabbinic Literature*, ed. C. E. Fonrobert and M. S. Jaffee (Cambridge: Cambridge University Press, 2007), 198–221, 203.

36 See Wolfson, *Venturing Beyond*, 273.

37 M. Idel, *Language, Torah, and Hermeneutics in Abraham Abulafia* (Albany, NY: State University of New York Press, 1989), 44.

38 Quoted in ibid.

39 Ibid.

40 This being said, the marble motif does not seem to appear in the tales of the prophets, where we might expect to find *Isrā'īliyyāt*. See e.g. al-Tha'labī, *'Arā 'is*, 336, where it is reported that the tablets were made from the lote-tree of paradise, which was made of green emerald.

41 See also M. Goodman, *A History of Judaism* (London: Allen Lane, 2018), 192, 195.

42 Jewish exegetes, by contrast, tend to interpret the motif in terms of God's stripping of free will from the individual(s) whose heart is said to be hardened. See M. ben Yashar, 'And I Will Harden the Heart of Pharaoh.' Bar-Ilan University, Daf Parashat Hashavua (Study Sheet on the Weekly Torah Portion, 1997).

43 Al-Qurṭubī, *al-Jāmi'*, 2:500 (Q 2:74); cf. Ali, *Holy Qur-an*, 37, note 82 (Q 2.27).

44 Al-Qāshānī, *Tafsīr*, 1:62 (Q 2.74).
45 Ibid. See also al-Tustarī, *Tafsīr*, 270 (Q 57.16); al-Qushayrī, *Laṭā'if*, 1:112 (Q 2.74); al-Qurṭubī, *al-Jāmi'*, 2:500 (Q 2.74).
46 See al-Jīlī, *al-Insān*, 96. Similarly, for Ibn 'Arabī, light is one of God's names, and the starting point of creation (*mabda' al-khalq*) and of perception (*mabda' al-idrāk*) (see al-Ḥakīm, *al-Mu'jam*, 1081–7).
47 Al-Jīlī, *al-Insān*, 119–20.
48 Compare al-Qāshānī, *Sharḥ*, 248: '[Moses'] station comes close to the station of comprehensiveness (*maqām al-jam'iyyah*) that our Prophet – May God bless him and grant him peace – was singled out for.'
49 See al-Ḥakīm, *al-Mu'jam*, 1193–5; Chodkiewicz, *Seal*, 47.
50 In keeping with the Qur'an-centred view (which arises out of, for example, Q 3.84 and Q 42.13), in al-Jīlī's view the pre-Muhammadan prophets can also be considered Muslims (in the sense that they submit to God); hence, they are able to attain the status of Perfect Humans.
51 Al-Jandī, *Sharḥ*, 65.
52 See e.g. al-Qurṭubī, *al-Jāmi'*, 6:60 (Q 5.3), 5:385 (Q 6.38), 10:200 (Q 17.12).
53 See e.g. ibid., 4:167 (Q 3.110); Ibn Kathīr, *Tafsīr*, 250 (Q 3.110).
54 See al-Jīlī, *al-Insān*, 260.
55 See Ibn 'Arabī, *Fuṣūṣ*, 70: 'For the Qur'an contains the Furqan, and not *vice versa*. It is for this reason that nobody was singled out for the Qur'an except Muhammad – Peace and prayers be upon him – and this *ummah* which is the best of communities (*khayr al-umam*) given to mankind.' See also Ibn 'Arabī, *al-Futūḥāt al-makkiyyah*, 3:400, quoted in al-Ḥakīm, *al-Mu'jam*, 1195: 'Muhammad was the greatest viceregent (*a'ẓam khalīfah*) and the greatest imam (*akbar imām*), and his community was the best community sent out to mankind, and God gave his heirs (*warathatahu*) the stations of the prophets and messengers, and so permitted for them independent working out of judgments (*al-ijtihād fī l-aḥkām*), which is legislation (*al-tashrī'*).'
56 Note in this regard, however, that the Qur'an translator and convert to Islam from Judaism Muhammad Asad (d. 1992) interprets Q 2.106 as a reference to the supersession and abrogation of the biblical scriptures by the Qur'an, rather than to intra-Qur'anic abrogation. See M. Asad, *The Message of the Qur'an* (Gibraltar: Dar al-Andalus, 1984), 22–3 (Q 2.106).
57 See e.g. Ibn Kathīr, *Tafsīr*, 705 (Q 13.38-39).
58 On the history of the interpretation of *khātam al-nabiyyīn*, see Friedmann, *Prophecy Continuous*, 49–82. For the conventional medieval view, see e.g. Ibn Kathīr, *Tafsīr*, 1061 (Q 33:40): 'This verse is a clear stipulation (*naṣṣ*) that there is no prophet after him, and if there is no prophet after him, then there is no messenger after him.' See also Ali, *Holy Qur-an*, 1119, note 3731 (Q 33.40): 'When a document is sealed, it is complete, and there can be no further addition. The holy Prophet Muhammad closed the long line of Apostles. God's teaching is and will always be continuous, but there has been and will be no Prophet after Muhammad.'
59 See al-Jīlī, *al-Insān*, 265.
60 See ibid., 211.
61 See e.g. Ibn Taymiyyah, *Majmū' al-fatāwá*, in thirty-seven volumes, ed. 'A. al-Jazzār and A. al-Bāz (Mansura: Dār al-Wafā', 1995), 11:226–7.
62 Al-Jīlī, *al-Insān*, 120–1.
63 See Lazarus-Yafeh, *Intertwined Worlds*, 35.
64 Friedmann, *Tolerance and Coercion*, 23.

65 See al-Qurṭubī, *al-Jāmiʿ*, 13:149 (Q 27.16): 'Every prophet who came after Moses, whether they were sent out or not, followed the law of Moses (*sharīʿat Mūsá*), until the Messiah – Peace be upon him – was sent out, for he abrogated it [i.e. the law of Moses] (*nasakhahā*).' See also al-Baghawī, *Maʿālim*, 3:60 (5.44): 'Among the prophets there were those who were not commanded by the ordinances of the Torah (*ḥukm al-Tawrāh*), such as Jesus – Peace be upon him.' Ibn Taymiyyah, *Majmūʿ al-fatāwá*, 11:224: 'Jesus referred them [i.e. his people] to the Torah for most of the law, and then came to complete it (*kammalahā*).'

66 See e.g. Mk 8.22-25, Mt. 20.29-34, Lk. 18.35-43, Jn 9.1-12 (healing of the blind), Mk 1.40-45, Mt. 8.1-4, Lk. 5.12-16, Lk. 17.11-19 (healing of lepers), Mk 5.21-42, Lk. 7.11-17, Jn 11.1-44 (reviving the dead), Syriac Infancy Gospel 1.2 (speaking in the cradle).

67 See e.g. al-Thaʿlabī, *ʿArāʾis*, 646, 648, 657, 661; al-Shahrastānī, *al-Milal wa-al-niḥal*, 2:244.

68 See e.g. Ibn ʿArabī, *Fuṣūṣ*, 139–40.

69 See al-Jīlī, *al-Insān*, 152, 269, 278.

70 Tustarī, *Tafsīr*, 237 (Q 40.81).

71 See A. Louth, *Introducing Eastern Common Theology* (London: SPCK), 60–5; A. McGrath, *Christian Theology: An Introduction* (Chichester and Malden, MA: Wiley-Blackwell, 2011), 16–18, 247–9.

72 For the use of this term in Arab Christian theology, see S. H. Griffith, 'The Concept of *al-ʿuqnūm* in ʿAmmār al-Baṣrī's Apology for the Doctrine of the Trinity', in *Actes du premier congrès international d'études arabes chrétiennes (Goslar, septembre 1980)*, ed. K. Samir (Rome: Pontificium Institutum Studiorum Orientalium, 1982); S. H. Griffith, *The Beginnings of Christian Theology in Arabic: Muslim-Christian Encounters in the Early Islamic Period* (Aldershot: Ashgate, 2002), 32, 180, 184–5.

73 See e.g. al-Warrāq, *Anti-Christian Polemic in Early Islam: Abū ʿĪsá al-Warrāq's 'Against the Trinity'*, ed. and tr. D. Thomas (Cambridge: Cambridge University Press, 1992), 76ff.; al-Shahrastānī, *al-Milal wa-al-niḥal*, 2:245; Ibn Taymiyyah, *al-Jawāb al-ṣaḥīḥ*, 2:244; Ṭūfī, *Muslim Exegesis*, 561, s.v. 'Hypostases'.

74 See Louth, *Introducing*, 57. For an overview of the early history and doctrines of the Melkites, see S. H. Griffith, *The Church in the Shadow of the Mosque: Christians and Muslims in the World of Islam* (Princeton, NJ and Oxford: Princeton University Press, 2008), 137–9.

75 See S. Noble and A. Treiger (eds.), *The Orthodox Church in the Arab World, 700-1700: An Anthology of Sources* (DeKalb, IL: NIU Press, 2014), 9. For an overview of the early history and doctrines of the Jacobites, see Griffith, *Church in the Shadow*, 134–6.

76 Al-Jīlī, *al-Insān*, 210.

77 See Griffith, *Church in the Shadow*, 8, and e.g. al-Warrāq, *Anti-Christian Polemic*, 47–8; al-Shahrastānī, *al-Milal wa-al-niḥal*, 2:247ff.; Ibn Ḥazm, al-Faṣl, 1:48; Stern, "Abd al-Jabbār's account'; Reynolds, *A Muslim Theologian*, 37, 204; Ibn Khaldūn, *The Muqaddimah*, 1:480.

78 See Noble and Treiger, *Orthodox Church*, 9; Griffith, *Church in the Shadow*, 131–4; Louth, *Introducing*, 62.

79 See e.g. al-Warrāq, *Anti-Christian Polemic*; al-Warrāq, *Early Muslim Polemic against Christianity: Abū ʿĪsá al-Warrāq's 'Against the Incarnation'*, ed. and tr. D. Thomas (Cambridge: Cambridge University Press, 2002); Reynolds, *A Muslim Theologian*; Siddiqui, *Christians, Muslims, & Jesus*, 106–12. Al-Shahrastānī, *al-Milal wa-al-niḥal*,

2:248ff., presents the Christologies of the three major Christian denominations in terms fairly similar to al-Jīlī's. The Melkites, he tells us, view the incarnation in terms of the 'mixing' (*imtizāj*) of God and Jesus; the Jacobites in terms of the divine 'appearance' or 'manifestation' (*ẓuhūr*) in Jesus; and the Nestorians in terms of Jesus' 'illumination' (*ishrāq*) by the divine light.

80 On the imputation of *kufr* (and *shirk*) to Christians in Islamic thought, see G. R. Hawting, *The Idea of Idolatry and the Emergence of Islam: From Polemic to History* (Cambridge: Cambridge University Press, 1999), 82–4; Friedmann, *Tolerance and Coercion*, 57.

81 See Goldziher, *Die Richtungen*, 222.

82 See Ibn 'Arabī, *Fuṣūṣ*, 141.

83 Al-Jīlī, *al-Insān*, 120.

84 See Izutsu, *Sufism and Taoism*, 48–67; Ahmed, *What Is Islam?*, 90; al-Jīlī, *al-Insān*, 60–1; Morrissey, 'An Introduction'; al-Jīlī, *Ibdā'*, 48.

85 See al-Jīlī, *al-Insān*, 42–7.

86 See Ibn 'Arabī, *Fuṣūṣ*, 70; Izutsu, *Sufism and Taoism*, 62.

87 See al-Jīlī, *Sharḥ*, 118–20.

88 See e.g. al-Shahrastānī, *al-Milal wa-al-niḥal*, 2:235–6, where he notes that while the Torah invokes 'an eye for an eye', and Jesus in the Gospel calls on mankind to 'turn the other cheek', the Qur'an (e.g. Q 2.178) plots a middle course, calling for *both* retribution and forgiveness. See also al-Qurṭubī, *al-Jāmi'*, 2:149 (Q 2.143), 'i.e. this [Islamic] community did not go to the extremes (*lam taghlu ghuluww*) of the Christians regarding their prophets, nor did they have a limited view (*qaṣṣarū*) of their prophets like the Jews'; al-Baghawī, *Tafsīr*, 2:314 (Q 3.171): 'Al-Ḥasan said, 'It is possible that [verse 3:171] was sent down with regard to both the Jews and Christians, for all of them went to extremes (*ghalū*) with regard to Jesus, the Jews by limiting [his status] (*bi-al-taqṣīr*), and the Christians by going beyond the limit (*bi-mujāwazat al-ḥadd*)'; Ibn Taymiyyah, *al-Jawāb al-ṣaḥīḥ*, 1:6–7, 2:62, 3:240ff., where he presents Islam as a middle path between the extremes of Jewish ultra-legalism and Christian permissiveness.

89 Izutsu, *Sufism and Taoism*, 62.

90 Al-Jīlī, *al-Insān*, 121–2.

91 See e.g. the statement of Shaykh al-Mufīd (d. 413/1022): '*Taqiyyah* is the concealing of the truth (*kitmān al-ḥl-m*), and covering up belief about it, and concealing it (*mukātamah*) from one's opponents.' Al-Mufīd, *Taṣḥīḥ al-i'tiqād bi-ṣawāb al-intiqād, aw, Sharḥ 'aqā'id al-Ṣadūq*, ed. H. Shahrastānī (Beirut: Dār al-Kitāb al-islāmī, 1983), 115. See also R. Strothmann, EI[2], s.v. 'Takiyya'; E. Kohlberg, 'Some Imāmī-shī'ī Views on Taqiyya', *Journal of the American Oriental Society* 95, no. 3 (1975), 395–402; L. Clarke, 'The Rise and Decline of *Taqiyya* in Twelver Shi'ism', in *Reason and Inspiration in Islam: Theology, Philosophy and Mysticism in Muslim Thought. Essays in Honour of Hermann Landolt*, ed. T. Lawson (London; New York: I.B. Tauris, 2005), 46–63; M. Ebstein, 'Secrecy in the Ismā'īlī Tradition and in the Mystical Thought of Ibn al-'Arabī', *Journal Asiatique* 298, no. 2 (2010), 303–43, 304–12. In the Qur'an, it should be noted, the root *k-t-m* generally connotes immoral deception. See Q 2.146, 3.71, and R. J. Khan, *Self and Secrecy in Early Islam* (Columbia, SC: University of South Carolina Press, 2008), 56. For those looking in from the outside of the esoteric traditions, this negative connotation generally holds true. Thus Ibn Taymiyyah (*Majmū' al-fatāwá*, 13:141) declares (Shī'ī) *taqiyyah* to be 'the slogan of hypocrisy' (*shi'ār al-nifāq*).

92 See Abū Zayd, *Hākadhā*, 89–121. Ebstein, 'Secrecy', 329–42, argues for the direct impact of this Shīʿī practice on Ibn ʿArabian Sufism.
93 Ibn Taymiyyah, *Majmūʿ al-fatāwá*, 11:16.
94 See Ibn ʿArabī, *Fuṣūṣ*, 210–11. See also Ibn ʿArabī's verses in his *al-Tanazzulāt al-Mawṣuliyyah* (quoted in Lipton, *Rethinking*, 52): 'If someone like me says "I am a lord," / Oh my friend – is that a major sin (*kabīra*)? / No, it is my right, for He and I are one! I did not even commit a minor sin (*ṣaghīra*).' According to Ibn Taymiyyah (*Majmūʿ al-fatāwá*, 11:244), the Ibn ʿArabian view on the relationship between God and creation was essentially the same as that of Pharaoh, 'who divested the Creator [of His divinity] (*ʿaṭṭala al-ṣāniʿ*)'.
95 In *al-Futūḥāt*, 4:393, Ibn ʿArabī places Pharaoh among the four groups of the damned, 'who will remain eternally in hell . . . because he entertained pretensions to divinity (*iddaʿa al-rubūbīyah li-nafsihi wa-nafāhā ʿan Allāh*)'. See E. Ormsby, 'The Faith of Pharaoh: A Disputed Question in Islamic Theology', *Reason and Inspiration in Islam*, 471–89, 472. For Ibn ʿArabī's controversial views on Pharaoh more generally, particularly on the question of his conversion to monotheism at his death, see Kātib Çelebī, *Balance*, 75–9; C. Ernst, 'Controversies Over Ibn al-ʿArabī's *Fuṣūṣ*: The Faith of Pharaoh', *Islamic Culture* 59 (1985), 259–66; Knysh, *Ibn ʿArabi*, 158–61; A. N. Lane, "Abd al-Ghanī al-Nābulusī's (1641-1731) Commentary on Ibn ʿArabī's Fuṣūṣ al-ḥikam: An Analysis and Interpretation' (DPhil diss., University of Oxford, 2001), 210–29; al-Jandī, *Sharḥ*, 537.
96 See al-Jīlī, *al-Insān*, 116–17.
97 Compare al-Sarrāj, *al-Lumaʿ*, 5–6, who identifies 'the knowledge of the realities of faith' (*ʿilm ḥaqāʾiq al-īmān*) with the knowledge of the Sufis.
98 See Goldziher, *Die Richtungen*, 182; Nwyia, *Exégèse*, esp. 141, quoting a hadith often cited by the Sufis: 'There is not a single verse of the Qur'an that does not have an outward (*ẓāhir*) and an inward (*bāṭin*) meaning'; K. Sands, *Ṣūfī Commentaries on the Qur'ān in Classical Islam* (London: Routledge, 2006), 7–13.
99 For exoteric interpretations, see e.g. al-Qurṭubī, *al-Jāmiʿ*, 15:325 (Q 41.53), 10:24 (Q 15.29); Ibn Kathīr, *Tafsīr*, 1204 (Q 45.13), 726 (Q 15.29).
100 See al-Jīlī, *al-Insān*, 130–1; see also ibid., 121, 150.
101 See e.g. Sands, *Ṣūfī Commentaries*, 44, 173, note 77; A. Keeler, *Sufi Hermeneutics: The Qur'an Commentary of Rashīd al-dīn Maybudī* (Oxford: Oxford University Press, 2006), 188; Abū Zayd, *Hākadhā*, 97; Ibn ʿArabī, *Fuṣūṣ*, 49, 69, 216; al-Qāshānī, *Tafsīr*, 2:242 (Q 46.3).
102 See al-Jīlī, *al-Insān*, 182–3, 261. For the Qur'anic signification of the terms, see esp. Q 11.105-108.
103 See Lane, *Lexicon*, 1:1798.
104 I. Poonawala, EI[2], s.v. 'Taʾwīl'. See also C. Gilliot, *Encyclopaedia of the Qurʾān*, s.v. 'Exegesis of the Qurʾān: Classical and Medieval'; Chittick, *Sufi Path of Knowledge*, 199; Tahānawī, *Kashshāf*, 376–7.
105 See Poonawala, EI[2], s.v. 'Taʾwīl'; Böwering, 'The Scriptural "Senses"'; Sands, *Ṣūfī Commentaries*, 7–13; G. Hourani, *Averroes on the Harmony of Religion and Philosophy* (Oxford: E. J. W. Gibb Memorial Trust, 2015), 22–8.
106 See e.g. al-Jīlī, *al-Insān*, 11, 79–80.
107 See al-Jīlī, *al-Insān*, 11. For Ibn Taymiyyah's critique of the notion that the knowledge attained via *kashf* can accord with the revealed knowledge of the Qur'an, see Sands, *Ṣūfī Commentaries*, 53.
108 See Hourani, *Averroes*.

109 See Tustarī, *Tafsīr*, 76; A. Knysh, *Encyclopaedia of the Qur'ān*, s.v. 'Sufism and the Qur'ān'; Böwering, 'The Scriptural "Senses"', 351–2. As Böwering points out, there is a parallel here with the four senses of scripture identified in medieval Christian and Jewish biblical exegesis, for which see E. A. Synan, 'The Four "Senses" and Four Exegetes', *With Reverence for the Word: Medieval Scriptural Exegesis in Judaism, Christianity, and Islam*, ed. J. D. McAuliffe, B. Walfish and J. Goering (Oxford: Oxford University Press, 2003), 225–36.

110 See Goldziher, *Die Richtungen*, 215.

111 See Chittick, *Sufi Path of Knowledge*, 364.

112 Hujwīrī, *Kashf al-maḥjūb*, 16. The early mystic al-Ḥakīm Tirmidhī (d. 255/869), similarly, identifies three levels of knowledge: knowledge of God, knowledge of God's organization of the world (*tadbīr*) and knowledge of God's commandments (*aḥkām*). See Nwyia, *Exégèse*, 142–4.

113 See Ibn 'Arabī, *Futūḥāt*, 1:139–40. See also Abū Zayd, *Hākadhā*, 105–6, for another threefold scheme put forward by Ibn 'Arabī in this context, namely his discussion of the creeds of the masses (*'aqīdat al-'awāmm*), of the elect of the people of God (*khawāṣṣ ahl Allāh*), and of the 'quintessence of the elect' (*khulāṣat al-khawāṣṣ*).

114 Al-Qāshānī, *Tafsīr*, 1:118 (Q 3:7).

115 See Ahmed, *What Is Islam?*, 167–8, 368–72; Hourani, *Averroes*, 114, note 191; Hodgson, *Venture*, 2:325. For the elitist mindset of the Ibn 'Arabian Sufis, see al-Qūnawī's comment: 'Hereafter let not every man seek to learn from the writings of the Sheykh or from mine, for that gate is barred to the majority of mankind.' Kātib Çelebī, *Balance*, 82.

116 See Hourani, *Averroes*, esp. 32–6, for Ibn Rushd's elaboration of the idea that there are three methods of logic/reasoning, namely, demonstration (*burhān*) – the method of the philosophers; dialectic (*jadal*) – the method of the theologians; and poetry (*shi'r*) and/or rhetoric (*khiṭāb*) – the method employed by scripture to sway the common people – a scheme that is ultimately rooted in the thought of al-Fārābī.

117 See L. Strauss, *Persecution and the Art of Writing* (Clencoe, IL: Free Press, 1952), esp. 34–6.

118 Al-Jīlī, *al-Insān*, 122.

119 Hence, as he explains in chapters thirteen to fifteen of *al-Insān al-kāmil* (pp. 64–78), the spiritually advanced individual first receives the manifestations of the names, then the manifestations of the attributes, and finally becomes a locus of manifestation for the essence.

120 See also ibid., 11, where he uses the term *dalla* to express the relationship between the names and the divine essence; al-Jīlī, *Sharḥ*, 140: 'In the language of the elect, "the guides" (*al-adillah*) are the divine names and attributes.'

121 Ibid., 126.

122 See ibid., 96.

123 See ibid., 207.

124 Chittick, *Self-Disclosure*, 6. See also Abū Zayd, *Hākadhā*, 95, quoting Ibn 'Arabī's definition of *ahl Allāh* as 'those who know Him by way of the divine gift' (*al-'ārifīn bihi min ṭarīq al-wahb al-ilāhī*). On the synonymity of *ahl al-ḥaqq* and *ahl Allāh* in the lexicon of Ibn 'Arabī, see Chittick, *Sufi Path of Knowledge*, 400, note 3.

125 See Chittick, *Self-Disclosure*, 6; al-Jīlī, *al-Insān*, 90. For this hadith, see Ibn Mājah, *Sunan*, 1:206–7; Ibn Ḥanbal, *Musnad*, 3:160, 3:161, 3:306.

126 Al-Jīlī, *al-Insān*, 90.

127 As noted previously, this image of creation as the mirror for the divine names, with man as the 'polishing of that mirror', is famously used by Ibn 'Arabī at the beginning of the *Fuṣūṣ* (pp. 48–9).

128 This is a different way of expressing the idea, which we saw in the previous chapter, that God's names and attributes leave their 'trace' or 'effect' (*athar*, *rasm*, *ḥukm*) on creation, and most completely on the Perfect Human.

129 Al-Jīlī, *al-Insān*, 91.

130 In Qur'anic orthography, *al-Tawrāh* is usually written in such a way that it can be read as '*al-tawriyah*'.

131 See S. A. Bonekbakker, EI^2, s.v. 'Tawriya.'

132 See e.g. his interpretation of *kufr* in accordance with the association of the root *k-f-r* with 'covering up', in Ibn 'Arabī, *Fuṣūṣ*, 141.

133 See al-Qurṭubī, *Jāmi'*, 4:9 (Q 3.3).

134 See e.g. ibid.; al-Zamakhsharī, *al-Kashshāf*, 1:335 (Q 3.3); Adang, *Encyclopaedia of the Qur'ān*, s.v. 'Torah'.

135 Al-Jīlī, *al-Insān*, 122–3.

136 See e.g. al-Ṭabarī, *Tafsīr*, 4:588 (Q 5.44); al-Zamakhsharī, *al-Kashshāf*, 1:636 (Q 5.44).

137 The classical exegetes, by contrast, tend to interpret the 'light' in this phrase in terms of the clarification of religious laws. See e.g. al-Ṭabarī, *Tafsīr*, 4:588 (Q 5.44); al-Zamakhsharī, *al-Kashshāf*, 1:636 (Q 5.44).

138 See al-Jīlī, *al-Insān*, 58. This hadith is recorded in Muslim, *Ṣaḥīḥ*, 2:12. It is conventionally employed to indicate that the Prophet did not see God during the *mi'rāj*.

139 See al-Jīlī, *al-Insān*, 60–1.

140 See ibid., 96.

141 See al-Ḥakīm, *al-Mu'jam*, 1081–7.

142 See al-Jīlī, *al-Insān*, 120.

143 See J. Neusner, *Understanding Jewish Theology: Classical Issues and Modern Perspectives* (Binghamton University: Global Publications (Classics in Jewish Studies), 2001), 13; D. E. Shapiro, 'Foundations of the Halakhah', *Understanding Jewish Theology*, 111–12.

144 Al-Jīlī, *al-Insān*, 123.

145 See al-Qushayrī, *al-Risālah al-Qushayriyyah*, ed. K. Manṣūr. Beirut: Dār al-Kutub al-'ilmiyyah, 2001), 108–9; al-Ḥakīm, *al-Mu'jam*, 492–5, 662; al-Qāshānī, *Mu'jam*, 181, 323; Tahānawī, *Kashshāf*, 834.

146 See D. B. Macdonald, EI^2, s.v. 'Ilhām'; Massignon, *Essay*, 31; Nwyia, *Exégèse*, 34; Sands, *Ṣūfī Commentaries*, 86.

147 See al-Qāshānī, *Mu'jam*, 65, 96; Tahānawī, *Kashshāf*, 554; Keeler, *Sufi Hermeneutics*, 20; Todd, *Sufi Doctrine*, 138.

148 See al-Ḥakīm, *al-Mu'jam*, 1059–60; Chittick, *Imaginal Worlds*, 68–70.

149 See al-Ḥakīm, *al-Mu'jam*, 720–35; al-Qāshānī, *Mu'jam*, 85; Tahānawī, *Kashshāf*, 1133–34.

150 See Karamustafa, *Sufism*, 8; and H. Corbin, *Mundus Imaginalis, Or, The Imaginary and the Imaginal* (Dallas: Spring Publications, 1972), 1, for the analogous Persian mystical concept of *nā-kojā-ābād*, 'the land of nowhere'.

151 See D. Gimaret, EI^2, s.v. 'Al-Milal wa'l-niḥal'. Wilfred Cantwell Smith, who is known for problematizing the concept of 'religion', asks whether *millah* 'is not the only word in any language or culture that designates a specific and transferable religion, one as distinct from others, and nothing else.' W. C. Smith, *The Meaning and End of Religion* (Minneapolis: Fortress Press, 1991), 294.

152 See al-Jīlī, *al-Insān*, 252–5.
153 For the table of nations, see D. Sperber, *Encyclopaedia Judaica*, s.v. 'Nations, the Seventy'. In Arabic translations of the Bible, *umam* (a term that al-Jīlī uses interchangeably with *milal*) is most often used to translate *gōyīm*.
154 Recorded in Tirmidhī, *al-Jāmiʿ*, 5:29 (no. 2906).
155 See L. Gardet, *EI*², s.v. "Ālam'.
156 See al-Qayṣarī, *Sharḥ-i muqaddamah-ʾi Qayṣarī bar Fuṣūṣ al-ḥikam-i Muḥyī al-Dīn Ibn ʿArabī*, ed. J. Āshtiyānī (Mashhad: Kitābfurūshī-yi bāstān, 1966), 447–8.
157 See al-Jīlī, *al-Insān*, 214.
158 Interestingly, the corresponding Hebrew term *malkhūt* appears in the technical vocabulary of Kabbalah to denote the tenth and last of the divine emanations (*sefirōt*), while the Kabbalists also set out a hierarchy of (four) worlds (*ʿōlamīm*). See D. C. Matt (tr.), *Zohar: The Book of Enlightenment* (Mahwah, NJ: Paulist Press, 1983), 36; D. M. Horwitz, *A Kabbalah and Jewish Mysticism Reader* (Philadelphia: Jewish Publication Society, 2016), 273–94. Though it is possible that al-Jīlī was aware of Jewish mystical interpretations of the Torah, it seems more likely that his view of the contents of the Torah is based on his reading of the Qur'an through the prism of his Sufi metaphysics.
159 See e.g. Q 23.100 (*al-barzakh*), 2.85, 2.113, 2.174 etc. (*al-qiyāmah*), 6.31, 6.40, 7.187 etc. (*al-sāʿah*), 101.6-11 (*al-mīzān*), 2.202, 3.19, etc. (*al-ḥisāb*), 2.35, 2.82, 2.111 (*al-jannah*), 2.24, 2.39, 2.80-81, etc. (*al-nār*). See also J. I. Smith, *Encyclopaedia of the Qur'ān*, s.v. 'Eschatology'; R. Tottoli, *EI*³, s.v. 'Afterlife'.
160 See M. Sells, *Encyclopaedia of the Qur'ān*, s.v. 'Memory'.
161 See Gardet, *EI*², s.v. "Ālam'.
162 See D. B. Macdonald, EI2, s.v. 'Malā'ika'; G. Webb, *Encyclopaedia of the Qur'ān*, s.v. 'Angel'.
163 See al-Jīlī, *Sharḥ*, 71. The use of the term *sirr* to denote the 'innermost self' of man is common in Sufi literature (see e.g. Keeler, *Sufi Hermeneutics*, 66).
164 Al-Jīlī, *al-Insān*, 123.
165 See Radtke, *Encyclopaedia of the Qur'ān*, s.v. 'Wisdom'. This association was picked up by the post-Qur'anic tradition, for which see Khalidi, *Muslim Jesus*, 21.
166 See al-Jīlī, *al-Insān*, 125–6.
167 On this point, see Nettler, *Sufi Metaphysics*, 128.
168 See e.g. chapter forty-one of *al-Insān al-kāmil*, 'On Mt. Sinai (*al-ṭūr*)' (p. 137), where al-Jīlī interprets the crumbling of the mountain depicted in the Qur'an (Q 7.143) as an expression of the 'annihilation' (*fanā'*) and 'obliteration and pulverization' (*saḥq wa-maḥq*) of Moses' self (*nafs*) in God. See also al-Jīlī's description of his encounter with Moses in the sixth heaven in chapter sixty-one (p. 238), where he describes Moses as 'drunk on the wine of the manifestation of lordship (*sakrān min khamr tajallī al-rubūbiyyah*), bewildered by the might of divinity (*ḥayrān min ʿizzat al-ulūhiyyah*): the forms of beings had been imprinted on the mirror of his knowledge, and the lordship of the Judge, the King had become manifest on his I-ness (*tajallat fī iniyyatihi rubūbiyyat al-malik al-dayyān*)', images which al-Jīlī again links to Q 7.143.
169 Nwyia, *Exégèse*, 83. For examples, see G. C. Anawati and L. Gardet, *Mystique musulmane: aspects et tendances, expériences et techniques* (Paris: J Vrin, 1961), 261–71; Knysh, *Sufism*, 75; Keeler, *Sufi Hermeneutics*, 250; al-Qāshānī, *Tafsīr*, 1:264–5 (Q 7.142-143); Johns, 'Moses in the Qur'an', 129–33; Keeler, 'Moses from a Muslim Perspective', 60–3.

170 See e.g. E. R. Goodenough, *By Light, Light: The Mystic Gospel of Hellenistic Judaism* (Amsterdam: Philo Press, 1969), 199–234, esp. 212–18; M. Idel, *Kabbalah: New Perspectives* (New Haven and London: Yale University Press, 1990), 67–8, 72, 95, 209, 227–8; J. Kugel, *Traditions of the Bible: A Guide to the Bible as It Was at the Start of the Common Era* (Cambridge, MA and London: Harvard University Press, 1998), 544–6, 635; J. Barton, 'Moses from a Christian Perspective', *Abraham's Children*, 49–54, 49–50; Knysh, *Sufism*, 131.

171 See A. M. Goichon, *EI*[2], s.v. 'Ḥikma'; Lane, *Lexicon*, 1:617; Hourani, *Averroes*, 21.

172 See D. Pingree, *EI*[2], s.v. "Ilm al-hay'a'; F. J. Ragep, *EI*[3], s.v. 'Astronomy'; A. I. Sabra, *EI*[2], s.v. "Ilm al-Ḥisāb'; R. Kruk, *EI*[2], s.v. 'Nabāt'.

173 See e.g. Ibn 'Arabī, *Futūḥāt*, 2:175; Todd, *Sufi Doctrine*, 62, note 92. The term appears in earlier Sufi thought (see e.g. Massignon, *Essay*, 55, 124), and in the work of Ibn Sīnā (see Goichon, *Lexique*, 7) and his follower, the Illuminationst philosopher Suhrawardī al-Maqtūl (d. 587/1191) (see S. H. Nasr and O. Leaman, *History of Islamic Philosophy*, in two vols (London: Routledge, 1996), 1:645).

174 Y. T. Langermann, 'Yemenite Philosophical Midrash as a Source for the Intellectual History of the Jews of Yemen', in *The Jews of Medieval Islam: Community, Society, & Identity*, ed. D. Frank (Leiden, New York and Köln: Brill, 1995), 335–48, 339. More generally, the Hebrew cognate *ḥākhām* is one of the traditional designations for a rabbi (see Goodman, *History of Judaism*, 160).

175 See Lane, *Lexicon*, 1:1169.

176 Quoted in Massignon, *Essay*, 99.

177 For the renunciant aspect of al-Jīlī's thought, see e.g. al-Jīlī, *al-Insān*, 151. Note also that in his *Risālah arba'īn mawṭin* al-Jīlī identifies *zuhd* as the sixth of the forty stations (*mawāṭin*) of the Sufi path. See al-Jīlī, 'Die Risāla arba'īn mawāṭin des 'Abdalkarīm al-Ǧīlī', ed. D. Mann (PhD diss., Saarbrücken, 1970), 8–10.

178 Al-Jīlī, *al-Insān*, 123–4.

179 See ibid., 89–90.

180 See al-Ṭabarī, *The History of al-Ṭabarī*, volume III: *The Children of Israel*, tr. W. M. Brinner (Albany, NY: State University of New York Press, 1991), 3:46, note 237.

181 This hadith is recorded in al-Tirmidhī, *al-Jāmi'* 4:414 (no. 2682); Ibn Mājah, *Sunan*, 1:213 (no. 222); Abū Dāwūd, *Sunan Abī Dāwūd*, ed. M.'A. Khālidī (Beirut: Dār al-Kutub al-'ilmiyyah, 2001), 578 (no. 3641).

182 See Ibn 'Arabī, *Fuṣūṣ*, 135; al-Ḥakīm, *al-Mu'jam*, 1193–5; Chodkiewicz, *Ocean*, 47.

183 The Bible prohibits various kinds of magic. See e.g. Deut. 18.10-12, 18.9-14 (divination, fortune telling, sorcery, charms, necromancy); Lev. 19.31, 20.27, Isa. 8.19 (necromancy).

184 The repeated claim of the unbelievers in the Qur'an that the revelation given to Muhammad is merely 'evident magic' (*siḥr mubīn*) (see e.g. Q 5.110, 6.7, 10.76) is meant to constitute a belittlement of the revelation. For the strong condemnation of magic in the hadith, see T. Fahd, *EI*[2], s.v. 'Siḥr'.

185 See ibid.; Ikhwān al-ṣafā', *On Magic: An Arabic Critical Edition and English Translation of Epistle 52a*, ed. and tr. G. de Callataÿ and. B. Hallfants (Oxford: Oxford University Press, 2011); M. Noble, 'The Perfection of the Soul in Fakhr al-Dīn al-Rāzī's *Al-Sirr al-maktūm*' (PhD diss., University of London, 2017).

186 See Knysh, *Sufism*, 53–7.

187 For Ibn Khaldūn's attitude towards Ibn 'Arabī and his followers, see Ibn Khaldūn, *The Muqaddimah*, 3:87–9; Ibn Khaldūn, *Ibn Khaldūn on Sufism: Remedy for the Questioner in Search of Answers (Shifā' al-Sā'il li-Tahdhīb al-Masā'il)*, tr. Y. Ozer

(Cambridge: Islamic Texts Society, 2017), 60–2, 67–9; Knysh, *Ibn 'Arabi*, 184–96; J. Morris, 'An Arab Machiavelli? Rhetoric, Philosophy and Politics in Ibn Khaldun's Critique of Sufism', *Harvard Middle Eastern and Islamic Review* 8 (2009), 242–91; F. Morrissey and R. Nettler, 'Ibn Khaldūn on Sufism: A Story of Truth vs. Falsehood in Three Parts', *The Maghreb Review* 44, no. 4 (2019), 403–30.

188 See Ibn Khaldūn, *Muqaddimah*, 3:171–227.

189 See Ibn 'Arabī, *Futūḥāt*, 1-231-2:89; al-Ḥakīm, *al-Mu'jam*, 76–8, 320–2; Ebstein, *Mysticism and Philosophy*, 97–122.

190 See al-Jīlī, *al-Insān*, 33–6, 40–1, 114; al-Jīlī, *Marātib*, 89–107; Atlagh, 'Le point'.

191 See L. Gardet, *EI*², s.v. 'Karāma'.

192 Al-Jīlī, *al-Insān*, 72.

193 Ibid., 124.

194 Schacht, *EI*², s.v. 'Aḥkām'.

195 For this principle in Islamic thought and practice, see M. Cook, *Commanding Right and Forbidding Wrong in Islamic Thought* (Cambridge: Cambridge University Press, 2000).

196 Schacht, *EI*², s.v. 'Aḥkām'; G. H. A. Juynboll, *EI*², s.v. 'Farḍ'.

197 See A. Layish & R. Shaham, *EI*², s.v. 'Tashrī''.

198 See e.g. al-Ṭabarī, *Tafsīr*, 6:57–8 (Q 7.145); al-Zamakhsharī, *al-Kashshāf*, 2:157 (Q 7.145); al-Shahrastānī, *al-Milal wa-al-niḥal*, 2:231.

199 For this attitude, see e.g. al-Andalusī, *Kitâb tabaqât al-umam, ou, Livre des catégories des nations*, ed. L. Cheikho (Beirut: Imprimerie Catholique, 1912), 87: 'As for the eighth community, the Children of Israel, they are not known for the philosophical sciences. Rather, their concern was for the sciences of the religious law (*'ulūm al-sharī'ah*) and the lives of the prophets (*siyar al-anbiyâ'*)'.

200 Al-Jīlī, *al-Insān*, 265.

201 See e.g. al-Shahrastānī, *al-Milal wa-al-niḥal*, 2:235–6; Ibn Taymiyyah, *al-Jawāb al-ṣaḥīḥ*, 1:6–7,

202 Al-Jīlī, *al-Insān*, 124.

203 See G. R. Hawting, *Encyclopaedia of the Qur'ān*, s.v. 'Worship'.

204 See al-Qushayrī, *al-Risālah*, 232–5.

205 See Chittick, *Sufi Path of Knowledge*, 309ff., esp. 310–11.

206 See Anṣārī, *Manāzil al-sā'irīn ilá al-ḥaqq jalla sha'nuh*, ed. I. 'Awaḍ (Cairo: Maktabat Ja'far al-ḥadīthah, 1977), 22–9.

207 Al-Jīlī thus seems to propose that Moses advocated something like the theological doctrine of *irjā'*, the 'deferral' of the punishment of the sinner to the afterlife, for which see W. Madelung, *EI*², s.v. 'Murdji'a'.

208 On the principle of retaliation in Islamic law, see J. Schacht, *EI*², s.v. 'Ḳiṣāṣ'.

209 Al-Jīlī, *al-Insān*, 124–5.

210 See al-Jīlī, *al-Insān*, 182–3, 261.

211 See e.g. al-Nawawī, *An-Nawawi's Forty Hadith* [= *al-Arba'ūn al-Nawawiyyah*], tr. E. Ibrahim and D. Johnson-Davies (Cairo: Dār al-Shurūq, 2002), 36–7.

212 See S. M. N. al-Attas, 'The Meaning and Experience of Happiness in Islam', in *Consciousness and Reality: Studies in Memory of Toshihiko Izutsu*, ed. J. Āshtiyānī (Leiden: Brill, 1999), 59–78.

213 As we shall see, al-Jīlī uses the same term to denote the condemnation of the Christians to hell. See al-Jīlī, *al-Insān*, 129–30.

214 See Khalil, *Islam and the Fate of Others*, 13–14, and note 52, where Khalil lists those prominent medieval Muslim thinkers who present the soteriologically exclusivist

position – that non-Muslims will be damned – as *ijmāʿ*. Khalil's book, it should be noted, however, is primarily devoted to those equally prominent, if more original, medieval Muslim thinkers (al-Ghazālī, Ibn ʿArabī, Ibn Taymiyyah) who had a somewhat different take on this question.

215 Muslim, *Ṣaḥīḥ*, 1:160. The hadith is quoted by the traditional Sunni exegetes, e.g. al-Qurṭubī, *al-Jāmiʿ*, 9:19; Ibn Kathīr, *Tafsīr*, 655 (Q 11.17).

216 See al-Jīlī, *al-Insān*, 259. The link between *qurb* and *saʿādah* is also made by Ibn ʿArabī (see Chittick, *Sufi Path of Knowledge*, 151).

217 See al-Qushayrī, *al-Risālah*, 116–18.

218 See al-Jīlī, *al-Insān*, 263–5.

219 See e.g. al-Qurṭubī, *al-Jāmiʿ*, 17:225 (Q 57.27), where he explicitly makes the link between *ibtadaʿū* and *bidʿah*.

220 On *bidʿah* and *bidʿah* literature, see J. Robson, *EI*[2], s.v. 'Bidʿah'; V. Rispler, 'Toward a New Understanding of the Term *bidʿa*', *Der Islam* 68, no. 2 (1991), 320–8; M. Fierro, 'The Treatises against Innovations (*kutub al-bidaʿ*)', *Der Islam* 69, no. 2 (1992), 204–6.

221 On the etymology of this term and the way it was narrowly understood in medieval Islam to mean 'monasticism', see C. Sahner, 'The Monasticism of My Community Is Jihad: A Debate on Asceticism, Sex, and Warfare in Early Islam', *Arabica* 64 (2017), 149–83, 158.

222 Thus Ibn Kathīr (*Tafsīr*, 1302 [Q 57:27]) interprets the verse to mean, 'The community of the Christians (*ummat al-naṣārá*) invented it.' See also S. Sviri, '*Wa-rahbānīyatan ibtadaʿūhā*: An Analysis of Traditions Concerning the Origin and Evaluation of Christian Monasticism', *Jerusalem Studies in Arabic and Islam* 13 (1990), 195–208; C. Sahner, 'Islamic Legends about the Birth of Monasticism: A Case Study on the Late Antique Milieu of the Qur'ān and Tafsīr', in *The Late Antique World of Early Islam: Muslims Among Christians and Jews in the East Mediterranean*, ed. R. Hoyland (Princeton, NJ: Darwin Press, 2005), 393–435, for the way in which Muslim exegetes used Q 57.27 in support of their argument about the decadence of Christianity. Cf. Massignon, *Essay*, 98–104, arguing that the verse was originally understood as a positive affirmation of Christian monasticism.

223 See Sahner, 'The Monasticism of My Community', 153–6, for the sources in which this hadith appears. Massignon, *Essay*, 99, argues that this hadith is of comparatively late invention, but cf. the response of Nwyia, *Exégèse*, 52–6.

224 Quoted in Chittick, *Sufi Path of Knowledge*, 337.

225 Al-Jīlī, *al-Insān*, 43.

226 See Lipton, *Rethinking*, 101–17, esp. 112–13.

227 See Lazarus-Yafeh, *EI*[2], s.v. 'Taḥrīf'.

228 See Adang, *Muslim Writers*, 229; Ibn Kathīr, *Tafsīr*, 322 (Q 4:46); Ali, *Holy Qur-an*, 194, note 565.

229 See al-Jīlī, *al-Insān*, 129.

230 See Madelung, *EI*[2], s.v. "Iṣmah'.

231 See L. Gardet, *EI*[2], s.v. 'Al-Ḳaḍāʾ wa-l-Ḳadar'; D. V. Frolov, *Encyclopaedia of the Qurʾān*, s.v. 'Freedom and Predestination'.

232 See al-Jīlī, *al-Insān*, 131, where he quotes Q 2:26 when making a similar point about the Christians' errors.

233 See e.g. Ibn Kathīr, *Tafsīr*, 28 (Q 1:7): 'He [i.e. God] was the one who led them [i.e. *al-ḍāllīn*, the Christians] into error (*aḍallahum*) with His decree (*bi-qadarihi*).'

234 See Saleh, 'Hebrew Bible', 410.

235 See al-Jīlī, *al-Insān*, 259–60.

236 See Lazarus-Yafeh, *Intertwined Worlds*, 76; Saleh, 'The Psalms', 289.

237 See D. Vishanoff, 'An Imagined Book Gets a New Text: Psalms of the Muslim David', *Islam and Christian-Muslim Relations* 22, no. 1 (2011), 85–99, for this idea in relation to Muslim views of the Psalms.

238 See Goldziher, *Die Richtungen*, 180–3; Sands, *Ṣūfī Commentaries*, 1. I do not presume to comment – as Goldziher or 'Afīfī do (see 'Afīfī, *Mystical Philosophy*, 192) – on the authenticity of the Sufi reading of scripture, that is, on whether it is 'genuine' exegesis or 'mere' eisegesis; I only note the tendency, in al-Jīlī's thought, to find his ideas in the scriptures.

Chapter 5

1 Saleh, 'The Psalms', 281–96, 281.

2 See e.g. al-Ya'qūbī, *Ibn-Wādhih qui dicitur al-Ja'qubī Historiae* [= *Tārīkh*], in two vols, ed. M. Th. Houtsma (Leiden: Brill, 1883), 1:57–9; al-Mas'ūdī, *Les prairies d'or*, in nine vols, ed. C. B. de Maynard and A. P. de Courteille (Paris: Imprimerie impériale, 1861–1917), 1:108–9; al-Qurṭubī, *al-Jāmi'*, 6:18 (Q 4.163); Schmidtke, 'Muslim Reception', 255–6; Adang, *Muslim Writers*, 155, 161; Vishanoff, 'An Imagined Book'; L. Cheikho, 'Quelques légendes islamiques apocryphes', *Mélanges de la Faculté Orientale, Université Saint-Joseph* 4 (1910), 5–56.

3 Saleh, 'The Psalms', 290–1. On al-Biqā'ī more generally, see W. Saleh, 'A Fifteenth-Century Muslim Hebraist: Al-Biqā'ī and His Defense of Using the Bible to Interpret the Qur'ān', *Speculum* 83, no. 3 (2008), 629–54.

4 See e.g. al-Ṭabarī, *Tafsīr*, 8:94 (Q 17:55); al-Qurṭubī, *al-Jāmi'*, 10:242 (Q 17.55), 6:18 (Q 4.163); Ibn Rabban, *Kitāb al-Dīn wa-al-dawlah*, ed. 'A. Nuwayhaḍ (Beirut: Dār al-āfāq al-jadīdah, 1973), 101; al-Mas'ūdī, *Les prairies*, 1:108–9.

5 Vishanoff, 'An Imagined Book'.

6 On medieval Muslims' knowledge of and interest in the Bible (or lack thereof), see N. Roth, 'Muslim Knowledge of the Hebrew Bible and Jewish Traditions in the Middle Ages', *The Maghreb Review* 16 (1991), 74–83; Saleh, 'The Psalms', 9; Griffith, *The Bible*, 175–203. A fragment of an eighth-century Arabic translation of the Psalms produced by a Christian in Syria is 'the oldest known specimen of Christian-Arabic literature' (Horovitz [Firestone], *EI*^{2}, s.v. 'Zabūr'), but it seems unlikely that this text was circulated among Muslims.

7 Al-Jīlī, *al-Insān*, 125.

8 See e.g. al-Ṭabarī, *Tafsīr*, 4:367 (Q 4.163), 21:105; al-Qurṭubī, *al-Jāmi'*, 6:18 (Q 4.163); 11:305 (Q 21.105).

9 A. Jeffrey, *The Foreign Vocabulary of the Qur'an* (Baroda: Oriental Institute, 1929), 5.

10 Ibid., 10. See e.g. al-Qurṭubī, *al-Jāmi'*, 1:104–5.

11 See al-Jandī, *Sharḥ*, 30–1.

12 Jeffrey, *Foreign Vocabulary*, 10.

13 A. Rippin, 'Syriac in the Qur'an: Classical Muslim Ideas', in *The Qur'an in Its Historical Context*, ed. G. S. Reynolds (London and New York: Routledge, 2008), 249–61.

14 Jeffrey, *Foreign Vocabulary*, 19–20.

15 Ibid.

16 Ibid., 23.

17 Having said that, it does seem that the term does in fact have a Syriac connection: Jeffery (Ibid., 148–9) thinks it is a corruption of the Hebrew *mizmōr* via the Syriac *mizmūr*.
18 Rippin, 'Syriac', 256.
19 Al-Mas'ūdī, *Les prairies*, 1:108–9.
20 Lane, *Lexicon*, 1:1216.
21 Al-Jīlī, *al-Insān*, 125.
22 Al-Zamakhsharī, *al-Kashshāf*, 336 (Q 3.3).
23 On this *ḥadīth*, which is not found in any of the six canonical books but does appear in later collections, see Cornell, *Realm of the Saint*, 344, note 55.
24 Al-Jīlī, *al-Insān*, 116.
25 Al-Mas'ūdī, *Les prairies*, 1:108–9; al-Qurṭubī, *al-Jāmi'*, 6:18 (Q 4.163); cf. the convert 'Abd Allāh Ibn Salām's (d. 43/663) reference to 150 *mazmūr*, using a cognate of the Hebrew term for 'psalm', *mizmōr*, in Cheikho, 'Quelques légendes', 41.
26 Al-Jīlī, *al-Insān*, 119.
27 Ibid., 120, 129, 130, 131.
28 Ibid., 131.
29 Ibid., 255.
30 Ibid.
31 This view fits with the traditional rabbinic view of the Mosaic Torah and the Davidic Psalms as 'the two essential poles of ancient Israel's faith: the word of God from on high and Israel's response in prayer, praise, and instruction.' W. P. Brown, 'The Psalms: An Overview', *The Oxford Handbook of the Psalms*, 1–24, 3.
32 Al-Jīlī, *al-Insān*, 125.
33 See Lane, *Lexicon*, 1:1600–2.
34 Al-Tirmidhī's (d. 279/892) famous collection of hadiths on the qualities of Muhammad, for instance, is known simply as *al-Shamā'il*.
35 See e.g. al-Ṭabarī, *Annales quos scripsit Abu Djafar Mohammed ibn Djarir at-Tabari: Tārīkh al-rusul wa-al-mulūk* [= *Tārīkh*], in fifteen volumes, ed. M. J. de Goeje et al. (Leiden: Brill, 1879-1901), 1:476; al-Ṭabarī, *Children of Israel*, 140; al-Tha'labī, *'Arā'is*, 462.
36 See e.g. al-Ṭabarī, *Tārīkh*, 1:478; al-Ṭabarī, *Children of Israel*, 143; al-Ya'qūbī, *Tārīkh*, 57; al-Tha'labī, *'Arā'is*, 462; Ibn Kathīr, *Qiṣaṣ al-anbiyā'*, ed. M. al-Fāḍilī (Beirut: al-Maktabah al-'Aṣriyyah, 2015), 327–8; Hujwīrī, *Kashf al-maḥjūb*, 402–3; Rūmī, *The Mathnawí*, 2:v. 1074, 3:v. 1014, 3:vv. 1470–3, 3:v. 2832, 3:vv. 4268–70; Maybudī, *The Unveiling of the Mysteries and the Provision of the Pious: Kashf al-asrār wa-'uddat al-abrār*, tr. W. Chittick (Louisville, KY: Fons Vitae, 2015), 435–6 (Q 39.33).
37 Al-Ṭabarī, *Tārīkh*, 1:478; al-Ṭabarī, *Children of Israel*, 143.
38 Ibn Kathīr, *Qiṣaṣ al-anbiyā'*, 327.
39 For Wahb, see R. G. Khoury, *Wahb b. Munnabih* (Weisbaden: O. Hassarrowitz, 1972).
40 Al-Ṭabarī, *Tafsīr*, 10:561 (Q 38.17). Cf. al-Ṭabarī, *Tārīkh*, 1:479. Ibn 'Arabī (*Fuṣūṣ*, 161) also notes that 'God gave him [i.e. David] strength (*quwwah*) and ascribed him with this attribute'.
41 P. Crone and M. Hinds, *God's Caliph: Religious Authority in the First Centuries of Islam* (Cambridge: Cambridge University Press, 2003), 44; al-Ṭabarī, *Children of Israel*, 145–6, 152–3; al-Tha'labī, *'Arā'is*, 471–2, 485–6; Lindsay, "Ali ibn 'Asakir', 69–70; Rūmī, *Mathnawí*, 3: vv. 2308–2503; Ibn Kathīr, *Qiṣaṣ al-anbiyā'*, 329.
42 In Sufi literature, particularly in the Persian tradition, David is also often presented as a mystical figure. See e.g. Maybudī, *Unveiling*, 75 (Q 2.223), 210 (Q 7.159), 221–2 (Q 8.24), 371 (Q 27.15); 'Aṭṭār, *Dīvān-i ghazaliyyāt va-qaṣāyid-i 'Aṭṭār*, ed. T. Tafaḍḍolī

(Tehran: Intishārāt-i Anjuman-i āthār-i millī, 1962), 692, *qaṣidah* 11, v. 10214; Rūmī, *Mathnawí*, 2: v. 493.

43 Al-Jīlī, *al-Insān*, 125.

44 See Ibn ʿArabī, *Fuṣūṣ*, 57–8 and *passim*. For the meaning of *ḥikmah* in Ibn ʿArabī's writings, see Rosenthal, 'Ibn ʿArabī', 13–14.

45 See Ibn ʿArabī, *Fuṣūṣ*, 214–26.

46 Al-Ṭabarī, *Tafsīr al-Ṭabarī: Jāmiʿ al-bayān ʿan taʾwīl āy al-Qurʾān*, in twenty-five volumes, ed. ʿA. al-Turkī (Cairo: Dār al-Hijr, 2001), 2:403 (Q 2.106). See also al-Qurṭubī, *al-Jāmiʿ*, 1:113–16, warning against weak hadiths on the subject.

47 See e.g. the hadiths quoted by Ibn Kathīr (*Tafsīr*, 15–16) in his exposition of 'the excellence (*faḍl*) of the *Fātiḥah*'.

48 See W. A. Graham, *Encyclopaedia of the Qurʾan*, s.v. 'Fātiḥa'.

49 Al-Jīlī, *al-Insān*, 125–6.

50 See al-Yaʿqūbī, *Tārīkh*, 57–9; Schmidtke, 'Muslim Reception', 255–6; Adang, *Muslim Writers*, 161.

51 Al-Ṭabarī, *Tafsīr*, 8:94 (Q 17.55); al-Qurṭubī, *al-Jāmiʿ*, 10:242 (Q 17.55), 6:18 (Q 4.163); Ibn Rabban, *Kitāb al-Dīn wa-al-dawlah*, 101; al-Masʿūdī, *Les prairies*, 1:108–9.

52 See al-Jīlī, *Marātib*, 9–14.

53 See al-Ḥakīm, *al-Muʿjam*, 1133; Nettler, *Sufi Metaphysics*, 9, and the references cited there.

54 See al-Jīlī, *Marātib*, 17–18; al-Jīlī, *al-Insān*, 5, 68, 113.

55 See Izutsu, *Sufism and Taoism*, 182–6.

56 See al-Tahānawī, *Kashshāf*, 402.

57 See Izutsu, *Sufism and Taoism*, 225. See also the title of Ibn ʿArabī's work *al-Tadbīrāt al-ilāhiyyah fi iṣlāḥ al-mamlakah al-insāniyyah*.

58 See e.g. al-Jīlī, *al-Insān*, 90, 115, 119; al-Jīlī, *Sharḥ*, 118, 253.

59 See al-Ḥakīm, *al-Muʿjam*, 353–6; al-Tahānawī, *Kashshāf*, 684–8.

60 See e.g. al-Jīlī, *al-Insān*, 211, where he explains that the Perfect Human is a microcosm of 'all the existential realities' (*jamīʿ al-ḥaqāʾiq al-wujūdiyyah*), which seems to mean everything that exists.

61 For Ibn ʿArabī's use of the terms, see Chittick, *Sufi Path of Knowledge*, 91–4; Izutsu, *Sufism and Taoism*, 33–5, 155, 159. For al-Jīlī's, see al-Jīlī, *al-Insān*, 151–2; 192; al-Jīlī, *Marātib*, 10.

62 See R. Wisnovsky, *Aspects of Avicenna* (Princeton, NJ: Markus Wiener, 2001), 116; Goichon, *Lexique*, 211–12.

63 See Ibn ʿArabī, *Fuṣūṣ*, 49, 59–60; Izutsu, *Sufism and Taoism*, 175.

64 See Ibn Khaldūn, *The Muqaddimah*, 3:111.

65 P. Lettinck, *EI*[2], s.v. 'Ṭabīʿiyyāt'. See also Ibn Khaldūn, *The Muqaddimah*, 3:147.

66 See e.g. al-Jīlī, *al-Insān*, 152, 256.

67 See Ibn Khaldūn, *The Muqaddimah*, 3:111–12.

68 Ibid., 111–12, 118–36. See also R. Rashed, *EI*[2], s.v. 'Riyāḍiyyāt'.

69 Aside from Ibn Khaldūn, the most prominent advocate of this idea was the great philosopher and musical theorist al-Fārābī. See T.-A. Druart, *Stanford Encyclopaedia of Islam*, s.v. 'al-Farabi: 4. Mathematics and Music'.

70 See Ibn Khaldūn, *The Muqaddimah*, 3:111.

71 See Ibid., 137ff.; K. El-Rouayheb, *Relational Syllogisms and the History of Arabic Logic, 900-1900* (Leiden: Brill, 2010), chapters one and two; A. Shihadeh, 'From al-Ghazālī to al-Rāzī: 6th/12th Century Developments in Muslim Philosophical Theology', *Arabic Sciences and Philosophy* 15, no. 1 (2005), 141–79, 168. R. Arnaldez,

EI[2], s.v. 'Manṭiḳ'; T. Street, *Stanford Encyclopaedia of Philosophy*, s.v. 'Arabic and Islamic Philosophy of Language and Logic'.

72 See Crone and Hinds, *God's Caliph*.

73 See Ibn 'Arabī, *Fuṣūṣ*, 48–55, 160–6.

74 Al-Jīlī, *al-Insān*, 211; Y. Ziedan, *al-Fikr al-ṣūfī 'ind 'Abd al-Karīm al-Jīlī* (Cairo: Dār al-Amīn, 1998), 108, for al-Jīlī's statement in *al-Kahf wa-al-raqīm* that the Perfect Human is the *khalīfah* referred to in Q 2.30.

75 Al-Jīlī, *al-Insān*, 162.

76 See Ahmed, *What Is Islam?*, 15–17.

77 Al-Jandī, *Sharḥ*, 66.

78 See T. F. Glick, S. J. Livesey and F. Wallis (eds), *Medieval Science: Technology, and Medicine: An Encyclopaedia* (Abingdon: Routledge, 2005), s.v. 'Physiognomy', 399–401.

79 See T. Fahd, *EI*[2], s.v. 'Firāsah'. For al-Rāzī's treatise, see Y. Mourad, 'La physiognomie arabe et le Kitāb al-firāsa de Fakhr al-Dīn al-Rāzī' (PhD diss., University of Paris, 1939); M. Viguera, *Dos cartillas de fisiognómica* (Madrid: Nacionel, 1977), 73–140.

80 Al-Tahānawī, *Kashshāf*, 1265. See also Ibn Khaldūn, *The Muqaddimah*, 1:222–3; Nwyia, *Exégèse*, 296–7.

81 See al-Ḥakīm, *al-Mu'jam*, 880; Rosenthal, 'Ibn 'Arabī', 20, note 87; Viguera, *Dos cartillas*, 27–70.

82 Al-Jīlī, *al-Insān*, 126.

83 On David's (and Solomon's) knowledge of the speech of the birds, see Q 27.16; S. Tlili, *Animals in the Qur'an* (Cambridge: Cambridge University Press, 2012), 177–81. On his piety, see Q 38.17; al-Ṭabarī, *Tārīkh*, 1:478; al-Ṭabarī, *Children of Israel*, 143; Lindsay, "Ali ibn 'Asakir', 64–8; Ibn Kathīr, *Qiṣaṣ al-anbiyā'*, 333.

84 Al-Ṭabarī, *Tārīkh*, 1:487; al-Ṭabarī, *Children of Israel*, 143.

85 Ibn Kathīr, *Qiṣaṣ al-anbiyā'*, 331.

86 See e.g. Maybudī, *Unveiling*, 34 (Q 2.77), 89 (Q 2.257), 148 (Q 4.103), 258 (Q 12.84).

87 See e.g. al-Ṭabarī, *Tārīkh*, 1:478; al-Ṭabarī, *Children of Israel*, 143; Ibn Kathīr, *Qiṣaṣ al-anbiyā'*, 327.

88 Al-Qurṭubī, *al-Jāmi'*, 13:151 (Q 27.16).

89 See al-Qushayrī, *al-Risālah*, 92–3.

90 For Ibn 'Arabī's use of the term in the same way, see al-Ḥakīm, *al-Mu'jam*, 641.

91 See e.g. al-Jīlī, *al-Insān*, 12; al-Jīlī, *Ibdā'*, 40.

92 A similar idea is found in the Persian Sufi Rūzbihān Baqlī's (d. 606/1209) commentary on Q 27.16. See R. Baqlī, *'Arā'is al-bayān fī ḥaqā'iq al-Qur'ān* (Q 27.16).

93 Al-Jīlī, *al-Insān*, 126.

94 See Ibn 'Arabī, *Fuṣūṣ*, 162.

95 See al-Jīlī, *al-Insān*, 153, 210.

96 See ibid., 91.

97 See al-Ḥakīm, *al-Mu'jam*, 876–78, 909–11; al-Tahānawī, *Kashshāf*, 1327–30; Chodkiewicz, *Seal*, 89–98.

98 See al-Jīlī, *al-Insān*, 162, 211.

99 See also Ibn 'Arabī, *Fuṣūṣ*, 162–3, where he appears to associate the term *khalā'if* with the prophets and *awliyā'*.

100 This distinction is in fact made explicitly in al-Tahānawī, *Kashshāf*, 757, who may be drawing directly upon al-Jīlī (as he does elsewhere in his lexicon).

101 See al-Jīlī, *Sharḥ*, 200; see also Ibid., 152–3. For Ibn 'Arabī's use of *taṣarruf* in the same way, see al-Ḥākim, *al-Mu'jam*, 694.

102 See al-Jīlī, *al-Insān*, 72.
103 For al-Jīlī's conception of *himmah* as the divine light placed in man by God, see ibid., 170–3 (chapter 55).
104 *Taḥaddī*, which literally means 'challenging', ordinarily in Islamic thought denotes the prophet's public announcement of his prophethood, the idea being that the prophet gives advance warning of the miracle that he will produce – in Muhammad's case, the Qur'an – and 'challenges' his opponents to produce something like it. See Ibn Khaldūn, *The Muqaddimah*, 1:188–9; al-Ījī, *al-Mawāqif*, 349. In Ash'arite theology, it is this challenge that distinguishes a prophetic miracle (*mu'jizah*) from a non-prophetic miracle (*karāmah*). See S. Schmidtke, *The Theology of al-'Allāma al-Ḥillī (d. 726/1325)* (Berlin: Klaus Schwarz Verlag, 1991), 149, note 48. The Qur'an itself is said to contain five '*taḥaddī*-verses': Q 2.23, 10.38, 11.13; 17.88; and 52.34. See Wild, 'We have sent down to thee', 138, note 7.
105 See in this regard Ibn Khaldūn, *The Muqaddimah*, 1:391–2, 422; Ibn Taymiyyah, *Majmū' al-fatāwá*, 11:180–2.
106 It should be noted that Ibn 'Arabī suggests that the *rāshidūn* caliphs, as well as Mu'āwiyah, Ḥasan. b. 'Alī, 'Umar II, and al-Mutawakkil also combined the spiritual viceregency with political rule (see Chodkiewicz, *Seal*, 95). Al-Jīlī, however, makes no reference to this.
107 Al-Jīlī, *al-Insān*, 126–7.
108 See ibid., 126, note 2.
109 Ibn 'Arabī, *Fuṣūṣ*, 152.
110 Al-Jīlī, *al-Insān*, 127.
111 It is often contrasted as well with '*ibārah*, 'clear expression'. See Nwyia, *EI*[2], s.v. '*Ishārah*'; Nwyia, *Exégèse*, 431, s.v. 'išāra'.
112 Nwyia, *EI*[2], s.v. '*Ishārah*'.
113 Gimaret, *EI*[2], *s.v.* 'Ṣifa'.
114 Ibid.
115 L. Gardet, *EI*[2], s.v. 'Fi'l'.
116 See al-Jīlī, *al-Insān*, 53.
117 See also al-Jīlī, *Marātib*, 25–6.
118 See al-Jīlī, *al-Insān*, 53.
119 See al-Jīlī, *al-Insān*, 53–4, where he tells us that the divine name *al-malik* appears at the level of *al-rubūbiyyah*, the sixth level, and al-Jīlī, *Marātib*, 22, where *malikiyyah* constitutes the seventh level, coming after *al-rubūbiyyah*.
120 Al-Jīlī, *al-Insān*, 113.
121 See e.g. Ibn Kathīr, *Qiṣaṣ al-anbiyā'*, 327; Lindsay, "Ali ibn 'Asakir', 59. Note also Ibn 'Arabī's (*Fuṣūṣ*, 166) spiritual interpretation of this motif.
122 Al-Jīlī, *al-Insān*, 116.
123 Ibid., 127.
124 For Ibn 'Arabī, as we have seen, *warāthah* is similarly connected to *walāyah*, following the hadith, 'The knowers (*al-'ulamā'*) are the heirs of the prophets (*warathat al-anbiyā'*).'
125 See P. Soucek, *Encyclopaedia of the Qur'ān*, s.v. 'Solomon'. For Ibn 'Arabī's treatment of the reasons behind David's failure to build the temple, see R. Nettler, 'Ibn 'Arabi's Gloss on the Prophet Yunus: Sufism and the Continuity of a Common Religious Culture', *The Religion of the Other: Essays in Honour of Mohamed Talbi*, ed. M. Ben-Madani (London: Maghreb Publications, 2013), 53–60, 57. Crone and Hinds (*God's Caliph*, 21–2, note 86), however, note that, in medieval Sunni thought, it was held

that only David (and, perhaps, the other prophets) should be referred to as *khalīfat Allāh*, an idea that is perhaps in the background here.

126 Al-Jīlī, *al-Insān*, 127–8.
127 See al-Jīlī, *al-Insān*, 97–8.
128 See Saleh, 'The Psalms', 281–4.
129 Al-Jīlī, *al-Insān*, 128.
130 Compare Ibn 'Arabī's use of this verse to warn against conceptualizing God in accordance with one's own self (see Chittick, *Sufi Path of Knowledge*, 337). It is a reflection of al-Jīlī's and Ibn 'Arabī's creative approach to the Qur'an that this verse in fact seems to refer to the unbelievers who reject the truth of divine revelation. For the more conventional interpretation, see e.g. Ibn Kathīr, *Tafsīr*, 474 (Q 6.91).
131 Again, Ibn 'Arabī uses the verse in a similar way, connecting it to *tanzīh* (see Chittick, *Sufi Path of Knowledge*, 75, 376).
132 Thus '*al-'ajz 'an dark al-idrāk idrāk*' is the last of the hundred and one *manāẓir* set out in *al-Manāẓir al-ilāhiyyah*. Al-Jīlī also quotes the saying on several occasions in *al-Insān al-kāmil* (19, 32, 105), and even composed a poem explaining its meaning. The saying is also often used by earlier Sufi thinkers, including al-Sarrāj (see al-Sarrāj, *al-Luma'*, 36), al-Ghazālī (see P. L. Heck, *Skepticism in Classical Islam: Moments of Confusion* (London: Routledge, 2014), 111) and Ibn 'Arabī (see Ibid., 54; Chittick, *Self-Disclosure*, 55, 64, 84, 191).
133 See P. Hadot, *What Is Ancient Philosophy?*, tr. M. Chase (Cambridge, MA and London: The Belknap Press of Harvard University Press, 2002), 25.
134 Al-Jīlī, *al-Insān*, 128.
135 These friends of God are 'Muhammadan' in two possible ways: first and most obviously, in their being Muslims (al-Jīlī sometimes uses *al-muḥammadiyyūn* and *al-muslimūn* interchangeably), and second, from an Ibn 'Arabian Sufi metaphysical perspective, in their being forms for the manifestation of the Muhammadan Reality. For Ibn 'Arabī's use of the term in this latter way, see Chittick, *Sufi Path of Knowledge*, 376.
136 See e.g. al-Jīlī, *al-Insān*, 203; al-Jīlī, *al-Manāẓir al-ilāhiyyah*, 164–5.
137 The saying is found in Ibn 'Arabī, *Futūḥāt*, 14:422–3.
138 For 'Abd al-Qādir's appearance in the writings of Ibn 'Arabī, see B. Abrahamov, *Ibn al-'Arabi and the Sufis* (Oxford: Anqa Publishing, 2014), 151–6.
139 Knysh, *Ibn 'Arabi*, 236.
140 See ibid.
141 See Goldziher, *Die Richtungen*, 217, who suggests that Ibn 'Arabī may have taken the motif from the *Iḥyā'* of al-Ghazālī.
142 See Y. Ziedan, *'Abd al-Karīm al-Jīlī: faylasūf al-ṣūfiyyah* (Cairo: al-Hay'ah al-Miṣriyyah 'āmmah li-l-kitāb, 1988), 47; Ziedan, *al-Fikr*, 45–6; al-Jīlī, *Ibdā'*, 36.
143 See al-Jīlī, *al-Insān*, 265–6.
144 See Chittick, *Sufi Path of Knowledge*, 258; Ibn 'Arabī, *Fuṣūṣ*, 134–5.
145 See al-Jīlī, *al-Insān*, 266.

Chapter 6

1 See Ali, *Holy Qur-an*, 286–7; McAuliffe, *Qur'anic Christians*, 180–1; Griffith, *Encyclopaedia of the Qur'ān*, s.v. 'Gospel'. Certain medieval Muslim scholars do

demonstrate knowledge of the contents of different books of the New Testament, including the four gospels. See de Vaux [Anawati], *EI*², s.v. 'Indjīl'; Stern, "Abd al-Jabbār's account', 137; al-Shahrastānī, *al-Milal wa-al-niḥal*, 2:246–7; Ibn Ḥazm, *al-Faṣl*, 2:2–3; Ṭūfī, *Muslim Exegesis*. The point, however, is that they do not view these 'gospels' as one and the same as the Gospel revealed to Jesus.

2 See Lazarus-Yafeh, *EI*², s.v. 'Taḥrīf'; Lazarus-Yafeh, *Intertwined Worlds*, 19–35; Adang, *Muslim Writers*, 223–48; Reynolds, 'On the Qur'anic Accusation', 184; McAuliffe, *Qur'anic Christians*, 111; and see McAuliffe, *Qur'anic Christians*, 168, note 42 for an overview of the other secondary literature.

3 See Khalidi, *Muslim Jesus*, 12–13; G. S. Reynolds, 'The Islamic Christ', *The Oxford Handbook of Christology*, ed. F. A. Murphy (Oxford: Oxford University Press, 2015), 183–98, 187–8.

4 See e.g. al-Warrāq, *Anti-Christian Polemic*; al-Warrāq, *Early Muslim Polemic*; Stern, "Abd al-Jabbār's Account'; Siddiqui, *Christians, Muslims, & Jesus*, 60–113.

5 On the titles of Jesus in the Qur'an and the Islamic tradition, see Parrinder, *Jesus in the Qur'an*, 16–54.

6 See Khalidi, *Muslim Jesus*, 12.

7 Al-Jīlī, *al-Insān*, 128.

8 Griffith, *Encyclopaedia of the Qur'ān*, s.v. 'Gospel'. See e.g. Stern, "Abd al-Jabbār's account', 135–6.

9 See e.g. al-Baghawī, *Tafsīr al-Baghawī: Ma'ālim al-tanzīl*, ed. M. al-Nimr, 'U. al-Ḍamīriyyah and S. al-Harsh, in eight volumes (Riyadh: Dār al-Ṭayyibah, 1989), 2:6 (Q 3.3): '*Al-Tawrāh* in Hebrew is *tūr*, which means "the law" (*al-sharī'ah*), and *al-injīl* in Syriac (*bi-al-sūriyāniyyah*) means "the crown" (*al-iklīl*)', which might imply that the original language of the Gospel was Syriac.

10 See Jāmī, *Precious Pearl*, 60.

11 See Welch, Paret, and Pearson, *EI*², s.v. 'Al-Ḳur'ān'; McAuliffe, 'Prediction and Prefiguration', 108.

12 Quoted in Adang, *Muslim Writers*, 170. See also Ibn Khaldūn, *The Muqaddimah*, 1:192–3.

13 Stern, "Abd al-Jabbār's Account', 136.

14 S. Stern, 'Quotations from Apocryphal Gospels in 'Abd al-Jabbār', *Journal of Theological Studies* 18 (1957), 34–57, 48.

15 See al-Jīlī, *al-Insān*, 260–1.

16 Ibid., 129.

17 This passage is quoted in full in Kātib Çelebī (Ḥājjī Khalīfah), *Kashf 'an asāmi al-kutub wa-al-funūn* [*Lexicon bibliographicum et encyclopædicum a Mustafa Ben Abdallah Katib Jelebi dicto et nomine Haji Khalfa celebrato compositum: ad codicum vindobonensium, parisiensium et berolinensis, fidem primum*], in seven vols, ed. G. Flugel (Leipzig: The Oriental Translation Fund for Great Britain and Ireland, 1835–1858), 1:452–3, in the section on *al-Injīl*, an indication of the influence of al-Jīlī's conception of the Gospel in later Islamic thought, as well of the centrality of this passage within al-Jīlī's treatment of the Gospel. For Kātib Çelebī's Qur'an-centred view of sacred history, including his insistence on the superiority of Muhammad over the other prophets, see Kātib Çelebī, *Balance*, 110–23, esp. 120.

18 He presents us with the same conception of the Trinity in the chapter on the Torah (see al-Jīlī, *al-Insān*, 120).

19 An earlier generation of scholars proposed that the Qur'an is here engaging with the Trinitarian doctrine of a heretical Christian sect (see Nicholson, *Studies*, 139), but

more recent scholars have rather seen in the reference to Jesus' mother a warning against the excessive veneration of Mary in the eastern Churches. See Ali, *Holy Qur-an*, 280, note 829; D. Thomas, *Encyclopaedia of the Qur'ān*, s.v. 'Trinity'.

20 Ibn Taymiyyah, *al-Jawāb al-ṣaḥīḥ*, 3:193.

21 Al-Baghawī, *Tafsīr*, 3:82 (Q 5.72).

22 See e.g. Stern, "Abd al-Jabbār's Account', 137; al-Shahrastānī, *al-Milal wa-al-niḥal*, 2:246–7; Rūmī, *The Mathnawí*, 7:35–6.

23 Ibid., 4:38 (Q 9:30). Sometime after al-Jīlī, meanwhile, Nūr al-Dīn al-Rānīrī (d. 1658) would refer in his critique of the Ibn 'Arabian Sufi metaphysics of Ḥamzah Fanṣūrī to the Christians' Trinity of Father, Mother, and Son. See Al-Attas, *Mysticism*, 70–1.

24 For the biblical roots of this formula, see Mt. 1.18-25; Lk. 1.26-38.

25 Ibn 'Arabī, *Fuṣūṣ*, 138–9.

26 See also a verse in the *Futūḥāt* (quoted in al-Ḥakīm, *al-Mu'jam*, 217), in which Ibn 'Arabī calls Jesus 'the son of the Spirit' (*ibn al-rūḥ*), which again suggests that the Spirit is Jesus' father.

27 On this phrase, see Griffith, *Encyclopaedia of the Qur'ān*, s.v. 'Christians and Christianity'.

28 See al-Jīlī, *al-Insān*, 121. See also in this regard the comments of al-Ḥakīm (al-Jīlī, *Ibdā'*, 37) on al-Jīlī's idea of esoteric scriptural interpretation (*ta'wīl*), which, she says, rests upon 'the necessity of the recipient [of scripture] not limiting himself to the apparent meaning of the terms (*allā yaqtaṣir al-mutalaqqī 'alá ẓāhir al-alfāẓ*), but rather passing beyond them to their inner meanings (*bawāṭin ma'ānīhā*)'. In line with this view, al-Jīlī implores the reader: 'Let not the apparent sense of the term suffice you (*la taktafi bi-ẓāhir al-lafẓ*), but seek what is behind that.'

29 See e.g. al-Jīlī, *al-Insān*, 26, 55–6; al-Jīlī, *Marātib*, 15–17.

30 See al-Jīlī, *al-Insān*, 113, 42.

31 On this title of Jesus, see Parrinder, *Jesus in the Qur'an*, 46–8.

32 Ibn 'Arabī, *Fuṣūṣ*, 139.

33 See al-Jīlī, *al-Insān*, 113.

34 See al-Jīlī, *Marātib*, 17.

35 See Louth, *Introducing*, 28.

36 See al-Jīlī, *al-Insān*, 42, 49.

37 An interesting parallel can be drawn between al-Jīlī's Sufi metaphysical interpretation of the Trinity and the interpretation of the Trinity put forward by the later Indian religious reformer Shāh Walī Allāh al-Dihlawī (d. 1176/1762), who was also heavily influenced by the Sufi metaphysics of Ibn 'Arabī. Shāh Walī Allāh interprets the three persons of the Trinity as representing the following metaphysical realities: the 'rational soul' (*al-nafs al-nāṭiqah*) or the 'universal soul' (*al-nafs al-kuliyyah*), the 'heavenly spirit' (*al-rūḥ al-sāmawī*) or the 'greatest manifestation' (*al-tajallī al-a'ẓam*), and the 'pure stone' (*al-ḥajar al-baḥt*) or the 'pure essence' (*al-dhāt al-baḥt*). See J. M. S. Baljon, *Religion and Thought of Shāh Walī Allāh Dihlawī: 1703-1762* (Leiden: Brill, 1986), 174, note 7. While al-Jīlī and Shāh Walī Allāh do not identify the three persons of the Trinity with the exact same metaphysical realities, nevertheless they both apply an Ibn 'Arabian Sufi metaphysical framework to their reading of the Trinitarian formula.

38 Al-Jīlī's first book on Sufi metaphysics – *al-Kahf wa-al-raqīm fī sharḥ bism Allāh al-raḥmān al-raḥīm* – is devoted to the metaphysical meaning of the *basmalah* (see Atlagh, 'Le Point'). See also al-Jīlī, *Sharḥ*, 138–9, on the 'mysteries (*asrār*) of the *basmalah*'.

39 See al-Jīlī, *al-Insān*, 146.
40 See Nwyia, *Exégèse*, 140.
41 Al-Jīlī, *al-Insān*, 129.
42 Khalidi, *Muslim Jesus*, 13.
43 Ibid., 12.
44 See Ibn ʿArabī, *Fuṣūṣ*, 146–9.
45 See Khalidi, *Muslim Jesus*, 12.
46 For this hadith, see J. Schacht, EI², s.v. ʻKhaṭaʼ.
47 The editor of the 1300/1882/3 Cairo edition of *al-Insān al-kāmil* was so scandalized by this expression that he declared it to be, in the words of Nicholson (*Studies*, 139–40), ʻan interpolation which only a heretic could have writtenʼ.
48 M. Shabistarī, *Gulshan-i rāz*, ed. Ṣ. Muwaḥḥid (Tehran: Intishārāt-i Ṭawrī, 2011), 121.
49 Ibn ʿArabī, *Fuṣūṣ*, 141. See also al-Ḥakīm, *al-Muʿjam*, 973.
50 See Qurʾān 4:48; D. Gimaret, EI², s.v. ʻShirkʼ.
51 See al-Jīlī, *al-Insān*, 121. Ibn ʿArabī also labels Christian theology as *kufr* and *shirk* in the context of his letter to the Seljuq Sultan of Konya Kaykāʾūs urging the strict application of the *dhimmī* laws (see Lipton, *Rethinking*, 55).
52 For the less charitable attitude of some of the most important exegetes towards the Christians of the Qurʾan, see McAuliffe, *Qurʾānic Christians*, *passim*.
53 Al-Jīlī, *al-Insān*, 129–30.
54 See M. Y. Dien, *EI²*, s.v. "Uḳūbaʼ; Tahānawī, *Kashshāf*, 1192.
55 See D. Gimaret, *EI²*, s.v. ʻShafāʿaʼ.
56 It is interesting to note that these names, according to al-Jīlī's scheme, are respectively a name of majesty (*jamāl*) and a name ʻsharedʼ (*mushtarak*) between majesty and mercy (see al-Jīlī, *al-Insān*, 96). This would appear to indicate that the divine forgiveness is not only a consequence of the names of divine mercy, such as the All-Forgiving (*al-ghaffār*), but is also connected to God's majesty and power.
57 This, as we would expect, is one of the names of divine majesty. See ibid., 97.
58 Ibn ʿArabī, *Fuṣūṣ*, 149.
59 Al-Jīlī, *al-Insān*, 130.
60 See Lane, *Lexicon*, 1:1798.
61 See e.g. Ibn Kathīr, *Tafsīr*, 28 (Q 1.7); al-Maḥallī and al-Suyūṭī, *al-Jalālayn*, 10 (Q 1.7).
62 See al-Jīlī, *al-Insān*, 182.
63 See Ibn ʿArabī, *Futūḥāt*, 4:327–9.
64 Ibn ʿArabī, *Fuṣūṣ*, 107–8. See also Chittick, *Imaginal Worlds*, 113–15; M. H. Khalil, *Islam and the Fate of Others: The Salvation Question* (Oxford: Oxford University Press, 2012), 62–7.
65 Al-Jīlī, *al-Insān*, 184.
66 Other Sufi authors also display empathy for Christianity, though usually on account of their association of Jesus with the renunciation of the world and the passions of the base self. See e.g. Shabistarī, *Gulshan*, 123; J. Nurbakhsh, *Jesus in the Eyes of the Sufis*, tr. T. Graham, L. Lewisohn and H. Mashkuri (London: Khaniqahi-Nimatullahi Publications, 1992), 39–48; Khalidi, *Muslim Jesus*, 41–3; M. Milani, ʻRepresentations of Jesus in Islamic Mysticism: Defining the "Sufi Jesus"ʼ, *Literature & Aesthetics* 21, no. 2 (2012), 45–65.
67 See e.g. Ibn Kathīr, *Tafsīr*, 352 (Q 5.119).
68 Al-Jīlī, *al-Insān*, 130.
69 See ibid., 50, 96.
70 See ibid., 48–50; al-Jīlī, *Marātib*, 19–20.

71 See ibid., 97–8.

72 The orthodox Christian formula is that the persons of the Trinity are 'of the same being' (*homōousia*). For the Christian doctrine of the Trinity, as understood by the Orthodox churches (which are of greater relevance here), see K. Ware, *The Orthodox Way* (Crestwood, NY: St. Vladimir's Seminary Press, 1995), 27–42; Louth, *Introducing*, 16–31. Al-Jīlī, following Ibn 'Arabī, would agree that the persons of the Trinity, as created forms, are of the same existence (*wujūd*) as God, yet he sees them as forms of limited existence (*al-wujūd al-muqayyad*), in contrast to the unlimited existence (*al-wujūd al-muṭlaq*) of the divine.

73 Al-Jīlī, *al-Insān*, 130.

74 See Lane, *Lexicon*, 1:761: s.v. '*khaṭa*": '*a wrong action; a mistake, or an error*; contr. of *ṣawāb*; . . . it signifies an *unintentional fault* or *offence* or *disobedience*.' Ibid., 1798, s.v. '*ḍalāl*': '*the going away from the right course*'; can be '*a state of perdition*'.

75 Ibn 'Arabī, *Fuṣūṣ*, 121. Similarly, as we have seen, Ibn 'Arabī warns against being limited (*tataqayyad*) by the 'knot' of a particular belief (ibid., 113).

76 Ibn Taymiyyah, *Majmū' al-fatāwá*, 11:242.

77 See Ibn 'Arabī, *Fuṣūṣ*, 141. My translation of the key term *taḍmīn* follows that of Shah-Kazemi (*The Other*, 221).

78 Al-Jandī, *Sharḥ*, 427.

79 On Hishām, see J. van Ess, *Theology and Society in the Second and Third Centuries of the Hijra: A History of Religious Thought in Early Islam*, in five vols., tr. J. O'Kane (Leiden: Brill, 2017), 1:410–48.

80 See Ibn Khaldūn, *The Muqaddimah*, 3:68: 'The anthropomorphists (*mujassimah*) did something similar in affirming that God has a body but not one like (ordinary human) bodies. . . . Thus, the anthropomorphists are more involved (than others) in innovation, and, indeed, in unbelief.'

81 See e.g. al-Zamakhsharī, *A Mu'tazilite creed of az-Zamaḫšarî (d. 538/1144): al-Minhâǧ fî uṣûl ad-dîn*, ed. and tr. S. Schmidtke (Stuttgart: Kommissionsverlag Franz Steiner, 1997), 13/52; al-Ash'arī, *The theology of al-Ash'arī*, 12/10.

82 See L. Massignon and G. C. Anawati, *EI*², s.v. 'Ḥulūl'; and see e.g. the title of the ninth-century CE Baghdadi writer Abū 'Īsá al-Warrāq's *Radd 'alá al-ittiḥād*; al-Shahrastānī, *al-Milal wa-al-niḥal*, 2:245, 254; Ibn Taymiyyah, *al-Jawāb al-ṣaḥīḥ*, 1:16, 18ff.; Ibn 'Arabī, *Fuṣūṣ*, 141.

83 See Massignon and Anawati, *EI*², s.v. 'Ḥulūl'; and see e.g. the titles of the Melkite theologian Theodore Abū Qurrah's (d. 820–5 CE) *Maymar fī al-radd 'alá man yunkir li-Allāh al-tajassud* and the Jacobite theologian Abū Rā'iṭah's (d. after 830 CE) *al-Risālah fī al-tajassud*.

84 Al-Jīlī, *al-Insān*, 144.

85 See Josef van Ess, *EI*², s.v. 'Tashbīh wa-Tanzīh'.

86 See al-Jīlī, *al-Insān*, 120.

87 Al-Jīlī, *Sharḥ*, 111–12.

88 Quoted in al-Jīlī, *Ibdā'*, 41.

89 The connection between *tashbīh* and *taqyīd* is also made by Ibn 'Arabī (see e.g. *Fuṣūṣ*, 69).

90 This being al-Jīlī's position, I do not agree with the statement of Nicholson, *Studies*, 140, that, in al-Jīlī's view, the Christians 'recognize the two complementary sides of true belief concerning God, namely that from the one point of view (*tanzíh*) He is above all likeness and that from the other (*tashbíh*) He reveals Himself in the forms of His creatures'.

91 Al-Jīlī, *al-Insān*, 130–1.

92 See also ibid., 151, 199, 267, 269, 271. For this meaning of *nāmūs* (which is one of many), see Lane, *Lexicon*, 1:2854. Given that al-Jīlī, as we have seen throughout this book, interprets the scriptures as forms of divine manifestation, his use of *nāmūs* in this way does not contradict its apparently original meaning of 'revealed law'. See H. Motzki, *Encyclopaedia of the Qur'ān*, s.v. 'Nāmūs'.

93 See R. Arnaldez, *EI*[2], s.v. 'Lāhūt and nāsūt'; al-Shahrastānī, *al-Milal wa-al-niḥal*, 2:245; Ibn Taymiyyah, *al-Jawāb al-ṣaḥīḥ*, 2:266, 3:73; Ibn Taymiyyah, *Majmū' al-fatāwá*, 2:107.

94 See Arnaldez, *EI*[2], s.v. 'Lāhūt and nāsūt'; Massignon, *Lexicon*, 31; al-Ḥallāj, *Kitāb al-ṭawāsīn*, ed. and tr. L. Massignon (Paris: Geuthner, 1913), 129–32; Takeshita, 'Ibn 'Arabī's Theory', 19.

95 See Arnaldez, *EI*[2], s.v. 'Lāhūt and nāsūt'; Izutsu, *Sufism and Taoism*, 149. The parallels between Christian and Sufi terminology, it should be noted, led some *'ulamā'* to accuse al-Ḥallāj, Ibn 'Arabī and other Sufis of professing the Christian doctrines of *ittiḥād* and *ḥulūl*. See e.g. Ibn Taymiyyah, *Majmū' al-fatāwá*, 2:281; Ibn Taymiyyah, *al-Jawāb al-ṣaḥīḥ*, 3:73; Ibn Khaldūn, *The Muqaddimah*, 3:85–6. This association between Sufi *ḥulūl* and the Christian doctrine of the Incarnation is in fact already found in al-Sarrāj (*al-Luma'*, 433).

96 Ibn 'Arabī, *Fuṣūṣ*, 138.

97 Al-Jīlī, *al-Insān*, 6.

98 As already noted, Ibn 'Arabī uses the term 'Muhammadans' in a technical sense to denote a specific class of *awliyā'*, namely those who embody the Muhammadan Reality. Yet, since al-Jīlī also refers to *al-muslimūn* here, and since, in the final chapter, he identifies *al-muslimūn* with *al-muḥammadiyyūn* (see al-Jīlī, *al-Insān*, 255), I do not think that he is using the term in this precise, Ibn 'Arabian technical sense. It does seem, however, to carry the connotation of *true* Muslims, that is, those who know the true, metaphysical meaning of the Muhammadan message.

99 Ibn 'Arabī (*Fuṣūṣ*, 49, 216) also alludes to this verse in the course of his elaboration of his cosmogony in the chapter on Adam at the beginning of the *Fuṣūṣ*, as well as in his discussion of the nature of Muhammad in the final chapter.

100 See al-Jīlī, *al-Insān*, 150 (in the chapter on *al-rūḥ al-quds*), where he describes how the divine breathing into Adam denotes 'the divine existence within created beings' (*al-wujūd al-ilāhī fī al-makhlūqāt*).

101 See e.g. Ibn 'Arabī, *Fuṣūṣ*, 69; al-Jīlī, *al-Insān*, 121; Sands, *Ṣūfī Commentaries*, 44, 173, note 77; Keeler, *Sufi Hermeneutics*, 188; Izutsu, *Sufism and Taoism*, 54; Chittick, *Sufi Path of Knowledge*, xv, 43, 92, 164, 245, 358, 399, note 21.

102 Al-Jīlī, *al-Insān*, 279.

103 Ibn 'Arabī uses Q 48.10 in a similar way (see Chittick, *Sufi Path of Knowledge*, 323–4).

104 Al-Jīlī, *al-Insān*, 131.

105 This connection is suggested by Q 57.16, which, as we saw in Chapter 4, links the *fāsiqīn* to those whose 'hearts have hardened'.

106 For these concepts in Sufi literature, see Keeler, *Sufi Hermeneutics*, 66; Tahānawī, *Kashshāf*, 1407–8.

107 See al-Jīlī, *Sharḥ*, 71.

108 See e.g. Ibn 'Arabī, *Futūḥāt*, 3:359; Goldziher, *Die Richtungen*, 224; Chittick, *Sufi Path of Knowledge*, 72, 148, 171, 247, 388, note 22; Abū Zayd, *Hākadhā*, 95–6. See also the similar usage by Rūzbihān Baqlī, quoted in Sands, *Ṣūfī Commentaries*, 10–11. Al-Jandī (*Sharḥ*, 30) in one instance uses the term for grammarians, that is, those

scholars who literally deal with the outward forms of words, rather than their inner meanings.

109 Al-Qāshānī, *Mu'jam*, 125.

110 Elsewhere in the book (*al-Insān*, 103, 188), al-Jīlī refers to the same group as *ahl al-ẓāhir*.

111 The majority of medieval Sunni exegetes interpret Q 48.10 as a reference to the so-called pledge of the tree (*bay'at al-shajarah*) or pledge of satisfaction (*bay'at al-riḍwān*) made to Muhammad by his Companions prior to the Treaty of Ḥudaybiyyah in 6/628, thus limiting the meaning of the verse to a particular historical event. Similarly, they interpret Q 4.80 in terms of the necessity of obeying the commandments and prohibitions of God, as expressed through His messenger Muhammad. See e.g. al-Ṭabarī, *Tafsīr*, 4:180 (Q 4.80), 11:338–9 (Q 48.10); Ibn Kathīr, *Tafsīr*, 335 (Q 4.80), 1225–7 (Q 48.10).

112 Al-Jīlī, *al-Insān*, 131.

113 See Chittick, *Sufi Path of Knowledge*, 4, 12, 20, 51, 89, 111, 122, 143, 277, 280, 343, 355. For al-Jīlī's interpretation, see al-Jīlī, *al-Insān*, 150–1, where he explains that the verse denotes how the 'sanctified spirit (*al-rūḥ al-muqaddas*) . . . is present, in its perfection, within [the universe] (*muta'ayyin bi-kamālihi fīhi*)'.

114 See al-Jīlī, *al-Insān*, 60.

115 See Chittick, *Sufi Path of Knowledge*, 84 (Q 51.21), 368 (Q 45.12).

116 For the hadith, see Bukhārī, *Le recueil*, 4:231. For Ibn 'Arabī's use of this *ḥadīth qudsī*, see W. A. Graham, *Divine Word and Prophetic Word in Early Islam: A Reconsideration of the Sources, With Special Reference to the Divine Saying or Hadîth qudsî* (The Hague: Mouton, 1977), 173–4; Chittick, *Sufi Path of Knowledge*, 176, 325–30.

117 See al-Jīlī, *al-Insān*, 215, 269, 278.

118 Ibid., 260.

Conclusion

1 See al-Ḥakīm, *al-Mu'jam*, 949–54.

2 See al-Qūnawī, *I'jāz al-bayān*, 10; Todd, *Sufi Doctrine*, 99.

3 See al-Qayṣarī, *Sharḥ*, 273.

4 See e.g. 'Afīfī, 'Ibn 'Arabī fī dirāsātī', 26; J. Morris, 'Ibn 'Arabī and His Interpreters', pt. 3, *Journal of the American Oriental Society* 107, no. 1 (1987), 101–20, 108.

5 If al-Jīlī's description of his mystical ascension in chapter sixty-one (*al-Insān*, 237–8) is a guide, then it can be said that he places Moses higher in the hierarchy of prophets than Jesus and David, for he puts Moses in the sixth heaven (as in traditional accounts of the Prophet's *mi'rāj*), and Jesus and David in the fourth. Muhammad's superiority over Moses, David and Jesus is reflected in al-Jīlī's placing him in the eighth heaven, for which see ibid., 194.

6 The following is based on F. Morrissey, "Abd al-Karīm al-Jīlī's Sufi View of Other Religions', *The Maghreb Review* 43, no. 2 (2018), 175–97, copyright @ *The Maghreb Review*, 2018. Reprinted with permission.

7 See al-Jīlī, *al-Insān*, 254–5.

8 Ibid., 252–3.

9 See ibid., 259–60.

10 See ibid., 260–1.

11 Ibid., 260.
12 Ibid., 261.
13 Ibid., 260.
14 Ibid.
15 Ibid.
16 See ibid., 263–80.
17 For Ibn ʿArabī's conception of the mysteries of the pillars of Islam, a topic dealt with in chapters sixty-eight to seventy-two of the *Futūḥāt*, see Abū Zayd, *Hākadhā*, 275–97.
18 See al-Jīlī, *al-Insān*, 263–4, 277–9.
19 Ibid., 261.
20 Ibid., 262.
21 See Strauss, *Persecution*.
22 Kātib Çelebī, *Balance*, 80.
23 Nicholson, *Studies*, 141.

Bibliography

Abrahamov, Binyamin. 'Signs', *Encyclopaedia of the Qur'ān*, vol. 5, edited by Jane Dammen McAuliffe. Leiden: Brill, 2006, 2–11.

Abrahamov, Binyamin. *Ibn al-'Arabī and the Sufis*. Oxford: Anqa Publishing, 2014.

Abū Dāwūd, Sulaymān. *Sunan Abī Dāwūd*, edited by Muhammad 'Abd al-'Azīz Khālidī. Beirut: Dār al-Kutub al-'ilmiyyah, 2001.

Abū Zayd, Naṣr Ḥāmid. *Falsafat al-ta'wīl: dirāsah fī ta'wīl al-Qur'ān 'ind Muḥyī al-dīn Ibn 'Arabī*. Beirut: Dār al-Tanwīr, 1983.

Abū Zayd, Naṣr Ḥāmid. *Hākadhā takallama Ibn 'Arabī*. Casablanca, Beirut: Dār al-Thaqāfī al-'Arabī, 2006.

Abū Zayd, Naṣr Ḥāmid. *Critique of Religious Discourse*, translated by Jonathan Wright. New Haven, CT: Yale University Press, 2018.

Adang, Camilla. *Muslim Writers on Judaism and the Bible: From Ibn Rabban to Ibn Hazm*. Leiden: Brill, 1996.

Adang, Camilla. 'Torah', *Encyclopaedia of the Qur'ān*, vol. 5, edited by Jane Dammen McAuliffe. Leiden: Brill, 2006, 300–11.

Addas, Claude. *The Quest For the Red Sulphur*, translated by Peter Kingsley. Cambridge: Islamic Texts Society, 1993.

Addas, Claude. '"At the Distance of Two Bows' Length or Even Closer": The Figure of the Prophet in the Work of 'Abd al-Karīm al-Jīlī', *Journal of the Muhyiddin Ibn 'Arabi Society*, pt. 1, 45 (2009), 65–88, pt. 2, 46 (2009), 1–26.

'Afīfī, Abū al-'Alá. *The Mystical Philosophy of Muhyid Dín Ibnul 'Arabí*. Cambridge: The Cambridge University Press, 1939.

'Afīfī, Abū al-'Alá. 'Ibn 'Arabī fī dirāsātī', in *Al-Kitāb al-tidhkārī Muḥy al-dīn Ibn 'Arabī: fī al-dhikrá al-mi'wiyyah al-thāminah li-mīlādihi*, edited by Ibrāhīm Madkūr. Cairo: al-Hay'ah al-Miṣriyyah al-'āmmah li-al-kitāb, 1969, 3–34.

'Afīfī, Abū al-'Alá. 'Al-A'yān al-thābitah fī madhhab Ibn 'Arabī wa-al-ma'dūmāt fī madhhab al-Mu'tazilah', in *al-Kitāb al-tidhkārī Muḥy al-dīn Ibn 'Arabī: fī al-dhikrá al-mi'wiyyah al-thāminah li-mīlādihi*, edited by Ibrāhīm Madkūr. Cairo: al-Hay'ah al-Miṣriyyah al-'āmmah li-al-kitāb, 1969, 183–208.

Ahmed, Shahab. *What Is Islam? The Importance of Being Islamic*. Princeton, NJ: Princeton University Press, 2016.

Akkach, Samer. *'Abd al-Ghani al-Nabulusi: Islam and the Enlightenment*. Oxford: Oneworld, 2007.

Akkach, Samer. *Intimate Invocations: Al-Ghazzī's Biography of 'Abd al-Ghanī al-Nābulusī*. Leiden: Brill, 2012.

Ali, Abdullah Yusuf (tr.). *The Holy Qur-an: Text, Translation and Commentary*. New York: Hafner Pub. Co., 1946.

Anawati, Georges C. and Gardet, Louis. *Mystique musulmane: aspects et tendances, expériences et techniques*. Paris: J Vrin, 1961.

Andalusī, Ṣa'īd. *Kitâb tabaqât al-umam, ou, Livre des catégories des nations*, edited by Louis Cheikho. Beirut: Imprimerie Catholique, 1912.

Anṣārī, ʿAbd Allāh. *Manāzil al-sāʾirīn ilá al-ḥaqq jalla shaʾnuh*, edited by Ibrāhīm ʿAwaḍ. Cairo: Maktabat Jaʿfar al-ḥadīthah, 1977.

Arkoun, Mohammed. *Islam: To Reform or Subvert?* London: Saqi Essentials, 2006.

Arnaldez, Roger. 'Ḳidm', in *Encyclopaedia of Islam*, second (new) edition, vol. 5, edited by B. Lewis, V. L. Ménage, Ch. Pellat and J. Schacht. Leiden: Brill, 1986, 95–9.

Arnaldez, Roger. 'Lāhūt and nāsūt', in *Encyclopaedia of Islam*, second (new) edition, vol. 5, edited by B. Lewis, V. L. Ménage, Ch. Pellat and J. Schacht. Leiden: Brill, 1986, 611–14.

Arnaldez, Roger. 'Manṭiḳ', in *Encyclopaedia of Islam*, second (new) edition, vol. 6, edited by C. E. Bosworth, E. van Donzel and Ch. Pellat. Leiden: Brill, 442–52.

Asad, Muhammad. *The Message of the Qur'an*. Gibraltar: Dar al-Andalus, 1984.

Ashʿarī, Abū al-Ḥasan. *The Theology of al-Ashʿarī: The Arabic Texts of al-Ashʿarī's Kitāb al-Lumaʿ and Risālat Istiḥsān al-khawḍ fī ʿilm al-kalām*, edited by Richard McCarthy. Beirut: Impr. catholique, 1953.

Atlagh, Riyadh. 'Le point et la ligne: Explication de la Basmala par la science des lettres chez ʿAbd al-Karīm al-Ǧīlī (m. 826 h.)', *Bulletin d'études orientales* 44 (1992), special edition: Sciences occultes et islam, 161–90.

Atlagh, Riyadh. 'Contribution à l'étude de la pensée mystique d'Ibn ʿArabī et son école à travers l'oeuvre de ʿAbd al-Karīm al-Jīlī', PhD diss., École pratique des hautes études, 2000.

ʿAṭṭār, Farīd al-dīn. *Dīvān-i ghazaliyyāt va-qaṣāyid-i ʿAṭṭār*, edited by Taqī Tafaḍḍolī. Tehran: Intishārāt-i Anjuman-i āthār-i millī, 1962.

Attas, Syed M. N. *The Mysticism of Ḥamzah Fanṣūrī*, PhD diss., School of Oriental and African Studies, 1966.

Attas, Syed M. N. 'The Meaning and Experience of Happiness in Islam', in *Consciousness and Reality: Studies in Memory of Toshihiko Izutsu*, edited by Jalāl al-Dīn Āshtiyānī. Leiden: Brill, 1999, 59–78.

Babinger, Franz. *Mehmed the Conqueror and His Time*, translated by Ralph Manheim, edited by William C. Hickman. Princeton, NJ: Princeton University Press, 1979.

Baghawī. *Tafsīr al-Baghawī: Maʿālim al-tanzīl*, edited by Muḥammad ʿAbd Allāh al-Nimr, ʿUthmān Jumʿah al-Ḍamīriyyah, and Sulaymān Muslim al-Harsh, in eight volumes. Riyadh: Dār al-Ṭayyibah, 1989.

Balić, Smail. *Das unbekannte Bosnien: Europas Brücke zur islamischen Welt*. Köln: Bölau, 1992.

Baljon, J. M. S. *Religion and Thought of Shāh Walī Allāh Dihlawī: 1703–1762*. Leiden: Brill, 1986.

Baqlī, Rūzbihān. *ʿArāʾis al-bayān fī ḥaqāʾiq al-Qurʾān*. Online edition, accessed via http://www.altafsir.com/Tafasir.asp?tMadhNo=3&tTafsirNo=32&tSoraNo=1&tAyahNo=1&tDisplay=yes&UserProfile=0&LanguageId=1 on 19 February 2018.

Barton, John. 'Moses from a Christian Perspective', in *Abraham's Children: Jews, Christians and Muslims in Conversation*, edited by Richard Harries, Norman Solomon and Timothy Winter. London and New York: T&T Clark, 2005, 49–54.

ben Yashar, Menachem. 'And I Will Harden the Heart of Pharaoh', Bar-Ilan University, Daf Parashat Hashavua (Study Sheet on the Weekly Torah Portion), 1997, accessed via https://www.biu.ac.il/JH/Parasha/eng/vaera/yashar.html, 23 January 2018.

Berenbaum, Michael and Skolnik, Fred (eds). 'Tablets of the Law', in *Encyclopaedia Judaica*, vol. 19. Detroit: Macmillan Reference USA in assoc. with Keter Pub. House, 2007, 425.

Berjak, Rafik. 'Bashar', in *The Qur'an: An Encyclopaedia*, edited by Oliver Leaman. London: Routledge, 2006, 115.

El-Bizri, Nader. 'God: Essence and Attributes', in *The Cambridge Companion to Classical Islamic Theology*, edited by T. Winter. Cambridge: Cambridge University Press, 2008, 121–40.

Bonebakker, Seger A. 'Tawriya', in *Encyclopaedia of Islam*, second (new) edition, vol. 10, edited by P. J. Bearman, Th. Bianquis, C. E. Bosworth, E. van Donzel and W. P. Heinrichs. Leiden: Brill, 2002, 395–6.

Böwering, Gerhard. 'The Scriptural "Senses" in Medieval Qur'an Exegesis', in *With Reverence for the Word: Medieval Scriptural Exegesis in Judaism, Christianity, and Islam*, edited by Jane Dammen McAuliffe, Barry Walfish and Joseph Goering. Oxford: Oxford University Press, 2003, 346–65.

Brinner, William M. 'An Islamic Decalogue', in *Studies in Islamic and Judaic Traditions*, edited by William M. Brinner and Stephen D. Ricks. Atlanta: Scholars Press, 1986, 67–84.

Brown, William P. 'The Psalms: An Overview', in *The Oxford Handbook of the Psalms*, edited by idem. Oxford: Oxford University Press, 2014, 1–24.

Bukhārī, Muḥammad. *Le recueil des traditions mahométanes*, in four volumes. Leiden: Brill, 1862–1908.

Burton, John. 'Abrogation', in *Encyclopaedia of the Qur'ān*, vol. 1, edited by Jane Dammen McAuliffe. Leiden: Brill, 2001, 11–19.

Casewit, Yousef. *The Mystics of al-Andalus: Ibn Barrajān and Islamic Thought in the Twelfth Century*. Cambridge: Cambridge University Press, 2018.

Cheikho, Louis. 'Quelques légendes islamiques apocryphes', *Mélanges de la Faculté Orientale*, Université Saint-Joseph 4 (1910), 5–56.

Chittick, William C. 'The Perfect Man as the Prototype of the Self in the Sufism of Jāmī', *Studia Islamica* 49 (1979), 135–57.

Chittick, William C. 'The Five Divine Presences: From al-Qūnawī to al-Qayṣarī', *The Muslim World* 72, no. 2 (1982), 107–28.

Chittick, William C. *The Sufi Path of Knowledge: Ibn al-'Arabi's Metaphysics of Imagination*. Albany, NY: State University of New York Press, 1989.

Chittick, William C. *Imaginal Worlds: Ibn al-'Arabī and the Problem of Religious Diversity*. Albany, NY: State University of New York Press, 1994.

Chittick, William C. *The Self-Disclosure of God: Principles of Ibn al-'Arabī's Cosmology*. Albany, NY: State University of New York Press, 1998.

Chittick, William C. 'The Central Point: Qûnawî's Role in the School of Ibn 'Arabî', *Journal of the Muyiddin Ibn 'Arabi Society* 35 (2004), 25–45.

Chittick, William C. *Science of the Cosmos, Science of the Soul: The Pertinence of Islamic Cosmology in the Modern World*. Oxford: Oneworld, 2007.

Chodkiewicz, Michel. *An Ocean Without a Shore: Ibn 'Arabî, the Book, and the Law*, translated by David Streight. Albany, NY: State University of New York Press, 1993.

Chodkiewicz, Michel. 'The Vision of God According to Ibn 'Arabi', *Prayer and Contemplation*, a special issue of the *Journal of the Muhyiddin Ibn 'Arabi Society* 14 (1993), 53–67.

Chodkiewicz, Michel. *Seal of Saints: Prophethood and Sainthood in the Doctrine of Ibn 'Arabī*, translated by Liadain Sherrard. Cambridge: Islamic Texts Society, 1999.

Clarke, Linda. 'The Rise and Decline of *Taqiyya* in Twelver Shi'ism', in *Reason and Inspiration in Islam: Theology, Philosophy and Mysticism in Muslim Thought. Essays in Honour of Hermann Landolt*, edited by Todd Lawson. London and New York: I.B. Tauris, 2005, 46–63.

Cook, Michael. *Commanding Right and Forbidding Wrong in Islamic Thought*. Cambridge: Cambridge University Press, 2000.

Corbin. *Terre céleste et corps de résurrection, de l'Iran mazdéen à l'Iran shī'ite*. Paris: Buchet/Chastel, 1960.
Corbin, Henry. *Mundus Imaginalis, Or, The Imaginary and the Imaginal*. Dallas: Spring Publications, 1972.
Corbin, Henry. *Spiritual Body and Celestial Earth: From Mazdean Iran to Shī'ite Iran*, translated by Nancy Pearson. Princeton, NJ: Princeton University Press, 1977.
Cornell, Vincent. *Realm of the Saint: Power and Authority in Moroccan Sufism*. Austin, TX: University of Texas Press, 1998.
Cornell, Vincent. 'Practical Sufism. An Akbarian Foundation for a Liberal Theology of Difference', *Journal of the Muhyiddin Ibn 'Arabi Society* 36 (2004), 59–84.
Cragg, Kenneth. *The Event of the Qur'ān: Islam in Its Scripture*. London: Allen & Unwin, 1971.
Crone, Patricia and Hinds, Martin. *God's Caliph: Religious Authority in the First Centuries of Islam*. Cambridge: Cambridge University Press, 2003.
Demiri, Lejla. "Abd al-Ghanī l-Nābulusī: *al-Kashf wa-al-bayān 'an asrār al-adyān fī kitāb al-Insān al-kāmil wa-kāmil al-insān*', in *Christian-Muslim Relations: A Bibliographical History*, vol. 12, edited by D. Thomas and J. Chesworth. Leiden and Boston: Brill, 2018, 121–4.
de Vaux, Carra [Anawati, Georges C.]. 'Indjīl', in *Encyclopaedia of Islam*, second (new) edition, vol. 3, edited by B. Lewis, V. L. Ménage, Ch. Pellat and J. Schacht. Leiden: Brill, 1971, 1205–8.
Dien, Mawil Y. "Uḳūba', in *Encyclopaedia of Islam*, second (new) edition, vol. 10, edited by P. J. Bearman, Th. Bianquis, C. E. Bosworth, E. van Donzel and W. P. Heinrichs. Leiden: Brill, 2000, 799–800.
Druart, Therese-Anne. *Stanford Encyclopaedia of Islam*, s.v. 'al-Farabi'. Accessed via https://plato.stanford.edu/entries/al-farabi/#MathMusi on 11 February 2020.
Ebstein, Michael. 'Secrecy in the Ismā'īlī Tradition and in the Mystical Thought of Ibn al-'Arabī', *Journal Asiatique* 298, no. 2 (2010), 303–43.
Ebstein, Michael. *Mysticism and Philosophy in al-Andalus: Ibn Masarra, Ibn al-'Arabī and the Ismā'īlī Tradition*. Leiden: Brill, 2014.
Elmore, Gerald. 'Review of *Sufi Metaphysics and Qur'ānic Prophets: Ibn 'Arabī's thought and method in the* Fuṣūṣ al-ḥikam', *Journal of Qur'anic Studies* 7, no. 1 (2005), 81–97.
El-Rouayheb, Khaled. *Relational Syllogisms and the History of Arabic Logic, 900-1900*. Leiden: Brill, 2010.
El-Rouayheb, Khaled. *Islamic Intellectual History in the Seventeenth Century*. Cambridge: Cambridge University Press, 2015.
Ernst, Carl W. 'Controversies Over Ibn al-'Arabī's *Fuṣūṣ*: The Faith of Pharaoh', *Islamic Culture* 59 (1985), 259–66.
Ernst, Carl W. *Words of Ecstasy in Sufism*. Albany, NY: State University of New York Press, 1985.
Ernst, Carl W. *Sufism: An Introduction to the Mystical Tradition of Islam*. Boston and London: Shambhala Publications, 2011.
Ernst, Carl W. 'Nasr Hamid Abu Zayd on Ibn 'Arabi and Modernity', *Journal of the Muhyiddin Ibn 'Arabi Society* 58 (2015), 1–16.
Fahd, Toufic. 'Firāsah', in *Encyclopaedia of Islam,* second (new) edition, vol. 2, edited by B. Lewis, V. L. Ménage, Ch. Pellat and J. Schacht. Leiden: Brill, 1965, 916–17.
Fahd, Toufic. 'Siḥr', in *Encyclopaedia of Islam*, second (new) edition, vol. 9, edited by C. E. Bosworth, E. van Donzel, W. P. Heinrichs and G. Lecomte. Leiden: Brill, 1997, 567–71.

Farghānī, Sa'd al-Dīn. *Muntahá al-madārik fī sharḥ Tā'iyyat Ibn al-Fāriḍ*, in two volumes, edited by 'Āṣim al-Kayyālī. Beirut: Dār al-Kutub al-'ilmiyyah, 2007.

Fierro, Maribel. 'The Treatises Against Innovations (*kutub al-bida'*)', *Der Islam* 69, no. 2 (1992), 204–46.

Freeden, Michael. *Ideology: A Very Short Introduction*. Oxford: Oxford University Press, 2003.

Friedmann, Yohanan. *Prophecy Continuous: Aspects of Aḥmadī Religious Thought and Its Medieval Background*. Berkeley, CA and London: University of California Press, 1989.

Friedmann, Yohanan. *Tolerance and Coercion in Islam: Interfaith Relations in the Muslim Tradition*. Cambridge: Cambridge University Press, 2003.

Frolov, Dmitry V. 'Freedom and Predestination', in *Encyclopaedia of the Qur'ān*, vol. 2, edited by Jane Dammen McAuliffe. Leiden: Brill, 2002, 267–71.

Gardet, Louis. "Ālam', in *Encyclopaedia of Islam*, second (new) edition, vol. 1, edited by H. A. R. Gibb, J. H. Kramers, E. Lévi-Provençal and J. Schacht. Leiden: Brill, 1960, 349–52.

Gardet, Louis. 'Fi'l', in *Encyclopaedia of Islam*, second (new) edition, vol. 2, edited by B. Lewis, V. L. Ménage, Ch. Pellat and J. Schacht. Leiden: Brill, 1965, 895–9.

Gardet, Louis. 'Al-Ḳaḍā' wa-l-Ḳadar', in *Encyclopaedia of Islam*, second (new) edition, vol. 5, edited by C. E. Bosworth, E. van Donzel, B. Lewis and Ch. Pellat. Leiden: Brill, 1978, 365–7.

Gardet, Louis. 'Karāma', in *Encyclopaedia of Islam*, second (new) edition, vol. 5, edited by C. E. Bosworth, E. van Donzel, B. Lewis and Ch. Pellat. Leiden: Brill, 1978, 615–16.

Gibb, Hamilton A. R. and Bowen, Harold. *Islamic Society and the West: A Study of the Impact of Western Civilization on Moslem Culture in the Near East*, in two volumes, London: Oxford University Press, 1950–57.

Gilliot, Claude. 'Exegesis of the Qur'ān: Classical and Medieval', in *Encyclopaedia of the Qur'ān*, vol. 2, edited by Jane Dammen McAuliffe. Leiden: Brill, 2002, 99–124.

Gimaret, Daniel. 'Al-Milal wa'l-niḥal', in *Encyclopaedia of Islam*, second (new) edition, vol. 7, edited by C. E. Bosworth, E. van Donzel, W. P. Heinrichs and Ch. Pellat. Leiden: Brill, 1993, 54–5.

Gimaret, Daniel. 'Shirk', in *Encyclopaedia of Islam*, second (new) edition, vol. 9, edited by C. E. Bosworth, E. van Donzel, W. P. Heinrichs and G. Lecomte. Leiden: Brill, 1997, 484–6.

Gimaret, Daniel. 'Ṣifa', in *Encyclopaedia of Islam*, second (new) edition, vol. 9, edited by C. E. Bosworth, E. van Donzel, W. P. Heinrichs and G. Lecomte. Leiden: Brill, 1997, 551–2.

Gimaret, Daniel. 'Shafā'a, in *Encyclopaedia of Islam*, second (new) edition, vol. 9, edited by C. E. Bosworth, E. van Donzel, W. P. Heinrichs and G. Lecomte. Leiden: Brill, 1997, 177–9.

Glick, Thomas F., Livesey, Steven J. and Wallis, Faith (eds). *Medieval Science: Technology, and Medicine: An Encyclopaedia*. Abingdon: Routledge, 2005.

Goichon, Amélie M. *Lexique de la langue philosophique d'Ibn Sīnā (Avicenne)*. Paris: Desclée de Brouwer, 1938.

Goichon, Amélie M. 'Ḥikma', in *Encyclopaedia of Islam*, second (new) edition, vol. 3, edited by B. Lewis, V. L. Ménage, Ch. Pellat and J. Schacht. Leiden: Brill, 1971, 377–8.

Goldziher, Ignaz. *Die Richtungen der islamischen Koranauslegung*. Leiden: Brill, 1920.

Goodenough, Erwin R. *By Light, Light: The Mystic Gospel of Hellenistic Judaism*. Amsterdam: Philo Press, 1969.

Graham William A. *Divine Word and Prophetic Word in Early Islam: A Reconsideration of the Sources, With Special Reference to the Divine Saying or Hadîth qudsî*. The Hague: Mouton, 1977.

Graham, William A. 'Fātiḥa', in *Encyclopaedia of the Qur'an*, vol. 2, edited by Jane Dammen McAuliffe. Leiden: Brill, 2002, 187–92.

Griffith, Sidney H. 'The Concept of *al-ʻuqnūm* in ʻAmmār al-Baṣrī's Apology for the Doctrine of the Trinity', in *Actes du premier* congrès international d'études arabes chrétiennes (Goslar, septembre 1980), edited by Khalil Samir. Rome: Pontificium Institutum Studiorum Orientalium, 1982.

Griffith, Sidney H. 'Christians and Christianity', in *Encyclopaedia of the Qur'ān*, vol. 1, edited by Jane Dammen McAuliffe. Leiden: Brill, 2001, 307–16.

Griffith, Sidney H. 'Gospel', in *Encyclopaedia of the Qur'ān*, vol. 2, edited by Jane Dammen McAuliffe. Leiden: Brill, 2002, 342–3.

Griffith, Sidney H. *The Beginnings of Christian Theology in Arabic: Muslim-Christian Encounters in the Early Islamic Period*. Aldershot: Ashgate, 2002.

Griffith, Sidney H. *The Church in the Shadow of the Mosque: Christians and Muslims in the World of Islam*. Princeton, NJ and Oxford: Princeton University Press, 2008.

Griffith, Sidney H. *The Bible in Arabic: The Scriptures of the 'People of the Book' in the Language of Islam*. Princeton, NJ: Princeton University Press, 2013.

Hadot, Pierre. *What Is Ancient Philosophy?*, translated by Michael Chase. Cambridge, MA and London: The Belknap Press of Harvard University Press, 2002.

Ḥakīm, Suʻād. *Al-Muʻjam al-ṣūfī: al-ḥikmah fī ḥudūd al-kalimah*. Beirut: Dandarah li-al-ṭabāʻah wa-al-nashr, 1981.

Ḥakīm, Suʻād. *Ibn ʻArabī: mawlid al-lughah al-jadīdah*. Beirut: Dandarah li-al-ṭabāʻah wa-al-nashr, 1991.

Ḥallāj, al-Ḥusayn. *Kitāb al-ṭawāsīn*, edited and translated by Louis Massignon. Paris: Geuthner, 1913.

Ḥaqqī, Ismāʻīl. *Kitāb tafsīr al-Qur'ān al-musammá Rūḥ al-bayān*. Būlāq: al-Maṭbaʻah al-ʻāmirah, 1870.

Hawting, Gerald R. *The Idea of Idolatry and the Emergence of Islam: From Polemic to History*. Cambridge: Cambridge University Press, 1999.

Hawting, Gerald R. 'Worship', in *Encyclopaedia of the Qur'ān*, vol. 5, edited by Jane Dammen McAuliffe. Leiden: Brill, 2006, 555–7.

Heck, Paul L. *Skepticism in Classical Islam: Moments of Confusion*. London: Routledge, 2014.

Ḥibshī, ʻAbd Allāh M. *Al-Ṣūfiyyah wa-al-fuqahā' fī al-Yaman*. Sana'a: Tawzīʻ maktabat al-jīl al-jadīd, 1976.

Hick, John. 'Religious Pluralism and Islam', Lecture delivered to the Institute for Islamic Culture and Thought, Tehran, February 2005. Accessed via http://www.johnhick.org.uk/article11.html on 19 January 2018.

Hodgson, Marshall. *The Venture of Islam: Conscience and History in a World Civilization*, in three volumes. Chicago and London: University of Chicago Press, 1974.

Hoffman, Valerie. 'Annihilation in the Messenger of God: The Development of a Sufi Practice', *International Journal of Middle East Studies* 31, no. 3 (1999), 351–69.

Hoover, Jon. 'Fiṭra', in *Encyclopaedia of Islam*, third edition (online), edited by Kate Fleet, Gudrun Krämer, Denis Matringe, John Nawas and Everett Rowon. Leiden: Brill, 2016. Accessed via http://ezproxy-prd.bodleian.ox.ac.uk:2134/entries/encyclopaedia-of-islam-3/fitra-COM_27155?s.num=0&s.f.s2_parent=s.f.book.encyclopaedia-of-islam-3&s.q=fitra on 18 January 2018.

Horovitz, Josef. 'Nabī', in *Encyclopaedia of Islam*, first edition, vol. 3, edited by M. Th. Houtsma, A. J. Wensinck, E. Levi-Provençal. Leiden: Brill, 1934, 802–3.

Horovitz, Josef [Firestone, Reuben]. 'Zabūr', in *Encyclopaedia of Islam*, second (new) edition, vol. 11. P. J. Bearman, Th. Bianquis, C. E. Bosworth, E. van Donzel and W. P. Heinrichs. Leiden: Brill, 2002, 372–3.

Horwitz, Daniel M. *A Kabbalah and Jewish Mysticism Reader*. Philadelphia: Jewish Publication Society. 2016.

Hourani, George. *Averroes on the Harmony of Religion and Philosophy*. Oxford: E.J.W. Gibb Memorial Trust, 2015.

Hujwīrī, 'Alī. *Kashf al-maḥjūb: the oldest Persian treatise on Ṣúfiism*, translated by Reynold Alleyne Nicholson. Leiden: Brill, 1911.

Ibn 'Arabī. *Al-Futūḥāt al-Makkiyyah*, in four volumes. Egypt: Dār al-Kutub al-'arabiyyah al-kubrá, 1329 AH [= 1911].

Ibn 'Arabī. *Fuṣūṣ al-ḥikam*, edited by Abū al-'Alá 'Afīfī. Beirut: Dār al-Kitāb al-'Arabī, 1946.

Ibn 'Arabī. *Al-Futūḥāt al-makkiyyah*, in 14 volumes, edited by 'Uthmān Yaḥyá. Cairo: al-Hay'ah al-Miṣriyyah al-'āmmah li-al-kitāb, 1972–1992.

Ibn 'Arabī. *The Bezels of Wisdom*, translated by Ralph W. J. Austin. Mahwah, NJ: Paulist Press, 1980.

Ibn 'Arabī. *Journey to the Lord of Power: A Sufi Manual on Retreat*, translated by Rabia Harris. London and The Hague: East West Publications, 1981.

Ibn Ḥanbal, Aḥmad. *Musnad al-Imām Aḥmad Ibn Ḥanbal*, in eight volumes, edited by Samīr Majdhūb and Muḥammad Samārah. Beirut, Damascus: al-Maktab al-islāmī, 1993.

Ibn Ḥazm. *al-Faṣl fī al-milal wa-al-ahwā' wa-al-niḥal*, in five volumes, edited by Muḥammad 'Alī Ṣubayḥ. Cairo: Maktabat al-Salām al-'ālamiyyah, no date listed.

Ibn Kathīr, Ismā'īl. *Tafsīr Ibn Kathīr*, edited by Muḥammad Khinn and Muṣṭafá Khinn. Beirut: Mu'assasat al-Risālah, 2000.

Ibn Kathīr, Ismā'īl. *Qiṣaṣ al-anbiyā'*, edited by Muḥammad 'Abd al-Qādir al-Fāḍilī. Beirut: al-Maktabah al-'Aṣriyyah, 2015.

Ibn Khaldūn. *The Muqaddimah: An Introduction to History*, in three volumes, translated by Franz Rosenthal. London: Routledge & Kegan Paul, 1958.

Ibn Khaldūn. *Shifā' al-sā'il wa-tahdhīb al-masā'il*, edited by Muḥammad al-Ḥāfiẓ. Damascus: Dār al-Fikr, 1996.

Ibn Khaldūn. *Muqaddimah*, in three volumes, edited by 'Alī 'Abd al-Wāḥid Wāfī. Cairo: Dār Nahdat Miṣr li-al-nashr, 2014.

Ibn Khaldūn. *Ibn Khaldūn on Sufism: Remedy for the Questioner in Search of Answers (Shifā' al-Sā'il li-Tahdhīb al-Masā'il)*, translated by Yumna Ozer. Cambridge: Islamic Texts Society, 2017.

Ibn Mājah, Muḥammad. *Sunan Ibn Mājah*, in five volumes, edited by Maḥmūd Naṣṣār. Beirut: Dār al-Kutub al-'ilmiyyah, 1998.

Ibn Rabban. *Kitāb al-Dīn wa-al-dawlah*, edited by 'Ādil Nuwayhaḍ. Beirut: Dār al-Āfāq al-jadīdah, 1973.

Ibn Rabban. *The Polemical Works of 'Alī al-Ṭabarī*, edited by Rifaat Ebied and David Thomas. Leiden and Boston: Brill, 2016.

Ibn Taymiyyah. *al-Jawāb al-ṣaḥīḥ li-man baddala dīn al-masīḥ*, four volumes in one, edited by 'Alī Ṣubḥ al-Madanī. Cairo: Maṭābi' al-Majd al-tijāriyyah, 1964.

Ibn Taymiyyah, Taqī al-dīn. *Majmū'ah al-Rasā'il al-kubrá*. No editor listed. Beirut: Dār Iḥyā' al-turāth al-'arabī, 1972.

Ibn Taymiyyah, Taqī al-dīn. *Majmū' al-fatāwá*, in thirty-seven volumes, edited by 'Āmir al-Jazzār and Anwar al-Bāz. Mansura: Dār al-Wafā', 1995.

Idel, Moshe. *Language, Torah, and Hermeneutics in Abraham Abulafia*. Albany, NY: State University of New York Press, 1989.

Idel, Moshe. *Kabbalah: New Perspectives*. New Haven and London: Yale University Press, 1990.

Ikhwān al-Ṣafā'. *On Magic: An Arabic Critical Edition and English Translation of Epistle 52a*, edited and translated by Godefroid de Callataÿ and Bruno Hallfants. Oxford: Oxford University Press, 2011.

Iqbal, Muhammad. *The Development of Metaphysics in Persia: A Contribution to the History of Muslim Philosophy*. London: Luzac & Co., 1908.

Iqbal, Muhammad. *Speeches, Writings and Statements of Iqbal*, in two parts, edited by Latif Ahmad Shirwani. Lahore: Iqbal Academy Pakistan, 2016.

Izutsu, Toshihiko. *The Structure of the Ethical Terms in the Koran; A Study in Semantics*. Tokyo: Keio Institute of Cultural and Linguistics Studies, 1959.

Izutsu, Toshihiko. *God and Man in the Koran: Semantics of the Koranic Weltanschauung*. Tokyo: Keio Institute of Cultural and Linguistics Studies, 1964.

Izutsu, Toshihiko. *Sufism & Taoism: A Comparative Study of Key Philosophical Concepts*. Berkeley and London: University of California Press, 1984.

Jāmī, 'Abd al-Raḥmān. *The Precious Pearl*, translated by Nicholas Heer. Albany, NY: State University of New York Press, 1979.

Jazā'irī, 'Abd al-Qādir. *Al-Mawāqif al-rūḥiyyah wa-al-fuyūḍāt al-subūḥiyyah*, in two volumes, edited by 'Āṣim Ibrāhīm al-Kayālī. Beirut: Dār al-kutub al-'ilmiyyah, 2004.

Jeffrey, Arthur. *The Foreign Vocabulary of the Qur'an*. Baroda: Oriental Institute, 1929.

Jīlī, 'Abd al-Karīm. *De l'homme universel: extraits du livre al-Insân al-kâmil*, translated by Titus Burckardt. Alger: Messerschmitt; Lyon: P. Derain, 1952.

Jīlī, 'Abd al-Karīm. 'Die Risāla arbaʿīn mawāṭin des ʿAbdalkarīm al-Ǧīlī', edited by Dagmar Mann. PhD diss., Saarbrücken, 1970.

Jīlī, 'Abd al-Karīm. *Al-Manāẓir al-ilāhiyyah*, edited by Najāh al-Ghunaymī. Cairo: Dār al-Manār, 1987.

Jīlī, 'Abd al-Karīm. *Al-Insān al-kāmil fī ma'rifat al-awākhir wa-al-awā'il*, edited by Ṣalāḥ Muḥammad 'Uwayḍah. Beirut: Dār al-Kutub al-'ilmiyyah, 1997.

Jīlī, 'Abd al-Karīm. *Al-Kamālāt al-ilāhiyyah fī al-ṣifāt al-muḥammadiyyah*, edited by Saʿīd ʿAbd al-Fattāḥ. Cairo: *'Ālam al-fikr*, 1997.

Jīlī, 'Abd al-Karīm. *Göttliche Vollkommenheit und die Stellung des Menschen: die Sichtweise ʿAbd al-Karīm al Ǧīlīs auf der Grundlage des 'Šarḥ muškilāt al-futūḥāt al-makkīya'*, edited by Angelika Al-Massri. Stuttgart: Deutsche Morganländische Gesellschaft, 1998.

Jīlī, 'Abd al-Karīm. *Al-Nādirāt al-'ayniyyah li-'Abd al-Karīm al-Jīlī, ma'a sharḥ al-Nābulusī*, edited by Youssef Ziedan. Cairo: Dār al-Amīn, 1999.

Jīlī, 'Abd al-Karīm. *Marātib al-wujūd wa-ḥaqīqat kull mawjūd*. No editor listed. Cairo: Maktabat al-Qāhirah, 1999.

Jīlī, 'Abd al-Karīm. *Sharḥ mushkilāt al-Futūḥāt al-Makkiyyah*, edited by Youssef Ziedan. Cairo: Dār al-Amīn, 1999.

Jīlī, 'Abd al-Karīm. *al-Isfār 'an Risālat al-anwār fī-mā yatajallá li-ahl al-dhikr min al-anwār*, edited by 'Āṣim al-Kayyālī. Beirut: Dār al-Kutub al-'ilmiyyah, 2004.

Jīlī, 'Abd al-Karīm. *Ibdā' al-kitābah wa-kitābat al-'ibdā'* (*'ayn 'alá al-'ayniyyah: sharḥ mu'āṣir li-'ayniyyat al-imām al-ṣūfī 'Abd al-Karīm al-Jīlī*) [= *al-Nādirāt al-'ayniyyah*], edited and commented on by Su'ād al-Ḥakīm. Beirut: Dār al-Burāq, 2004.

Jīlī, 'Abd al-Karīm. *I Nomi divini e il Profeta alla luce del sufismo* (Al-Kamālāt al-ilāhiyyah fī al-ṣifāt al-muḥammadiyyah), translated by Claudio Marzullo. Turin: Il leone verde, 2015.

Johns, Anthony H. 'Moses in the Qur'an: Finite and Infinite Dimensions of Prophecy', in *The Charles Strong Lectures: 1972–1984*, edited by Robert B. Crotty. Leiden: Brill, 1987, 123–38.

Juynboll, G. H. A. 'Farḍ', in *Encyclopaedia of Islam*, second (new) edition, vol. 2, edited by B. Lewis, V. L. Ménage, Ch. Pellat and J. Schacht. Leiden: Brill, 1965, 789–90.

Karamustafa, Ahmet T. *Sufism: The Formative Period*. Berkeley: University of California Press, 2007.

Kātib Çelebī (Ḥājjī Khalīfah). *Kashf al-ẓunūn ʿan asāmi al-kutub wa-al-funūn* [*Lexicon bibliographicum et encyclopædicum a Mustafa Ben Abdallah Katib Jelebi dicto et nomine Haji Khalfa celebrato compositum: ad codicum vindobonensium, parisiensium et berolinensis, fidem primum*], in seven volumes, edited by Gustav Flugel. Leipzig: The Oriental Translation Fund for Great Britain and Ireland, 1835–1858.

Keeler, Annabel. 'Moses from a Muslim Perspective', in *Abraham's Children: Jews, Christians and Muslims in Conversation*, edited by Richard Harries, Norman Solomon, and Timothy Winter. London and New York: T&T Clark, 2005, 55–66.

Keeler, Annabel. *Sufi Hermeneutics: The Qur'an Commentary of Rashīd al-dīn Maybudī*. Oxford: Oxford University Press, 2006.

Keller, C.-A. 'Perceptions of Other Religions in Sufism', in *Muslim Perceptions of Other Religions*, edited by Jacques Waardenburg. Oxford: Oxford University Press, 1999, 181–94.

Keller, Nur H. M. 'On the Validity of All Religions in the Thought of Ibn Al–'Arabi and Emir 'Abd al-Qadir: A Letter to 'Abd al-Matin', (1996) Accessed via http://www.masud.co.uk/ISLAM/nuh/amat.htm on 1 February 2018.

Kermani, Navid. 'From Revelation to Interpretation: Nasr Hamid Abu Zayd and the Literary Study of the Qur'an', in *Modern Muslim Intellectuals and the Qur'an*, edited by Suha Taji-Farouki. Oxford: Oxford University Press, 2004, 169–224.

Khalidi, Tarif. *The Muslim Jesus: Sayings and Stories in Islamic Literature*. Cambridge, MA and London: Harvard University Press, 2001.

Khalil, Mohammad H. *Islam and the Fate of Others: The Salvation Question*. Oxford and New York: Oxford University Press, 2013.

Khan, Ruqayya J. *Self and Secrecy in Early Islam*. Columbia, SC: University of South Carolina Press, 2008.

Khoury, Raif G. *Wahb b. Munnabih*. Weisbaden: O. Hassarrowitz, 1972.

Knysh, Alexander. "Orthodoxy' and 'Heresy' in Mediaeval Islam: An Essay in Reassessment', *The Muslim World* 53, no. 1 (1993), 48–67.

Knysh, Alexander. *Ibn 'Arabi in the Later Islamic Tradition: The Making of a Polemical Image in Medieval Islam*. Albany, NY: State University of New York Press, 1999.

Knysh, Alexander. 'Sufism and the Qur'ān', *Encyclopaedia of the Qur'ān*, vol. 5, edited by Jane Dammen McAuliffe. Leiden: Brill, 2006, 137–59.

Knysh, Alexander. *Sufism: A New History of Islamic Mysticism*. Princeton, NJ: Princeton University Press, 2018.

Kohlberg, Etan. 'Some Imāmī-shīʿī Views on Taqiyya', *Journal of the American Oriental Society* 95, no. 3 (1975), 395–402.

Kruk, Remke. 'Nabāt', in *Encyclopaedia of Islam*, second (new) edition, vol. 6, edited by C. E. Bosworth, E. van Donzel and Ch. Pellat. Leiden: Brill, 1991, 831–4.

Kugel, James L. *Traditions of the Bible: A Guide to the Bible as It Was at the Start of the Common Era*. Cambridge, MA and London: Harvard University Press, 1998.

Lane, Andrew N. ''Abd al-Ghanī al-Nābulusī's (1641–1731) Commentary on Ibn 'Arabī's Fuṣūṣ al-ḥikam: An Analysis and Interpretation', DPhil diss., University of Oxford, 2001.

Lane, Edward W. *Arabic-English Lexicon*, in two volumes, supplemented by Stanley Lane-Poole. Cambridge: Islamic Texts Society, 1984.

Langermann, Y. Tzvi. 'Yemenite Philosophical Midrash as a Source for the Intellectual History of the Jews of Yemen', in *The Jews of Medieval Islam: Community, Society, & Identity*, edited by Daniel Frank. Leiden, New York and Köln: Brill, 1995, 335–48.

Lala, Ismail. 'The Term 'Huwiyya' in Muḥyī al-Dīn ibn 'Arabī and 'Abd al-Razzāq al-Qāshānī's Sufi Thought', Dphil. diss., University of Oxford, 2017.

Layish, Aharon and Shaham, Ron. 'Tashrī'', in *Encyclopaedia of Islam*, second (new) edition, vol. 10, edited by P. J. Bearman, Th. Bianquis, C. E. Bosworth, E. van Donzel and W. P. Heinrichs. Leiden: Brill, 2000, 353–4.

Lazarus-Yafeh, Hava. *Intertwined Worlds: Medieval Islam and Bible Criticism*. Princeton, NJ: Princeton University Press, 1992.

Lazarus-Yafeh, Hava. 'Taḥrīf', in *Encyclopaedia of Islam*, second (new) edition, vol. 10, edited by P. J. Bearman, Th. Bianquis, C. E. Bosworth, E. van Donzel and W. P. Heinrichs. Leiden: Brill, 2000, 111–12.

Lazarus-Yafeh, Hava. 'Tawrāt', in *Encyclopaedia of Islam*, second (new) edition, vol. 10, edited by P. J. Bearman, Th. Bianquis, C. E. Bosworth, E. van Donzel and W. P. Heinrichs. Leiden: Brill, 2000, 393–5.

Lettinck, Paul. 'Ṭabī'iyyāt', in *Encyclopaedia of Islam*, second (new) edition, vol. 12 (supplement), edited by P. J. Bearman, Th. Bianquis, C. E. Bosworth, E. van Donzel and W. P. Heinrichs. Leiden: Brill, 2004, 769–70.

Lindsay, James E. "Alī Ibn 'Asākir as a Preserver of *Qiṣaṣ al-Anbiyā*': The Case of David ibn Jesse', *Studia Islamica* 82 (1995), 45–82.

Lings, Martin. *What Is Sufism?* London: George Allen & Unwin, 1975.

Lipton, Gregory. *Rethinking Ibn 'Arabi*. New York: Oxford University Press, 2018.

Lo Polito, Nicholas. "Abd al-Karīm al-Jīlī: Tawḥīd, Transcendence, and Immanence', PhD diss., University of Birmingham, 2010.

Louth, Andrew. *Introducing Eastern Orthodox Theology*. London: SPCK, 2013.

Macdonald, Duncan B. 'Fiṭra', in *Encyclopaedia of Islam*, second (new) edition, vol. 2, edited by B. Lewis, V. L. Ménage, Ch. Pellat and J. Schacht. Leiden: Brill, 1965, 931–2.

Macdonald, Duncan B. 'Ilhām', in *Encyclopaedia of Islam*, second (new) edition, vol. 3, edited by B. Lewis, V. L. Ménage, Ch. Pellat and J. Schacht. Leiden: Brill, 1971, 1119–20.

Macdonald, Duncan B. 'Malā'ika', in *Encyclopaedia of Islam*, second (new) edition, vol. 6, edited by C. E. Bosworth, E. van Donzel and Ch. Pellat. Leiden: Brill, 1991, 216–19.

Madelung, Wilferd. "Iṣmah', in *Encyclopaedia of Islam*, second (new) edition, vol. 4, edited by E. van Donzel, B. Lewis and Ch. Pellat. Leiden: Brill, 1978, 182–4.

Madelung, Wilferd. 'Murdji'a', in *Encyclopaedia of Islam*, second (new) edition, vol. 7, edited by C. E. Bosworth, E. van Donzel, W. P. Heinrichs and Ch. Pellat. Leiden: Brill, 1993, 605–7.

Madigan, Daniel. 'Preserved Table', in *Encyclopaedia of the Qur'ān*, vol. 4, edited by Jane Dammen McAuliffe. Leiden: Brill, 2004, 261–3.

Madigan, Daniel. 'Revelation and Inspiration', in *Encyclopaedia of the Qur'ān*, vol. 4, edited by Jane Dammen McAuliffe. Leiden: Brill, 2004, 437–48.

Maḥallī, Jalāl al-Dīn and Suyūṭī, Jalāl al-Dīn. *Tafsīr al-Jalālayn*, in two volumes, edited by Ṣafī Mubārakfūrī. Riyadh: al-Dār, 2002.

Mahmoud, Mohamed. *Quest for Divinity: A Critical Examination of the Thought of Mahmud Muhammad Taha*. Syracuse, NY: Syracuse University Press, 2007.

Martin, Richard C. 'Createdness of the Qur'ān', in *Encyclopaedia of the Qur'ān*, vol. 1, edited by Jane Dammen McAuliffe. Leiden: Brill, 2001, 467–72.

Mas'ūdī, *Les prairies d'or*, in nine volumes, edited by C. Barbier de Maynard and A. Pavet de Courteille. Paris: Imprimerie impériale, 1861–1917.

Massignon, Louis. *Essay on the Origins of the Technical Language of Islamic Mysticism*, translated by Benjamin Clark. Notre Dame, IN: University of Notre Dame Press, 1997.

Massignon, Louis and Anawati, Georges. 'Ḥulūl', in *Encyclopaedia of Islam*, second (new) edition, vol. 3, edited by B. Lewis, V. L. Ménage, Ch. Pellat and J. Schacht. Leiden: Brill, 1971, 570–1.

Matt, Daniel C. (tr.). *Zohar: The Book of Enlightenment*. Mahwah, NJ: Paulist Press, 1983.

Matt, Daniel C. (tr.). *The Zohar*, in nine volumes. Stanford: Stanford University Press, 2004–2016.

Maybudī, Rashīd al-dīn. *The Unveiling of the Mysteries and the Provision of the Pious: Kashf al-asrār wa-'uddat al-abrār*, translated by William C. Chittick. Louisville, KY: Fons Vitae, 2015.

McAuliffe, Jane. *Qur'ānic Christians: An Analysis of Classical and Modern Exegesis*. Cambridge: Cambridge University Press, 1991.

McAuliffe, Jane D. 'The Prediction and Prefiguration of Muḥammad', in *Bible and Qur'ān: Essays in Scriptural Intertextuality*, edited by John C. Reeves. Atlanta, GA: Society of Biblical Literature, 2003, 107–32.

McGinnis, Jon. *Avicenna*. New York and Oxford: Oxford University Press, 2009.

McGrath, Alister E. *Christian Theology: An Introduction*. Chichester and Malden, MA: Wiley-Blackwell, 2011.

McGregor, Richard. *Sanctity and Mysticism in Medieval Egypt: The Wafā' Sufi Order and the Legacy of Ibn 'Arabī*. Albany, NY: State University of New York Press, 2004.

Milani, Milad. 'Representations of Jesus in Islamic Mysticism: Defining the "Sufi Jesus"', *Literature & Aesthetics* 21, no. 2 (2012), 45–65.

Mir, Mustansir. 'Names of the Qur'ān', in *Encyclopaedia of the Qur'ān*, vol. 3, edited by Jane Dammen McAuliffe. Leiden: Brill, 2003, 505–15.

Morris, James W. 'Ibn 'Arabī and His Interpreters', pt 3, *Journal of the American Oriental Society* 107, no. 1 (1987), 101–20.

Morris, James W. 'An Arab Machiavelli? Rhetoric, Philosophy and Politics in Ibn Khaldun's Critique of Sufism', *Harvard Middle Eastern and Islamic Review* 8 (2009), 242–91.

Morrissey, Fitzroy. 'An Introduction to 'Abd al-Karīm al-Jīlī's Commentary on the *Futūḥāt*', *The Maghreb Review* 41, no. 4 (2016), 499–526.

Morrissey, Fitzroy. "Abd al-Karīm al-Jīlī's Sufi View of Other Religions', The *Maghreb Review* 43, no. 2 (2018), 175–97.

Morrissey, Fitzroy and Nettler, Ronald L. 'Ibn Khaldūn on Sufism: A Story of Truth vs. Falsehood in Three Parts', *The Maghreb Review* 44, no. 4 (2019), 403–30.

Morrissey, Fitzroy. *Sufism and the Perfect Human: From Ibn 'Arabī to al-Jīlī*. Abingdon: Routledge, 2020.

Motzki, Harald. 'Nāmūs', in *Encyclopaedia of the Qur'ān*, vol. 3, edited by Jane Dammen McAuliffe. Leiden: Brill, 2003, 515–16.

Mourad, Youssef. 'La physiognomie arabe et le Kitāb al-firāsa de Fakhr al-Dīn al-Rāzī', PhD diss., University of Paris, 1939.

Mufīd, Muḥammad. *Taṣḥīḥ al-iʿtiqād bi-ṣawāb al-intiqād, aw, Sharḥ ʿaqāʾid al-Ṣadūq*, edited by Hibat al-Dīn Shahrastānī. Beirut: Dār al-Kitāb al-islāmī, 1983.

Murata, Sachiko. *The Tao of Islam: A Sourcebook on Gender Relationships in Islamic Thought*. Albany, NY: State University of New York, 1992.

Murata, Sachiko. *Chinese Gleams of Sufi Light*. Albany, NY: State University of New York Press, 2000.

Muslim, Abū al-Ḥusayn. *Ṣaḥīḥ Muslim*, eighteen volumes in nine, edited by Muḥammad ʿAbd al-Bāqī. Beirut: Dār al-Kutub al-ʿilmiyyah, 1995.

Nabhānī, Yūsuf. *Jawāhir al-biḥār fī faḍāʾil al-nabī al-mukhtār*, in four volumes, edited by Muḥammad al-Ḍannāwī. Beirut: Dār al-Kutub al-ʿilmiyyah, 1998.

Nasr, Seyyed H. *An Introduction to Islamic Cosmological Doctrines: Conceptions of Nature and Methods Used for Its Study by the Ikhwān al-Ṣafāʾ, al-Bīrūnī and Ibn Sīnā*. London: Thames and Hudson, 1978.

Nasr, Seyyed H. and Leaman, Oliver. *History of Islamic Philosophy*, in two volumes. London: Routledge, 1996.

Nasr, Seyyed H. *Islam in the Modern World: Challenged by the West, Threatened by Fundamentalism, Keeping Faith with Tradition*. New York: Harper Collins, 2011.

Nawawī, Yaḥyá. *An-Nawawi's Forty Hadith* [= *al-Arbaʿūn al-Nawawiyyah*], translated by Ezzeddin Ibrahim and Denys Johnson-Davies. Cairo: Dār al-Shurūq, 2002.

Nettler, Ronald L. 'Ibn ʿArabī's Notion of Allah's Mercy', *Israel Oriental Studies* 8 (1978), 219–29.

Nettler, Ronald L. *Sufi Metaphysics and Qur'ānic Prophets: Ibn ʿArabī's Thought and Method in the* Fuṣūṣ al-ḥikam. Cambridge: Islamic Texts Society, 2003.

Nettler, Ronald L. 'Ibn ʿArabi's Gloss on the Prophet Yunus: Sufism and the Continuity of a Common Religious Culture', in *The Religion of the Other: Essays in Honour of Mohamed Talbi*, edited by Mohamed Ben-Madani. London: Maghreb Publications, 2013, 53–60.

Neusner, Jacob (ed.). *Understanding Jewish Theology: Classical Issues and Modern Perspectives*. Binghamton University: Global Publications (Classics in Jewish Studies), 2001.

Nicholson, Reynold A. *The Mystics of Islam*. London: G. Bell & Sons, 1914.

Nicholson, Reynold A. *Studies in Islamic Mysticism*. Richmond, Surrey: Curzon Press, 1921.

Noble, Samuel and Treiger, Alexander (eds). *The Orthodox Church in the Arab World, 700-1700: An Anthology of Sources*. DeKalb, IL: NIU Press, 2014.

Noble, Michael. 'The Perfection of the Soul in Fakhr al-Dīn al-Rāzī's *Al-Sirr al-maktūm*', PhD diss., University of London, 2017.

Nurbakhsh, Javad. *Jesus in the Eyes of the Sufis*, translated by Terry Graham, Leonard Lewisohn and Hamid Mashkuri. London: Khaniqahi-Nimatullahi Publications, 1992.

Nwyia, Paul. *Exégèse coranique et langage mystique; nouvel essai sur le lexique technique des mystiques musulmans*. Beirut: Dar el-Machreq, 1970.

Nwyia, Paul. 'Ishārah', in *Encyclopaedia of Islam*, second (new) edition, vol. 4, edited by E. van Donzel, B. Lewis and Ch. Pellat. Leiden: Brill, 1978, 113–14.

Padwick, Constance. *Henry Martyn: Confessor of the Faith*. London: Student Christian Movement, 1922.

Ormsby, Eric. 'The Faith of Pharaoh: A Disputed Question in Islamic Theology', *Reason and Inspiration in Islam: Theology, Philosophy and Mysticism in Muslim Thought. Essays in Honour of Hermann Landolt*, edited by Todd Lawson. London and New York: I.B. Tauris, 2005, 471–89.

Parrinder, Geoffrey. *Jesus in the Qur'an*. London: Oneworld, 2003.

Pingree, David. "Ilm al-hay'a', in *Encyclopaedia of Islam*, second (new) edition, vol. 3, edited by B. Lewis, V. L. Ménage, Ch. Pellat and J. Schacht. Leiden: Brill, 1971, 1135–38.

Poonawala, Ismail. 'Ta'wīl', in *Encyclopaedia of Islam*, second (new) edition, vol. 10, edited by P. J. Bearman, Th. Bianquis, C. E. Bosworth, E. van Donzel and W. P. Heinrichs. Leiden: Brill, 2000, 390–2.

Qāshānī, 'Abd al-Razzāq. *Sharḥ 'alá al-Fuṣūṣ al-ḥikam*. No editor listed. Egypt: al-Maṭba'ah al-Yamaniyyah, no date listed.

Qāshānī, 'Abd al-Razzāq. *Mu'jam iṣṭilāḥāt al-ṣūfiyyah*, edited by 'Abd al-'Āl Shāhīn. Cairo: Dār al-Manār, 1992.

Qāshānī, 'Abd al-Razzāq ['Ibn al-'Arabī']. *Tafsīr al-Qur'ān al-karīm*, in two volumes, edited by 'Abd al-Wārith Muḥammad 'Alī. Beirut: Dār al-Kutub al-'ilmiyyah, 2001.

Qayṣarī, Dāwūd. *Sharḥ-i muqaddamah-'i Qayṣarī bar Fuṣūṣ al-ḥikam-i Muḥyī al-Dīn 'Arabī*, edited by Jalāl al-Dīn Āshtiyānī. Mashhad: Kitābfurūshī-yi bāstān, 1966.

Qūnawī, Ṣadr al-dīn. *I'jāz al-bayān fī tafsīr umm al-Qur'ān*, edited by Jalāl al-Dīn Āshtiyānī. Qom: Mu'assasah-yi Būstān-i Kitāb-i Qom, 1423 AH [= 2002].

Qurṭubī, Muḥammad. *Al-Jāmi' li-aḥkām al-Qur'ān: tafsīr al-Qurṭubī*, twenty volumes in ten. Beirut: Dār al-Kitāb al-'Arabī, 1997.

Qushayrī, Abū al-Qāsim. *Laṭā'if al-ishārāt: tafsīr Ṣūfī kāmil li-al-Qur'ān al-Karīm*, in four volumes, edited by Ibrāhīm Basyūnī. Cairo: al-Hay'ah al-Miṣriyyah al-'āmmah li-al-kitāb, 2000.

Qushayrī, Abū al-Qāsim. *Al-Risālah al-Qushayriyyah*, edited by Khalīl Manṣūr. Beirut: Dār al-Kutub al-'ilmiyyah, 2001.

Race, Alan. *Christians and Religious Pluralism: Patterns in Christian Theology*. London: SCM Press, 1983.

Race, Alan. *Making Sense of Religious Pluralism: Shaping Theology of Religions for our Times*. London: SPCK, 2013.

Radtke, Bernd. 'Wisdom', in *Encyclopaedia of the Qur'ān*, vol. 5, edited by Jane Dammen McAuliffe. Leiden: Brill, 2006, 483–4.

Ragep, F. Jamil. 'Astronomy', in *Encyclopaedia of Islam*, third edition (online), edited by Kate Fleet, Gudrun Krämer, Denis Matringe, John Nawas and Everett Rowon. Leiden: Brill, 2009. Accessed via http://ezproxy-prd.bodleian.ox.ac.uk:2134/entries/encyclopaedia-of-islam-3/astronomy-COM_22652?s.num=2&s.f.s2_parent=s.f.cluster.Encyclopaedia+of+Islam&s.q=astronomy on 26 January 2018.

Rahman, Fazlur. *Major Themes of the Qur'ān*. Minneapolis, MA: Bibliotheca Islamica, 1989.

Rashed, Roshdi. 'Riyāḍiyyāt', in *Encyclopaedia of Islam*, second (new) edition, vol. 8, edited by C. E. Bosworth, G. Lecomte, E. J. van Donzel, Wolfhart Heinrichs, and Peri Bearman. Leiden: Brill, 1995, 549–62

Rāzī, Najm al-dīn. *The Path of God's Bondsmen from Origin to Return* (Merṣād al-'ebād men al-mabdā' elā'l-ma'ād): *A Sufi Compendium*, translated by Hamid Algar. Delmar, NY: Caravan Books, 1982.

Reynolds, Gabriel S. *A Muslim Theologian in a Sectarian Milieu*: 'Abd al-Jabbār *and the Critique of Christian Orgins*. Leiden: Brill, 2004.

Reynolds, Gabriel S. 'On the Qur'anic Accusation of Scriptural Falsification (*taḥrīf*) and Christian Anti-Jewish Polemic', *Journal of the American Oriental Society* 130 (2010), 189–202.

Reynolds, Gabriel S. 'The Islamic Christ', in *The Oxford Handbook of Christology*, edited by Francesca Aran Murphy. Oxford: Oxford University Press, 2015, 183–98.

Rippin, Andrew. 'Syriac in the Qur'an: Classical Muslim Theories', in *The Qur'an in Its Historical Context*, edited by Gabriel S. Reynolds. London and New York: Routledge, 2008, 249–61.

Rispler, Vardit. 'Toward a New Understanding of the Term *bid'a*', *Der Islam* 68, no. 2 (1991), 320–8.

Robson, James. 'Bid'ah', in *Encyclopaedia of Islam*, second (new) edition, vol. 1, edited by H. A. R. Gibb, J. H. Kramers, E. Lévi-Provençal and J. Schacht. Leiden: Brill, 1960, 1169.

Rosenthal, Franz. 'Ibn 'Arabī Between "Philosophy" and "Mysticism": "Sūfism and Philosophy Are Neighbors and Visit Each Other", *fa-inna at-taṣawwuf wa-t-tafalsuf yatajāwarāni wa-yatazāwarāni*', *Oriens* 31 (1988), 1–35.

Roth, Norman. 'Muslim Knowledge of the Hebrew Bible and Jewish Traditions in the Middle Ages', *The Maghreb Review* 16, no. 1–2 (1991), 74–83.

Rubin, Uri. 'Jews and Judaism', in *Encyclopaedia of the Qur'ān*, vol. 3, edited by Jane Dammen McAuliffe. Leiden: Brill, 2003, 21–34.

Rubin, Uri. 'Muhammad', in *Encyclopaedia of the Qur'ān*, vol. 3, edited by Jane Dammen McAuliffe. Leiden: Brill, 2003, 440–58.

Rubin, Uri. 'Oft-Repeated', in *Encyclopaedia of the Qur'ān*, vol. 3, edited by Jane Dammen McAuliffe. Leiden: Brill, 2003, 574–6.

Rubin, Uri. 'Prophets and Prophethood', in *Encyclopaedia of the Qur'ān*, vol. 4, edited by Jane Dammen McAuliffe. Leiden: Brill, 2004, 289–306.

Rūmī, Jalāl al-dīn. *The Mathnawí of Jalálu'ddín Rúmí*, in eight volumes, edited by R. A. Nicholson. London: Luzac & Co., 1925–1940.

Rundgren, Frithiof. 'The Preface of the *Futûhât al-Makkiyya*', in *Muhyiddin Ibn 'Arabi: A Commemorative Volume*, edited by Stephen Hirtenstein and Michael Tiernan. Shaftesbury: Element for the Muhyiddin Ibn 'Arabi Society, 1993.

Rustom, Mohammed. 'Ibn 'Arabī's Letter to Fakhr al-Dīn al-Rāzī: A Study and Translation', *Journal of Islamic Studies* 25, no. 2 (2014), 113–37.

Sabra, Abdelhamid I. "Ilm al-Ḥisāb', in *Encyclopaedia of Islam*, second (new) edition, vol. 3, edited by B. Lewis, V. L. Ménage, Ch. Pellat and J. Schacht. Leiden: Brill, 1971, 1138–41.

Sahner, Christian. 'Islamic Legends About the Birth of Monasticism: A Case Study on the Late Antique Milieu of the Qur'ān and Tafsīr', in *The Late Antique World of Early Islam: Muslims Among Christians and Jews in the East Mediterranean*, edited by Robert Hoyland. Princeton, NJ: Darwin Press, 2015, 393–435.

Sahner, Christian. 'The Monasticism of My Community Is Jihad: A Debate on Asceticism, Sex, and Warfare in Early Islam', *Arabica* 64 (2017), 149–83.

Saleh, Walid. 'A Fifteenth-Century Muslim Hebraist: Al-Biqā'ī and His Defense of Using the Bible to Interpret the Qur'ān', *Speculum* 83, no. 3 (2008), 629–54.

Saleh, Walid. 'The Psalms in the Qur'an and the Islamic Tradition', in *The Oxford Handbook of the Psalms*, edited by William P. Brown. Oxford: Oxford University Press, 2014, 281–96.

Saleh, Walid. 'The Hebrew Bible in Islam', in *The Cambridge Companion to the Hebrew Bible/Old Testament*, edited by Stephen B. Chapman and Martin A. Sweeney. Cambridge: Cambridge University Press, 2016, 407–25.

Sands, Kristin Zahra. *Ṣūfī Commentaries on the Qur'ān In Classical Islam*. London: Routledge, 2006.

Sarrāj, Abū Naṣr. *Kitāb al-Luma' fī al-taṣawwuf*, edited by Reynold Alleyne Nicholson. Leiden: Brill, 1914.

Schacht, Joseph. *The Origins of Muhammadan Jurisprudence*. London: Oxford University Press, 1950.
Schacht, Joseph. 'Aḥkām', in *Encyclopaedia of Islam*, second (new) edition, vol. 1, edited by H. A. R. Gibb, J. H. Kramers, E. Lévi-Provençal and J. Schacht. Leiden: Brill, 1960, 257.
Schacht, Joseph. 'Khaṭa'', in *Encyclopaedia of Islam*, second (new) edition, vol. 5, edited by C. E. Bosworth, E. van Donzel, B. Lewis and Ch. Pellat. Leiden: Brill, 1978, 1100–102.
Schacht, Joseph. 'Ḳiṣāṣ', in *Encyclopaedia of Islam*, second (new) edition, vol. 5, edited by B. Lewis, V. L. Ménage, Ch. Pellat and J. Schacht. Leiden: Brill, 1986, 766–72.
Schimmel, Annemarie. *Mystical Dimensions of Islam*. Chapel Hill, NC: University of North Carolina Press, 1975.
Schippers, Arie. 'Psalms', in *Encyclopaedia of the Qur'ān*, vol. 4, edited by Jane Dammen McAuliffe. Leiden: Brill, 2004, 314–18.
Schlosser, Dominik. 'Ibn Qayyim al-Jawziyya's Attitude Toward Christianity in *Hidāyat al-ḥayārā fī ajwibat al-yahūd wal-naṣārā*', in *Islamic Theology, Philosophy and Law: Debating Ibn Taymiyya and Ibn Qayyim al-Jawziyya*, edited by Birgit Krawietz and Georges Tamer. Berlin and Boston: Walter de Gruyter, 2013, 422–60.
Schmidtke, Sabine. *The Theology of al-'Allāma al-Ḥillī (d. 726/1325)*. Berlin: Klaus Schwarz Verlag, 1991.
Schmidtke, Sabine. 'The Muslim Reception of Biblical Materials: Ibn Qutayba and His *A'lām al-nubuwwa*', *Islam and Christian-Muslim Relations* 22, no. 3 (2011), 249–74.
Schöck, Cornelia. 'Moses', in *Encyclopaedia of the Qur'ān*, vol. 3, edited by Jane Dammen McAuliffe. Leiden: Brill, 2003, 411–26.
Sells, Michael. 'Ascension', in *Encyclopaedia of the Qur'ān*, vol. 1, edited by Jane Dammen McAuliffe. Leiden: Brill, 2001, 176–81.
Sells, Michael. 'Memory', in *Encyclopaedia of the Qur'ān*, vol. 3, edited by Jane Dammen McAuliffe. Leiden: Brill, 2003, 372–4.
Shabistarī, Maḥmūd. *Gulshan-i rāz*, edited by Ṣamad Muwaḥḥid. Tehran: Intishārāt-i Ṭawrī, 2011.
Shahrastānī, Ibn 'Abd al-Karīm. *Al-Milal wa-al-niḥal*, three volumes in one, edited by Aḥmad Fahmī Muḥammad. Beirut: Dār al-Kutub al-'ilmiyyah, 1992.
Shapiro, David E. 'Foundations of the Halakhah', in *Understanding Jewish Theology: Classical Issues and Modern Perspectives*, edited by Jacob Neusner. Binghamton University: Global Publications (Classics in Jewish Studies), 2001.
Shihadeh, Aymen. 'From al-Ghazālī to al-Rāzī: 6th/12th Century Developments in Muslim Philosophical Theology', *Arabic Sciences and Philosophy* 15, no. 1 (2005), 141–79.
Siddiqui, Mona. *Christians, Muslims, & Jesus*. New Haven, CT and London: Yale University Press, 2013.
Sirriyeh, Elizabeth. *Sufi Visionary of Ottoman Damascus: 'Abd al-Ghanī al-Nabulusī, 1641–1731*. Abingdon: RoutledgeCurzon, 2005.
Skinner, Quentin. 'Meaning and Understanding in the History of Ideas', *History and Theory* 8, no. 1 (1969), 3–53.
Smith, Jane I. 'Eschatology', in *Encyclopaedia of the Qur'ān*, vol. 2, edited by Jane Dammen McAuliffe. Leiden: Brill, 2002, 44–54.
Smith, Margaret. *Readings from the Mystics of Islam; Translations from the Arabic and Persian, Together with a Short Account of the History and Doctrines of Ṣūfism and Brief Biographical Notes on Each Ṣūfī Writer*. London: Luzac, 1950.
Smith, Wilfred C. *The Meaning and End of Religion*. Minneapolis: Fortress Press, 1991.
Soucek, Priscilla. 'Solomon', in *Encyclopaedia of the Qur'ān*, vol. 5, edited by Jane Dammen McAuliffe. Leiden: Brill, 2006, 76–8.

Sperber, Daniel. 'Nations, the Seventy', in *Encyclopaedia Judaica*, vol. 15. Detroit: Macmillan Reference USA in assoc. with Keter Pub. House, 2007, 30–2.

Stern, Samuel M. 'Quotations from Apocryphal Gospels in 'Abd al-Jabbār', *Journal of Theological Studies* 18 (1957), 34–57.

Stern, Samuel M. ''Abd al-Jabbār's Account of How Christ's Religion Was Falsified by the Adoption of Roman Customs', *Journal of Theological Studies* 19 (1958), 128–85.

Street, Tony. *Stanford Encyclopaedia of Philosophy*, s.v. 'Arabic and Islamic Philosophy of Language and Logic'. Accessed via http://plato.stanford.edu/entries/arabic-islamic-language/#GhaLog, on 10 November 2016.

Strothmann, Rudolf. 'Taḳiyya', in *Encyclopaedia of Islam*, second (new) edition, vol. 10, edited by P. J. Bearman, Th. Bianquis, C. E. Bosworth, E. van Donzel and W. P. Heinrichs. Leiden: Brill, 2000, 134–6.

Strauss, Leo. *Persecution and the Art of Writing*. Clencoe, IL: Free Press, 1952.

Suyūṭī, Jalāl al-dīn. *Al-Durr al-manthūr fī al-tafsīr al-ma'thūr: wa-huwa mukhtaṣar tafsīr Tarjumān al-Qur'ān*, in six volumes. Beirut: Dār al-Kutub al-'ilmiyyah, 1990.

Sviri, Sara. '*Wa-rahbānīyatan ibtadaʿūhā*: An Analysis of Traditions Concerning the Origin and Evaluation of Christian Monasticism', *Jerusalem Studies in Arabic and Islam* 13 (1990), 195–208.

Swartz, Michael D. 'Jewish Visionary Tradition in Rabbinic Literature', in *The Cambridge Companion to the Talmud and Rabbinic Literature*, edited by Charlotte Elisheva Fonrobert and Martin S. Jaffee. Cambridge: Cambridge University Press, 2007, 198–221.

Synan, Edward A. 'The Four "Senses" and Four Exegetes', in *With Reverence for the Word: Medieval Scriptural Exegesis in Judaism, Christianity, and Islam*, edited by Jane Dammen McAuliffe, Barry Walfish and Joseph Goering. Oxford: Oxford University Press, 2003, 225–36.

Ṭabarī, Abū Jaʿfar. *Annales quos scripsit Abu Djafar Mohammed ibn Djarir at-Tabari: Tārīkh al-rusul wa-al-mulūk*, in fifteen volumes, edited by M. J. de Goeje, Jakob Barth, Theodor Nöldeke, Pieter de Jong, Eugen Prym, Heinrich Thorbecke, Siegmund Fränkel, Ignazio Guidi, David Müller, M. Th. Houtsma, Stanislas Guyard and V. R. Rozen. Leiden: Brill, 1879–1901.

Ṭabarī, Abū Jaʿfar. *The History of al-Ṭabarī*, volume III: *The Children of Israel*, translated by William M. Brinner. Albany, NY: State University of New York Press, 1991.

Ṭabarī, Abū Jaʿfar. *Tafsīr al-Ṭabarī: al-musammá Jāmiʿ al-bayān fī ta'wīl al-Qur'ān*, in thirteen volumes. Beirut: Dār al-Kutub al-'ilmiyyah, 1999.

Ṭabarī, Abū Jaʿfar. *Tafsīr al-Ṭabarī: Jāmiʿ al-bayān 'an ta'wīl āy al-Qur'ān*, in twenty-five volumes, edited by 'Abd Allāh b. 'Abd al-Muḥsin al-Turkī. Cairo: Dār al-Hijr, 2001.

Tahānawī, Muḥammad. *Kashshāf iṣṭilāḥāt al-funūn*, edited by Luṭfī 'Abd al-Badīʿ, 'Abd al-Munʿim Ḥusayn and Amīn Khūlī. Cairo: al-Mu'assasah al-Miṣriyyah al-ʿāmmah li-al-ta'līf wa-al-tarjamah wa-al-ṭibāʿah wa-al-nashr, 1963.

Taji-Farouki, Suha. *Beshara and Ibn 'Arabi: A Movement of Sufi Spirituality in the Modern World*. Oxford: Anqa, 2007.

Takeshita, Masataka. 'Ibn 'Arabī's Theory of the Perfect Man and Its Place in the History of Islamic Thought', PhD diss., University of Chicago, 1987.

Thaʿlabī, Aḥmad. *'Arā'is al-majālis fī qiṣaṣ al-anbiyā', or, 'Lives of the Prophets'*, translated and annotated by William M. Brinner. Leiden: Brill, 2002.

Thomas, David. 'Trinity', in *Encyclopaedia of the Qur'ān*, vol. 5, edited by Jane Dammen McAuliffe. Leiden: Brill, 2006, 369–70.

Tirmidhī, Muḥammad. *Al-Jāmiʿ al-kabīr*, in six volumes, edited by Bashshār Maʿrūf. Beirut: Dār al-Gharb al-islāmī, 1998.

Tlili, Sara. *Animals in the Qur'an*. Cambridge: Cambridge University Press, 2012.
Todd, Richard. *The Sufi Doctrine of Man: Ṣadr al-Dīn al-Qūnawī's Metaphysical Anthropology*. Leiden: Brill, 2014.
Tottoli, Roberto. *Biblical Prophets in the Qur'ān and Muslim Literature*. Richmond: Curzon, 2002.
Tottoli, Roberto. 'Afterlife', in *Encyclopaedia of Islam*, third edition (online), edited by Kate Fleet, Gudrun Krämer, Denis Matringe, John Nawas and Everett Rowon. Leiden: Brill, 2009. Accessed via http://ezproxy-prd.bodleian.ox.ac.uk:2134/entries/encyclopaedia-of-islam-3/afterlife-COM_22930?s.num=0&s.f.s2_parent=s.f.cluster.Encyclopaedia+of+Islam&s.q=tottoli+resurrection on 17 January 2018.
Trimingham, J. Spencer. *The Sufi Orders in Islam*. Oxford: Clarendon Press, 1971.
Ṭūfī, Najm al-Dīn. *Muslim Exegesis of the Bible in Medieval Cairo: Najm al-Dīn al-Ṭūfī's (d. 716/1316) Commentary on the Christian Scriptures*, edited, translated and introduced by Lejla Demiri. Leiden: Brill, 2013.
Tustarī, Sahl. *Tafsīr al-Qur'ān al-'aẓīm*, edited by Ṭāhā 'Abd al-Ra'ūf Sa'd and Sa'd Ḥasan Muḥammad 'Alī. Cairo: Dār al-Ḥaram li-al-turāth, 2004.
van Ess, Josef. 'Tashbīh wa-Tanzīh', in *Encyclopaedia of Islam*, second (new) edition, vol. 10, edited by P. J. Bearman, Th. Bianquis, C. E. Bosworth, E. van Donzel and W. P. Heinrichs. Leiden: Brill, 2000, 341–4.
van Ess, Josef. 'Tolerance and Pluralism in Classical Islam', in *The Religion of the Other*, edited by Mohamed Ben-Madani. London: Maghreb Publications, 2013, 27–32.
van Ess, Josef. *Theology and Society in the Second and Third Centuries of the Hijra: A History of Religious Thought in Early Islam*, in five volumes, translated by John O'Kane. Leiden: Brill, 2017–20.
Viguera, Maria J. *Dos cartillas de fisiognómica*. Madrid: Nacionel, 1977.
Vishanoff, David. 'An Imagined Book Gets a New Text: Psalms of the Muslim David', *Islam and Christian-Muslim Relations* 22, no. 1 (2011), 85–99.
Waardenburg, Jacques. 'Muslim Studies of Other Religions: 2. The Medieval Period: 650–1500', in *Muslim Perceptions of Other Religions: A Historical Survey*, edited by *Jacques Waardenburg*. New York and Oxford: Oxford University Press, 1999, 18–69.
Waardenburg, Jacques. *Muslims as Actors: Islamic Meanings and Muslim Interpretations in the Perspective of the Study of Religions*. Berlin and New York: Walter de Gruyter, 2007.
Ware, Kallistos (Timothy). *The Orthodox Way*. Crestwood, NY: St. Vladimir's Seminary Press, 1995.
Warrāq, Abū 'Īsá. *Anti-Christian Polemic in Early Islam: Abū 'Īsá al-Warrāq's 'Against the Trinity'*, edited and translated by David Thomas. Cambridge: Cambridge University Press, 1992.
Warrāq, Abū 'Īsá. *Early Muslim Polemic Against Christianity: Abū 'Īsá al-Warrāq's 'Against the Incarnation'*, edited and translated by David Thomas. Cambridge: Cambridge University Press, 2002.
Webb, Gisela. 'Angel', *Encyclopaedia of the Qur'ān*, vol. 1, edited by Jane Dammen McAuliffe. Leiden: Brill, 2001, 84–92.
Welch, Alford T., Paret, Rudi and Pearson, James D. 'Al-Ḳur'ān', in *Encyclopaedia of Islam*, second (new) edition, vol. 5, edited by B. Lewis, V. L. Ménage, Ch. Pellat and J. Schacht. Leiden: Brill, 1986, 400–432.
Wensinck, Arent J. 'Rasūl', in *Encyclopaedia of Islam*, second (new) edition, vol. 8, edited by C. E. Bosworth, E. van Donzel, W. P. Heinrichs and G. Lecomte. Leiden: Brill, 1995, 454–5.

Wild, Stefan. "We Have Sent Down to Thee the Book with the Truth . . .': Spatial and Temporal Implications of the Qur'anic Concepts of nuzūl, tanzīl, and 'inzāl', *The Qur'an as Text*, edited by Stefan Wild. Leiden: Brill, 1996, 137–53.
Winter, Michael. 'A Polemical Treatise by 'Abd al-Ġanī al-Nābulusī Against a Turkish Scholar on the Religious Status of the Dimmīs', *Arabica* 35 (1988), 92–103.
Winter, Timothy. 'Ibn Kemāl (d. 940/1534) on Ibn 'Arabī's Hagiology', in *Sufism and Theology*, edited by Ayman Shihadeh. Edinburgh: Edinburgh University Press, 2007, 137–57.
Wisnovsky, Robert. *Aspects of Avicenna*. Princeton, NJ: Markus Wiener, 2001.
Wisnovsky, Robert. 'Heavenly Book', in *Encyclopaedia of the Qur'ān*, vol. 2, edited by Jane Dammen McAuliffe. Leiden: Brill, 2002, 412–14.
Woerner-Powell, Tom. *Another Road to Damascus: An Integrative Approach to 'Abd al-Qādir al-Jazā'irī*. Berlin and Boston: Walter de Gruyter, 2017.
Wolfson, Elliot R. *Venturing Beyond – Law and Morality in Kabbalistic Mysticism*. New York: Oxford University Press, 2006.
Ya'qūbī, Aḥmad. *Ibn-Wādhih qui dicitur al-Ja 'qubī Historiae*, in two volumes, edited by M. Th. Houtsma. Leiden: Brill, 1883.
Zahniser, A. H. Matthias. 'Messenger', in *Encyclopaedia of the Qur'ān*, vol. 3, edited by Jane Dammen McAuliffe. Leiden: Brill, 2003, 380–3.
Zamakhsharī, Maḥmūd. *Al-Kashshāf 'an ḥaqā 'iq ghawāmiḍ al-tanzīl wa- 'uyūn al-aqāwīl fī wujūh al-ta 'wīl: wa-huwa tafsīr al-Qur 'ān al-karīm*, in four volumes. Beirut: Dār al-Kitāb al-'Arabī, 1947.
Zamakhsharī, Maḥmūd. *A Mu'tazilite creed of az-Zamaḫšarî (d. 538/1144): al-Minhâğ fî uṣûl ad-dîn*, edited and translated by Sabine Schmidtke. Stuttgart: Kommissionsverlag Franz Steiner, 1997.
Zarkashī, Badr al-Dīn. *Al-Burhān fī 'ulūm al-Qur'ān*, in four volumes. Cairo: Dār al-Turāth, 1984.
Ziedan, Youssef. *'Abd al-Karīm al-Jīlī: faylasūf al-ṣūfiyyah*. Cairo: al-Hay'ah al-Miṣriyyah 'al-āmmah li-al-kitāb, 1988.
Ziedan, Youssef. *Al-Fikr al-ṣūfī 'ind 'Abd al-Karīm al-Jīlī*. Cairo: Dār al-Amīn, 1998.
Ziedan, Youssef. *Dawwāmāt al-tadayyun*. Cairo: Dār al-Shurūq, 2013.
Ziedan, Youssef. *Al-Lāhūt al-'arabī wa-uṣūl al-'unf al-dīnī*. Cairo: Dār al-Shurūq, 2015.

Index

'Abd al-Jabbār 21, 137–8
Abraham 24, 64–4, 135
abrogation (*naskh*)
  earlier religions/scriptures 22–6, 70
  Gospel/Christianity 72, 151
  Judaism/Torah 59–60, 67, 69–72, 75, 83, 100, 140, 151
Abulafia, Abraham 65–66
Abū Zayd, Naṣr Hāmid 30, 37–8
Akiva (Rabbi) 65–6
Akkach, Samer 29–30
'Alī (Imam) 80
alteration of scripture (*tabdīl*), *see under* corruption of scripture (*taḥrīf*)
Āmulī, Ḥaydar 28
Anṣārī, 'Abd Allāh 95
Ash'arites 114, 123, 154, 155
Averroes, *see under* Ibn Rushd
Avicenna, *see under* Ibn Sina

al-Baghawī 139
al-Biqā'ī 103
Brahmans 87, 170
Brethren of Purity 92
al-Būnī, Aḥmad 92
Burckhardt, Titus 1

Casewit, Youssef 25
Chittick, William 28
Chodkiewicz, Michel 25
Christians and Christianity
  abrogation (*naskh*) 25, 69, 71–2, 100
  corruption (*taḥrīf*) 21–3, 59, 99, 135–6, 139–40, 157–8
  denominational differences 71–4, 138
  doctrine of divine comparability (*tashbīh*) 71, 74–5, 85–6, 95, 152–9, 162, 164, 169
  forgiveness 145–50, 164, 171
  Gospel 20, 59, 135–65
  hierarchy of religions 169
  Incarnation 21–2, 73–4, 135–6, 148–50, 152–9, 164, 169
  Jesus' people 71–5, 77–8, 107, 138, 142–50, 159–62, 164, 169–71
  language 104
  literalism 79, 81, 138–45, 154–6, 164
  military victories 30
  monasticism 90, 97–9
  Moses 90
  one manifestation of a single religion 30
  People of Scripture (*ahl al-kitāb*) 21, 59
  permissiveness 94
  punishment 78, 97, 145–9, 153, 172
  rituals 103, 170
  Trinity (*see under* Trinity)
concealment (*kitmān, katm*) 76–81
Corbin, Henry 1
Cornell, Vincent 29
corruption of scripture (*taḥrīf*) 21–4
  Christian 59, 99, 135–6, 139–40, 157–8
  Jewish 24, 59–60, 61, 94, 98, 140

David
  attributes 107–9, 116–19
  birds 107–8, 113–19
  kingship (*mulk*) 107, 113, 119–21, 124–6, 128, 132
  people 107
  Perfect Human 108–10, 126, 133, 167, 169
  piety 116–17
  Psalms 20, 103–3
  Solomon 103, 119–21, 126–7, 132–3
  viceregency (*khilāfah*) 111, 114–15, 119–21, 124–9, 132
dissimulation (*taqiyyah*) 77, *see also* concealment (*kitmān*)

esoteric interpretation (*ta'wīl*) 76–81, 131

al-Fārābī 114
al-Farghānī, Sa'd al-Dīn 38
fixed entities/essences (*al-a'yān al-thābitah*) 35, 36, 113
Friends of God (*awliyā'*)
  David 127
  general prophethood 44–5, 70, 130–2
  heirs of Muhammad 64, 68, 70
  hierarchy 120
  knowledge 80, 129–30
  miracles 72, 93, 120
  'Mosaic' 14–15, 84, 92
  'Muhammadan' 13–14, 70, 83–4, 130–1
  Muhammadan Reality 16, 64
  revelation 44, 49
  viceregency 121, 126

Gabriel (angel) 44, 139–40
Goldziher, Ignaz 104
Gospel (*al-Injīl*)
  abrogation 22, 24–6, 59, 69–72, 83, 100, 151
  corruption (*taḥrīf*) 21–3, 59, 135–6, 139–40, 157–8
  hierarchy of scriptures 82–3, 124, 133, 168–9
  al-Jīlī's presentation 1, 3, 7, 135–65
  language 105, 136–8
  legal content 94
  metaphysical meaning 16, 82–3, 123, 150–2, 156–7, 163, 167–9
  miracles 72
  mysteries 81
  opening formula 138–42
  revelation 20, 75, 106, 136–8
  Torah 59
Griffith, Sidney 136

al-Ḥakīm, Su'ād 2
Hebrew 87, 88, 90, 103–5, 136–7
Hujwīrī 80

Ibn 'Abbās 39, 51, 80
Ibn 'Abd al-Raḥmān, Yūnus 154
Ibn 'Arabī
  Adam 25, 33, 38, 43, 110, 114
  David 114, 119
  divine incomparability (*tanzīh*) and comparability (*tashbīh*) 74–5, 155, 169
  epistemology 61, 80, 98
  Fuṣūṣ al-ḥikam 5, 28, 43, 91, 110, 132, 168
  al-Futūḥāt al-Makkiyyah 5, 24–8, 40, 80, 98, 115, 130–1
  influence 1, 5, 8, 168
  Jesus 139–40, 143, 145, 147, 153–4, 157–8
  modern scholarship 3, 25, 26, 28–31
  Moses 26
  Muhammad 24–5, 33, 40, 110
  mysteries of the pillars of Islam 171
  occult sciences 92–3
  Perfect Human 15–16, 38, 119–20, 163
  Pharaoh 77
  prophecy 44–5, 70, 110, 130–2
  Qur'an 24, 35, 40, 69
  Solomon 122
  Sufi metaphysics 8–9
  terminology 2, 27, 35, 44, 48, 67, 83, 90, 91, 112–15, 144, 155, 157, 161, 168
  Torah 24
  universal mercy 11, 15, 53, 96, 149, 171
  universal monotheism 26–7, 30, 144, 150
Ibn Barrajān 24
Ibn al-Fāriḍ 38
Ibn al-Ḥakam, Hishām 154
Ibn Ḥazm 20, 21, 111
Ibn Jamīl, Abū al-Ghayth 130–1
Ibn Kathīr 21, 23, 108, 117
Ibn Khaldūn 8–9, 21, 22, 92, 93, 114
Ibn Qayyim al-Jawziyyah 21
Ibn Qutaybah 111, 137
Ibn Rushd 79–81
Ibn Sīnā 114, 115
Ibn Taymiyyah 21, 22, 70–1, 77, 139, 153
Idel, Moshe 65
idol-worshippers 26, 66, 144, 170
Izutsu, Toshihiko 8, 26, 35, 42, 75

al-Jabartī, Ismā'īl 5, 38, 131
Ja'far al-Ṣādiq 80
Jāmī, 'Abd al-Raḥmān 136
al-Jandī, Mu'ayyad al-Dīn 5, 26–7, 68–9, 104, 115, 153–4
al-Jazā'irī, 'Abd al-Qādir 28

Jeffrey, Arthur 104
Jesus
  defence of his people 142–7
  disclosure of mysteries 71–2, 74–8
  Fuṣūṣ al-ḥikam 139–40, 143, 145, 147, 153, 157–8
  Gospel 20, 22, 135–65
  innocence 71, 74, 99, 142–5
  knowledge 63–4, 145
  language 136
  legislative prophethood 94
  manifestation of God 145–7, 149–52, 154, 167
  miracles 71–2, 74–5, 89
  Moses 71–3, 100
  Muhammad 23
  Muslim views 135–6, 143
  New Testament 66, 72
  people 71–5, 77–8, 107, 138, 142–50, 159–62, 164, 169, 170–1
  Perfect Human 151–2, 167, 169
  titles 135, 140
Jews and Judaism
  abrogation (*naskh*) 25, 60, 69, 72, 100
  corruption of scripture (*taḥrīf*) 21–4, 59–61, 94, 98, 140
  doctrine of divine incomparability (*tanzīh*) 74–5, 85–6, 100, 162, 169
  hardness of heart 63, 66–7
  hierarchy of religions 72, 169
  imperfection 67–9, 79, 97
  Isrāʾīliyyāt 62, 66, 108
  law 93–4
  monasticism 96–8
  mysticism 65–6, 90
  one manifestation of a single religion 30
  People of Scripture (*ahl al-kitāb*) 21, 59
  Psalms 103, 107
  punishment 97, 172
  rabbis 91–2
  rituals 99, 103, 170–1
  Torah 20, 59–101, 107
al-Jīlānī, ʿAbd al-Qādir 130–1
al-Jīlī, ʿAbd al-Karīm
  influence of Ibn ʿArabī 1–2, 5, 8–9, 12–13, 168
  Gospel 135–65
  al-Insān al-kāmil (book) 1, 6–17
  life 5
  modern scholarship 1, 5, 28–31, 170, 172–3
  originality 168
  other religions 1–3, 29–31, 87, 170–2
  Psalms 103–33
  Qurʾan 33–57
  soteriology 78, 88, 96–7, 145–50, 171–2
  Sufi metaphysics 3, 8–17, 167–9
  Torah 59–101
  works 1, 5–6
John (prophet) 91

Kātib Çelebī (Ḥājjī Khalīfah) 172
Kaykāʾūs (Seljuq Sultan of Rūm) 27, 30

Lazarus-Yafeh, Hava 59–60
levels of existence (*marātib al-wujūd*) 3, 9–15, 27, 37, 78, 115, 167
  Gospel 150–1, 165, 167, 169
  hierarchy of scriptures 16, 40, 82–3, 151, 155, 168–9
  Marātib al-wujūd (book) 6
  Perfect Human 16, 44, 48, 68
  Psalms 124, 151, 167, 169
  Qurʾan 34–5, 42, 43, 54, 151, 167, 169
  Torah 67, 82, 101, 151, 167, 169
  Trinity 140–2
Lings, Martin 46
Lipton, Gregory 3, 25

magic 91–3
manifestation (*tajallī*, *ẓuhūr*), *see under* universal theophany
Mary 71, 73, 138–43, 151–2, 158, 162, 164
Massignon, Louis 24
al-Masʿūdī 105, 106, 112
Maybudī, Rashīd al-Dīn 117
Mir, Mustansir 42
Moses
  heirs 14, 83–4, 91–2
  Ibn ʿArabī 26, 110
  innocence 96, 99–100
  Jesus 71–3
  Muhammad 23, 24
  mystic 90, 100

Perfect Human 61, 167, 169
people 24, 26, 60–2, 66–9, 76–7, 79, 87, 89, 93–100, 107, 170–1
Pharaoh 76–7, 94–5
propagation of revelation 50–62, 64–7, 76–81, 86, 89, 169
Torah 20, 59–101
Mother of the Book (*umm al-kitāb*) 7, 20, 34–5, 37–8, 59, 106, 140, *see also* Preserved Tablet (*al-lawḥ al-maḥfūẓ*)
Muhammad
Muhammadan Reality (*al-ḥaqīqah al-muḥammadiyyah*) 16, 33, 39, 45, 49, 56, 73, 169
Perfect Human 6, 14, 16, 39, 49, 56–7, 110, 158–9, 169
Qur'an 20, 35–41, 48–50, 56, 76–9, 169
seal of prophets 20, 22, 67–8, 70
superiority 3, 17, 22–5, 67–71, 109–10, 121–2, 129–30, 169, 171–3
viceregents 45, 70, 114
Mu'tazilites 21, 23, 106, 123, 137, 154, 155

al-Nābulusī, 'Abd al-Ghanī 6, 29
Nasafī, 'Azīz 35
Nicholson, R.A. 1, 43, 173
Nwyia, Paul 90

Paul (the Apostle) 66, 139
Perennialist school 28, 30
Perfect Human (*al-insān al-kāmil*)
comprehensiveness 16, 46–9
David 108–10, 167
divine attributes 12, 15–16, 52–3, 68, 83, 114, 128, 151–2
divine essence 36–40, 50–1, 53, 83, 128
esoteric interpretation (*ta'wīl*) 80
Gospel 157
governing of world 113
incarnationism (*tajsīm*) 154
al-Insān al-kāmil (book) 1
Jesus 167
al-Jīlī 1, 3, 6, 15–17, 38–9
microcosm 16, 48, 64, 68
miracles 72, 75, 93, 118–20, 131
Muhammad 6, 14, 16, 39, 49, 56–7, 110, 158–9, 169
'Muhammadan' 13–14, 70, 83–4, 130–1
'Mosaic' 14, 83–4, 92
Moses 61, 167
Muslims 68–9, 79
'Perfect Ones' (*al-kummal*) 16, 44, 67, 83
Pole (*al-quṭb*) 38, 119–20, 127
Qur'an 156–9, 162–3
'realization' (*taḥqīq*) 44, 51, 76–7, 119
Torah 83–4, 87
Pharaoh 66, 76–7, 94–5
preparedness (*isti'dād*) 27, 44, 67, 75, 78, 111, 113, 144, 161
Preserved Tablet (*al-lawḥ al-maḥfūẓ*) 6, 7, 51, *see also* Mother of the Book (*umm al-kitāb*)
Psalms (*al-Zabūr*)
contents 103, 111–16, 167
etymology 103–5
hierarchy of scriptures 122–4, 133, 168–9
al-Jīlī's presentation 103–3
language 105, 136
metaphysical meaning 122–4, 167–9
revelation 105–7
Torah 112

al-Qāshānī, 'Abd al-Razzāq
commentary on *Fuṣūṣ* 5, 25, 28
esoteric interpretation (*ta'wīl*) 81
hardness of heart 66
knowledge of the Perfect Humans 81
Qur'an commentary 28, 35, 52–3, 62, 66, 81
scholars of external forms (*'ulamā' al-rusūm*) 161
seven oft-repeated verses 52–3, 62
superiority of Muhammad 25
al-Qayṣarī, Dā'ūd 5, 88, 168
al-Qūnawī, Ṣadr al-Dīn 35, 168
Qur'an
confirmation of earlier scriptures 20–2
esoteric interpretation (*ta'wīl*) 76–81

Furqan 14–15, 33, 54–5, 123
al-Jīlī's presentation 33–57
metaphysical meaning 14, 34–6, 83, 123, 167–9
sacred history 2–3, 17, 19–31, 124
superiority 3, 17, 22–4, 56–7, 67–71, 75, 109–11, 124, 169, 172–3
translation 137
vocabulary 2, 6, 33
al-Qurṭubī 42, 72, 84, 112, 118
al-Qushāshī, Aḥmad 29
al-Qushayrī, Abū al-Qāsim 24–5, 95

Rahman, Fazlur 35
al-Rāzī, Fakhr al-Dīn 21, 92, 114, 115
Rāzī, Najm al-Dīn 26
receptivity (*qābiliyyah*), *see under* preparedness (*isti'dād*)
Rippin, Andrew 104

sacred history
al-Jīlī's view 16–17, 31, 49, 56–7, 70, 75, 83, 99–101, 110, 122–4, 133, 151, 163–5, 168–9, 172–3
Qur'an-centred view of 2, 17, 19–23, 34, 45, 59–60, 99, 103, 135–6
Sufi views of 24–7, 173
saints and sainthood, *see under* Friends of God (*awliyā'*)
scholars of external forms (*'ulamā' al-rusūm*) 140, 160–2
Shabistarī, Maḥmūd 144
al-Shāfi'ī 23
Shah-Kazemi, Reza 28–9, 31
al-Shahrastānī 21, 22, 59
al-Shiblī 119–20
Sinai, Mt. 7, 59, 65, 89–90, 94
Smith, Margaret 1
Solomon
birds 114, 116–18, 121
David 103, 109, 114, 116–21, 126–7
jinni 121–2, 130
kingship (*mulk*) 119–22, 127–30, 132
knowledge 109
miraculous powers 119–21
Muhammad 121–2, 129–30
Perfect Human 133
viceregency (*khilāfah*) 119–22, 125, 132
wind 113, 127
Strauss, Leo 172
al-Suhrawardī, 'Umar 80
al-Sulamī 80
al-Suyūṭī 62, 104–5
Syriac 103–5, 117, 119, 136–7

al-Ṭabarī 108, 110, 112, 117
al-Tha'labī 62
Torah (*al-Tawrāh*)
abrogation 22–6, 59–60, 67, 69–72, 75, 83, 100, 140, 151
contents 63–5, 85–99, 167
corruption (*taḥrīf*) 21–4, 59–60, 94, 98, 100
Furqan 54, 59
Gospel 59, 71–2
Hebrew 136
hierarchy of scriptures 82–3, 124, 133, 168–9
incompleteness 61–2, 64–5, 67–71, 79, 99, 100, 116
al-Jīlī's presentation 59–101
law 63, 93–6, 112
metaphysical meaning 81–5, 122–3, 167–9
names 59
Oral Torah 94
Qur'an 20, 63–4, 76–81, 85–99
revelation 20, 60–2, 106
tablets 60–7, 85–99
Traditionalist school, *see under* Perennialist school
Trinity
Christian interpretation 71–4, 138–40, 142–5, 148, 152–6, 161, 162, 164, 169, 171
al-Jīlī's interpretation 140–5, 150–2, 167, 168, 170
Qur'an-centred view 21–2, 73, 135–6, 139
al-Ṭūfī, Najm al-Dīn 22
Tustarī, Sahl 24, 72, 80

universal mercy 11, 15, 53, 96, 149–50, 171–2

universal monotheism 13, 26, 144–5, 147, 150, 170–2
universal theophany 3, 8–9, 135, 154
  humans as loci of divine manifestation 77, 128, 132–3, 152
  Qur'anic basis 78, 156–9, 162–3
  scriptures 16, 56, 84, 87, 101, 112–13, 115, 157, 162, 165, 167, 172
  universal monotheism 26, 144–5, 147, 150, 172

Wafā', Muhammad 53
Wolfson, Elliot R. 65

al-Ya'qūbī 111

al-Zamakhsharī 23, 106
Ziedan, Youssef 30–1
Zohar 65
Zoroastrians 87, 170

www.ingramcontent.com/pod-product-compliance
Lightning Source LLC
Chambersburg PA
CBHW072145290426
44111CB00012B/1976